ENGLISH–SPANISH
SPANISH–ENGLISH
MEDICAL DICTIONARY

DICCIONARIO MÉDICO
INGLÉS–ESPAÑOL
ESPAÑOL–INGLÉS

ENGLISH–SPANISH
SPANISH–ENGLISH
MEDICAL DICTIONARY

DICCIONARIO MÉDICO
INGLÉS–ESPAÑOL
ESPAÑOL–INGLÉS

Glenn T. Rogers, M.D.

Los Angeles County
University of Southern California
  Medical Center
Los Angeles, California

McGraw-Hill, Inc.
HEALTH PROFESSIONS DIVISION

New York   St. Louis   San Francisco   Auckland
Bogotá   Caracas   Lisbon   London   Madrid
Mexico   Milan   Montreal   New Delhi   Paris
San Juan   Singapore   Sydney   Tokyo   Toronto

ENGLISH-SPANISH SPANISH-ENGLISH MEDICAL DICTIONARY

123456789   DOCDOC   987654321

ISBN   0-07-053537-X

This book was set in Times Roman.
The editors were Edward M. Bolger, Mariapaz Ramos-Englis, and Catherine Lizza; the production supervisor was Richard Ruzycka.
R. R. Donnelley and Sons Company was printer and binder.

Library of Congress Cataloging-in-Publication Data

Rogers, Glenn T.
   English-Spanish Spanish-English medical dictionary / Glenn T. Rogers.
     p. cm.
   ISBN 0-07-053537-X :
   1. Medicine—Dictionaries.   2. English language—Dictionaries—
Spanish.   3. Medicine—Dictionaries—Spanish.   4. Spanish
language—Dictionaries—English.   5. Dictionaries, Medical—Spanish.
I. Title.
   [DNLM: W 13 R726e]
   R121.R626 1991
   610′.3—dc20
   DNLM/DLC
   for Library of Congress   90-13709
                                                     CIP

CONTENTS—MATERIAS

PREFACE

Good medicine requires a good history. Few experiences are more frustrating for the health practitioner than to greet a patient and realize that the practitioner and the patient have no common language. For the patient, the experience must be equally frustrating and also frightening. Stories abound regarding the mishaps that occur due to ineffective communication. One such story, which appeared in the Oakland Tribune, involves an Oakland woman who returned to her native Mexico to die, believing she had leukemia. In fact, her doctors had told her she was anemic.

The rapid growth of the Spanish-speaking population presents a special challenge to health workers in the United States. Courses in medical Spanish are now available at many medical centers, and more than a dozen books have been published which offer medical Spanish instruction in the form of sample phrases, exercises, and the like. Notably absent has been a comprehensive medical Spanish dictionary to reinforce these other efforts. This dictionary is the first of its kind.

With over fourteen thousand entries, this dictionary contains virtually every health-related term likely to occur in a conversation between a health worker and a Spanish-speaking patient. There are technical terms which could be important to certain patients (e.g., "white blood cell count," "glucose monitor"), common terms (e.g., "stomachache," "to go to the bathroom"), recently coined terms, colloquialisms, and slang. The colloquialisms form an important feature of this dictionary, as they are used frequently by Latins to describe their ailments and can be quite frustrating when offered in response to the practitioner's carefully-crafted textbook Spanish. Many of these colloquialisms are recorded here for the first time.

Another unique feature of this dictionary is its focus on Spanish as it is spoken in the United States. The great majority of Spanish-speaking people in this country come from Mexico, Central America, Cuba, Puerto Rico, and the Dominican Republic, and translations have been chosen which will be best understood by the people of these areas. Terms peculiar to a particular country carry regional labels.

Over thirty doctors from eleven Spanish American countries assisted with the extensive verification and editing of this dictionary. Four Latin dentists reviewed the dental terms. Translations are based on current usage at major Spanish American medical centers and in the Spanish American medical literature. Multiple revisions were made to ensure completeness and accuracy.

Many people helped with various aspects of the production of this book. I would like to thank my wife Cynda Valle Rogers for her patience, Richard Blum for his help with the data management, and my parents for wiring me money to pay my Mexico City hotel bill when my credit card was suddenly and inexplicably declined. I would also like to thank Peter Beren, José de la Torres, Victor Guerrero, Antonio Gutiérrez, Gabriel Lerman, Camilo Leslie, Victor Marrero, Allan Ortejarai, Dan Poynter, Rolando Valdez, Gustavo Valero, and Vicente Valero.

PREFACIO

La mayoría de la literatura médica de importancia aparece en inglés y el estudiante de medicina, médico u otro practicante de la salud que quiere acceder a ella debe saber inglés médico básico. Un obstáculo a esta meta ha sido la falta de un práctico diccionario médico bilingüe. Hasta ahora no ha existido ninguno suficientemente extenso, preciso, económico y de tamaño conveniente. Este diccionario viene a llenar ese espacio vacío.

Abarcando más de 14.000 términos, este diccionario contiene la mayoría de los términos que se encuentran en artículos médicos. Además, contiene muchos modismos, los cuales podrían ser muy útiles para los que quieren practicar su profesión en Los Estados Unidos o que tienen contacto con pacientes de habla inglesa. Las formas irregulares de los plurales, comparativos, superlativos, pretéritos y participios pasados aparecen al igual que indicaciones de las funciones gramaticales y del nivel lingüístico. Para aquellos médicos que intentan presentarse al "FLEX" o a los "National Boards" este diccionario será indispensable.

Más de treinta médicos y otros especialistas han asistido en la redacción de este diccionario para asegurar la exactitud de las traducciones. Su tamaño conveniente lo hace ideal para ser llevado al hospital o a la biblioteca. Los principiantes del inglés médico podrán usar el diccionario para aumentar su vocabulario, mientras que los estudiantes más avanzados lo podrán usar como referencia. El propósito de este diccionario es llegar a servir como una autoridad para todo lo vinculado a la traducción médica.

Muchos me han ayudado en la realización de esta obra. Quisiera dar gracias en particular a mi esposa Cynda Valle Rogers por su paciencia, a Richard Blum por su consejo sobre computadoras, y a mis padres por haberme enviado con prontitud dinero para pagar la cuenta de mi hotel en Mexico, D.F., cuando mi tarjeta de crédito fue repentina e inexplicablemente rechazada. Quiero dar gracias también a Peter Beren,

José de la Torres, Victor Guerrero, Antonio Gutiérrez, Gabriel Lerman, Camilo Leslie, Victor Marrero, Allan Ortejarai, Dan Poynter, Rolando Valdez, Gustavo Valero, y Vicente Valero.

HOW TO USE THIS DICTIONARY

Terms are listed in alphabetical order. Note that the Spanish-English section contains separate headings for *ch*, *ll*, and *ñ*, and that *callo* follows *calzado*, for example, according to Spanish rules for alphabetization.

Terms consisting of more than one word and phrases are listed either as individual entries or as run-ons under the key word of the term or phrase. When the entry word is repeated in a run-on, it is replaced by a dash (———). "Rigor mortis," "tardive dyskinesia," and "endoscopic retrograde cholangiopancreatography (ERCP)" are examples of terms which are listed as individual entries. By contrast, "nerve block" is listed as a run-on under "nerve," "pernicious anemia" is listed as a run-on under "anemia," and "to give birth" is listed as a run-on under "birth". For the convenience of the reader, many phrases are listed under more than one word. All chemicals, including medications, acids, and oils, are listed according to the first word of the term.

Entries are followed by an indication of the part of speech and plural form when it applies. In the Spanish-English section, noun entries are followed by *m* if they are masculine, by *f* if they are feminine, and by *mf* if they vary according to context, as with *cardiólogo -ga*, *doctor -ra*, and *adolescente* (*el adolescente* or *la adolescente*). The indication *m&f* applies to a few Spanish nouns, such as *azucar*, which may be considered either masculine or feminine.

In the English-Spanish section, the same indications of gender noted above follow translated nouns save for masculine nouns ending in *-o* or modified by an adjective ending in *-o* and feminine nouns ending in *-a* or modified by an adjective ending in *-a*.

For a given entry, translations are listed in order of preference according to accuracy, level of usage, and likelihood of being understood by a broad range of Latins. When a term has more than one meaning, only those meanings which apply to medicine are translated. Synonymous or nearly synonymous translations are separated by commas; translations of distinct meanings are separated by semicolons.

Abbreviations for region, level of usage, and field of medicine appear in italics between parentheses. When they precede a translation, they apply to the entry term; when they follow a translation, they apply to the translation. This same principle applies to parenthetical explanations. The label (*fam*) applies to colloquial terms used frequently in speech and rarely in writing. Some of these terms could seem overly familiar or inappropriate, particularly to a highly educated or aristocratic Latin when used on first meeting. On the other hand, such a term may be the only term understood by a less educated Latin and should be tried when a more formal term fails to make the point. Terms labeled (*form*) will not be understood by many Latins. The label (*vulg*) applies to slang terms, including drug jargon, and to terms considered by most people to be crude. They will be used from time to time, particularly by male patients with little education, but should rarely if ever be used by a health practitioner.

Parentheses are used occasionally to enclose optional portions of a translation. In this case the material between parentheses is not italicized. "Airsickness," for example, is translated as "mareo (en avión)". Speaking out of context, one would have to say "mareo en avión" to convey airsickness, however if one were already talking about air travel, "mareo" could be sufficient. The reflexive "se" is enclosed in parentheses when it is optional or dependent on context. For example, "bathe" is translated as "*vt, vi* bañar(se)". In this situation "se" would be used with the intransitive case of the verb, but not the transitive case.[*]

---

[*] Recall that a transitive verb form takes an object, while an intransitive verb form does not. Consider the two example sentences: "The nurse will bathe your baby,"and, "Use a mild soap when you bathe." In the first sentence "bathe" is transitive ("your baby" is the object); in the second it is intransitive.

COMO USAR ESTE DICCIONARIO

Los artículos se presentan en orden alfabético. Términos o frases que tienen más de una palabra se encuentran como entradas individuales o a continuación de la palabra más importante. Cuando la entrada está repetida en una continuación, está reemplazada por un guión largo (——). "Rigor mortis," "discinesia tardía," y "colangiopancreatografía retrógrada endoscópica" son ejemplos de términos que se encuentran como entradas individuales. En cambio, "trabajo de parto" se encuentra a continuación de "parto," "en polvo" se encuentra a continuación de "polvo," y "enfermedad de Graves" se encuentra a continuación de "enfermedad". Para vocablos que tienen varios significados, solo los que pertenecen a la salud han sido traducidos. Sinónimos se separan por coma; significados distintos se separan por punto y coma.

Las abreviaturas de región, nivel lingüístico, y campo aparecen entre paréntesis en letra cursiva. Cuando aparecen antes de la traducción, quiere decir que modifican la entrada; cuando aparecen después de la traducción, quiere decir que modifican la traducción. Lo mismo aplica a frases explicativas entre paréntesis. La etiqueta (*fam*) aplica a términos que se usan mucho al hablar, raras veces al escribir, y que podrían ser a veces inapropiados, especialmente al utilizarse en el primer encuentro con un paciente mayor o muy formal. Traducciones denotadas como (*form*) serán desconocidas para alguna gente. La etiqueta (*vulg*) aplica a jerga y a términos que se consideran ofensivos para la mayoría de la gente.

Se usan paréntesis de vez en cuando para encerrar aclaraciones opcionales de una traducción. En este caso la aclaración entre paréntesis aparece en letra redonda. Por ejemplo "médico residente" se traduce como "resident (physician)". Esto quiere decir que, fuera de contexto, uno tendría que decir "resident physician" para comunicar "médico residente," pero ya hablando del personal médico de un hospital, por ejemplo, sería suficiente decir sencillamente "resident".

MEDICAL SPANISH TIPS

- The most important advice I can give to anyone learning a foreign language is to try to master the pronunciation at an early stage. This has a double benefit. Not only will you be understood more easily, but you will be better able to identify and retain words and phrases of the foreign language as you hear them. This will remarkably accelerate the learning process. As you hear the foreign language being spoken by a native speaker, repeat key phrases over and over in your mind—or even aloud if possible—comparing your pronunciation to the memory of the correctly spoken sounds. Experiment with your tongue, lips, and palate to create sounds which may be unfamiliar to you. Take a deep breath and pronounce the soft "i" of "sin," then slowly modulate it to the "ee" of "seen". Go back and forth between these two sounds. Somewhere in between is the *i* as it sounds in Spanish, for example in *cinco*. Pronounce the English "d" sound over and over again and gradually modulate it to the "th" of "the". Somewhere in between is the Spanish *d*. Prounounce the English "h" sound over and over again and gradually modulate it to the English "k". Somewhere in between is a close facsimile of the Spanish *j*. Exercises like these will improve your pronunciation tremendously.

- On the subject of pronunciation, note that Spanish vowels are short and pure. Never linger on a vowel as in English. Say the sentence, "No way!" with some feeling and notice how the vowel sounds are drawn out. This rarely happens in Spanish; Spanish is much more staccato in its delivery. Note also that there is no schwa sound in Spanish. The schwa sound is the "uh" sound so often given to unaccented syllables in English. For example the first, third, and possibly fifth syllables of **acetaminophen** are schwa sounds. In Spanish vowels retain their characteristic sounds whether or not they are accented. *Acetaminofén* is pronounced ah-ceh-tah-mee-noh-FEHN, not uh-ceh-tuh-mee-nuh-FEHN. It is often helpful first to practice a word without consonants. *Acetaminofén* without consonants would be *ah-eh-ah-ee-ah-EH*. When you have mastered the vowel changes for a given word, it is usually a simple matter to fill in the consonants. Learn to say *cah-BEH-sah*, not *cuh-BEH-suh*; *meh-dee-SEE-nah*, not *meh-duh-SEE-nuh*.

- When referring to a part of the body in Spanish, it is common to use the definite article instead of the possessive adjective, provided it is clear whose body is involved. The Spanish definite articles, recall, are *el* and *la*. *Me duele la cabeza* is the best translation of "My head hurts." *Me duele mi cabeza* sounds redundant in Spanish.

- The indirect object* is used much more often in Spanish than in English. Health workers are frequently doing things to patients and this requires the use of *le* or, in familiar speech, *te*.

  > *Quiero tomarle el pulso*...I want to take your pulse.
  > *Voy a escucharle el corazón*...I'm going to listen to your heart.
  > *Tenemos que operarte la pierna*...We need to operate on your leg.

  It would not be correct to say, *Quiero tomar su pulso, Voy a escuchar su corazón*, etc.

---

* Recall that a *direct* object may be any type of object and receives the direct action of the verb, while the *indirect* object is always a person (or other living being) *to* whom or *for* whom the action is being performed. In the sentence "Juan owes Carlos five dollars," "five dollars" is the direct object, while "Carlos" is the indirect object. Generally, if you can rearrange a sentence so as to put a "to" or a "for" in front of an object without changing the essential meaning, then that object is an indirect object. (Juan owes five dollars *to* Carlos.) In the sentence "Jane bought Barbara a soda," "soda" is the direct object while "Barbara" is the indirect object (Jane bought a soda *for* Barbara.)

- English-speaking people are often confused by the choices available for the direct object in Spanish. *Te* is always correct when speaking informally, for instance to a child.

  Voy a examinarte, Juanito..I'm going to examine you, Johnny.

  When speaking formally, most Spanish Americans use *lo* for males and *la* for females.

  Voy a examinarlo, señor..I'm going to examine you, sir.
  Voy a examinarla, señora..I'm going to examine you, ma'am.

  There are a few exceptions to this rule, for instance the verb *pegar*, when it means "to hit" takes *le* for a direct object.

  ¿Le pegó?..Did it hit you?

  Some Spanish Americans will use *le* for *all* (formal) second person direct objects, male or female.

  Voy a examinarle, señor..I'm going to examine you, sir.
  Voy a examinarle, señora..I'm going to examine you, ma'am.

  This style is especially common in Mexico.

- Some verbs require that the subject and object be inverted when translating between English and Spanish. The Spanish student is likely to encounter this for the first time when learning to translate the verb "to like". "I like coffee" would be *Me gusta el café*. The subject and object are inverted. This particular construction is a stumbling block to fluency and even advanced students often have to think for a couple seconds in order to conjugate the verb correctly and choose the correct object pronouns.

  Me falta el aire..I am short of breath.
  Les falta el aire..They are short of breath.
  Le salieron los dientes..His teeth came in.

Me dio un catarro..I caught a cold.
Me dieron náuseas..I got nauseated.
¿Le fluye la nariz?..Do you have a runny nose?
¿Cuándo le salieron granos?..When did you get pimples?
¿Le salieron moretones?..Did you get bruised?
Te falta hierro..You're low on iron.

Notice that the English subject corresponds to the Spanish *indirect* object in all these cases.

- Many Spanish verbs are used in the reflexive form when applied to medicine. The use of the reflexive pronoun *se* in some way turns the action of the verb back on the verb's subject.

Orinó..He urinated.
Se orinó..He urinated on himself.

Corté el pan..I cut the bread.
Me corté el dedo..I cut my finger.

Puede vestirla..You can dress her.
Puede vestirse..You can get dressed (*literally* dress yourself).

La enfermera le va a inyectar..The nurse will give you an injection.
La enfermera le va a enseñar como inyectarse..The nurse will teach you how to inject yourself.

A reflexive construction is often used when an English-speaking person would use the past participle preceded by "to get," "to be," or "to become".

Tiene que internarse..You need to be admitted.
Se cansa..He gets tired..He becomes tired.
Ud. se curó..You were cured..You got cured.
Se mejoró..She got better.
Se dislocó..It became dislocated.

Se infectó..It became infected..It got infected.

- Most Spanish nouns which end in -*o* are masculine and most which end in -*a* are feminine, however there are some important exceptions in medical Spanish. For instance, most Spanish words which end in -*ma* are derived from Greek and retain their original masculine gender.

  un problema médico..a medical problem
  el electrocardiograma..the electrocardiogram

  Other medical terms which end in -*a* and are masculine include *aura, día, cólera* (the disease), *herbicida, insecticida, pesticida, raticida, spermaticida,* and *vermicida.*

  The word *mano,* which comes from the Latin *manus,* retains its original feminine gender—despite the fact it ends in -*o*.

  Tengo las manos frías..My hands are cold.

  A source of confusion to Spanish students is the construction *"el agua".* Although *agua* is feminine (and requires feminine modifiers), *el* is used instead of *la* to avoid the awkward double-*ah* sound of *"la agua"*. This rule applies to any word which begins with an accented *ah* sound.

  el agua fría..the cold water
  terapista del habla..speech therapist

  This rule also applies to the indefinite article.

  un afta..a canker sore
  un arma blanca..a sharp weapon

  This rule does not apply to plural forms, since the double-*ah* sound is then broken up by an *s* sound.

las aguas frías..the cold waters
unas aftas..some canker sores

Other medical Spanish terms which begin with an accented *ah* sound include *ámpula, área, asma,* and *hambre.*

■ When comparing quantities, use *de.*

más de dos pastillas..more than two pills
menos de una taza..less than a cup

In all other situations use *que.*

más alto que tu hermano..taller than your brother
más que pesabas hace dos meses..more than you weighed two months ago
menos que siempre..less than usual
menos que nunca..less than ever

■ Health practitioners should be aware that the Spanish word *alcohol* is often considered a synonym for "hard liquor". Many Latin beer and wine drinkers will answer no in all sincerity to the question, *¿Toma alcohol?* A broader question would be *¿Acostumbra tomar bebidas alcohólicas?* To avoid all misunderstandings, you could then follow a negative answer with *¿Cerveza?..¿Vino?*

SPANISH PRONUNCIATION

a   Like the English **a** in **father** (e.g., *padre, cama*).

b   Similar to the English **b**. At the beginning of a breath group or following an *m* or *n*, the Spanish *b* sounds like the **b** in **bite** (e.g., *boca, embarasada*). In all other situations the Spanish *b* lies somewhere between the English **b** and the English v (e.g., *tubo, jarabe*). Allow a little air to escape between slightly parted lips as you make this latter sound.

c   Like the English **c**. Before *a*, *o*, or *u* it is hard (e.g., *cara*); before *e* or *i* it is soft (e.g., *ácido*). (In Castilian Spanish, *c* is pronounced differently, however this form of Spanish is rarely spoken by Spanish Americans.)

ch Like the English **ch** in **touch** or **chill**.

d   Similar to the English **d**. At the beginning of a breath group or following *l* or *n*, the Spanish *d* sounds like the English **d** in **dizzy** (e.g., *dosis, venda*). In all other situations the Spanish *d* lies somewhere between the English **d** and the **th** in **this** (e.g., *mudo, nacido*). Allow a little air to escape between the tip of your tongue and upper teeth as you make the latter sound.

e   Similar to the **ey** in **they** (e.g., *peso, absceso*), unless followed by a consonant in the same syllable, in which case it is closer to the **e** in **sepsis** (e.g., *esperma, recto*).

f   Like the English **f**.

g   When followed by *a*, *o*, *u*, or a consonant, the Spanish *g* is similar to the English **g** in **gout** (e.g., *gota, grasa*). Allow a little air to escape between your tongue and palate as you make this sound. When followed by *e* or *i*, the Spanish *g* may be approximated by the **h** in **hospital**, although the true sound has in addition some of the quality of the English **k** (e.g., *gen*, *gingivitis*).

h Silent (e.g., *hombre. almohada*).

i Like the **i** in **saline** or **latrine** (e.g., *orina*, *signo*, *sífilis*). Preceding another vowel, the Spanish *i* sounds like the English **y**. *Siesta* is pronounced *SYES-tah*, **sodio** is pronounced *SO-dyoh*, *viudo* is pronounced *VYOO-doh*, etc. Following another vowel, *i* forms individual diphthongs: *ai* sounds like the **y** in **cry** (e.g., *aire*, *aislar*); *ei* sounds like the **ay** in **tray** (e.g., *aceite*, *afeitar*); *oi* sounds like the **oy** in **boy** (e.g., *toxoide*, *coloide*); and *ui* sounds like the **ui** in **suite** (e.g., *cuidado*, *ruido*).

j May be approximated by the **h** in **hospital**, although the true sound has in addition some of the quality of the English **k** (e.g., *jugo, bajar*). The Spanish *j* is pronounced the same as the Spanish *g* followed by *e* or *i* (See above).

k Like the English **k**. (*k* is not included in the Spanish alphabet and appears only in foreign words.)

l Similar to the English **l** (e.g., *lado*, *pelo*). The Spanish *l* is articulated rapidly, never drawn out as in English.

ll Somewhere between the **ll** of **million** and the **y** of **kayak**.

m Like the English **m**.

n Like the English **n**. Before *b*, *p*, or *v* the Spanish *n* sounds like the English **m** (e.g., *convalecerse*, *vinblastina*). Before *m* it is silent (e.g., *inmunidad*).

ñ Like the **ni** in **bunion** (e.g., *baño*, *sueño*).

o   Similar to the English **o** in **coma**.

p   Like the English **p** in **spit**. Hold your hand in front of your mouth as you say **spit** and then **pit**. Notice that less air is expelled in pronouncing **spit**. The Spanish *p* is not aspirated, which means little air should be expelled. It is a shorter, more explosive sound than the English **p**.

q   Like the English **k**. The Spanish *q* is always followed by *u*, but lacks the **w** sound of the English **qu**. *Quinina* is pronounced *kee-NEE-nah*, not *kwee-NEE-nah*. The **kw** sound of **quit** is represented in Spanish by *cu*, as in *cuarto*, *cuidado*, etc.

r   Similar to the **tt** of **butter**. At the beginning of a word the Spanish *r* is trilled. The Spanish *rr* is always trilled.

s   Like the English **s**. Before voiced consonants, the Spanish *s* sounds like the English **z** (e.g., *rasgar*, *espasmo*).

t   Like the English **t** in **stent**. Hold your hand in front of your mouth as you say **stent** and then **tent**. Notice that less air is expelled in pronouncing **stent**. The Spanish *t* is not aspirated, which means little air should be expelled. It is a shorter, more explosive sound than the English **t**, made by quickly tapping the tip of the tongue against the back of the upper front teeth.

u   Like the English **u** in **flu** or **rule**, never like the **u** in **acute** or **use**. The Spanish *u* has a **w** sound when it precedes another vowel (e.g., *agua*, *cuello*), except in the case of *gue*, *gui*, *que*, and *qui*, when it is silent (e.g., *inguinal*, *quebrar*). The **w** sound is retained in *güe* and *güi* (e.g., *agüita*, *ungüento*). The diphthong *au* sounds like the **ow** of **brow** (e.g., *aura*, *trauma*). The diphthong *iu* sounds like the **u** in **acute** or **use** (e.g., *viudo*, *diurético*).

v   Identical to the Spanish *b*. See above.

x   Like the English **x** in **flex**. Before consonants, the Spanish *x* is often pronounced like the English s (e.g., *extra, expediente*).

y   Similar to the English y (e.g., *yeso, yodo*). Note that the Spanish word *y* (= **and**) is pronounced like the **ee** in **see**.

z   Like the English s (e.g., *nariz, brazo*).

ABBREVIATIONS—ABREVIATURAS

abbr	abbreviation	abreviatura
adj	adjective	adjetivo
adv	adverb	adverbio
anat	anatomy	anatomía
Ang	Anglicism	anglicismo
ant	antiquated	antiguo
arith	arithmetic	aritmética
bot	botany	botánica
CA	Central America	Centroamérica
card	cardiology	cardiología
Carib	Caribbean	caribe
chem	chemistry	química
comp	comparative	comparativo
Cub	Cuba	Cuba
dent	dentistry	odontología
derm	dermatology	dermatología
ES	El Salvador	El Salvador
esp.	especially	especialmente
f	feminine	femenino
fam	familiar	familiar
fig	figurative	figurado
form	formal	formal
fpl	feminine plural	femenino plural
frec	frequently	frecuentemente
ger	gerund	gerundio
gyn	gynecology	ginecología
m	masculine	masculino
Mex	Mexico	México
micro	microbiology	microbiología
mpl	masculine plural	masculino plural
n	noun	nombre *o* sustantivo
neuro	neurology	neurología
Nic	Nicaragua	Nicaragua
npl	noun plural	nombre plural

obst	obstetrics	obstetricia
ortho	orthopedics	ortopedia
path	pathology	patología
ped	pediatrics	pediatría
pharm	pharmacology	farmacología
physio	physiology	fisiología
pl	plural	plural
pp	past participle	participio pasado
PR	Puerto Rico	Puerto Rico
prep	preposition	preposición
pret	preterit	pretérito
psych	psychology	psicología
SA	South America	Sudamérica
SD	Santo Domingo	Santo Domingo
super	superlative	superlativo
surg	surgery	cirugía
US	United States	Estados Unidos
V.	See	Véase
var	variation	variación
vi	verb, intransitive	verbo intransitivo
vr	verb, reflexive	verbo reflexivo
vt	verb, transitive	verbo transitivo
vulg	slang	vulgar

ENGLISH-SPANISH

INGLÉS-ESPAÑOL

A

AA *V.* **Alcoholics Anonymous.**
abdomen *n* abdomen *m*, estómago (*fam*)
abdominal supporter *n* faja, cinturón *m* (*para prevenir hernias*)
ability *n* (*pl* **-ties**) habilidad *f*, capacidad *f*
abnormal *adj* anormal
abnormality *n* (*pl* **-ties**) anormalidad *f*
abort *vt, vi* abortar
abortion *n* aborto (*esp. inducido*); **accidental** —— aborto accidental; **habitual** —— aborto habitual; **incomplete** —— aborto incompleto; **spontaneous** —— aborto espontáneo; **therapeutic** —— aborto terapéutico; **threatened** —— amenaza de aborto; **to have an** —— tener un aborto, abortar
abrasion *n* abrasión *f* (*form*), raspón *m*, raspadura
abrasive *adj & n* abrasivo
abscess *n* absceso, (*dent*) postemilla (*Mex, CA*)
absence *n* ausencia, falta
absent *adj* ausente
absent-minded *adj* distraído, olvidadizo
absorb *vt* absorber
absorbable *adj* absorbible
absorbent *adj* absorbente
absorption *n* absorción *f*
abstinence *n* abstinencia
abuse *n* abuso; **child** —— abuso infantil; **substance** —— abuso de substancias tóxicas
access *n* acceso; **wheelchair** —— acceso para sillas de rueda
accident *n* accidente *m*, (*automobile*) choque *m*
accident-prone *adj* propenso a sufrir accidentes
accumulate *vt, vi* acumular(se)
accuracy *n* exactitud *f*, precisión *f*
accurate *adj* exacto, preciso
acetaminophen *n* acetaminofén *m*
acetic acid *n* ácido acético
acetone *n* acetona
achalasia *n* acalasia
ache *n* dolor *m*, dolor persistente; **stomach** —— dolor de estómago; *vi* doler
achondroplasia *n* acondroplasia

acid *adj & n* ácido; **fatty** —— ácido graso; **gastric** —— ácido gástrico
acidity *n* acidez *f*
acne *n* acné *f*
acoustic *adj* acústico
acquire *vt* adquirir
acromegaly *n* acromegalia
act *n* acto; *vi* (*to behave*) comportarse; **to** —— **out** (*psych*) expresar impulsos reprimidos en conducta sin inhibiciones
ACTH *abbr* **adrenocorticotropic hormone.** *V.* **hormone.**
actinomycosis *n* actinomicosis *f*
action *n* acción *f*
activate *vt* activar
active *adj* activo
activity *n* actividad *f*; **strenuous** —— actividad fuerte
acuity *n* agudeza; **visual** —— agudeza visual
acupuncture *n* acupuntura
acute *adj* agudo
acyclovir *n* aciclovir *m*
Adam's apple *n* manzana de Adán
adapt *vt, vi* adaptar(se)
adaptation *n* adaptación *f*
add *vt* (*arith*) sumar; **How much is four and seven?..**¿Cuánto es cuatro más siete?
addict *n* adicto -ta *mf*, vicioso -sa *mf*; **drug** —— farmacodependiente *mf* (*form*), drogadicto -ta *mf*; *vt* enviciar; **to become addicted** enviciarse, volverse adicto
addiction *n* adicción *f*
addictive *adj* adictivo, que crea hábito
additive *adj & n* aditivo
address *n* dirección *f*, domicilio
adenitis *n* adenitis *f*
adenocarcinoma *n* adenocarcinoma *m*
adenoidectomy *n* (*pl* **-mies**) adenoidectomía
adenoiditis *n* adenoiditis *f*
adenoids *npl* vegetaciones adenoides *fpl*, adenoides *fpl*
adenoma *n* adenoma *m*; **villous** —— adenoma velloso
adequate *adj* adecuado, suficiente
adhesion *n* adherencia
adhesive *adj* adhesivo; —— **tape** tela *or* cinta adhesiva

adjust *vt* ajustar, modificar
adjustable *adj* ajustable
adjustment *n* ajuste *m*, corrección *f*, modificación *f*
adjuvant *adj* adyuvante, coadyuvante
administration *n* administración *f*
admission *n* (*to the hospital*) admisión *f*, ingreso
admit *vt* (*pret* & *pp* **admitted**; *ger* **admitting**) (*to the hospital*) internar, ingresar; **to be admitted** internarse, ingresarse; **He was admitted yesterday..** Se internó ayer...**You need to be admitted.**.Ud. necesita ser internado.
Admitting *n* Admisión *f*, Ingresos
adolescence *n* adolescencia
adolescent *adj* & *n* adolescente *mf*
adopt *vt* adoptar
adoption *n* adopción *f*
adoptive *adj* adoptivo
adrenaline *n* adrenalina
adult *adj* & *n* adulto -ta *mf*
advance *n* avance *m*
advantage *n* ventaja
aerobics *npl* aeróbicos, aerobics *mpl* (*Ang*)
aerosol *n* aerosol *m*
aerosolized *adj* en aerosol
affect *n* (*psych*) afecto; *vt* afectar
affection *n* afecto, cariño
affectionate *adj* afectuoso, cariñoso
affinity *n* (*pl* **-ties**) afinidad *f*
affliction *n* mal *m*, achaque *m*
afraid *adj* **to be** —— tener miedo; **Are you afraid of injections?**..¿Tiene miedo a las inyecciones?
afterbirth *n* (*fam*) placenta, secundinas (*fam*)
afternoon *n* tarde *f*
aftertaste *n* sabor *m* que queda después de tomar un medicamento o alimento
agammaglobulinemia *n* agammaglobulinemia
age *n* edad *f*; **bone** —— edad ósea; **middle** —— edad madura *or* mediana; **old** —— vejez *f*
agency *n* (*pl* **-cies**) agencia
agent *n* agente *m*
aggravate *vt* agravar
aggression *n* agresión *f*
aggressive *adj* agresivo
aging *n* envejecimiento
agitate *vt* agitar; **to become agitated** agitarse
agoraphobia *n* agorafobia
aid *n* ayuda, auxilio; *vt* ayudar, asistir
aide *n* asistente *mf*, ayudante *mf*, auxiliar *mf*; **nurse's** —— asistente de enfermera
AIDS *abbr* **acquired immunodeficiency syndrome.** *V.* **syndrome.**
ailment *n* mal *m*, achaque *m*, padecimiento
air *n* aire *m*
air conditioning *n* aire acondicionado
airsickness *n* mareo (en avión)

airway *n* vía respiratoria
alanine *n* alanina
albinism *n* albinismo
albino *adj* albino; *n* (*pl* **-nos**) albino -na *mf*
albumin *n* albúmina
albuterol *n* albuterol *m*
alcaptonuria *var de* **alkaptonuria**
alcohol *n* alcohol *m*, bebidas alcohólicas (*incluyendo vino y cerveza*); **Do you drink alcohol?**..¿Toma Ud. bebidas alcohólicas? **denatured** —— alcohol desnaturalizado; **rubbing** —— alcohol para fricciones
alcoholic *adj* & *n* alcohólico -ca *mf*
Alcoholics Anonymous (AA) *n* Alcohólicos Anónimos
alcoholism *n* alcoholismo
aldosterone *n* aldosterona
aldosteronism *n* aldosteronismo
alert *adj* alerta
algae *npl* algas
alienated *adj* aislado emocionalmente, incapaz de establecer relaciones con los demás
alienation *n* aislamiento emocional, incapacidad *f* para establecer relaciones con los demás
align *vt, vi* alinear(se)
alignment *n* alineamiento
alimentary *adj* alimentario
alive *adj* vivo, con vida
alkali *n* álcali *m*
alkaline *adj* alcalino; —— **phosphatase** fosfatasa alcalina
alkalosis *n* alcalosis *f*
alkaptonuria *n* alcaptonuria
allergic *adj* alérgico; **Are you allergic to any medicine?**..¿Es Ud. alérgico a algún medicamento?
allergy *n* (*pl* **-gies**) alergia
alleviate *vt* aliviar
allopurinol *n* alopurinol *m*
aloe *n* áloe *m*
alpha *n* alfa; —— **fetoprotein** alfa feto proteína
alprazolam *n* alprazolam *m*
alternate *adj* alterno; —— **days** días alternos; *vt, vi* alternar
altitude *n* altitud *f*
aluminum *n* aluminio
alveolus *n* (*pl* **-li**) alveolo *or* alvéolo
amalgam *n* (*dent*) amalgama
Amanita Amanita
amantadine *n* amantadina
ambulance *n* ambulancia
ambulatory *adj* ambulatorio
ameba *n* (*pl* **-bas** *o* **-bae**) amiba
amebiasis *n* amibiasis *f*
amebic *adj* amibiano
amenorrhea *n* amenorrea
American *adj* americano, norteamericano, estadounidense; *n* americano -na *mf*,

norteamericano -na *mf*
amiloride *n* amilorida
amino acid *n* aminoácido
aminoglycoside *n* aminoglucósido
aminophylline *n* aminofilina
amitriptyline *n* amitriptilina
ammonia *n* amoniaco *or* amoníaco
amnesia *n* amnesia
amniocentesis *n* (*pl* -ses) amniocentesis *f*
amnionitis *n* amnionitis *f*
amoxacillin *n* amoxacilina
amphetamine *n* anfetamina
amphotericin B *n* anfotericina B
ampicillin *n* ampicilina
ampule *n* ampolleta, ámpula
amputate *vt* amputar
amputation *n* amputación *f*
amylase *n* amilasa
amyloidosis *n* amiloidosis *f*
amyotrophic lateral sclerosis *n* esclerosis lateral amiotrófica
anabolic *adj* anabólico
anaerobic *adj* anaerobio
anal *adj* anal
analgesia *n* analgesia
analgesic *adj & n* analgésico
analysis *n* (*pl* -ses) análisis *m*
analyst *n* (*fam*) psicoanalista *mf*
analyze *vt* analizar
anaphylactic *adj* anafiláctico
anaphylaxis *n* anafilaxis *f*
anatomical, anatomic *adj* anatómico
anatomy *n* anatomía
ancestor *n* antepasado
androgen *n* andrógeno
anemia *n* anemia; **aplastic** —— anemia aplásica; **hemolytic** —— anemia hemolítica; **iron deficiency** —— anemia ferropriva (*form*), anemia por deficiencia de hierro; **pernicious** —— anemia perniciosa; **sickle cell** —— anemia de células falciformes, anemia drepanocítica; **sideroblastic** —— anemia sideroblástica
anemic *adj* anémico
anencephaly *n* anencefalia
anergy *n* anergia
anesthesia *n* anestesia; **general** —— anestesia general; **local** —— anestesia local; **regional** —— anestesia regional
anesthesiologist *n* anestesiólogo -ga *mf*
anesthesiology *n* anestesiología
anesthetic *adj & n* anestésico
anesthetist *n* anestesista *mf*
anesthetize *vt* anestesiar
aneurysm *n* aneurisma *m*; **dissecting** —— aneurisma disecante; **micotic** —— aneurisma micótico
angel dust *n* polvo de angel (*Ang*)
anger *n* ira, enojo
angina *n* angina (de pecho); **Prinzmetal's** —— angina de Prinzmetal; **unstable** —— angina inestable

angiodysplasia *n* angiodisplasia
angiogram *n* angiograma *m*, angiografía
angiography *n* angiografía
angioma *n* angioma *m*
angioplasty *n* (*pl* -ties) angioplastia; **percutaneous transluminal coronary** —— angioplastia transluminal percutánea coronaria
angiosarcoma *n* angiosarcoma *m*
angle *n* ángulo
angry *adj* enojado; **to get** —— enojarse
aniline *n* anilina
animal *n* animal *m*; —— **fat** grasa de animal
ankle *n* tobillo
anklebone *n* hueso del tobillo
ankylosis *n* anquilosis *f*
annoying *adj* molesto, fastidioso
annual *adj* anual
annular *adj* anular
anointing of the sick *n* santos óleos
anomaly *n* (*pl* -lies) anomalía
anorexia *n* anorexia; —— **nervosa** anorexia nervosa
anovulation *n* anovulación *f*
anovulatory *adj* anovulatorio
ant *n* hormiga
antacid *adj & n* antiácido
anterior *adj* anterior
anthelminthic *adj & n* antihelmíntico
anthrax *n* ántrax *m*
antiarrhythmic *adj & n* antiarrítmico
antibacterial *adj* antibacteriano
antibiotic *adj & n* antibiótico; **broad spectrum** —— antibiótico de amplio espectro
antibody *n* (*pl* -dies) anticuerpo
anticholinergic *adj* anticolinérgico
anticoagulant *adj & n* anticoagulante *m*
anticoagulate *vt* anticoagular
anticonvulsant *adj & n* anticonvulsivo, anticonvulsivante *m*
antidepressant *adj & n* antidepresivo; **tricyclic** —— antidepresivo tricíclico
antidote *n* antídoto
antiemetic *adj & n* antiemético
antifreeze *n* anticongelante *m*
antigen *n* antígeno
antihistamine *n* antihistamínico
antihypertensive *adj & n* antihipertensivo
antiinflammatory *adj* antiinflamatorio
antimicrobial *adj & n* antimicrobiano
antipsychotic *adj & n* antipsicótico
antipyretic *adj & n* antipirético
antiseptic *adj & n* antiséptico
antiserum *n* (*pl* -ra *o* -rums) antisuero
antisocial *adj* antisocial
antispasmodic *adj & n* antiespasmódico, antiespástico
antitoxin *n* antitoxina
anus *n* (*pl* anus *o* anuses) ano
anxiety *n* ansiedad *f*, desesperación *f*,

nervios (*fam*)
anxious *adj* ansioso
aorta *n* aorta
aortic *adj* aórtico
apathetic *adj* apático
apathy *n* apatía, indiferencia
Apgar score *n* índice *m or* valoración *f* de Apgar
aphasia *n* afasia
apnea *n* apnea; **sleep** —— apnea del sueño
apparatus *n* (*pl* -tus *o* -tuses) aparato
appearance *n* apariencia, aspecto
appendectomy *n* (*pl* -mies) apendicectomía
appendicitis *n* apendicitis *f*
appendix *n* (*pl* -dixes *o* -dices) apéndice *m*
appetite *n* apetito
apple *n* manzana
applicator *n* aplicador *m*
appointment *n* cita
appropriate *adj* apropiado, adecuado
approximately *adv* aproximadamente
apraxia *n* apraxia
apron *n* delantal *m*
aptitude *n* aptitud *f*
aqueous *adj* acuoso
ARC *abbr* **AIDS-related complex.** *V.* **complex.**
arch *n* arco; —— **of the foot** arco del pie
ARDS *abbr* **adult respiratory distress syndrome.** *V.* **syndrome.**
area *n* área
Argentine, Argentinean *adj* & *n* argentino -na *mf*
arginine *n* arginina
arm *n* brazo
armpit *n* axila, sobaco (*fam*)
arouse *vt* (*from sleep*) despertar; (*sexually, etc.*) excitar
arrest *n* paro; **cardiac** —— paro cardiaco; **respiratory** —— paro respiratorio
arrhythmia *n* arritmia
arsenic *n* arsénico
arteriosclerosis *n* arteriosclerosis *f*
arteriovenous *adj* arteriovenoso
arteritis *n* arteritis *f*; **temporal** *o* **giant cell** —— arteritis temporal
artery *n* (*pl* -ries) arteria; **brachial** —— arteria braquial; **carotid** —— arteria carótida; **coronary** —— arteria coronaria; **femoral** —— arteria femoral; **iliac** —— iliaca; **radial** —— arteria radial; **subclavian** —— arteria subclavia
arthritic *adj* artrítico
arthritis *n* artritis *f*; **juvenile** —— artritis juvenil; **rheumatoid** —— artritis reumatoide
arthrogram *n* artrograma *m*, artrografía
arthrography *n* artrografía
arthroscopy *n* (*pl* -pies) artroscopia *or* (*esp. spoken*) artroscopía
artificial *adj* artificial, postizo
asbestos *n* asbesto

ascariasis *n* ascariasis *f*, ascaridiasis *f*
Ascaris Ascaris
ascending *adj* ascendente
ascites *n* ascitis *f*
ascorbic acid *n* ácido ascórbico
ASD *abbr* **atrial septal defect.** *V.* **defect.**
aseptic *adj* aséptico
asleep *adj* dormido; **to fall** —— dormirse; **My foot fell asleep..**Se me durmió el pie.
asparagine *n* asparagina
aspergillosis *n* aspergilosis *f*
asphyxia *n* asfixia
asphyxiate *vt, vi* asfixiar(se)
aspirate *vt* aspirar
aspiration *n* aspiración *f*; **joint** —— aspiración articular; **needle** —— aspiración con aguja
aspirin *n* aspirina
assault *n* asalto; *vt* asaltar
assist *vt* asistir
assistant *n* asistente *mf*, ayudante *mf*, auxiliar *mf*; **nursing** —— asistente de enfermera
associate *n* socio -cia *mf*
association *n* asociación *f*
asthma *n* asma
asthmatic *adj* & *n* asmático -ca *mf*
astigmatism *n* astigmatismo
astringent *adj* & *n* astringente *m*
asylum *n* asilo; **insane** —— (*ant*) manicomio
ataxia *n* ataxia
ataxic *adj* atáxico
ate *pret de* eat
atenolol *n* atenolol *m*
atherosclerosis *n* aterosclerosis *f*
athlete *n* atleta *mf*; **athlete's foot** pie *m* de atleta
athletic supporter *n* suspensorio
atmosphere *n* atmósfera
atrial *adj* auricular
atrioventricular (A-V) *adj* auriculoventri-cular (AV)
atrium *n* (*pl* atria) (*of the heart*) aurícula
atrophy *n* atrofia; *vi* (*pret* & *pp* -phied) atrofiarse
atropine *n* atropina
attack *n* ataque *m*, acceso; **heart** —— ataque cardiaco *or* al corazón; **transient ischemic** —— isquemia cerebral transitoria; *vt* atacar
attend *vt* (*a clinic, class, etc.*) asistir a
attention *n* atención *f*
attenuated *adj* atenuado
atypical *adj* atípico
audiogram *n* audiograma *m*
audiologist *n* audiólogo -ga *mf*
audiology *n* audiología
audiometer *n* audiómetro
audiometry *n* audiometría
audition *n* audición *f*
auditory *adj* auditivo; —— **tube** conducto

auditivo
aunt *n* tía
aura *n* aura *m*
autism *n* autismo
autistic *adj* autístico; *n* autista *mf*
autoclave *n* autoclave *m*
autoimmune *adj* autoinmune
autoimmunity *n* autoinmunidad *f*
autologous *adj* autólogo
automobile *n* automóvil *m*
autopsy *n* (*pl* -sies) autopsia
autosomal *adj* autosómico
autumn *n* otoño

A-V *V.* **atrioventricular.**
available *adj* disponible
average *adj* promedio (*invariant with respect to gender*); —— **height** altura promedio; *n* promedio
aversion *n* aversión *f*
avoid *vt* evitar; **You should avoid salt**..Debe evitar la sal.
awake *adj* despierto
axilla *n* (*pl* -lae) axila
axillary *adj* axilar
azathioprine *n* azatioprina

B

babble *n* (*sounds made by baby*) balbuceo; *vi* balbucear
baby *n* (*pl* -bies) bebé *m*, criatura
bacillus *n* (*pl* -li) bacilo; **Calmette-Guérin** —— (**BCG**) bacilo de Calmette-Guérin (BCG)
back *adj* de atrás; *n* espalda; (*of the hand*) dorso; **the back of**..la parte de atrás de; **lower** —— parte baja de la espalda
backache *n* dolor *m* de espalda
backbone *n* columna vertebral, espina dorsal, columna (*fam*)
backup *n* respaldo
backward *adv* hacia atrás
bacon *n* tocino
bacteria *pl de* **bacterium**
bacterial *adj* bacteriano
bacterium *n* (*pl* -ria) bacteria (*en inglés se emplea casi siempre la forma plural:* **bacteria**); **Bacteria cause disease**..Las bacterias causan enfermedades.
Bacteroides Bacteroides
bad *adj* (*comp* **worse**; *super* **worst**) malo; **Salt is bad for you**..La sal le hace mal...a **bad cold**..un resfriado fuerte; —— **for one's health** malo *or* nocivo para la salud
bag *n* bolsa; —— **of waters** fuente *f*, bolsa de las aguas; **bags under one's eyes** bolsas bajo los ojos; **doctor's** —— maletín (médico); **hot-water** —— bolsa de agua caliente
baked *adj* horneado, (cocido) al horno
baker *n* panadero -ra *mf*
balance *n* (*equilibrium*) equilibrio
bald *adj* calvo
baldness *n* calvicie *f*

balloon *n* (*of a Foley catheter, etc.*) balón *m*
balls *npl* (*vulg*) testículos, huevos (*vulg*), cojones *mpl* (*vulg*)
balm *n* bálsamo; **lip** —— crema para los labios
bandage *n* vendaje *m*, (*material*) venda; **Mr. Mata's bandage is dirty**..El vendaje del señor Mata está sucio...**We need a new bandage**..Necesitamos una nueva venda; **adhesive** —— venda adhesiva; **elastic** —— venda elástica
Band-Aid *n* Curita *m&f* (*Both terms are trademarks. Los dos términos son marcas.*)
bands *npl* frenos, frenillos
barber *n* peluquero -ra *mf*, barbero
barbiturate *n* barbitúrico
barefoot *adj* descalzo, sin zapatos
barf (*vulg*) *n* vómito; *vt*, *vi* arrojar, devolver, deponer (*Mex*), tener basca, vomitar
barium *n* bario
barrel *n* (*of a syringe*) barril *m*
barrier *n* barrera
basal ganglia *npl* ganglios basales
base *n* (*chem, pharm, etc.*) base *f*; **oil-based** a base de aceite; **water-based** a base de agua
baseline *adj* basal; *n* (*behavior, physical exam*) estado habitual (*para el paciente*); (*lab value*) nivel habitual
bashful *adj* tímido
basic *adj* básico
basin *n* palangana, vasija; **emesis** —— riñón *m*, riñonera, escupidera
bassinet *n* moisés *m*
bat *n* (*zool*) murciélago

bath *n* baño; **sitz** —— baño de asiento; **steam** —— baño de vapor; **to take a** —— bañarse
bathe *vt, vi* bañar(se)
bathroom *n* baño; **to go to the** —— ir al baño
bathtub *n* tina (de baño), bañera, bañadera (*Cub*)
BCG *abbr* **Calmette-Guérin bacillus.** *V.* **bacillus.**
beam *n* (*light, X-ray, etc.*) rayo
beans *npl* frijoles *mpl*
bear *vt* (*pret* **bore**; *pp* **borne** *o* **born**) (*a child*) dar a luz, parir (*esp. Carib, fam*); (*to endure*) tolerar, aguantar; *vi* **to** —— **down** pujar; **Bear down as if you were having a bowel movement**..Puje como si estuviera defecando.
beard *n* barba
beat *n* (*of the heart*) latido; *vi* (*pret* **beat**; *pp* **beaten** *o* **beat**) latir
beclomethasone *n* beclometasona
bed *n* cama; (*sickbed, deathbed, fig*) lecho; **to stay in** —— guardar cama, quedarse en cama; **vascular** —— lecho vascular
bedbug *n* chinche *f*
bedclothes *npl* ropa de cama
bedding *n* ropa de cama
bedpan *n* bacinilla, pato, cómodo (*Mex*)
bedrail *n* barandal *m*, baranda
bedridden *adj* postrado en cama
bedroom *n* cuarto, dormitorio, recámara
bedside *n* lado de la cama
bedsore *n* llaga (*debida a permanecer mucho tiempo sin cambiar de posición*)
bed-wetting *n* enuresis *f* (*form*); (el) orinarse en la cama
bee *n* abeja; **Africanized** *or* **killer** —— abeja africana *or* asesina
beef *n* carne *f* de res, res *f*
beeper *n* bíper *m* (*Ang*)
beer *n* cerveza
beginning *n* comienzo, principio
behavior *n* conducta, comportamiento; —— **modification** modificación de la conducta
belch *vi* eructar
belief *n* creencia
belladonna *n* belladona
Bell's palsy *n* parálisis *f* de Bell, parálisis facial
belly *n* (*pl* **-lies**) vientre *m*, barriga, panza, estómago (*fam*)
bellybutton *n* (*fam*) ombligo
bellyache *n* dolor *m* de barriga
belt *n* cinto, cinturón *m*, correa
bend *n* curva, ángulo; *vt* (*pret & pp* **bent**) doblar; **Bend your knee**..Doble la rodilla; **to** —— **one's head down** bajar *or* agachar la cabeza; **Bend your head down**..Baje la cabeza; *vi* doblarse; **to** —— **over** *o* **down** doblarse; **Bend over**..Dóblese.

bends *n* enfermedad *f* por descompresión
beneficial *adj* benéfico
benefit *n* bien *m*, beneficio; **for your** —— por su bien
benign *adj* benigno
bent *pret & pp de* **bend**
benzedrine *n* bencedrina
benzene *n* benceno
benzodiazepine *n* benzodiacepina
benzoyl peroxide *n* peróxido de benzoílo
beriberi *n* beriberi *m*
beta *n* beta; —— **blocker** beta bloqueador *m*
beta-hemolytic *adj* beta hemolítico
better *adj & adv* (*comp de* **good** *y* **well**) mejor; **to get** —— mejorarse
bicarbonate *n* bicarbonato
biceps *n* bíceps *m*
bicuspid *adj & n* bicúspide *m*
bicycle *n* bicicleta
bifocals *npl* bifocales *mpl*
big *adj* (*comp* **bigger**; *super* **biggest**) grande; **How big was it?**..¿Qué tan grande era? **to get bigger** crecer, ponerse más grande
bile *n* bilis *f*
biliary *adj* biliar
bilingual *adj* bilingüe
bilirubin *n* bilirrubina
bill *n* (*charges*) cuenta, cobro
bind *vi* (*clothing, etc.*) apretar
binge *n* borrachera (*esp. por varios días seguidos*)
biochemical *adj* bioquímico
biochemistry *n* bioquímica
biodegradable *adj* biodegradable
biofeedback *n* biorretroalimentación *f*
biological, biologic *adj* biológico
biology *n* biología
biopsy *n* (*pl* **-sies**) biopsia; **needle** —— biopsia con aguja; **open** —— biopsia abierta
biorhythm *n* ritmo biológico
biostatistics *n* bioestadística
bipolar *adj* bipolar
bird *n* pájaro
birth *n* nacimiento; (*childbirth*) parto; —— **canal** canal *m* del parto; —— **certificate** certificado *or* acta de nacimiento; —— **control** control *m* de la natalidad; —— **control pill** píldora anticonceptiva; **natural** —— parto natural; **to give** —— dar a luz, aliviarse (*Mex, fam*); **She gave birth to a baby girl**..Dio a luz una niña.
birthday *n* cumpleaños *m*; **Happy birthday!**..¡Feliz cumpleaños!
birthing *n* parto natural
birthmark *n* marca de nacimiento, lunar *m*
bisexual *adj* bisexual
bismuth *n* bismuto
bite *n* mordida, mordedura; (*insect*) piquete *m*, picadura; *vt, vi* (*pret* **bit**; *pp* **bitten** *o* **bit**) morder; (*insect*) picar; **Bite**

down..Apriete los dientes.
bitter *adj* amargo
black *adj* negro; *n* (*person*) negro -gra *mf*, moreno -na *mf*; **to —— out** desmayarse, perder el conocimiento
black-and-blue *adj* amoratado, moreteado
black eye *n* ojo morado
black widow *n* viuda negra
blackhead *n* espinilla
blackout *n* (*faint*) desmayo; (*lapse of memory*) laguna mental
bladder *n* vejiga
blade *n* hoja
bland *adj* (*food*) no picante, sin sabor fuerte
blanket *n* frazada, cobija (*Mex*), friza (*PR, SD*); **electric ——** frazada *or* cobija eléctrica, cobertor eléctrico
bleach *n* blanqueador *m*, cloro
bled *pret & pp de* **bleed**
bleed *n* hemorragia, sangrado, (*cerebral*) derrame *m*; *vi* (*pret & pp* **bled**) sangrar
bleeding *adj* sangrante; **—— ulcer** úlcera sangrante; *n* hemorragia, sangrado
bleomycin *n* bleomicina
blew *pret de* **blow**
blind *adj* ciego
blindness *n* ceguera; **color ——** daltonismo (*form*), dificultad *f* para diferenciar ciertos colores; **night ——** ceguera nocturna
blink *n* parpadeo; *vi* parpadear
blister *n* ampolla, vesícula; **fever ——** fuego, ampolla en los labios (*debida al herpes*)
bloated *adj* hinchado; (*stomach*) hinchado, inflado (del estómago); **She looks bloated**..Se ve hinchada...**Do you get bloated after you eat?**..¿Se le hincha el estómago después de comer?
block *n* bloqueo; **bundle branch ——** bloqueo de rama; **heart ——** bloqueo cardiaco; *vt* (*pharm, physio*) bloquear; (*anat, surg*) obstruir (*form*), tapar (*fam*)
blockage *n* obstrucción *f*
blocker *n* bloqueador *m*; **beta —— beta** bloqueador; **calcium channel ——** bloqueador de los canales de calcio; **H₂-blocker** bloqueador de los receptores H₂
blond *adj* rubio, güero (*Mex*); *n* rubio, güero (*Mex*)
blonde *n* rubia, güera (*Mex*)
blood *n* sangre *f*; **—— bank** banco de sangre; **—— flow** flujo sanguíneo (*form*), circulación *f*; **—— poisoning** envenenamiento de la sangre; **—— pressure** presión *f* arterial (*form*), presión (de la sangre) (*fam*); **—— pressure cuff** esfigmomanómetro, baumanómetro, tensiómetro, aparato para medir la presión (*fam*); **—— type** grupo sanguíneo (*form*), tipo de sangre; **—— vessel** vaso sanguíneo; **arterial —— gas** gasometría, gases *mpl* arteriales

blood-borne *adj* transmitido a través de la sangre
bloodstream *n* torrente sanguíneo
bloody nose *n* sangrado por la nariz, hemorragia nasal
bloody show (*obst*) *n* sangrado vaginal (*antes de la expulsión del feto*)
blot *vt* (*pret & pp* **blotted**; *ger* **blotting**) secar por presión con material absorbente
blouse *n* blusa
blow *n* (*stroke*) golpe *m*; *vt* (*pret* **blew**; *pp* **blown**) **to —— one's nose** sonarse *or* soplarse (*Carib*) la nariz; *vi* (*to breathe out air forcefully*) soplar; **Blow as hard as you can**..Sople lo más fuerte que pueda.
blue *adj* azul; (*fam, sad*) triste; *n* **the blues** (*fam*) tristeza, melancolía
blur *vi* (*pret & pp* **blurred**; *ger* **blurring**) (*one's vision*) empañarse *or* borrarse (*la vista*)
blurred *adj* empañado, borroso; **—— vision** vista empañada, visión borrosa; **Do you get blurred vision?**..¿Se le empaña la vista?
blurry *adj* empañado, borroso
BM *abbr* bowel movement. *V.* **bowel**.
body *n* (*pl* **bodies**) cuerpo; **—— image** imagen *f* corporal
bodybuilder *n* fisicoculturista *mf*
boil *n* furúnculo (*form*), absceso (de la piel), nacido (*esp. Carib*); *vt* (*water*) hervir, hacer hervir; (*meat, etc.*) cocer, hacer cocer; *vi* hervir
Bolivian *adj & n* boliviano -na *mf*
bomb *n* bomba; **atomic —— bomba** atómica
bond (*psych, obst*) *n* vínculo, enlace *m*; *vi* formar un vínculo *or* enlace (con)
bonding (*psych, obst*) *n* formación *f* de un vínculo *or* enlace, enlazamiento (*form*)
bone *adj* óseo; **—— marrow** médula ósea; *n* hueso
booklet *n* folleto
booster *adj* de refuerzo; **—— shot** revacunación *f*, inyección *f* de refuerzo
boot *n* bota
booze *n* (*vulg*) bebida alcohólica
border *n* (*edge, margin*) borde *m*, margen *m*
bore *pret de* **bear**
boric acid *n* ácido bórico
born (*pret & pp de* **bear**) *adj* nacido; **to be —— nacer**
borne *pp de* **bear**
bother *vt* molestar; **Is your neck bothering you?**..¿Le molesta el cuello?
bottle *n* botella; (*for pills*) frasco, pomo; **hot-water ——** bolsa de agua caliente; **nursing —— *o* baby's ——** biberón *m*, mamadera, pacha (*CA*)
bottom *n* (*fam*) nalgas, sentaderas (*fam*)
botulism *n* botulismo
bovine *adj* bovino

bowel *n* intestino, tripa (*often pl*); —— **movement (BM)** defecación *f* (*form*), evacuación *f*, deposición *f* (*SA*); **large** —— intestino grueso; **small** —— intestino delgado; **to have a** —— **movement** defecar (*form*) evacuar, obrar (*Mex, CA*), hacer popó *or* pupú (*fam, esp. ped*), hacer del baño (*Mex, fam*), dar del cuerpo (*Carib, fam*); **When did you have your last bowel movement?**..¿Cuándo fue la última vez que evacuó?

bowl *n* plato hondo

bowlegged *adj* con las piernas arqueadas, zambo

boy *n* niño, muchacho

boyfriend *n* novio, amigo (íntimo)

bra *V.* **brassiere.**

brace *n* aparato ortopédico

braces *npl* frenos, frenillos

bradycardia *n* bradicardia

Braille *n* Braille *m*

brain *n* cerebro; —— **wave** onda cerebral

brainstem *n* tallo cerebral

bran *n* salvado, afrecho

brand *n* marca

brassiere *n* brassiere *m*, sostén *m*, ajustador *m* (*Cub*)

Brazilian *adj & n* brasileño -ña *mf*

bread *n* pan *m*

break *n* (*ortho*) fractura, quebradura; (*chromosome*) rompimiento; *vt, vi* (*pret* **broke**; *pp* **broken**) (*ortho*) fracturar(se), quebrar(se), romper(se) (*esp. Carib*), partir(se) (*Cub*); **My foot broke**..Se me quebró el pie...**I broke my foot**..Me quebré el pie...**How did you break your foot?**..¿Cómo se quebró el pie? **to** —— **out** (*one's skin*) salirle granos *or* barros; **When did your skin break out?**..¿Cuándo le salieron granos?

breakdown *n* colapso; **nervous** —— choque *or* colapso nervioso, crisis nerviosa

breakfast *n* desayuno; **to have** —— desayunar(se)

breast *n* mama, seno, pecho; —— **pump** tiraleche *m*, sacaleche *m*

breastbone *n* esternón *m* (*form*), hueso del pecho

breast-feed *vt* amamantar (*form*), dar pecho, dar de mamar; **Are you breastfeeding him?**..¿Le está dando pecho?

breast-feeding *n* lactancia maternal, (el) dar pecho

breath *n* aliento; **bad** —— mal aliento; **shortness of** —— falta del aire, sensación *f* de ahogo; **to be short of** —— faltarle la respiración *or* el aire; **Are you short of breath?**..¿Le falta la respiración?...**Do you get short of breath when you walk?**..¿Le falta el aire cuando camina?...**How many blocks can you walk before you get short of breath?**..¿Cuántas cuadras puede

caminar antes que le falte el aire? **to hold one's** —— detener *or* aguantar la respiración; **Hold your breath**..Detenga la respiración; **to take a deep** —— respirar profundo, hacer una respiración profunda; **Take a deep breath**..Respire profundo.

breathe *vt, vi* respirar; **to** —— **in** inspirar (*form*), respirar (*fam*), tomar aire (*fam*); **Breathe in**..Respire..Tome aire; **to** —— **out** expulsar el aire (*form*), sacar aire (*esp. Mex, CA; fam*), botar aire (*esp. Carib, SA; fam*)

breech presentation *n* presentación pélvica (*form*), presentación de nalgas

bridge *n* (*dent, etc.*) puente *m*

brief *adj* breve

bring *vt* **to** —— **on** (*pain, etc.*) provocar, causar

broiled *adj* asado, asado a la parrilla

broke *pret de* **break**

broken (*pp de* break) *adj* quebrado, roto

bromocriptine *n* bromocriptina

bronchial *adj* bronquial

bronchiectasis *n* bronquiectasia

bronchiole *n* (*pl* -li) bronquiolo

bronchiolitis *n* bronquiolitis *f*

bronchitis *n* bronquitis *f*

bronchodilator *n* broncodilatador *m*

bronchogenic *adj* broncogénico *or* broncógeno

bronchopneumonia *n* bronconeumonía

bronchoscopy *n* broncoscopia *or* (*esp. spoken*) broncoscopía

bronchospasm *n* broncospasmo *or* broncoespasmo

bronchus *n* (*pl* -chi) bronquio

broth *n* caldo

brother *n* hermano

brother-in-law *n* (*pl* **brothers-in-law**) cuñado

brow *n* frente *f*

brown *adj* café, marrón

brucellosis *n* brucelosis *f*

bruise *n* contusión *f* (*form*), moretón *m*, morete *m*, magulladura, lastimadura; *vt* causar moretones; *vi* hacerse moretones; **Do you bruise easily?**..¿Se le hacen moretones fácilmente?

bruised *adj* (*one place*) que tiene moretón, (*all over*) amoratado, moreteado

brunette *adj* moreno, trigueño; *n* morena, trigueña

brush *n* cepillo; *vt* cepillar; **to** —— **one's hair** cepillarse el pelo; **to** —— **one's teeth** cepillarse los dientes

brushing *n* cepillado

bubble *n* burbuja

bubo *n* (*pl* **buboes**) bubón *m*

bubonic *adj* bubónico

buckle *n* hebilla; *vt* abrochar(se)

buckteeth *n* dientes salidos

buffer *n* tampón *m*, amortiguador *m*, buffer

m; —— **solution** solución amortiguadora
buffered *adj* amortiguado
bug *n* (*fam*) insecto; (*fam*) microbio
build *n* físico, complexión *f*; *vt* to —— **up**
(*one's strength, muscles, etc.*) fortalecer;
(*one's resistance*) aumentar (*las defensas*);
vi to —— **up** acumularse
buildup *n* depósito, acumulación *f*
bulb syringe *n* perilla, pera
bulimia *n* bulimia
bulimic *adj* bulímico
bullet *n* bala
bump *n* protuberancia (*form*), bola, bolita,
pelota, (*due to trauma, esp. about the
head*) chichón *m*
bunion *n* juanete *m*
burn *n* quemadura; *vt* (*pret & pp* **burned** *o*
burnt) quemar; **Did you burn your
hand?**..¿Se quemó la mano? **to ——
oneself** *o* **to get burned** quemarse; **Did
you burn yourself?**..¿Se quemó? *vi* arder;
Does it burn when your urinate?..¿Le

arde al orinar?
burning *adj* ardiente, quemante; *n* ardor *m*
burp *vt* (*a baby*) sacar el aire, hacer eructar;
**You should burp your baby after each
meal**..Debe sacarle el aire a su bebé
después de cada comida; *vi* eructar
burr *n* (*plant*) espina, cadillo; (*metal*)
rebaba, astilla (de metal)
bursa *n* bolsa
bursitis *n* bursitis *f*
burst *vt*, *vi* (*pret & pp* **burst**) reventar(se)
bust *n* busto
busulfan *n* busulfán *m*
butcher *n* carnicero -ra *mf*
butt *n* (*vulg*) nalgas
butter *n* mantequilla
buttock *n* glúteo, nalga (*fam*)
button *vt* (*también* to —— **up**) abotonar(se),
abrochar(se)
buzz *n* zumbido; *vi* zumbar
buzzing *n* zumbido
bypass *n* bypass *m* (*Ang*), puente (cor~~ario)

C

cactus *n* (*pl* **-tuses** *o* **-ti**) cacto
cadaver *n* cadáver *m*
cadmium *n* cadmio
caffeine *n* cafeína
calamine *n* calamina
calcify *vt*, *vi* (*pret & pp* **-fied**) calcificar(se)
calcitonin *n* calcitonina
calcium *n* calcio; —— **carbonate** carbonato
de calcio; —— **channel blocker**
bloqueador *m* de los canales de calcio;
—— **gluconate** gluconato de calcio
calf *n* (*pl* **calves**) (*anat*) pantorrilla
calibrate *vt* calibrar
calisthenics *n* calistenia
call, on de guardia
callus *n* (*pl* **-luses**) callo, (*thin*) callosidad *f*
calm *adj* tranquilo, quieto; *n* calma; *vt*
calmar; *vi* to —— **down** calmarse
calomel *n* calomel *m*
calorie *n* caloría
campaign *n* campaña
camphor *n* alcanfor *m*
Campylobacter Campylobacter
can *n* lata, bote *m*
canal *n* canal *m*, conducto; **auditory ——**
canal auditivo; **birth ——** canal del parto;
semicircular —— conducto semicircular

cancel *vt* (*pret & pp* **-celed** *o* **-celled**; *ger*
-celing *o* **-celling**) cancelar
cancer *n* cáncer *m*; **breast ——** cáncer de la
mama (*form*), cáncer del seno *or* pecho;
lung ——, **prostate ——**, etc. cáncer del
pulmón, cáncer de la próstata, etc.
cancerous *adj* canceroso
Candida Candida
candidiasis *n* candidiasis *f*
candy *n* (*pl* **-dies**) (*one piece*) dulce *m*,
(*collective*) dulces
cane *n* bastón *m*
canker sore *n* afta, pequeña úlcera en la
boca
cannula *n* cánula; **nasal ——** cánula nasal
cap *n* (*of a bottle*) tapa; (*of a needle*)
protector *m* (*para una aguja*); (*dent*)
corona; (*surg, head covering*) gorro;
cervical —— capuchón *m* cervical; **safety
——** tapa de seguridad
capable *adj* capaz
capacity *n* (*pl* **-ties**) capacidad *f*
capillary *n* (*pl* **-ries**) capilar *m*
capsule *n* cápsula
captopril *n* captopril *m*
car *n* coche *m*, carro
carat *n* quilate *m*; **14 —— gold** oro de 14

quilates
carbamazepine *n* carbamazepina
carbidopa *n* carbidopa
carbohydrate *n* carbohidrato
carbon *n* (*element*) carbono; —— **dioxide**
bióxido *or* dióxido de carbono; ——
monoxide monóxido de carbono; ——
tetrachloride tetracloruro de carbono
carbonate *n* carbonato
carbuncle *n* carbunco
carcinoembryonic antigen *n* antígeno
carcinoembriónico
carcinoid *adj* & *n* carcinoide *m*
carcinoma *n* carcinoma *m*; **basal cell** ——
carcinoma basocelular; **oat cell** ——
carcinoma de células en avena; **small cell**
—— carcinoma de células pequeñas;
squamous cell —— carcinoma espinocelular *or* de células escamosas
card *n* (*hospital, business, etc.*) tarjeta
cardiac *adj* cardiaco *or* cardíaco
cardiogenic *adj* cardiogénico *or* cardiógeno
cardiologist *n* cardiólogo -ga *mf*
cardiology *n* cardiología
cardiomyopathy *n* cardiomiopatía; **dilated**
—— cardiomiopatía dilatada; **hypertrophic** —— cardiomiopatía hipertrófica;
restrictive —— cardiomiopatía restrictiva
cardiopulmonary resuscitation (CPR) *n*
resucitación *f or* reanimación *f* cardiopulmonar (RCP)
cardiovascular *adj* cardiovascular
cardioversion *n* cardioversión *f*
carditis *n* carditis *f*
care *n* cuidado; **health** —— atención
médica, servicios médicos; **intensive** ——
cuidados intensivos, terapia intensiva;
prenatal —— atención *f* prenatal;
primary —— atención primaria *or* del
primer nivel; **tertiary** —— atención *f* del
tercer nivel; **to take** —— **of** cuidar a,
atender a; **Who takes care of your
mother at home?**..¿Quién cuida a su
madre en casa? **to take** —— **of oneself**
cuidarse; **You should take care of
yourself better**..Debe cuidarse más; *vi* **to**
—— **for** cuidar a, atender a
careful *adj* **to be** —— tener cuidado; **Be
careful with this medicine**..Tenga
cuidado con esta medicina.
caregiver *n* cuidador -ra *mf*
careless *adj* descuidado
carelessness *n* descuido
caretaker *n* cuidador -ra *mf*
caries *n* caries *f*
carotid *adj* carótido
carpal *adj* carpiano
carpenter *n* carpintero
carrier *n* portador -ra *mf*
carsickness *n* mareo (en un vehículo)
cartilage *n* cartílago
case *n* caso; **nine out of ten cases**..nueve de

diez casos; **just in** —— por si acaso, para
estar seguro, por precaución
cast *n* (*ortho*) yeso; **urinary** —— cilindro
urinario
castor oil *n* aceite *m* de ricino
castrate *vt* castrar
castration *n* castración *f*
cat *n* gato
CAT *abbr* **computerized axial tomography.**
V. **tomography.**
cataract *n* catarata
catatonia *n* catatonía
catch *vt* (*pret* & *pp* **caught**) (*a disease*)
darle (*a uno*), pegarle (*a uno*), coger; **I
caught a cold**..Me dio un catarro; **to** ——
one's breath agarrar aire, tomar aire
catching (*fam*) *adj* contagioso
catgut *n* catgut *m*
catheter *n* catéter *m*, sonda; **Foley** ——
sonda Foley; **Hickman** —— catéter
Hickman; **Tenckhoff** —— catéter
Tenckhoff
catheterization *n* cateterismo; **cardiac** ——
cateterismo cardiaco
caught *pret* & *pp de* **catch**
causalgia *n* causalgia
cause *n* causa; *vt* causar
caustic *adj* cáustico
cauterize *vt* cauterizar
cavity *n* (*pl* **-ties**) cavidad *f*; **You have a
cavity**..Tiene un diente picado..Tiene una
cavidad...**You have cavities**..Tiene caries.
cc. *V.* **cubic centimeter.**
cecum *n* (*pl* **ceca**) ciego
cefaclor *n* cefaclor *m*
cefotaxime *n* cefotaxima
ceftriaxone *n* ceftriaxona
celiac *adj* celiaco *or* celíaco
celibate *adj* que no tiene relaciones sexuales
cell *n* célula; **B** —— célula B; **plasma** ——
célula plasmática; **red blood** —— glóbulo
rojo; **T** —— célula T; **white blood** ——
glóbulo blanco
cellulite *n* celulitis *f*
cellulitis *n* celulitis *f*
center *n* centro; **day-care** —— guardería
infantil (*esp. para niños de madres que
trabajan durante el día*); **healthcare** ——
centro de salud
centigrade *adj* centígrado
centimeter (cm.) *n* centímetro (cm.); ——
cubed *o* **cubic** —— (**cc.**) centímetro
cúbico (cc.)
centipede *n* ciempiés *m*
central *adj* central; —— **line** catéter *m*
central
cephalic *adj* cefálico
cephalosporin *n* cefalosporina
cephalothin *n* cefalotina
cerclage *n* cerclaje *m*
cereal *n* cereal *m*
cerebellum *n* (*pl* **-la**) cerebelo

cerebral *adj* cerebral; —— **palsy** parálisis *f* cerebral
cerebrovascular *adj* cerebrovascular
cerebrum *n* (*pl* -**brums** *o* -**bra**) cerebro
certificate *n* certificado, partida; **birth** —— certificado *or* acta de nacimiento; **death** —— certificado de defunción
cervical *adj* cervical
cervicitis *n* cervicitis *f*
cervix *n* (*pl* -**vixes** *o* -**vices**) cérvix *f*, cuello de la matriz
cesarean section *n* operación cesárea
chafe *n* rozadura; *vt, vi* rozar(se)
chair *n* silla
chalazion *n* (*pl* -**zia**) chalazión *m*
chamber *n* cámara
chancre *n* chancro; **soft** —— chancro blando
chancroid *n* chancroide *f*
change *n* cambio; —— **of life** cambio de vida; *vt, vi* cambiar
chap *vi* agrietarse, partirse (*debido a la resequedad*)
chapped *adj* agrietado, partido (*debido a la resequedad*)
Chap Stick *n* (*marca*) crema para los labios, lápiz *m* para labios partidos
characteristic *adj* característico; *n* característica
charcoal *n* carbón *m*; **activated** —— carbón activado
charge *n* costo, cobro
charlatan *n* charlatán -na *mf*
charley horse (*fam*) *n* calambre *m*
chart *n* tabla; (*medical record*) expediente *m*; **eye** —— carta de examen visual; **Snellen** —— carta de Snellen
chatter *vi* (*one's teeth*) castañetear
checkup *n* chequeo
cheek *n* mejilla; (*fam, buttock*) nalga
cheekbone *n* pómulo
cheerful *adj* alegre
cheese *n* queso
chemical *adj* químico; *n* substancia química
chemistry *n* química
chemotherapy *n* (*pl* -**pies**) quimioterapia
chest *n* pecho
chew *vt, vi* masticar
chewable *adj* masticable
chewing gum *n* chicle *m*
chicken *n* pollo
chickenpox *n* varicela, viruelas locas (*Mex, CA*)
chigger *n* nigua
child *n* (*pl* **children**) niño -ña *mf*
childbirth *n* parto
childhood *n* niñez *f*
childproof *adj* a prueba de niños
Chilean *adj* & *n* chileno -na *mf*
chill *n* escalofrío
chin *n* barba, mentón *m*
chip *n* pedacito, astilla; *vt, vi* astillar(se), quebrar(se)
chiropodist *n* quiropodista *mf*, podíatra *or* podiatra *mf*
chiropractic *n* quiropráctica
chiropractor *n* quiropráctico -ca *mf*
Chlamydia Chlamydia
chloral hydrate *n* hidrato de cloral
chlorambucil *n* clorambucilo
chloramphenicol *n* cloranfenicol *m*
chlordane *n* clordano
chloride *n* cloruro
chlorinated *adj* clorado
chlorination *n* cloración *f*
chlorine *n* cloro
chloroform *n* cloroformo
chlorpromazine *n* cloropromacina
chlorpropamide *n* clorpropamida
chocolate *n* chocolate *m*
choke *vt* estrangular; *vi* (*due to fumes, lack of air, etc.*) asfixiarse, sofocarse, ahogarse; **to** —— **on** (*food, etc.*) atragantarse con
cholangiocarcinoma *n* colangiocarcinoma *m*
cholangiogram *n* colangiograma *m*, colangiografía
cholangiography *n* colangiografía; **percutaneous transhepatic** —— (PTC) colangiografía transhepática percutánea
cholangitis *n* colangitis *f*
cholecystectomy *n* (*pl* -**mies**) colecistectomía
cholecystitis *n* colecistitis *f*
cholera *n* cólera *m*
cholesterol *n* colesterol *m*
cholestyramine *n* colestiramina
chondrosarcoma *n* condrosarcoma *m*
chorea *n* corea; **Huntington's** —— corea de Huntington
chorioretinitis *n* coriorretinitis *f*
chromium *n* cromo
chromosome *n* cromosoma *m*
chronic *adj* crónico
cigar *n* puro, tabaco (*esp. Carib*)
cigarette *n* cigarro, cigarrillo
cimetidine *n* cimetidina
ciprofloxacin *n* ciprofloxacina
circle *n* círculo; (*under one's eye*) ojera
circulation *n* circulación *f*; **collateral** —— circulación colateral; **fetal** —— circulación fetal; **pulmonary** —— circulación pulmonar; **systemic** —— circulación sistémica *or* mayor
circulatory *adj* circulatorio
circumcise *vt* circuncidar
circumcised *adj* circunciso
circumcision *n* circuncisión *f*
cirrhosis *n* cirrosis *f*
cirrhotic *adj* & *n* cirrótico -ca *mf*
cisplatin *n* cisplatin *m*
citrate *n* citrato
citrus fruit *n* fruta cítrica
clamp *n* pinza *or* pinzas; *vt* pinzar
clap *n* (*vulg*) gonorrea

class *n* clase *f*
classic *adj* clásico
claudication *n* claudicación *f*; **intermittent**
——— claudicación intermitente
claustrophobia *n* claustrofobia
clavicle *n* clavícula
clean *adj* limpio; *vt* limpiar
cleaning *n* (*dent, etc.*) limpieza
cleanliness *n* limpieza
clear *adj* claro, transparente; *vi* **to** ———
one's throat garraspear *or* carraspear; **to**
——— **up** (*a rash, illness, etc.*) resolverse
cleft palate *n* paladar hendido
clench *vt* (*teeth, fist*) apretar *or* cerrar fuerte
(*los dientes, el puño*)
click *n* (*card*) chasquido; *vi* (*joint*) tronar;
My knee clicks when I bend it..Me
truena la rodilla al doblarla.
climate *n* clima *m*
climax *n* orgasmo
clindamycin *n* clindamicina
clinic *n* clínica; **urgent care** ——— clínica de
urgencias
clinical *adj* clínico
clinician *n* médico clínico
clip (*surg*) *n* pinza; *vt* pinzar
clitoris *n* (*pl* **-rides**) clítoris *m*
clofazimine *n* clofazimina
clofibrate *n* clofibrato
clomiphene *n* clomifén *m*
clonazepam *n* clonacepam *m*
clone *n* clona
clonic *adj* clónico
clonidine *n* clonidina
clonus *n* clonus *m*, clono
close *vt* cerrar; **Close your eyes**..Cierre los
ojos; *vi* cerrar(se)
Clostridium Clostridium
clot *n* coágulo; *vt, vi* (*pret & pp* **clotted**; *ger*
clotting) coagular(se)
cloth *n* (*for compress, etc.*) lienzo, paño
clothes *npl* ropa
clothing *n* ropa
clotrimazole *n* clotrimazol *m*
cloud *vi* (*también* **to** ——— **up**) (*one's vision*)
nublarse
cloudy *adj* (*comp* **-ier**; *super* **-iest**) (*vision*)
nublado; (*urine*) turbio
clubfoot *n* (*pl* **-feet**) pie deforme congénito
clumsy *adj* torpe
cm. *V.* **centimeter.**
CNS *abbr* **central nervous system.** *V.*
system.
coagulate *vt, vi* coagular(se)
coagulation *n* coagulación *f*; **disseminated**
intravascular ——— (**DIC**) coagulación
intravascular diseminada
coagulopathy *n* coagulopatía
coal *n* carbón *m*
coal tar *n* alquitrán *m* de hulla
coarctation *n* coartación *f*
coat *n* abrigo; *vt* (*one's stomach, etc.*) cubrir,

revestir, recubrir
coated *adj* cubierto, revestido, que tiene
capa
coating *n* capa, revestimiento, recubrimiento
cobalt *n* cobalto
coca *n* (*bot*) coca
cocaine *n* cocaína
coccidioidomycosis *n* coccidioidomicosis *f*
coccus *n* (*pl* **-ci**) coco
coccyx *n* (*pl* **-cyges**) cóccix *m*
cochlea *n* (*pl* **-leae**) cóclea
cockroach *n* cucaracha
cocoa butter *n* manteca de cacao
coconut *n* coco; ——— **oil** aceite *m* de coco
codeine *n* codeína
cod-liver oil *n* aceite *m* de hígado de
bacalao
coffee *n* café *m*; ——— **grounds** posos del
café, café molido
coitus *n* coito; ——— **interruptus** coito
interrumpido
coke (*vulg*) *n* cocaína, coca (*vulg*)
colchicine *n* colchicina
cold *adj* frío; **to be** ——— (*the weather*) hacer
frío; **Do your joints hurt more when it's**
cold?..¿Sus huesos le duelen más cuando
hace frío? **to be** *o* **feel** ——— tener *or*
sentir frío; **Are you cold?**..¿Tiene frío? *n*
frío; (*illness*) resfriado, catarro
cold cream *n* crema limpiadora
cold sore *n* fuego, úlcera en los labios
(*debida al herpes*)
cold turkey *adv* (*fam*) bruscamente
(*refiriéndose a la suspensión de un hábito*
o una adicción)
colectomy *n* (*pl* **-mies**) colectomía
colic *adj* (*anat*) cólico; *n* cólico
colitis *n* colitis *f*; **pseudomembranous** ———
colitis seudomembranosa; **ulcerative** ———
colitis ulcerosa
collagen *n* colágeno, colágena
collapse *n* colapso; *vi* desplomarse, caerse,
sufrir un colapso; (*a lung*) colapsarse
collar *n* cuello; **cervical** ——— (*hard or soft*)
collarín, collar cervical, (*rígido o blando*)
collateral *adj* colateral
colloid *n* coloide *m*
Colombian *adj & n* colombiano -na *mf*
colon *n* colon *m*; **spastic** ——— colon
espástico
colonic *adj* colónico; *n* (*fam*) enema *m&f*
colonization *n* colonización *f*
colonoscopy *n* (*pl* **-pies**) colonoscopia *or*
(*esp. spoken*) colonoscopía
color *n* color *m*; ——— **blindness** daltonismo
(*form*), dificultad *f* para diferenciar ciertos
colores
color-blind *adj* daltónico (*form*), que no
diferencia bien ciertos colores
colostomy *n* colostomía
colostrum *n* calostro
colposcopy *n* (*pl* **-pies**) colposcopia *or* (*esp.*

spoken) colposcopía
coma *n* coma *m*
comatose *adj* comatoso (*form*), en coma
comb *n* peine *m*; *vt* peinar; **to** —— **one's hair** peinarse
combination *n* combinación *f*
come *vi* **to** —— **and go** ir y venir; **Does the pain come and go?**..¿Le va y le viene el dolor? **to** —— **down** bajar(se); **Your sugar came down**..Se bajó el azucar; **to** —— **on** (*to begin*) empezar; **When did the pain come on?**..¿Cuándo empezó el dolor?
comfort *n* comodidad *f*
comfortable *adj* cómodo, confortable
commode *n* inodoro portátil (*para inválidos, etc.*)
common *adj* común
communicable *adj* transmisible
communication *n* comunicación *f*
community *adj* comunitario; *n* comunidad *f*
compassion *n* compasión *f*
compatible *adj* compatible
compensate *vt, vi* compensar
complain *vi* quejarse
complaint *n* queja
complement *n* complemento
complete *adj* completo
complex *n* complejo; **AIDS-related** —— (**ARC**) complejo relacionado con el SIDA; **Oedipal** —— complejo de Edipo
complexion *n* cutis *m*, tez *f*
complication *n* complicación *f*
component *n* componente *m*
compound *n* compuesto
compress *n* compresa; *vt* comprimir
compression *n* compresión *f*; **chest compressions** masaje cardiaco externo (**MCE**), compresiones torácicas
compromise *vt* comprometer
compulsion *n* compulsión *f*
compulsive *adj* compulsivo
computer *n* computadora
concave *adj* cóncavo
conceive *vi* concebir
concentrate *n* concentrado; *vt, vi* concentrar(se)
concentrated *adj* concentrado
concentration *n* concentración *f*
conception *n* concepción *f*
concussion *n* concusión *f*, conmoción *f*
condition *n* condición *f*, estado
conditioned *adj* condicionado
condom *n* condón *m*, preservativo
cone *n* cono
confabulation *n* confabulación *f*
confidence *n* confianza
confidential *adj* confidencial
conflict *n* conflicto
confuse *vt* confundir; **to become confused** confundirse
confusion *n* confusión *f*

congenital *adj* congénito
congested *adj* congestionado
congestion *n* congestión *f*
congestive *adj* congestivo
congratulations *interj* (*obst, etc.*) ¡Felicidades!
conjugated *adj* conjugado
conjunctiva *n* (*pl* -vae) conjuntiva
conjunctivitis *n* conjuntivitis *f*
conscience *n* conciencia; **guilty** —— conciencia culpable
conscious *adj* consciente
consciousness *n* conciencia, conocimiento; **to lose** —— perder el conocimiento *or* la conciencia; **to regain** —— volver en sí
consecutive *adj* consecutivo
consent *n* consentimiento, permiso; *vi* consentir; **to** —— **to** consentir en
consequence *n* consecuencia
conservative *adj* (*measures, etc.*) conservador
consistency *n* (*pl* -cies) consistencia
consommé *n* consomé *m*
constant *adj* constante
constipate *vt* estreñir
constipated *adj* estreñido; **to become** —— estreñirse
constipation *n* estreñimiento
constitution *n* constitución *f*
constrict *vt* apretar
consult *vt* consultar
consultation *n* consulta
consumption *n* consumo
contact *n* contacto; —— **lens** (*hard or soft*) lente *m&f* de contacto (*duro o blando*)
contagious *adj* contagioso
container *n* recipiente *m*
contaminate *vt* contaminar; **to become contaminated** contaminarse
contamination *n* contaminación *f*
content, contents *n, npl* contenido
continual *adj* continuo
contour *n* contorno
contraception *n* anticoncepción *f*, contracepción *f*
contraceptive *adj & n* anticonceptivo
contract *vt, vi* contraer(se)
contraction *n* contracción *f*; (*obst*) contracción, dolor *m* del parto; **premature atrial** —— (**PAC**) contracción auricular prematura; **premature ventricular** —— (**PVC**) contracción ventricular prematura
contracture *n* contractura
contraindication *n* contraindicación *f*
contrast medium *n* medio de contraste
control *n* control *m*; **birth** —— control de la natalidad; **out of** —— fuera de control; *vt* (*pret & pp* -trolled; *ger* -trolling) controlar
contusion *n* contusión *f*
convalesce *vi* convalecerse
convalescence *n* convalecencia

convalescent *adj* convaleciente
conversion *n* conversión *f*; —— **reaction** reacción conversiva
convex *adj* convexo
convulsion *n* convulsión *f*, ataque *m* (*fam*)
coo *vi* (*pret & pp* **cooed**) arrullar
cook *n* cocinero -ra *mf*; *vt, vi* cocinar
cookie *n* galleta
cool *adj* fresco
cooperate *vi* cooperar
cooperative *adj* cooperativo
coordination *n* coordinación *f*
COPD *abbr* **chronic obstructive pulmonary disease.** *V.* **disease.**
cope *vi* **to** —— **with** enfrentarse a, hacer frente a
copper *n* cobre *m*; —— **sulfate** sulfato de cobre
coral *n* coral *m*
cord *n* cordón *m*, cuerda; **spinal** —— médula espinal; **umbilical** —— cordón umbilical; **vocal** —— cuerda vocal
core *n* corazón *m*
corn *n* maíz *m*; (*on the foot*) callo; —— **oil** aceite *m* de maíz
cornea *n* córnea
coronary *adj* coronario
coroner *n* médico forense; oficial *m* del gobierno que investiga casos de muerte
corpse *n* cadáver *m*, difunto -ta *mf*
corpuscle *n* corpúsculo
correct *adj* correcto; *vt* corregir, ajustar
correction *n* corrección *f*, ajuste *m*
corrective *adj* correctivo
correlation *n* correlación *f*
corrosive *adj* corrosivo
cortex *n* (*pl* **-tices**) corteza
cortical *adj* cortical
corticosteroid *n* corticosteroide *m*
cortisol *n* cortisol *m*
cortisone *n* cortisona
cosmetic *adj & n* cosmético
Costa Rican *adj & n* costarricense *mf*
costochondritis *n* costocondritis *f*
cottage cheese *n* requesón *m*
cotton *n* algodón *m*; —— **ball** bolita de algodón, torunda (de algodón) (*esp. Mex, CA*)
couch *n* (*psych*) diván *m*
cough *n* tos *f*; —— **drop** pastilla para la tos; —— **syrup** jarabe *m* para la tos; **dry** —— tos seca; **hacking** —— tos fuerte; *vt* **to** —— **up** expectorar (*form*), desgarrar; **Are you coughing up phlegm?**..¿Desgarra flema?..¿Cuándo tose, saca flema?.. ¿Tiene flema al toser?...**Try to cough up phlegm from your lungs**..Trate de desgarrar flema de sus pulmones..Trate de toser y sacar flema de sus pulmones; *vi* toser; **Cough hard**..Tosa fuerte.
coumarin *n* cumarina
counseling *n* consejo

counselor *n* consejero -ra *mf*
count *n* recuento; **blood** —— biometría hemática, recuento sanguíneo; **white blood cell** —— recuento de glóbulos blancos; *vt, vi* contar
counteract *vt* contrarrestar
country *n* (*pl* **-tries**) país *m*; (*rural area*) campo
county *n* (*US*) condado
couple *n* pareja; **married** —— matrimonio
course *n* (*of a disease, etc.*) transcurso, curso; (*educational*) curso
cousin *n* primo -ma *mf*
cover *vt* cubrir, tapar; **Cover your right eye**..Tape su ojo derecho.
coverage *n* cobertura
cow *n* vaca
CPR *abbr* **cardiopulmonary resuscitation.** *V.* **resuscitation.**
crab louse *n* ladilla
crack *n* (*bone, teeth*) fisura, (*skin*) grieta; (*cocaine*) crack *m* (*Ang*), forma de cocaína que se fuma; *vt* (*one's joints, one's back*) tronar(se) (*los huesos, la espalda*); *vi* agrietarse, partirse
cracker *n* galleta
cradle *n* cuna, moisés *m*
cramp *n* calambre *m*; (*abdominal*) retorcijón *or* retortijón *m*; (*menstrual*) dolor *m* menstrual, cólico menstrual; (*postpartum*) entuertos; *vi* **My leg is cramping**..Tengo un calambre en la pierna.
cranial *adj* craneal
craniopharyngioma *n* craneofaringioma *m*
cranium *n* (*pl* **-nia**) cráneo
craving *n* (*obst*) antojo
crawl *vi* (*ped*) gatear
craziness *n* locura
crazy *adj* (*comp* **-ier**; *super* **-iest**) loco; **to drive** (*someone*) —— volver loco (*a alguien*), trastornar; **His mother drove him crazy**..Su madre lo volvió loco; **to go** —— volverse loco, enloquecer(se)
cream *n* crema; **hand** —— crema para las manos
creatinine *n* creatinina
cretin *n* cretino
cretinism *n* cretinismo
crib *n* cuna
cried *pret & pp de* **cry**
cries *pl de* **cry**
cripple *vt* lisiar
crippled *adj* lisiado, tullido
crisis *n* (*pl* **-ses**) crisis *f*; **blast** —— crisis blástica; **identity** —— crisis de identidad; **midlife** —— crisis de la edad madura
critical *adj* crítico
cromolyn sodium *n* cromoglicato de sodio
crooked *adj* torcido, chueco (*Mex*)
crop-dust *vt, vi* fumigar con avioneta
cross-eyed *adj* bizco
crossmatch *n* prueba cruzada; *vt* hacer

prueba(s) cruzada(s), cruzar (la sangre) (*fam*)
crotch *n* entrepiernas *or* entrepierna
croup *n* crup *m*
crown *n* (*anat, dent*) corona
crush *vt* aplastar, (*one's finger, hand, etc.*) machucar; (*a tablet*) triturar (*form*), moler, desbaratar
crushing *adj* (*sensation, pain*) opresivo, aplastante
crust *n* costra
crutch *n* muleta
cry *n* (*pl* **cries**) (*with tears*) llanto, lloro, (*yell*) grito; *vi* (*pret & pp* **cried**) llorar, gritar
cryotherapy *n* crioterapia
Cryptococcus Cryptococcus
cryptorchidism *n* criptorquidia
crystal *n* cristal *m*
CSF *abbr* **cerebrospinal fluid.** *V.* **fluid.**
CT *abbr* **computed tomography.** *V.* **tomography.**
Cuban *adj & n* cubano -na *mf*
cubic centimeter (cc.) *n* centímetro cúbico (cc.)
culdocentesis *n* (*pl* -**ses**) culdocentesis *f*
culdoscopy *n* (*pl* -**pies**) culdoscopia *or* (*esp. spoken*) culdoscopía
culture *n* cultura; (*micro*) cultivo; **blood** —— hemocultivo; **stool** —— coprocultivo; **urine** —— urocultivo; *vt* cultivar
cumulative *adj* acumulativo
cunnilingus *n* cunilinguo
cup, cupful *n* (*pl* -**fuls**) taza
curable *adj* curable
curative *adj* curativo
cure *n* cura, remedio, curación *f*; *vt* curar; **to be cured** curarse
curettage *n* curetaje *m*, legrado (*fam*), raspado (*fam*)
curve *n* curva; **growth** —— curva de crecimiento
cushion *n* cojín *m*, almohada
cuspid *n* (diente) canino, colmillo (*fam*)
cut *n* cortada, cortadura, corte *m*; *vt* (*pret &*

pp **cut**; *ger* **cutting**) cortar; **Did you cut your finger?**..¿Se cortó el dedo? **to** —— **down (on)** (*fam*) disminuir; **You have to cut down on salt.**.Tiene que tomar menos sal; **to** —— **off** cortar, amputar; **to** —— **one's hair** cortarse el pelo; **to** —— **one's nails** cortarse las uñas; **to** —— **oneself** cortarse; **Did you cut yourself?**..¿Se cortó?
cutaneous *adj* cutáneo
cutdown *n* venodisección *f*
cuticle *n* cutícula
cyanide *n* cianuro
cyanosis *n* cianosis *f*
cyanotic *adj* cianótico, morado (*fam*), amoratado (*fam*)
cyclamate *n* ciclamato
cycle *n* ciclo; **anovulatory** —— ciclo anovulatorio; **menstrual** —— ciclo menstrual; **ovulatory** —— ciclo ovulatorio; **reproductive** —— ciclo reproductor
cyclic, cyclical *adj* cíclico
cyclophosphamide *n* ciclofosfamida
cyst *n* quiste *m*; **Baker's** —— quiste de Baker; **Bartholin's** —— quiste de Bartholin; **dermoid** —— quiste dermoide; **hydatid** —— quiste hidatídico; **ovarian** —— quiste ovárico; **pilonidal** —— quiste pilonidal; **popliteal** —— quiste poplíteo; **sebaceous** —— quiste sebáceo; **thyroglossal duct** —— quiste del conducto tirogloso
cystectomy *n* (*pl* -**mies**) cistectomía
cysteine *n* cisteína
cystic *adj* quístico; (*duct, artery*) cístico
cysticercosis *n* cisticercosis *f*
cystic fibrosis *n* fibrosis quística
cystinuria *n* cistinuria
cystitis *n* cistitis *f*, infección *f* de la vejiga
cystocele *n* cistocele *m*
cystoscopy *n* (*pl* -**pies**) cistoscopia *or* (*esp. spoken*) cistoscopía
cytomegalovirus *n* citomegalovirus *m*
cytotoxic *adj* citotóxico

D

D&C *V.* dilation and curettage.
dacryocystitis *n* dacriocistitis *f*
dad *n* papá *m*
damage *n* daño; *vt* dañar, hacer daño
damp *adj* húmedo, mojado
dampness *n* humedad *f*
danazol *n* danazol *m*
dandruff *n* caspa
danger *n* peligro
dangerous *adj* peligroso
dangle *vt, vi* colgar; **Sit with your legs dangling**..Siéntese con las piernas colgando.
dapsone *n* dapsona
dark *adj* oscuro; *(complexion)* moreno
dark-skinned *adj* moreno
data *n o npl* datos, información *f*
date *n* fecha
daughter *n* hija
daughter-in-law *n* *(pl* **daughters-in-law)** nuera
day *n* día *m*; —— **care** cuidado para niños durante el día *(esp. niños de madres que trabajan)*; **every** —— todos los días; **every other** —— cada dos días; **the** —— **after** *o* **the following** —— el día siguiente; **the** —— **after tomorrow** pasado mañana; **the** —— **before** el día anterior; **the** —— **before yesterday** anteayer
daydream *vi* *(pret & pp* -dreamed *o* -dreamt)* soñar despierto
daze *n* estado de confusión o desorientación sin agitación; **in a** —— aturdido, atarantado; *vt* aturdir, atarantar
dazed *adj* atarantado, aturdido; **to become** —— atarantarse, aturdirse
DDT *V.* dichlorodiphenyltrichloroethane.
dead *adj* muerto
deaf *adj* sordo
deaf-and-dumb *adj* *(vulg)* sordomudo
deaf-mute *n* sordomudo -da *mf*
deafmutism *n* sordomudez *f*
deafness *n* sordera
death *n* muerte *f*, —— **certificate** certificado de defunción; **brain** —— muerte cerebral
debilitated *adj* debilitado
debilitating *adj* debilitante
debilitation *n* debilitación *f*
debridement *n* desbridamiento
decay *n* tooth —— caries *f*
deceased *adj & n* difunto -ta *mf*
decibel *n* decibel *m*
deciliter *n* decilitro

decision *n* decisión *f*
decongestant *adj* descongestivo, descongestionante; *n* descongestionante *m*, descongestivo
decrease *n* disminución *f*; *vt, vi* disminuir(se)
deep *adj* profundo, hondo
deep-fried *adj* frito con mucho aceite
defecate *vi* defecar
defect *n* defecto; **atrial septal** —— **(ASD)** comunicación *f* interauricular (CIA); **birth** —— defecto de nacimiento; **neural tube** —— defecto del tubo neural; **ventricular septal** —— **(VSD)** comunicación *f* interventricular (CIV)
defense mechanism *n* mecanismo de defensa
defibrillate *vt* desfibrilar
defibrillation *n* desfibrilación *f*
deficiency *n* *(pl* -cies)* carencia, deficiencia
deficient *adj* deficiente
deficit *n* déficit *m*
definitive *adj* definitivo
deformed *adj* deforme
deformity *n* *(pl* -ties)* deformidad *f*
degenerate *vi* degenerar
degenerative *adj* degenerativo
degree *n* grado
dehumanizing *adj* deshumanizante
dehydrated *adj* deshidratado
dehydration *n* deshidratación *f*
delay *n* *(developmental)* retraso, retardo; *vt* retrasar, retardar
delayed *adj* tardío, retardado, retrasado
deletion *n* deleción *f*
delicate *adj* delicado, frágil
delirious *adj* delirante; **to be** —— delirar; **He's delirious**..Está delirante..Está delirando.
delirium *n* delirio; —— **tremens** delirium tremens
deliver *(obst)* *vt* dar a luz; *(action performed by doctor or midwife)* atender (un parto); **Mrs. Mata delivered a baby boy at four in the morning**..La señora Mata dio a luz un niño a las cuatro de la madrugada...**Dr. Ford delivered Mrs. Mata**..El doctor Ford atendió el parto de la señora Mata..El Dr. Ford atendió a la señora Mata...**Dr. Ford delivered the twins**..El Dr. Ford atendió el parto de los gemelos..El Dr. Ford atendió a los gemelos; *vi* dar a luz, aliviarse *(Mex, fam)*
delivery *n* *(pl* -ries)* parto; —— **room** sala de partos
delta *n* delta

deltoid *n* deltoides *m*
delusion *n* falsa creencia patológica
demented *adj* demente
dementia *n* demencia
demonstrate *vt* demostrar
demoralize *vt* desmoralizar; **to become demoralized** desmoralizarse, desalentarse, desanimarse
demyelinating *adj* desmielinizante
dengue *n* dengue *m*, fiebre *f* rompehuesos
denial *n* negación *f*
dental *adj* dental; —— **floss** hilo dental
dentist *n* dentista *mf*, odontólogo -ga *mf*
dentistry *n* odontología
denture *n* dentadura postiza
deodorant *n* desodorante *m*
deoxyribonucleic acid (DNA) *n* ácido desoxirribonucleico (ADN *or* DNA)
department *n* departamento
dependence *n* dependencia, (*on drugs*) farmacodependencia
dependency *n* dependencia, (*on drugs*) farmacodependencia
dependent *adj* dependiente
depersonalization *n* despersonalización *f*
depigmentation *n* despigmentación *f*
depilatory *adj & n* depilatorio
deplete *vt* agotar
deposit *n* depósito, sedimento; *vt, vi* depositar(se)
depot *adj* (*pharm*) de depósito
depressant *adj & n* depresor *m*
depressed *adj* deprimido, decaído; **to get —— deprimirse**
depression *n* depresión *f*
depressive *adj* depresivo
depth *n* profundidad *f*; —— **perception** visión profunda, percepción *f* de la profundidad
deranged *adj* (*mentally*) trastornado, loco
dermatitis *n* dermatitis *f*; **contact ——** dermatitis por contacto
dermatologist *n* dermatólogo -ga *mf*
dermatology *n* dermatología
dermatomyositis *n* dermatomiositis *f*
DES *V.* **diethylstilbestrol.**
descendant *n* descendiente *mf*
descending *adj* descendente
describe *vt* describir
desensitization *n* desensibilización *f*
desensitize *vt* desensibilizar
desiccant *adj & n* desecante *m*
desire *n* deseo; *vt* desear
desperate *adj* desesperado; **to become ——** desesperarse
despondent *adj* abatido, deprimido, desalentado, desanimado
dessert *n* postre *m*
destroy *vt* destruir
destructive *adj* destructivo
detect *vt* detectar
detectable *adj* perceptible

detection *n* detección *f*
detergent *adj & n* detergente *m*
deteriorate *vi* (*condition of patient*) empeorar(se), deteriorarse; (*substance*) deteriorarse
deterioration *n* deterioro
detoxification *n* desintoxicación *f*
develop *vt, vi* desarrollar(se)
development *n* desarrollo
device *n* aparato, dispositivo
dexamethasone *n* dexametasona
diabetes *n* diabetes *f*; —— **insipidus** diabetes insípida; —— **mellitus** diabetes mellitus
diabetic *adj & n* diabético -ca *mf*
diagnose *vt* diagnosticar
diagnosis *n* (*pl* **-ses**) diagnóstico, diagnosis *f*
diagnostic *adj* diagnóstico
diagram *n* diagrama *m*
dialysis *n* diálisis *f*; **peritoneal ——** diálisis peritoneal
diameter *n* diámetro
diaper *n* pañal *m*; —— **rash** dermatitis *f* por pañal, salpullido *or* sarpullido
diaphragm *n* (*anat, gyn*) diafragma *m*
diarrhea *n* diarrea; **traveler's ——** diarrea del viajero
diastolic *adj* diastólico
diazepam *n* diazepam *m*
DIC *abbr* **disseminated intravascular coagulation.** *V.* **coagulation.**
dichlorodiphenyltrichloroethane (DDT) . diclorodifeniltricloroetano (DDT)
dicloxacillin *n* dicloxacilina
die *vi* (*pret & pp* **died**; *ger* **dying**) morir(se), fallecer
dieldrin *n* dieldrín *m*
diet *n* dieta, régimen *m*; *vi* (*también* **to be on a ——**) estar a dieta
dietary *adj* dietético, de dieta
diethylstilbestrol (DES) *n* dietilestilbestrol *m* (DES)
dietician *n* dietista *mf*
diffusion *n* difusión *f*
digest *vt* digerir
digestible *adj* digerible
digestion *n* digestión *f*
digestive *adj* digestivo
digital *adj* digital
digitalis *n* (*pharm*) digital *f*
digoxin *n* digoxina
dilate *vt, vi* dilatar(se)
dilation *n* dilatación *f*; —— **and curettage (D&C)** dilatación y legrado
dilator *n* dilatador *m*
dildo *n* (*pl* **-dos**) consolador *m* (*fam*)
diltiazem *n* diltiazem *m*
dilute *adj* diluido; *vt* diluir
dim *adj* (*comp* **dimmer**; *super* **dimmest**) oscuro, indistinto
dimension *n* dimensión *f*

dimethyl sulfoxide (DMSO) *n* dimetilsulfóxido

dimethyltryptamine (DMT) *n* dimetiltriptamina (DMT)

diminish *vt, vi* disminuir(se)

dimple *n* hoyuelo

dinner *n* cena

dioxide *n* bióxido *or* dióxido

diphenhydramine *n* difenhidramina

diphtheria *n* difteria

diplococcus *n* (*pl* -ci) diplococo

dipstick *n* (*for urine, etc.*) tira reactiva

direction *n* dirección *f*, instrucción *f*

dirt *n* suciedad *f*

dirty *adj* (*comp* -ier; *super* -iest) sucio; **to get** —— ensuciar(se)

disability *n* (*pl* -ties) incapacidad *f*

disabled *adj* inválido, incapacitado, inhabilitado; —— **person** inválido -da *mf*

disadvantage *n* desventaja

disappear *vi* desaparecerse

discharge *n* secreción *f*; *vt* (*from the hospital*) dar de alta; **We are going to discharge you the day after tomorrow.**..Lo vamos a dar de alta pasado mañana.

discomfort *n* molestia; **You're going to feel a little discomfort.**..Va a sentir un poco de molestia.

discontinue *vt* descontinuar, (*a medication*) dejar de tomar

discourage *vt* desalentar, desanimar; **to get discouraged** desalentarse, desanimarse

disease *n* enfermedad *f*, mal *m*; **Addison's** —— enfermedad de Addison; **Alzheimer's** —— enfermedad de Alzheimer; **benign breast** —— enfermedad mamaria benigna; **cat-scratch** —— enfermedad por arañazo de gato; **celiac** —— enfermedad celiaca; **Chagas'** —— enfermedad de Chagas; **chronic obstructive pulmonary** —— (COPD) enfermedad pulmonar obstructiva crónica (EPOC); **collagen-vascular** —— enfermedad colágenovascular *or* del colágeno; **connective tissue** —— enfermedad del tejido conectivo *or* conjuntivo; **Crohn's** —— enfermedad de Crohn; **Cushing's** —— enfermedad de Cushing; **degenerative joint** —— enfermedad articular degenerativa; **fibrocystic** —— enfermedad fibroquística; **fifth** —— quinta enfermedad; **Gaucher's** —— enfermedad de Gaucher; **Gilbert's** —— enfermedad de Gilbert; **glycogen storage** —— enfermedad de almacenamiento de glucógeno; **graft-versus-host** —— enfermedad or reacción *f* del injerto contra el huésped; **Graves'** —— enfermedad de Graves; **hand-foot-and-mouth** —— enfermedad de mano, pie y boca; **Hansen's** —— enfermedad de Hansen; **Hirschsprung's** —— enfermedad

de Hirschsprung; **Hodgkin's** —— enfermedad de Hodgkin; **Huntington's** —— enfermedad de Huntington; **hyaline membrane** —— enfermedad de membrana hialina; **interstitial lung** —— enfermedad intersticial pulmonar; **Kawasaki's** —— enfermedad de Kawasaki; **Legionnaire's** —— enfermedad de los legionarios; **Lyme** —— enfermedad de Lyme; **minimal change** —— enfermedad de lesiones mínimas; **Paget's** —— enfermedad de Paget; **Parkinson's** —— enfermedad de Parkinson; **pelvic inflammatory** —— (PID) enfermedad inflamatoria pélvica, infección pélvica; **peripheral vascular** —— enfermedad vascular periférica; **Pott's** —— enfermedad de Pott; **rheumatic heart** —— cardiopatía reumática; **sexually transmitted** —— (STD) enfermedad de transmisión sexual (*form*), enfermedad venérea; **sickle cell** —— enfermedad de células falciformes, drepanocitemia; **venereal** —— (VD) (*ant*) enfermedad venérea; **von Willebrand's** —— enfermedad de von Willebrand; **Whipple's** —— enfermedad de Whipple; **Wilson's** —— enfermedad de Wilson

disinfect *vt* desinfectar

disinfectant *adj & n* desinfectante *m*

disk *n* disco; **herniated** —— disco herniado; **slipped** —— disco desplazado

dislocate *vt* dislocar(se), zafar(se) (*fam*); **Did you dislocate your ankle?**..¿Se dislocó el tobillo?

dislocation *n* dislocación *f*, zafada (*fam*)

disopyramide *n* disopiramida

disorder *n* trastorno, desorden *m*; **bipolar** —— trastorno bipolar; **personality** —— trastorno de la personalidad; **posttraumatic stress** —— trastorno del estrés postraumático; **sleep** —— trastorno del sueño

disoriented *adj* desorientado

dispense *vt* (*pharm*) dispensar

disposable *adj* desechable

disseminate *vt, vi* diseminar(se)

disseminated *adj* diseminado

dissociation *n* (*psych*) disociación *f*

dissolve *vt, vi* disolver(se)

distend *vt* distender; *vi* distender(se)

distilled *adj* destilado

distinguish *vt* distinguir

distress *n* aflicción *f*

disturbance *n* trastorno, alteración *f*; **sleep** —— trastorno del sueño

disulfiram *n* disulfiramo

diuresis *n* diuresis *f*

diuretic *adj & n* diurético

diverticulitis *n* diverticulitis *f*

diverticulosis *n* diverticulosis *f*

diverticulum *n* (*pl* -la) divertículo

divorce *n* divorcio; *vt, vi* divorciar(se)
dizziness *n* mareo, sensación *f* de desmayo
dizzy *adj* (*comp* -zier; *super* -ziest) mareado; **to make** —— dar mareo
DMSO *V.* **dimethyl sulfoxide.**
DMT *V.* **dimethlytryptamine.**
DNA *V.* **deoxyribonucleic acid.**
doctor *n* médico, doctor -ra *mf*; **family** —— médico de cabecera *or* de la familia; **private** —— médico privado
Doctor of Medicine (M.D.) *n* médico
dog *n* perro
dominant *adj* dominante
Dominican *adj & n* dominicano -na *mf*
donate *vt* donar
donor *adj* donado; *n* donante *mf*, donador -ra *mf*
dope (*vulg*) *n* narcótico
Doppler *n* Doppler *m*
dorsal *adj* dorsal
dosage *n* dosificación *f*
dose *n* dosis *f*
double *adj & adv* doble; —— **chin** papada; —— **vision** visión *f or* vista doble; *vt* doblar
double-jointed *adj* hiperextensible
douche *n* ducha; *vi* ducharse
doxycycline *n* doxiciclina
drain *n* dren *m*, drenaje *m*; *vt* drenar, vaciar; *vi* drenarse, salir; **Is it draining pus?**..¿Le sale pus?
drainage *n* drenaje *m*, (*from a wound, etc.*) secreción *f*
drank *pret de* **drink**
draw *vt* **to** —— **blood** sacar sangre
dream *n* sueño; *vt, vi* (*pret & pp* **dreamed** *o* **dreamt**) soñar; **to** —— **of** *o* **about** soñar con
dress *n* vestido; *vt* vestir; (*a wound*) vendar; *vi* vestirse
dressing *n* venda, apósito
drill (*dent*) *n* taladro; *vt* taladrar
drink *n* bebida; *vt, vi* (*pret* **drank**; *pp* **drunk**) tomar, beber; **Do you drink alcohol?**..¿Acostumbra Ud. tomar bebidas alcohólicas?
drinker *n* bebedor -ra *mf*
drinking fountain *n* fuente *f* para beber, bebedero
drip *vi* gotear
drive *n* (*sex, hunger, etc.*) instinto; *vt, vi* (*pret* **drove**; *pp* **driven**) (*a vehicle*) manejar, conducir
drool *n* baba; *vi* babear
droop *vi* (*eyelids, etc.*) caerse
drop *n* gota; (*in level of something being measured*) baja; *vi* bajar(se); **Your sugar dropped**..Se bajó el azucar.
dropper *n* gotero
drove *pret de* **drive**
drown *vt, vi* ahogar(se)
drowsy *adj* (*comp* -sier; *super* -siest) soñoliento, somnoliento, adormilado
drug *n* droga, medicamento; *vt* drogar
druggist *n* farmacéutico -ca *mf*, boticario -ria *mf*
drugstore *n* farmacia, botica
drunk (*pp de* **drink**) *adj* borracho; **to get** —— emborracharse; *n* (*person*) borracho -cha *mf*; (*binge*) borrachera
dry *adj* seco, reseco; —— **heaves** (*fam*) (el) vomitar sin nada que expulsar; —— **mouth** resequedad *f or* sequedad *f* de boca; *vt* secar; *vi* (*también* **to get** —— *o* **to** —— **out**) secar(se), resecar
dryness *n* resequedad *f*, sequedad *f*
d.t.'s, the *npl* alucinaciones (*debidas a la suspensión del alcohol*), visiones *fpl* (*fam*); **Have you ever had the d.t.'s?**..¿Ha tenido visiones alguna vez (al dejar de tomar alcohol)?..¿Ha delirado alguna vez?
duct *n* conducto
ductus arteriosus *n* conducto arterioso; **patent** —— —— **(PDA)** conducto arterioso persistente
due to, debido a
dull *adj* (*pain*) sordo; *vt* (*pain*) calmar
duodenal *adj* duodenal
duodenitis *n* duodenitis *f*
duodenum *n* duodeno
durable *adj* duradero
duration *n* duración *f*
dust *n* polvo
dwarf *n* enano -na *mf*
dwarfism *n* enanismo
dye *n* colorante *m*
dying *ger de* **die**
dyscrasia *n* discrasia; **blood** —— discrasia sanguínea
dysentery *n* disentería
dysfunction *n* disfunción *f*
dyslexia *n* dislexia
dysphasia *n* disfasia
dysplasia *n* displasia

E

ear *n* oreja, (*organ of hearing*) oído; ——, nose, and throat (ENT) oídos, nariz, y garganta; external —— oído externo; inner —— oído interno; middle —— oído medio
earache *n* dolor *m* de oído
eardrum *n* tímpano
earlobe *n* lóbulo (del oído), pulpejo
earring *n* arete *m*
earthquake *n* temblor *m*, sismo, (*severe*) terremoto
earwax *n* cerilla
eat *vt, vi* (*pret* ate; *pp* eaten) comer
EBV *abbr* Epstein-Barr virus. *V.* virus.
ECG *V.* electrocardiogram.
Echinococcus Echinococcus
echocardiogram *n* ecocardiograma *m*, ecocardiografía
eclampsia *n* eclampsia
ECT *abbr* electroconvulsive therapy. *V.* therapy.
ectopic *adj* ectópico; —— pregnancy embarazo ectópico
Ecuadoran *adj & n* ecuatoriano -na *mf*
eczema *n* eccema *m&f*
edema *n* edema *m*; pulmonary —— edema pulmonar
edge *n* borde *m*, margen *m*
educate *vt* educar
education *n* educación *f*; health —— educación para la salud
EEG *V.* electroencephalogram.
effect *n* efecto; adverse —— efecto adverso; side —— efecto colateral; to take —— hacer efecto
effective *adj* eficaz, efectivo
effeminate *adj* afeminado
efficient *adj* eficiente
effort *n* esfuerzo
effusion *n* derrame *m*; pericardial —— derrame pericardiaco; pleural —— derrame pleural
egg *n* huevo; (*small, e.g., of a parasite*) huevecillo; (*fam, ovum*) óvulo, huevo (*fam*); —— yolk yema de huevo
ego *n* (*pl* egos) ego *m*, (el) yo
egocentric *adj* egocéntrico
ejaculate *vi* eyacular
ejaculation *n* eyaculación *f*; premature —— eyaculación precoz
EKG *V.* electrocardiogram.
elastic *adj & n* elástico
elbow *n* codo
elderly *adj* anciano

electric, electrical *adj* eléctrico
electrocardiogram (ECG *o* EKG) *n* electrocardiograma *m* (ECG), electrocardiografía
electrocute *vt* electrocutar
electroencephalogram (EEG) *n* electroencefalograma *m* (EEG)
electrolyte *adj* electrolítico; *n* electrólito *or* (*esp. spoken*) electrolito
electromyography (EMG) *n* electromiografía (EMG)
electrophoresis *n* electroforesis *f*
element *n* elemento; trace —— oligoelemento
elephantiasis *n* elefantiasis *f*
elevate *vt* elevar
elevation *n* elevación *f*
eligible *adj* elegible
eliminate *vt* eliminar
emaciated *adj* severamente enflaquecido, demacrado
embarrassment *n* vergüenza
embarrass *vt* Don't feel embarrassed..No le dé vergüenza.
embolectomy *n* (*pl* -mies) embolectomía
embolism *n* embolia; pulmonary —— embolia pulmonar
embolus *n* (*pl* -li) émbolo
embrace *n* abrazo; *vt* abrazar
embryo *n* (*pl* -os) embrión *m*
embryology *n* embriología
emergency *n* (*pl* -cies) emergencia; —— room (ER) sala de emergencia *or* urgencias
emesis basin *n* riñón *m*, riñonera, escupidera
emetic *adj & n* emético
EMG *V.* electromyography.
emotion *n* emoción *f*
emotional *adj* emocional; (*person*) emotivo
empathy *n* empatía
emphysema *n* enfisema *m*
employer *n* empleador -ra *mf*, patrón -na *mf*, jefe -fa *mf*
employment *n* empleo
empty *adj* vacío; *vt* vaciar
empyema *n* empiema *m*
enalapril *n* enalapril *m*
enamel *n* esmalte *m*
encephalitis *n* encefalitis *f*
encephalomyelitis *n* encefalomielitis *f*
encephalopathy *n* encefalopatía; Wernicke's —— encefalopatía de Wernicke
end *n* fin *m*
endarterectomy *n* endarterectomía

endemic *adj* endémico
endocarditis *n* endocarditis *f*
endocardium *n* endocardio
endocrine *adj* endocrino
endocrinologist *n* endocrinólogo -ga *mf*
endocrinology *n* endocrinología
endometriosis *n* endometriosis *f*
endometritis *n* endometritis *f*
endometrium *n* endometrio
endorphin *n* endorfina
endoscopic retrograde cholangiopancreatography (ERCP) *n* colangiopancreatografía
retrógrada endoscópica
endoscopy *n* (*pl* -pies) endoscopia *or* (*esp.
spoken*) endoscopía
endotracheal *adj* endotraqueal
endure *vt* aguantar
enema *n* enema *m&f*, lavativa (*fam*);
barium —— enema de bario
energetic *adj* enérgico
energy *n* energía
engineering *n* ingeniería; genetic ——
ingeniería genética
enlarge *vt* agrandar, aumentar
enriched *adj* enriquecido
ENT *abbr* ear, nose, and throat. *V.* ear.
enteric *adj* entérico
enteritis *n* enteritis *f*; regional —— enteritis
regional
enterococcus *n* (*pl* -ci) enterococo
enterocolitis *n* enterocolitis *f*
enteropathy *n* enteropatía; protein-losing
—— enteropatía con pérdida de proteínas
enterotoxin *n* enterotoxina
entrance *n* entrada
entrapment *n* compresión *f*; peripheral
nerve —— compresión de un nervio
periférico
environment *n* medio ambiente
environmental *adj* ambiental
enzyme *n* enzima
eosinophil *n* eosinófilo
ephedrine *n* efedrina
epidemic *adj* epidémico; *n* epidemia
epidemiology *n* epidemiología
epididymis *n* (*pl* -mides) epidídimo
epididymitis *n* epididimitis *f*
epidural *adj* epidural
epiglottis *n* epiglotis *f*
epiglottitis *n* epiglotitis *f*
epilepsy *n* epilepsia
epinephrine *n* epinefrina
episiotomy *n* (*pl* -mies) episiotomía
episode *n* episodio
epispadias *n* epispadias *m*
epulis *n* épulis *m*
equilibrium *n* equilibrio
eradicate *vt* erradicar
ERCP *V.* endoscopic retrograde
cholangiopancreatography.
erect *adj* erecto
erection *n* erección *f*

ergocalciferol *n* ergocalciferol *m*
ergotamine *n* ergotamina
erode *vt, vi* erosionar(se)
erogenous *adj* erógeno
erosion *n* erosión *f*
erotic *adj* erótico
eruption *n* erupción *f*
erysipelas *n* erisipela
erythema *n* eritema *m*; —— infectiosum
eritema infeccioso; —— multiforme
eritema multiforme; —— nodosum
eritema nodoso
erythrocyte *n* eritrocito
erythromycin *n* eritromicina
Escherichia coli Escherichia coli
esophagitis *n* esofagitis *f*; reflux ——
esofagitis por reflujo
esophagus *n* (*pl* -gi) esófago
essential *adj* esencial
estradiol *n* estradiol *m*
estriol *n* estriol *m*
estrogen *n* estrógeno
ethambutol *n* etambutol *m*
ethanol *n* etanol *m*
ether *n* éter *m*
ethical *adj* ético
ethionamide *n* etionamida
ethnic *adj* étnico
ethosuximide *n* etosuximida
ethyl *n* etilo
ethyl alcohol *n* alcohol etílico
ethylene glycol *n* etilenglicol *m*
eunuch *n* eunuco
euphoria *n* euforia
Eustachian tube *n* trompa de Eustaquio
euthanasia *n* eutanasia
evacuate *vt* evacuar
evaluate *vt* evaluar, valorar
evaluation *n* evaluación *f*, valoración *f*
evaporate *vi* evaporarse
evaporation *n* evaporación *f*
even *adj* liso, parejo, plano
evening *adj* vespertino (*form*), (*early*) de la
tarde, (*after dark*) de noche; *n* tarde *f*,
noche *f*
eventually *adv* con el tiempo
evil eye *n* mal *m* de ojo
evolution *n* evolución *f*
exact *adj* exacto
exam *V.* examination.
examination *n* examen *m*, revisión *f*; breast
—— examen de los senos; eye ——
examen visual; pelvic —— examen
ginecológico, revisión *f* de (sus) partes
(*fam*); physical —— examen físico;
rectal —— tacto rectal
examine *vt* examinar, revisar; May I
examine your leg?..¿Puedo examinarle la
pierna?
exanthem subitum *n* exantema súbito
excess *n* exceso
excessive *adj* excesivo

excite *vt* excitar
excuse *n* excusa; work —— certificado para
no trabajar, incapacidad *f* de trabajo (*Mex*)
exercise *n* ejercicio; *vt* hacer ejercicio con;
You need to exercise your arm..Tiene
que hacer ejercicio con su brazo; *vi* hacer
ejercicio
exert *vt* to —— oneself esforzarse
exertion *n* esfuerzo, actividad *f* fuerte
exhale *vt*, *vi* exhalar
exhausted *adj* exhausto, agotado; to become
—— agotarse
exit *n* salida
expect *vt* esperar
expectorant *adj* & *n* expectorante *m*
expel *vt* expeler, expulsar
experiment *n* experimento; *vi* experimentar
experimental *adj* experimental
expert *adj* & *n* experto -ta *mf*
expiration date *n* fecha de caducidad
expire *vt*, *vi* (*to breathe out*) espirar; (*to die*)
fallecer, expirar
exploratory *adj* (*surg*) explorador,
exploratorio
explore *vt* (*surg*) explorar
expose *vt* exponer; Have you been exposed
to tuberculosis?..¿Ha estado expuesto a la
tuberculosis?..¿Ha estado en contacto con
algún enfermo de tuberculosis?
exposure *n* exposición *f*

expulsion *n* expulsión *f*
extend *vt*, *vi* extender(se)
extension *n* extensión *f*, prolongación *f*
extensive *adj* extenso
exterior *adj* & *n* exterior *m*
external *adj* externo
extra *adj* extra
extract *n* (*pharm*) extracto; *vt* (*to remove,
take out*) extraer, sacar
extraction *n* extracción *f*
extreme unction *n* santos óleos
extremity *n* extremidad *f*
extrovert *n* extrovertido -da *mf*
extroverted *adj* extrovertido
eye *n* ojo; —— chart carta de examen
visual; angle *o* corner of the —— ángulo
del ojo
eyedropper *n* gotero
eyeball *n* globo ocular (*form*), globo del ojo
eyebrow *n* ceja; Raise your eyebrows..Le-
vante las cejas.
eyeglasses *npl* lentes *mpl*, anteojos
eyelash *n* pestaña
eyelid *n* párpado
eyesight *n* vista, visión *f*
eyestrain *n* vista cansada, cansancio visual
eyewash *n* colirio
eyewear *n* lentes *mpl*; protective ——
lentes protectores

F

face *n* cara
facedown *adj* boca abajo
face-lift *n* cirugía plástica *or* estética (*para
eliminar las arrugas de la cara*)
faceup *adj* boca arriba
facial *adj* facial; *n* tratamiento *or* masaje *m*
facial
factor *n* factor *m*; intrinsic —— factor
intrínseco; Rh —— factor Rh; risk ——
factor de riesgo
Fahrenheit *adj* Fahrenheit
fail *vi* fracasar, fallar
failure *n* (*treatment*) fracaso; (*organ*)
insuficiencia, falla; heart ——, kidney
——, respiratory ——, etc. insuficiencia
cardiaca, renal, respiratoria, etc.
faint *adj* mareado, débil, que tiene sensación
de desmayo; Do you feel faint?..¿Se
siente mareado?..¿Tiene sensación de
desmayo? *n* desmayo; *vi* desmayarse,

desvanecerse
fair *adj* (*complexion*) blanco, güero (*Mex*)
faith healer *n* curandero -ra *mf*
faith healing *n* curanderismo
fall *n* caída; (*in level of something being
measured*) baja; (*season*) otoño; *vi* (*pret
fell*; *pp fallen*) caerse; bajar(se)
false *adj* falso, (*tooth, eye, etc.*) postizo;
—— teeth dientes postizos, dentaduras
postizas
familial *adj* familiar
family *adj* familiar; *n* (*pl* -lies) familia; ——
member familiar *m*; —— planning
planificación *f* familiar; —— practice
medicina familiar
famotidine *n* famotidina
fan *n* abanico, (*electric*) ventilador *m*
fang *n* colmillo
fantasy *n* (*pl* -sies) fantasía
farmer's lung *n* enfermedad *f* pulmonar de

los granjeros
farsighted *adj* hipermétrope (*form*), que tiene dificultad para ver los objetos cercanos
fascia *n* (*pl* -ciae) fascia
fasciitis *n* fascitis *f*
fascioliasis *n* fascioliasis *f*
fasciotomy *n* (*pl* -mies) fasciotomía
fast *n* ayuno; *vi* ayunar
fasting *adj* en ayunas; —— **glucose** glucosa en ayunas *or* en ayuno; *n* ayuno, (el) ayunar
fat *adj* (*comp* **fatter**; *super* **fattest**) gordo; **to get** —— engordar; *n* grasa, (*lard*) manteca
fatal *adj* fatal, mortal
father *n* padre *m*
father-in-law *n* (*pl* **fathers-in-law**) suegro
fatigue *n* fatiga, cansancio
fatty *adj* (*comp* -tier; *super* -tiest) grasoso; —— **acid** ácido graso
fear *n* miedo, temor *m*
features *npl* facciones *fpl*, rasgos
febrile *adj* febril
feces *npl* heces *fpl* fecales, heces
fed *pret* & *pp de* **feed**
fee *n* honorarios
feeble *adj* débil
feed *vt* (*pret* & *pp* **fed**) alimentar (*form*), dar de comer
feedback *n* retroalimentación *f*
feeding *n* alimentación *f*
feel *vt* (*pret* & *pp* **felt**) (*touch, pinprick, etc.*) sentir; **Can you feel the cotton?..¿Puede sentir el algodón?** *vi* (*sick, tired, well, etc.*) sentirse; **How do you feel?..¿Cómo se siente?...Do you feel sick?..¿Se siente enfermo?**
feeling *n* (*sensation*) sensación *f*; (*emotion*) sentimiento, emoción *f*
feet *pl de* **foot**
fell *pret de* **fall**
fellatio *n* felación *f*, coito bucal *or* oral
felon *n* panadizo
felt *pret* & *pp de* **feel**
female *adj* & *n* hembra
feminization *n* feminización *f*
femoral *adj* femoral
femur *n* fémur *m*
fentanyl *n* fentanil *m*
ferric *adj* férrico
ferrous sulfate *n* sulfato ferroso
fertile *adj* fértil
fertilization *n* fertilización *f*, fecundación *f*
fertilize *vt* fecundar
fester *vi* enconarse
fetal *adj* fetal
fetish *n* fetiche *m*
fetishism *n* fetichismo
fetus *n* feto
fever *n* fiebre *f*, calentura; **breakbone** —— fiebre rompehuesos; **dengue** —— dengue *m*; **hay** —— fiebre del heno, alergia al

polen; **paratyphoid** —— fiebre paratifoidea; **Q** —— fiebre Q; **relapsing** —— fiebre recurrente; **rheumatic** —— fiebre reumática; **Rocky Mountain spotted** —— fiebre manchada de las Montañas Rocosas; **scarlet** —— fiebre escarlatina; **trench** —— fiebre de las trincheras; **typhoid** —— fiebre tifoidea; **yellow** —— fiebre amarilla
fever blister *n* fuego, ampolla en los labios (*debida al herpes*)
feverish *adj* acalenturado
few *adj* pocos; **just a few times**..unas pocas veces
fiancé *n* novio
fiancée *n* novia
fiber *n* fibra; **muscle** —— fibra muscular; **nerve** —— fibra nerviosa
fiberoptic *adj* de fibra óptica
fibrillation *n* fibrilación *f*; **atrial** —— fibrilación auricular; **ventricular** —— fibrilación ventricular
fibrinogen *n* fibrinógeno
fibroadenoma *n* fibroadenoma *m*
fibrocystic *adj* fibroquístico
fibroid *n* (*of the uterus*) mioma *or* fibromioma uterino (*form*), tumor (benigno) del útero, bolita del útero (*fam*)
fibroma *n* fibroma *m*
fibromyalgia *V.* **fibrositis.**
fibrosis *n* fibrosis *f*
fibrositis *n* fibrositis *f*
fibrotic *adj* fibrótico
fibula *n* peroné *m*
field *n* campo; **visual** —— campo visual
figure *n* (*of a person*) figura
filariasis *n* filariasis *f*
file *n* (*for nails*) lima; (*patient chart*) expediente *m*; *vt* limar
fill *vt* llenar; (*a prescription*) surtir; (*a tooth*) obturar (*form*), rellenar, tapar
filling *n* (*dent*) empaste *m*, relleno
film *n* capa, tela; (*X-ray*) placa
filter *n* filtro; *vt, vi* filtrar(se)
filtration *n* filtración *f*
final *adj* final
finding *n* hallazgo
finger *n* dedo (de la mano); —— **cot** dedo de hule; —— **pad** yema del dedo; **index** —— dedo índice; **little** —— dedo meñique; **middle** —— dedo medio; **ring** —— dedo anular
fingernail *n* uña (*de un dedo de la mano*)
fingerstick *n* punción *f* digital (*form*), pinchazo del dedo, piquete *m* del dedo (*esp. Mex*)
fingertip *n* punta del dedo
fire *n* fuego, incendio; —— **department** cuerpo de bomberos; —— **extinguisher** extinguidor *m*
fireman *n* (*pl* -men) bombero
firm *adj* firme

first *adj* primero; —— **aid** primeros auxilios; **first-aid kit** botiquín *m* de primeros auxilios
fish *n* (*pl* **fish** *o* **fishes**) pez *m*; (*after being caught, as a food*) pescado
fish bone *n* espina
fisherman *n* (*pl* **-men**) pescador *m*
fishhook *n* anzuelo
fissure *n* fisura
fist *n* puño; **to make a** —— apretar el puño, cerrar la mano
fistula *n* (*pl* **-lae** *o* **-las**) fístula
fit *adj* (*comp* **fitter**; *super* **fittest**) en forma; *n* (*attack*) ataque *m*, acceso; *vt* (*glasses, etc.*) ajustar
fix *vt* arreglar, reparar
fixation *n* fijación *f*
flabby *adj* (*comp* **-bier**; *super* **-biest**) fláccido, flojo
flaccid *adj* fláccido
flake (*skin*) *n* escama; *vi* descamarse (*form*), caerse en escamas
flaky *adj* (*comp* **-ier**; *super* **-iest**) escamoso
flammable *adj* inflamable
flank *n* flanco
flap *n* colgajo
flare *vi* **to** —— **up** agravar(se), volver(se) a agravar (*una enfermedad*)
flask *n* frasco, pomo
flat *adj* (*comp* **flatter**; *super* **flattest**) plano
flatfoot *n* (*pl* **-feet**) pie plano
flatulence *n* flatulencia
flatworm *n* platelminto, gusano plano
flavor *n* sabor *m*, gusto; **cherry-flavored, banana-flavored, etc.** sabor a cereza, sabor a plátano, etc.
flea *n* pulga
fleeting *adj* (*pain, etc.*) pasajero, momentáneo, fugaz
flesh *n* carne *f*
flex *vt, vi* flexionar(se) (*form*), doblar(se)
flexible *adj* flexible
flies *pl de* **fly**
floater *n* (*in the eye*) estrellita, lucecita
flood *n* inundación *f*, diluvio
flora *n* (*pl* **-ras** *o* **-rae**) flora
floss *n* hilo dental; *vt, vi* limpiar (*los dientes*) con hilo dental
flour *n* harina
flow *n* flujo; **blood** —— flujo sanguíneo (*form*), circulación *f*; **menstrual** —— flujo *or* sangrado menstrual; *vi* fluir
flu *n* gripe *f*, influenza; **Asian** —— gripe asiática
fluctuate *vi* fluctuar, variar
fluid *n* líquido, fluido; **amniotic** —— líquido amniótico; **cerebrospinal** —— (**CSF**) líquido cefalorraquídeo (**LCR**); **pleural** —— líquido pleural; **seminal** —— líquido seminal; **synovial** —— líquido sinovial
fluke *n* duela

fluorescent *adj* fluorescente
fluoridation *n* fluorización *f*
fluoride *n* fluoruro
fluoroscopy *n* (*pl* **-pies**) fluoroscopia *or* (*esp. spoken*) fluoroscopía
fluorouracil *n* fluorouracilo
fluphenazine *n* flufenacina
flurazepam *n* fluracepam *m*
flush (*physio*) *n* rubor *m*, bochorno; *vi* ruborizarse, sonrojarse
flutter *n* aleteo; **atrial** —— aleteo auricular
fly *n* (*pl* **flies**) mosca; (*of trousers*) bragueta
foam *n* espuma
foamy *adj* (*comp* **-ier**; *super* **-iest**) espumoso
focal *adj* focal
focus *n* (*pl* **foci** *o* **focuses**) foco; *vt* (*pret & pp* **focused** *o* **focussed**; *ger* **focusing** *o* **focussing**) enfocar
fold *n* pliegue *m*; **skin** —— pliegue cutáneo; *vt* **to** —— **one's arms** cruzar los brazos
folic acid *n* ácido fólico
follicle *n* folículo; **hair** —— folículo piloso; **ovarian** —— folículo ovárico
folliculitis *n* foliculitis *f*
follow *vt* (*to take care of*) atender; **Who follows you for your diabetes?**..¿Quién la atiende de su diabetes?
follow-up *n* seguimiento, atención médica subsecuente, vigilancia
fontanel, fontanelle *n* fontanela, mollera
food *n* comida, alimento(s); —— **poisoning** intoxicación alimenticia *or* alimentaria; **baby** —— comida para niños; **canned** —— alimentos enlatados; **fast** —— comida rápida, comida preparada en un restaurant de servicio rápido; **processed** —— alimentos procesados
food-borne *adj* transmitido por los alimentos
foot *n* (*pl* **feet**) pie *m*; —— **drop** pie péndulo
footpad *n* (*fam*) plantilla
footwear *n* calzado (*zapatos, botas*)
force *n* fuerza
forceps *n* (*pl* **-ceps** *o* **-cipes**) (*obst*) fórceps *m*; (*surg*) pinzas (*de disección*)
forearm *n* antebrazo
forehead *n* frente *f*
foreign body *n* cuerpo extraño
forensic *adj* forense
foreplay *n* caricias eróticas que anteceden al acto sexual
foreskin *n* prepucio
form *n* forma; (*paper to fill out*) formulario; *vt, vi* formar(se)
formaldehyde *n* formaldehido
formation *n* formación *f*
formula *n* fórmula
formulary *n* formulario
fortify *vt* fortificar, fortalecer
forward *adv* adelante, hacia adelante
fossa *n* fosa
foster care *n* (*US*) crianza de huérfanos por

alguien que no es padre adoptivo y que recibe remuneración del gobierno

fox *n* zorro

fracture *n* fractura; **closed** —— fractura cerrada; **comminuted** —— fractura conminuta; **compound** —— fractura expuesta *or* abierta; **compression** —— fractura por compresión; **cranial** —— fractura del cráneo; **hairline** —— fisura; **open** —— fractura expuesta *or* abierta; **skull** —— fractura del cráneo; **spiral** —— fractura en espiral *or* espiroidea; **stress** —— fractura por esfuerzo; *vt, vi* fracturar(se), quebrar(se) (*fam*); You fractured your neck?..¿Se fracturó el cuello?

fragile *adj* frágil, quebradizo

fragment *n* fragmento

frail *adj* frágil, débil

frambesia *n* frambesia

fraternal *adj* fraterno

freckle *n* peca

free *adj* (*loose, unattached*) suelto, libre; *vt* soltar

freebase *n* (*cocaine*) base *f* libre de cocaína, coca en pasta

freeze *vt, vi* (*pret* **froze**; *pp* **frozen**) congelar(se)

frequency *n* (*pl* **-cies**) frecuencia

fresh *adj* (*food, air*) fresco

friction *n* fricción *f*

fried *adj* frito

front *adj* de enfrente; *n* the —— of..la parte de enfrente de

frontal *adj* frontal

frostbite *n* congelación *f*

frothy *adj* (*comp* **-ier**; *super* **-iest**) espumoso

frown *vi* fruncir el ceño *or* el entrecejo

froze *pret de* **freeze**

frozen *pp de* **freeze**

fructose *n* fructosa

fruit *n* (*pl* **fruit** *o* **fruits**) fruta(s); You can eat fruit..Puede comer frutas.

fry *vt* freír

FSH *abbr* **follicle-stimulating hormone**. *V.* **hormone**.

fuel *n* combustible *m*

full *adj* lleno; I feel full..Me siento lleno.

fullness *n* plenitud *f* (*form*), llenura

fumes *npl* humo, vapor *m*, gas *m*

fumigate *vt* fumigar

function *n* función *f*

funeral home *n* funeraria

fungal *adj* relativo a los hongos

fungus *n* (*pl* **-guses** *o* **-gi**) hongo

funny bone *n* (*fam*) codo

furosemide *n* furosemida

furuncle *n* furúnculo

fuse *vi* (*ortho*) soldar

fusion *n* fusión *f*

G

gag *vt* (*pret & pp* **gagged**; *ger* **gagging**) (*también* **to make** ——) provocar náusea(s); *vi* sentir náusea(s)

gain *n* ganancia, aumento; *vt* **to** —— **weight** aumentar de peso

gait *n* marcha (*form*), forma de andar

galactose *n* galactosa

galactosemia *n* galactosemia

gallbladder *n* vesícula biliar, vesícula (*fam*)

gallium *n* galio

gallop *n* (*card*) galope *m*

gallstone *n* cálculo biliar

gamma *n* gamma

gancyclovir *n* ganciclovir *m*

ganglion *n* (*pl* **-glia** *o* **-glions**) ganglio

ganglioneuroma *n* ganglioneuroma *m*

gangrene *n* gangrena; **dry** —— gangrena seca; **gas** —— gangrena gaseosa

gardener *n* jardinero -ra *mf*

Gardnerella vaginalis Gardnerella vaginalis

gargle *vi* hacer gárgaras

gas *n* gas *m*; (*fam*) gasolina; **arterial blood** —— gasometría, gases arteriales; **natural** —— gas natural; **tear** —— gas lacrimógeno; **to have** —— tener gas; **to pass** —— tirar gases *or* vientos, pasar gas

gash *n* tajo, cuchillada

gasoline *n* gasolina

gasp *vi* hacer esfuerzos para respirar, jalar aire

gastrectomy *n* (*pl* **-mies**) gastrectomía

gastric *adj* gástrico

gastrin *n* gastrina

gastrinoma *n* gastrinoma *m*

gastritis *n* gastritis *f*

gastrocnemius *n* gastrocnemio

gastroenteritis *n* gastroenteritis *f*

gastroenterologist *n* gastroenterólogo -ga *mf*

gastroenterology n gastroenterología
gastrointestinal (GI) adj gastrointestinal
gauze n gasa
gave pret de **give**
gay adj & n homosexual mf
gaze n mirada, el acto de mantener fija la vista en una dirección determinada
gel n gel m
gelatin n gelatina
gemfibrozil n gemfibrosilo
gender n género
gene n gen m
generic adj genérico
genetic adj genético; —— **engineering** ingeniería genética
genetics n genética
genital adj genital; n **genitals** genitales mpl
genius n genio
gentamicin n gentamicina
gentle adj suave, ligero
geriatrician n geriatra mf
geriatrics n geriatría
germ n germen m
German measles n sarampión m alemán, rubeola or rubéola
gerontologist n gerontólogo -ga mf
gerontology n gerontología
gestation n gestación f
gestational adj gestacional
get vt (pret got; pp gotten; ger getting) (a disease) darle (a uno), pegarle (a uno); **I got the flu**..Me dio la gripe; **to —— over** (an illness, etc.) recobrarse, recuperarse; **to —— up** levantarse
GH abbr **growth hormone. V. hormone.**
GI V. **gastrointestinal.**
Giardia Giardia
giardiasis n giardiasis f
giddy adj (comp **-dier**; super **-diest**) mareado
gigantism n gigantismo
Gila monster n monstruo de Gila
gingiva n (pl **-vae**) gingiva, encía
gingivitis n gingivitis f; **acute necrotizing ulcerative ——** gingivitis ulcerosa necrosante aguda
girdle n faja, corsé m
girl n niña, muchacha
girlfriend n novia, amiga (íntima)
give vt (pret **gave**; pp **given**) (a disease) contagiar, pegar; **Don't give me your cold!**..¡No me pegue su resfriado! **to —— up** (smoking, etc.) dejar de; **You have to give up smoking**..Tiene que dejar de fumar; **to —— up on** (diet, treatment, etc.) abandonar
gland n glándula; **adrenal ——** glándula suprarrenal; **endocrine ——** glándula endocrina; **parathyroid ——** glándula paratiroides; **parotid ——** glándula parótida; **pineal ——** glándula pineal; **pituitary ——** glándula pituitaria;

salivary —— glándula salival; **thyroid ——** glándula tiroides
glass n (material) vidrio; (tumbler) vaso; **a glass of milk**..un vaso con leche
glasses npl lentes mpl, anteojos
glaucoma n glaucoma m
glioblastoma n glioblastoma m
glioma n glioma m
glipizide n glipizida
globulin n globulina; **gamma ——** globulina gamma; **immune ——** globulina inmune
glomerulonephritis n glomerulonefritis f
glossitis n glositis f
glottis n glotis f
glove n guante m; **sterile gloves** guantes estériles
glucagon n glucagón m
glucose n glucosa; —— **monitor** aparato para medir la glucosa
glutamic acid n ácido glutámico
glutamine n glutamina
gluten n gluten m
glyburide n gliburida
glycerin n glicerina, glicerol m
glycerol n glicerina, glicerol m
glycine n glicina
gnat n jején m, mosquito
GnRH abbr **gonadotropin-releasing hormone. V. hormone.**
go vi **to —— away** (pain, etc.) quitarse; **The pain went away**..El dolor se me quitó; **to —— down** (temperature, blood glucose, etc.) bajar(se); **to —— up** subir(se)
goal n meta
goat n cabra
goggles npl lentes protectores
goiter n bocio
gold n oro
gonad n gónada
gonadotropin n gonadotropina; **human chorionic ——** (HCG) gonadotropina coriónica humana
gonococcus n (pl **-ci**) gonococo
gonorrhea n gonorrea
good adj (comp **better**; super **best**) bueno; n bien m; **for your own ——** por su propio bien
good-looking adj bien parecido, guapo
goose pimples npl piel f de gallina
got pret de **get**
gotten pp de **get**
gout n gota
gouty adj gotoso
gown n bata
grade n (degree) grado
gradually adv poco a poco
graft n injerto; **skin ——** injerto cutáneo; vt injertar
grain n (pharm) grano; (cereal) grano, cereal m
gram n gramo
Gram-negative adj gramnegativo

Gram-positive *adj* grampositivo
grandchild *n* (*pl* **-children**) nieto -ta *mf*
granddaughter *n* nieta
grandfather *n* abuelo
grandiose *adj* grandioso, pomposo
grandmother *n* abuela
grandparent *n* abuelo -la *mf*; **grandparents** abuelos
grandson *n* nieto
granulation *n* granulación *f*
granulocyte *n* granulocito
granuloma *n* granuloma *m*
granulomatosis *n* granulomatosis *f*; **Wegener's** —— granulomatosis de Wegener
graph *n* gráfica *or* gráfico
grasp *n* prensión *f*; *vt* agarrar, coger
grass *n* hierba; (*fam*) marihuana *or* marijuana
gratification *n* gratificación *f*
grave *adj* grave
gray *adj* gris; —— **hair** cana(s); —— **matter** substancia gris
graze *n* rozón *m*; *vt* rozar(se)
grease *n* grasa, manteca
greasy *adj* (*comp* **-ier**; *super* **-iest**) grasoso, grasiento
green *adj* verde
grew *pret de* **grow**
grief *n* pesar *m*, aflicción *f*, pena
grieve *vi* afligirse
grilled *adj* asado a la parrilla
grind *vt* (*a pill, etc.*) moler, triturar
grip *n* prensión *f*; *vt* agarrar, coger

griseofulvin *n* griseofulvina
grit *vt* (*one's teeth*) rechinar (*los dientes*)
groan *n* gemido; *vi* gemir
groin *n* ingle *f*
group *n* grupo; **support** —— grupo de apoyo
grow *vi* (*pret* **grew**; *pp* **grown**) crecer; **to** —— **old** envejecer(se); **to** —— **out of** (*a habit*) quitarse (*a uno*), perder; **They will outgrow it**..Se les quitará; **to** —— **up** crecer, volverse adulto
growl *vi* (*one's stomach*) gruñir, sonar, tronar; **My stomach is growling**..Me gruñen las tripas.
growth *n* crecimiento; (*on the skin*) tumor *m*, tumorcito
grunt *n* gruñido; *vi* gruñir
guard *n* protector *m*
guardian *n* (*legal*) tutor -ra *mf*
Guatemalan *adj* & *n* guatemalteco -ca *mf*
guide *n* guía; —— **dog** perro guía
guideline *n* pauta
guilt *n* culpa; —— **feelings** sentimientos de culpa
guinea pig *n* cobayo, (*esp. fig*) conejillo de Indias
gum *n* goma; (*anat*) encía; **chewing** —— chicle *m*
gumma *n* goma *m*
gun *n* pistola; (*rifle*) fusil *m*
gurgle *n* gorgoteo; *vi* gorgotear
gut *n* intestino, tripa (*often pl*)
gynecologist *n* ginecólogo -ga *mf*
gynecology *n* ginecología

H

habit *n* hábito, costumbre *f*; **bad** —— vicio
habit-forming *adj* que crea hábito
habituation *n* habituación *f*
Haemophilus Haemophilus
hair *n* pelo, cabello; **body** —— vello
haircut *n* corte *m* de pelo; **to get a** —— cortarse el pelo
haircutter *n* peluquero -ra *mf*
half *adj* medio; —— **asleep** medio dormido; —— **brother** medio hermano; —— **sister** media hermana; —— **the** la mitad de; **Take half the medicine now**..Tome la mitad de la medicina ahora; **a** —— *o* —— **a** medio; **Take a half pill every morning**..Tome media pastilla todas las mañanas

half-life *n* vida media
halfway house *n* (*US*) casa de rehabilitación (*esp. para farmacodependientes y alcohólicos después de tratamiento y antes de volver a la sociedad*)
halitosis *n* halitosis *f*, mal aliento
hall, hallway *n* corredor *m*, pasillo
hallucination *n* alucinación *f*
haloperidol *n* haloperidol *m*
halothane *n* halotano
ham *n* jamón *m*
hamartoma *n* hamartoma *m*
hammer *n* martillo
hamstring *n* tendón *m* de la corva

hand *n* mano *f*
hand-held *adj* manual
handkerchief *n* pañuelo
handwriting *n* escritura, letra
hang *vt* (*pret* & *pp* hanged *o* hung) (*by the neck*) ahorcar; to —— oneself ahorcarse; *vi* colgar
hangnail *n* padrastro, uñero (*fam*)
hangover *n* resaca, cruda (*Mex*), goma (*CA*); to have a —— tener una resaca, tener una cruda (*Mex*), estar crudo (*Mex*), estar de goma (*CA*)
happiness *n* felicidad *f*
happy *adj* feliz, contento
hard *adj* duro; —— of hearing que no oye bien, medio sordo
harm *n* daño; *vt* dañar, hacer daño
harmful *adj* nocivo, dañino
harmless *adj* inofensivo, no dañino, que no hace daño
harsh *adj* áspero
hashish *n* hachís *m*
hat *n* sombrero
hate *n* odio; *vt* odiar
hay *n* heno
hazard *n* peligro
hazardous *adj* peligroso
HCG *abbr* human chorionic gonadotropin. *V.* gonadotropin.
HDL *abbr* high density lipoprotein. *V.* lipoprotein.
head *n* cabeza; (*of an abscess*) centro; (*of a bed*) cabecera; to come to a —— (*abscess*) madurar
headache *n* cefalea (*form*), dolor *m* de cabeza; cluster —— cefalea en grupos; migraine —— migraña, jaqueca; tension —— cefalea por tensión *or* tensional; vascular —— cefalea vascular
heal *vt, vi* curar(se), sanar
healing *n* curación *f*, (el) curar; Steroids can retard healing..Los esteroides pueden retardar la curación...the art of healing..el arte de curar
health *n* salud *f*, salubridad *f*; mental —— salud mental; public —— salud pública
healthcare *n* atención médica, servicios médicos
Health Department *n* departamento de salud
healthy *adj* (*comp* -ier; *super* -iest) sano, saludable
hear *vt, vi* (*pret* & *pp* heard) oír
hearing *n* (*sense*) oído, audición *f* (*form*); How's your hearing?..¿Cómo escucha?..¿Cómo oye? —— aid audífono
heart *n* corazón *m*; —— attack ataque cardiaco *or* al corazón; —— disease enfermedad *f* del corazón; —— murmur soplo cardiaco; congestive —— failure insuficiencia cardiaca congestiva
heartbeat *n* latido del corazón

heartburn *n* agruras, acidez *f* (estomacal), acedía
heat *n* calor *m*; *vt* (*también* to —— up) calentar
heater *n* calentador *m*
heating *n* calefacción *f*
heating pad *n* cojín eléctrico
heatstroke *n* insolación *f*, golpe *m* de calor
heaviness *n* pesadez *f*
heavy *adj* (*comp* -ier; *super* -iest) pesado
heavyset *adj* robusto, fornido
heel *n* talón *m*; (*of a shoe*) tacón *m*
height *n* altura
helium *n* helio
helmet *n* casco
help *interj* ¡Auxilio!, ¡Socorro!; *n* ayuda, auxilio, socorro; *vt, vi* ayudar
hemangioma *n* hemangioma *m*; cavernous —— hemangioma cavernoso
hematocrit *n* hematócrito
hematologist *n* hematólogo -ga *mf*
hematology *n* hematología
hematoma *n* hematoma *m*; subdural —— hematoma subdural
hemiplegia *n* hemiplejía
hemisphere *n* hemisferio
hemochromatosis *n* hemocromatosis *f*
hemodialysis *n* hemodiálisis *f*
hemoglobin *n* hemoglobina
hemolytic *adj* hemolítico
hemophilia *n* hemofilia
hemorrhage *n* hemorragia; subarachnoid —— hemorragia subaracnoidea
hemorrhagic *adj* hemorrágico
hemorrhoid *n* hemorroide *f*, almorrana
hemosiderosis *n* hemosiderosis *f*
heparin *n* heparina
hepatic *adj* hepático; —— insufficiency insuficiencia hepática
hepatitis *n* hepatitis *f*; —— A; B; non-A, non-B; etc. hepatitis A, B, no A no B, etc.
hepatoma *n* hepatoma *m*
hepatorenal *adj* hepatorrenal
herb *n* hierba; —— shop botánica, hierbería
herbal *adj* herbario
herbalist *n* hierbero -ra *mf*
herbicide *n* herbicida *m*
hereditary *adj* hereditario
heredity *n* herencia
hermaphrodite *adj* & *n* hermafrodita *mf*
hernia *n* hernia; incarcerated —— hernia incarcerada; inguinal —— hernia inguinal; hiatal —— hernia hiatal; strangulated —— hernia estrangulada; umbilical —— hernia umbilical
heroin *n* heroína
herpangina *n* herpangina
herpes *n* herpes *m*; —— simplex herpes simple; —— zoster herpes zoster, zona
herpetic *adj* herpético
heterosexual *adj* & *n* heterosexual *mf*

hiccup *n* hipo; *vi* (*pret & pp* -cuped *o* -cupped; *ger* -cuping *o* -cupping) (*también* **to have the hiccups**) tener hipo
hickey *n* chupete *m*, chupón *m*, marca roja en la piel debida a un beso fuerte
high *adj* alto; (*fam*) intoxicado por drogas, drogado
high-heeled *adj* de tacón alto
high-pitched *adj* de tono alto, agudo
hip *n* cadera
hipbone *n* hueso de la cadera
hip-joint *n* articulación *f* de la cadera
hiplength *adj* de largo hasta el muslo
Hippocratic Oath *n* juramento hipocrático
histamine *n* histamina
histidine *n* histidina
histiocytosis X *n* histiocitosis *f* X
histology *n* histología
histoplasmosis *n* histoplasmosis *f*
history *n* (*pl* -ries) (*medical*) historia clínica
histrionic *adj* histriónico
HIV *abbr* **human immunodeficiency virus.** *V.* **virus.**
hives *npl* ronchas
hoarse *adj* ronco
hoarseness *n* ronquera
hobby *n* (*pl* -bies) pasatiempo
hold *vt* **to —— one's breath** detener *or* aguantar la respiración; **to —— one's nose** taparse la nariz
hole *n* hoyo, agujero
home *n* casa, hogar, domicilio; **at ——** en casa
homeless *adj* sin hogar
homemaker *n* ama de casa
homeopath *n* homeópata *mf*
homeopathy *n* homeopatía
homesick *adj* **to be —— sentir nostalgia (*a la tierra de uno*)
homesickness *n* nostalgia (*a la tierra de uno*)
homosexual *adj & n* homosexual *mf*
Honduran *adj & n* hondureño -ña *mf*
hooked *adj* (*on drugs*) prendido (*esp. Mex*), adicto
hookworm *n* uncinaria
hop *n* brinco, salto; *vi* (*pret & pp* **hopped**; *ger* **hopping**) brincar, saltar; **Hop on one foot..Brinque en un pie.**
hope *n* esperanza; **to lose —— perder la esperanza, desesperarse; *vi* esperar; **to —— for** esperar
hopeless *adj* desesperado, sin esperanza
hormonal *adj* hormonal
hormone *n* hormona; **adrenocorticotropic —— (ACTH)** hormona adrenocorticotrópica; **follicle-stimulating —— (FSH)** hormona estimulante del folículo; **gonadotropin-releasing —— (GnRH)** hormona liberadora de gonadotropinas; **growth —— (GH)** hormona del crecimiento; **luteinizing —— (LH)** hormona

luteinizante; **parathyroid —— (PTH)** hormona paratiroidea; **thyroid ——** hormona tiroidea; **thyroid-stimulating —— (TSH)** hormona estimulante del tiroides
hornet *n* avispón *m*
horsefly *n* (*pl* -flies) tábano
hose *n* (*pl* **hose**) (*stocking*) media
hose *n* (*tube*) manguera
hospice *n* asilo para pacientes con enfermedades terminales
hospital *n* hospital *m*; **—— administration** administración *f* del hospital; **community —— hospital de la comunidad; **county —— (*US*) hospital del condado; **general —— hospital general; **mental —— hospital psiquiátrico; **private —— hospital privado; **public —— hospital público; **Veteran's Administration (VA) —— hospital para veteranos
hospitalize *vt* hospitalizar, internar; **Have you ever been hospitalized before?..¿Ha estado hospitalizado alguna vez antes?**
hostile *adj* hostil
hostility *n* hostilidad *f*
hot *adj* (*comp* **hotter**; *super* **hottest**) caliente; (*to the taste*) picante; **to be *o* feel —— tener *or* sentir calor; **Do you feel hot more often than other people?..¿Ud. siente calor más frecuente que otras personas? **—— flash** calor *m*, bochorno, sensación repentina de calor (*esp. durante la menopausia*); **—— springs** aguas *fpl* termales
hot-water bottle *o* **bag** *n* bolsa de agua caliente
hour *n* hora; **office hours** horas de oficina *or* de consulta; **visiting hours** horas de visita
housecleaner *n* sirviente -ta *mf*, limpiador -ra *mf* de casas
housefly *n* (*pl* -flies) mosca doméstica
housewife *n* (*pl* -wives) ama de casa
hug *n* abrazo; *vt* (*pret & pp* **hugged**; *ger* **hugging**) abrazar
hum *n* (*buzz or ringing*) zumbido; *vt* (*pret & pp* **hummed**; *ger* **humming**) (*a note*) canturrear; *vi* zumbar, canturrear
human *adj* humano; **—— being** ser humano; *n* humano
humanitarian *adj* humanitario
humerus *n* húmero
humid *adj* húmedo
humidifier *n* humidificador *m*
humidify *vt* (*pret & pp* -fied) humedecer
humidity *n* humedad *f*
hump *n* (*on the back*) joroba
humpback *n* jorobado -da *mf*
hung *pret & pp* de **hang**
hunger *n* hambre *f*
hungover *adj* crudo (*Mex*); **to be —— tener una resaca, tener una cruda (*Mex*), estar

crudo (*Mex*), estar de goma (*CA*)
hungry *adj* **to be** —— tener hambre; **Are you hungry?**..¿Tiene hambre?
hurricane n huracán *m*
hurt *vt* (*pret & pp* **hurt**); (*to cause pain*) doler, causar dolor; (*to injure*) lastimar, herir; (*to harm*) hacer daño; **This won't hurt you**..Esto no le va a doler...**I'm not going to hurt you**..No voy a causarle dolor...**Did you hurt your finger?**..¿Se lastimó el dedo?...**Eating oranges won't hurt you**..El comer naranjas no le hará daño; **to** —— **oneself** *o* **to get** —— lastimarse; **Did you hurt yourself?**..¿Se lastimó? *vi* doler, sentir dolor; **Where does it hurt?**..¿Dónde le duele?...**Tell me when it hurts**..Dígame cuando sienta dolor.
husband *n* esposo, marido
hydatid *adj* hidatídico
hydralazine *n* hidralacina
hydrocarbon *n* hidrocarburo
hydrocele *n* hidrocele *m*
hydrocephalus *n* hidrocéfalo
hydrocephaly *n* hidrocefalia
hydrochloric acid *n* ácido clorhídrico
hydrochlorothiazide *n* hidroclorotiazida
hydrocortisone *n* hidrocortisona
hydrogen peroxide *n* peróxido de hidrógeno (*form*), agua oxigenada
hydronephrosis *n* hidronefrosis *f*
hydrophobia *n* hidrofobia
hydrotherapy *n* hidroterapia
hygiene *n* higiene *f*, aseo; **oral** —— aseo oral *or* bucal
hygienic *adj* higiénico
hygienist *n* higienista *mf*
hymen *n* himen *m*
hyoid bone *n* hioides *m*
hyperactive *adj* hiperactivo
hyperactivity *n* hiperactividad *f*
hyperalimentation *n* hiperalimentación *f*
hyperbaric *adj* hiperbárico; —— **chamber** cámara hiperbárica
hypercalcemia *n* hipercalcemia
hyperglycemia *n* hiperglucemia

hyperlipidemia *n* hiperlipemia *or* hiperlipidemia
hyperlipoproteinemia *n* hiperlipoproteinemia
hyperosmolar *adj* hiperosmolar
hyperparathyroid *adj* hiperparatiroideo
hyperparathyroidism *n* hiperparatiroidismo
hyperplasia *n* hiperplasia
hypersensitive *adj* hipersensible
hypersensitivity *n* hipersensibilidad *f*
hypertension *n* hipertensión *f*, alta presión (*fam*); **malignant** —— hipertensión maligna; **portal** —— hipertensión portal; **pulmonary** —— hipertensión pulmonar
hyperthermia *n* hipertermia
hyperthyroid *adj* hipertiroideo
hyperthyroidism *n* hipertiroidismo
hypertrophy *n* hipertrofia; **benign prostatic** —— hipertrofia prostática benigna
hyperventilate *vi* respirar demasiado rápido
hypnosis *n* hipnosis *f*
hypnotic *adj & n* hipnótico
hypnotism *n* hipnotismo
hypnotist *n* hipnotizador -ra *mf*
hypnotize *vt* hipnotizar
hypoallergenic *adj* hipoalergénico
hypochondriac *adj & n* hipocondríaco *or* (*esp. spoken*) hipocondriaco
hypodermic *adj* hipodérmico
hypoglycemia *n* hipoglucemia
hypoglycemic *adj* hipoglucémico; **oral** —— **agent** hipoglucemiante *m* oral
hypoparathyroid *adj* hipoparatiroideo
hypoparathyroidism *n* hipoparatiroidismo
hypospadias *n* hipospadias *m*
hypotension *n* hipotensión *f*
hypothalamus *n* hipotálamo
hypothermia *n* hipotermia
hypothyroid *adj* hipotiroideo
hypothyroidism *n* hipotiroidismo
hysterectomy *n* (*pl* -**mies**) histerectomía; **abdominal** —— histerectomía abdominal; **vaginal** —— histerectomía vaginal
hysteria *n* histeria
hysterical *adj* histérico

I

I&D *V.* **incision and drainage**.
ibuprofen *n* ibuprofén *m*
ice *n* hielo; —— **chips** pedacitos de hielo;
  —— **cream** helado, nieve (*Mex*); ——
  pack bolsa con hielo
id *n* (*psych*) id *m*
ideal *adj* ideal
identification *n* identificación *f*; ——
  bracelet brazalete *m* para identificación
identify *vt* identificar; *vi* **to** —— **with**
  (*psych*) identificarse con
identity *n* (*pl* -**ties**) identidad *f*; —— **crisis**
  crisis *f* de identidad
idiopathic *adj* idiopático
ileum *n* íleon *m*
ileus *n* íleo
iliac *adj* iliaco
ilium *n* hueso iliaco
ill *adj* enfermo, malo
illegal *adj* ilegal
illiteracy *n* analfabetismo
illiterate *adj* analfabeto
illness *n* enfermedad *f*, mal *m*; **mental** ——
  enfermedad mental
illusion *n* ilusión *f*
image *n* imagen *f*
imbalance *n* desequilibrio
imipenem *n* imipenem *m*
imipramine *n* imipramina
immature *adj* inmaduro
immediate *adj* inmediato
immediately *adv* inmediatamente
immobile *adj* inmóvil
immobilization *n* inmovilización *f*
immobilize *vt* inmovilizar
immune *adj* inmune
immunity *n* inmunidad *f*
immunization *n* inmunización *f*
immunize *vt* inmunizar
immunocompetent *adj* inmunocompetente
immunocompromised *adj* inmunocomprometido
immunodeficiency *n* inmunodeficiencia
immunodepressed *adj* inmunodeprimido
immunodepression *n* inmunodepresión *f*
immunoglobulin *n* inmunoglobulina
immunological, immunologic *adj* inmunológico
immunologist *n* inmunólogo -ga *mf*
immunology *n* inmunología
immunosuppressant *n* inmunosupresor *m*
immunosuppressive *adj* inmunosupresor
immunotherapy *n* inmunoterapia
impacted *adj* impactado

impaction *n* impactación *f*
impaired *adj* dañado; **hearing** —— **que**
  tiene dificultad para oír
imperforate *adj* imperforado
impetigo *n* impétigo
implant *n* implante *m*; *vt* implantar
implantation *n* implantación *f*
impotence *n* impotencia
impotent *adj* impotente
improve *vt, vi* mejorar(se)
improvement *n* mejoría
impulse *n* impulso
impulsive *adj* impulsivo
impure *adj* impuro
impurity impureza
inactive *adj* inactivo
inactivity *n* inactividad *f*
inappropriate *adj* inapropiado
incapable *adj* incapaz
incapacitating *adj* incapacitante
incest *n* incesto
inch *n* pulgada
incidence *n* incidencia
incision *n* incisión *f*, corte *m*, herida
incisor *n* diente incisivo
incoherent *adj* incoherente
incompatible *adj* incompatible
incompetent *adj* incompetente
incomplete *adj* incompleto
incontinence *n* incontinencia, incapacidad *f*
  para retener la orina o el excremento;
  stress —— incontinencia de esfuerzo
incontinent *adj* (*of urine or stool*)
  incontinente, incapaz de retener la orina o
  el excremento
increase *n* aumento; *vt, vi* aumentar
incubator *n* incubadora
incurable *adj* incurable
independent *adj* independiente
index *adj & n* (*pl* **indexes** *o* **indices**) índice
  m
indication *n* indicación *f*
indifference *n* indiferencia
indigestion *n* indigestión *f*
indisposition *n* indisposición *f*
indistinct *adj* indistinto
indomethacin *n* indometacina
induce *vt* inducir
ineffective *adj* ineficaz
ineligible *adj* inelegible
infant *n* infante *m*, criatura
infantile *adj* infantil
infarct *n* infarto
infarction *n* infarto, acción *f* y efecto de un

infarto; **myocardial** —— infarto de miocardio
infect *vt, vi* infectar(se)
infection *n* infección *f*; **urinary tract** —— **(UTI)** infección del tracto urinario, mal *m* de orín (*fam*)
infectious *adj* infeccioso
inferior *adj* (*anat*) inferior
infertile *adj* estéril
infertility *n* infertilidad *f*, esterilidad *f*
infest *vt* infestar
infestation *n* infestación *f*
infiltrate *vt, vi* infiltrar(se)
infirmary *n* enfermería
inflamed *adj* inflamado; **to become** —— inflamarse
inflammable *adj* inflamable
inflammation *n* inflamación *f*
influenza *n* influenza, gripe *f*
information *n* información *f*
infrared *adj* infrarrojo
infuse *vt* infundir
infusion *n* infusión *f*
ingest *vt* ingerir
ingredient *n* ingrediente *m*
ingrown nail *n* uña enterrada *or* encarnada, uñero
inguinal *adj* inguinal
INH *V.* isoniazid.
inhale *vt, vi* inhalar
inhaler *n* aerosol *m*, inhalador *m*, espray *m* (*Ang*); **metered dose** —— aerosol dosificador
inherit *vt* heredar
inherited *adj* heredado
inhibit *vt* inhibir
inhibited *adj* inhibido, cohibido
inhibition *n* inhibición *f*, cohibición *f*
initial *adj* inicial; *n* inicial *f*
inject *vt* inyectar
injectable *adj* inyectable
injection *n* inyección *f*; **The nurse will give you an injection**..La enfermera lo va a inyectar..La enfermera le va a poner una inyección.
injure *vt* herir, lastimar
injury *n* (*pl* **-ries**) herida, lesión *f*
inlay *n* (*dent*) incrustación *f*
inner *adj* interno
inoculate *vt* inocular
inoperable *adj* inoperable
inorganic *adj* inorgánico
insane *adj* loco
insanity *n* locura
insect *n* insecto
insecticide *n* insecticida *m*
insecure *adj* inseguro
insecurity *n* inseguridad
inseminate *vt* inseminar
insemination *n* inseminación *f*; **artificial** —— inseminación artificial
insert *vt* introducir, meter

inside *adj* interior, interno; *adv* dentro, adentro; *n* interior *m*; *prep* dentro de; **inside your body**..dentro de su cuerpo
insole *n* plantilla
insomnia *n* insomnio
inspire *vt, vi* inspirar
instep *n* empeine *m* (del pie)
instinct *n* instinto
instruction *n* instrucción *f*
instrument *n* instrumento
insufficiency *n* insuficiencia; **aortic** ——, **renal** ——, **venous** ——, etc. insuficiencia aórtica, renal, venosa, etc.
insulin *n* insulina; **lente** —— insulina lenta; **NPH** —— insulina NPH *or* de acción intermedia; **regular** —— insulina de acción rápida; **semilente** —— insulina semilenta; **ultralente** —— insulina ultralenta
insurance *n* seguro (*often pl*)
intact *adj* intacto
intellect *n* intelecto
intellectual *adj* intelectual
intelligence *n* inteligencia; —— **quotient (IQ)** cociente *m* de inteligencia (CI)
intense *adj* intenso
intensive *adj* intensivo
interact *vi* interactuar
interaction *n* interacción *f*
intercourse *n* relación *f* (sexual), acto sexual; **When was the last time you had intercourse?**..¿Cuándo fue la útima vez que tuvo relaciones?
interferon *n* interferón *m*
interior *adj* & *n* interior *m*
intermediate *adj* intermedio
intermittent *adj* intermitente
intern *n* médico interno, interno -na *mf*
internal *adj* interno
internist *n* internista *mf*
interpersonal *adj* interpersonal
interpret *vt, vi* interpretar
interpreter *n* intérprete *mf*
interstitial *adj* intersticial
interval *n* intervalo
intestinal *adj* intestinal
intestine *n* intestino, tripa (*often pl*); **large** —— intestino grueso; **small** —— intestino delgado
intolerance *n* intolerancia
intoxication *n* intoxicación *f*
intraarticular *adj* intraarticular
intracranial *adj* intracraneal
intramuscular *adj* intramuscular
intraocular *adj* intraocular
intrauterine device (IUD) *n* dispositivo intrauterino (DIU), aparato (*fam*)
intravenous (IV) *adj* intravenoso (IV), endovenoso
intrinsic factor *n* factor intrínseco
introvert *n* introvertido -da *mf*
introverted *adj* introvertido

intubate *vt* intubar
intubation *n* intubación *f*
intussusception *n* intususcepción *f*
invalid *n* (*ant*, **disabled person** *es preferido*) inválido -da *mf*
invasive *adj* invasor
investigational *adj* (*medication, etc.*) en investigación
involuntary *adj* involuntario
iodine *n* yodo
ipecac *n* ipecacuana
IQ *V.* **intelligence quotient.**
iris *n* (*pl* **irides**) iris *m*
iritis *n* iritis *f*
iron *n* hierro
irradiate *vt* irradiar, tratar con radiación
irregular *adj* irregular
irreversible *adj* irreversible
irrigate *vt* irrigar
irritability *n* irritabilidad *f*
irritable *adj* irritable
irritant *n* irritante *m*
irritate *vt* irritar; **to become irritated** irritarse
irritating *adj* irritante, molesto
irritation *n* irritación *f*
ischemia *n* isquemia
ischemic *adj* isquémico
isolate *vt* aislar
isolation *n* aislamiento
isoleucine *n* isoleucina
isoniazid (INH) *n* isoniacida
isosorbide dinitrate *n* dinitrato de isosorbide
itch *n* picazón *f*, comezón *f*; *vi* picar, tener picazón *or* comezón; **Where does it itch?..¿Dónde le pica?...Does your arm itch?..¿Le pica el brazo?...Do you itch?..¿Tiene picazón?**
itching, itchiness *n* picazón *f*, comezón *f*
ITP *abbr* **idiopathic thrombocytopenic purpura.** *V.* **purpura.**
IUD *V.* **intrauterine device.**
IV *V.* **intravenous.**
IVP *abbr* **intravenous pyelogram.** *V.* **pyelogram.**

J

jabbing *adj* punzante
jacket *n* chaqueta, chamarra (*Mex*); (*dent*) corona
jail *n* cárcel *f*
jaundice *n* ictericia (*form*), coloración amarilla de la piel, piel amarilla (*fam*)
jaw *n* mandíbula, quijada (*fam*); **lower ——** maxilar *m* inferior, mandíbula, quijada; **upper ——** maxilar *m* superior
jawbone *n* mandíbula, quijada
Jehovah's Witnesses *npl* Testigos de Jehová
jejunal *adj* yeyunal
jejunum *n* yeyuno
jelly *n* (*pl* **-lies**) jalea
jellyfish *n* (*pl* **-fish** *o* **-fishes**) medusa, aguamala
jigger *n* nigua
job *n* trabajo, empleo
jock itch *n* (*fam*) tiña inguinal
jockstrap *n* (*fam*) suspensorio
jog *vi* (*pret & pp* **jogged**; *ger* **jogging**) trotar
join *vt* (*two objects*) ligar, juntar; *vi* unirse, juntarse
joint *n* articulación *f*, coyuntura, hueso (*esp. Mex, CA; fam, used as plural*); **Do your joints hurt?..¿Le duelen las coyunturas?..¿Le duelen los huesos?**
jugular *adj* yugular
juice *n* jugo, zumo; **fruit ——** jugo de fruta; **orange ——** jugo de naranja
junk *n* (*vulg*) heroína
junkie (*vulg*) *n* persona que se inyecta heroína
juvenile *adj* juvenil

K

keloid n queloide m
keratotomy n queratotomía; radial —— queratotomía radiada
ketoacidosis n cetoacidosis f
ketoconazole n ketoconazol m
ketone n cetona
ketotic adj cetónico
kid n (fam, child) niño -ña mf
kidney n riñón m; —— disease enfermedad f de los riñones; —— failure insuficiencia renal; polycystic —— riñón poliquístico
kidney belt n (fam) faja, cinturón m (para prevenir hernias)
kill vt matar
kilogram n kilogramo
kiss n beso; vt besar
kissing bug n chinche f (vector de la enfermedad de Chagas)

kit n botiquín m; first-aid —— botiquín de primeros auxilios
Klebsiella Klebsiella
knee n rodilla; —— jerk reflejo patelar or rotuliano; back of the —— corva
kneecap n rótula
kneelength adj de largo hasta la rodilla
kneepad n rodillera
knife n (pl knives) cuchillo
knife-like adj (pain) punzante
knit vi (ortho) soldar
knock-kneed adj con las rodillas hacia adentro, patizambo
knuckle n nudillo
kwashiorkor n kwashiorkor or cuasiorcor m
kyphoscoliosis n cifoscoliosis f
kyphosis n cifosis f

L

lab V. laboratory.
label n etiqueta
labetolol n labetolol m
labium n (pl labia) labio (genital)
labor n trabajo de parto; —— pain dolor m del parto; to be in —— estar en trabajo de parto
laboratory n (pl -ries) laboratorio
labyrinth n laberinto
labyrinthitis n laberintitis f
laceration n laceración f
lack n deficiencia, falta
lactase n lactasa
lactate vi lactar, salirle leche (fam)
lactation n lactancia
lactic acid n ácido láctico
lactic dehydrogenase n deshidrogenasa láctica
lactose n lactosa
lactulose n lactulosa
lag n retraso; vi (pret & pp lagged; ger lagging) retrasarse

lain pp de lie
lamb n (carne f de) cordero
lame adj cojo
lamp n lámpara
lance vt abrir con bisturí (un absceso)
lancet n lanceta
language n (referring to structure and development) lenguaje m
lanolin n lanolina
lanugo n lanugo
lap n (of a person) regazo
laparoscopy n (pl -pies) laparoscopia or (esp. spoken) laparoscopía
laparotomy n (pl -mies) laparotomía
lapse n lapso
lard n manteca
large adj grande
larva n (pl -vae) larva
larva migrans n larva migrans
laryngeal adj laríngeo
laryngectomy n (pl -mies) laringectomía
laryngitis n laringitis f

laryngoscopy n (pl -**pies**) laringoscopia or (esp. spoken) laringoscopía
larynx n (pl -**inges**) laringe f
laser n rayo láser, láser m
last adj último; **your last period**..su última regla; vi durar; **How long did the pain last?**..¿Cuánto tiempo le duró el dolor?
last rites npl santos óleos
late adj (development, etc.) tardío
latent adj latente
lateral adj lateral
latex n látex m
latrine n letrina
laugh n risa; vi reir(se)
laughing gas n gas m hilarante
lavage n lavado; **bronchoalveolar** —— lavado broncoalveolar; **gastric** —— lavado gástrico; **peritoneal** —— lavado peritoneal
lavatory n (pl -**ries**) lavatorio
lawsuit n demanda (legal)
laxative adj & n laxante m; **bulk** —— laxante que aumenta el bolo fecal
lay adj lego, popular, no profesional; —— **opinion** opinión popular or no profesional
lay pret de **lie**
layer n capa
lb. V. **pound.**
LDL abbr **low density lipoprotein.** V. **lipoprotein.**
lead n plomo
lean adj (person) flaco; (meat) magro; vi inclinarse; **Lean forward**..Inclínese hacia adelante.
learning n aprendizaje m; —— **disability** dificultad f del aprendizaje
leathery adj correoso
lecithin n lecitina
leech n sanguijuela
left adj izquierdo; n (left-hand side) izquierda
left-handed adj zurdo
leg n pierna
legume n legumbre f
leiomyoma n leiomioma or liomioma m
leiomyosarcoma n leiomiosarcoma or liomiosarcoma m
leishmaniasis n leishmaniasis f
length n longitud f, largo
lengthen vt alargar, hacer más largo
lens n lente m&f; (of the eye) cristalino; **contact** —— (hard or soft) lente de contacto (duro o blando)
leprosy n lepra
leptospirosis n leptospirosis f
lesbian n lesbiana
lesion n lesión f
lethal adj letal
lethargy n letargo
leucine n leucina
leukemia n leucemia; **acute lymphocytic** —— leucemia linfocítica aguda; **chronic**

myelogenous —— leucemia mielógena crónica; **granulocytic** —— leucemia granulocítica; **lymphoblastic** —— leucemia linfoblástica; **myeloid** —— leucemia mieloide
leukocyte n leucocito
level n nivel m
LGV V. **lymphogranuloma venereum.**
LH abbr **luteinizing hormone.** V. **hormone.**
libido n libido f, deseo sexual
lice pl de **louse**
lichen planus n liquen plano
lick vt lamer
lidocaine n lidocaína
lie vi (pret **lay**; pp **lain**; ger **lying**) **to** —— **down** acostarse
life n vida; —— **expectancy** expectativa or esperanza de vida
lifestyle n estilo de vida
life-threatening adj que amenaza la vida
lift vt levantar; **to** —— **weights** levantar pesas
ligament n ligamento
ligation n ligadura; **tubal** —— ligadura de las trompas, amarre m de las trompas (fam)
light adj (case of disease) leve; (touch) ligero; (weight) liviano; n luz f
lightheaded adj mareado, que tiene sensación de desmayo; **to feel** —— tener mareo, estar mareado, tener sensación de desmayo
lightheadedness n mareo, sensación f de desmayo
lightning n relámpago
limb n (arm or leg) miembro
limit n límite m; **lower** —— **of normal** límite inferior normal **upper** —— **of normal** límite superior normal; vt limitar
limp adj flojo; vi cojear, renquear
lindane n lindano
line n línea; vt (the intestine, etc.) revestir; **to** —— **up** alinear; vi **to** —— **up** alinearse
liniment n linimento
lining n (of the stomach, etc.) revestimiento
linoleic acid n ácido linoleico
lip n labio; (genital) labio
lipase n lipasa
lipid n lípido
lipoma n lipoma m
lipoprotein n lipoproteína; **high density** —— **(HDL)** lipoproteína de alta densidad (LAD); **low density** —— **(LDL)** lipoproteína de baja densidad (LBD); **very low density** —— **(VLDL)** lipoproteína de muy baja densidad (LMBD)
liposuction n liposucción f
lipread vi (pret & pp -**read**) leer los labios
liquid adj & n líquido
liquor n licor m, alcohol m
lisinopril n lisinopril m

lisp *n* ceceo; *vi* cecear
listen *vi* escuchar; **I'm going to listen to your lungs..**Voy a escucharle los pulmones.
listeriosis *n* listeriosis *f*
liter *n* litro
lithium *n* litio
lithotripsy *n* litotripsia
litter *n* camilla
little *adj* pequeño, chico; poco; **a little tumor..**un tumor pequeño...**a little milk..**un poco de leche...**little time..**poco tiempo; —— **by** —— poco a poco
live *adj* (*virus, vaccine*) vivo; *vi* vivir
liver *n* hígado; —— **disease** enfermedad *f* del hígado; —— **failure** insuficiencia hepática
lives *pl de* **life**
lobar *adj* lobar
lobe *n* lóbulo
lobectomy *n* (*pl* -**mies**) lobectomía
local *adj* local
lockjaw *n* (*fam*) trismo
lodge *vi* alojarse
long *adj* largo; *adv* **How long have you had diabetes?..**¿Desde cuándo tiene diabetes?..¿Hace cuánto que tiene diabetes?...**How long did you have nausea?..**¿Cuánto tiempo tuvo náusea?
long-acting *adj* de acción prolongada
longevity *n* longevidad *f*
long-term *adj* a largo plazo
look *vi* mirar; **Look upward..**Mire hacia arriba.
loop *n* lazo
loose *adj* flojo, suelto
loosen *vt* aflojar, soltar, (*clothing*) desabrochar(se); **Loosen your pants..**Desabroche su pantalón.
loperamide *n* loperamida
lorazepam *n* loracepam *m*
lordosis *n* lordosis *f*
lordotic *adj* lordótico
lose *vt* (*pret & pp* lost) perder; **to** —— **consciousness** perder el conocimiento *or* la conciencia; **to** —— **weight** perder peso, bajar de peso
loss *n* pérdida; **hair** —— caída del pelo; **hearing** —— pérdida de la audición
lot *n* (*pharm*) lote *m*; **a** —— mucho; **Do you sleep a lot?..**¿Duerme mucho? **a** —— **of** (*fam*) mucho(s); **a lot of milk..**mucha leche...**a lot of pimples..**muchos granos

lotion *n* loción *f*, crema; **hand** —— crema para las manos; **suntan** —— loción bronceadora, crema para el sol
louse *n* (*pl* **lice**) piojo
lovastatin *n* lovastatina
love *n* amor *m*; *vt, vi* amar, querer
loved one *n* ser amado
loving *adj* cariñoso, afectuoso
low *adj* bajo; **Your potassium is low..**Su potasio está bajo; **to be** —— **on** faltarle (*a uno*); **You are low on iron..**Le falta hierro.
lower *adj* (*anat*) inferior (*form*), bajo, de abajo; —— **back** parte baja de la espalda; *vt* (*one's blood sugar, one's arm*) bajar
low-pitched *adj* grave
lozenge *n* trocisco, pastilla para chupar
LSD *V.* **lysergic acid diethylamide.**
lubricant *adj & n* lubricante *m*
lubricate *vt* lubricar
lukewarm *adj* tibio
lumbar *adj* lumbar
lump *n* bola, bolita, pelota, (*due to trauma, esp. about the head*) chichón *m*
lumpectomy *n* lumpectomía (*Ang*)
lumpy *adj* (*comp* -**ier**; *super* -**iest**) que tiene bolitas
lunch *n* comida al mediodía, almuerzo, comida (*Mex*); **to have** —— comer al mediodía, almorzar, comer (*Mex*)
lung *n* pulmón *m*
lupus *n* lupus *m*; **systemic** —— **erythematosus (SLE)** lupus eritematoso generalizado *or* sistémico
luteal *adj* luteínico
lye *n* lejía
lying *ger de* **lie**
lymph *n* linfa; —— **node** ganglio linfático
lymphadenitis *n* linfadenitis *f*
lymphangitis *n* linfangitis *f*
lymphatic *adj* linfático
lymphocyte *n* linfocito; **B** —— linfocito B; **helper T** —— linfocito T ayudante; **suppressor T** —— linfocito T supresor
lymphogranuloma venereum (LGV) *n* linfogranuloma venéreo *or* inguinal
lymphoid *adj* linfoide
lymphoma *n* linfoma *m*; **non-Hodgkin's** —— linfoma no Hodgkin
lyophilized *adj* liofilizado
lysergic acid diethylamide (LSD) *n* dietilamida del ácido lisérgico (LSD)
lysine *n* lisina

M

macrobiotic *adj* macrobiótico
mad *adj (comp* **madder;** *super* **maddest)**
enojado; *(crazy)* loco; **to get** ——
enojarse
maggot *n* cresa, gusano
magnesium *n* magnesio; —— **sulfate**
sulfato de magnesio
magnetic resonance imaging (MRI) *n*
imágenes *fpl* por resonancia magnética,
resonancia magnética nuclear
magnifying glass *n* lupa
maintain *vt* mantener
maintenance *n* mantenimiento
major *adj* mayor
make-up *n (cosmetics)* maquillaje *m*
malabsorption *n* malabsorción *f*
malady *n (pl* **-dies)** enfermedad *f*, mal *m*
malaise *n* malestar *m*
malaria *n* paludismo, malaria
malathion *n* malatión *m*
mal del pinto *n* mal *m* del pinto, pinta
male *adj* masculino; *n* varón *m*
malformation *n* malformación *f*
malignancy *n* malignidad *f*
malignant *adj* maligno
malinger *vi* fingirse enfermo
malnourished *adj* desnutrido
malnutrition *n* desnutrición *f*
malpractice *n* negligencia médica
mammary *adj* mamario
mammogram *n* mamografía, mamograma *m*
mammography *n* mamografía
man *n (pl* **men)** hombre
manage *vt* manejar
management *n* manejo
mandible *n* mandíbula
maneuver *n* maniobra; *vt, vi* maniobrar
mania *n* manía
manic-depressive *adj* maniacodepresivo
manicure *n* manicura
manifestation *n* manifestación *f*
manipulate *vt* manipular
manometry *n* manometría
manual *adj* manual; *n (booklet)* manual *m*
many *adj* muchos; **many times..**muchas
veces
margarine *n* margarina
margin *n* margen *m*
marijuana *n* marihuana *or* marijuana
mark *n* marca
marrow *n* médula; **bone** —— médula ósea
masculine *adj* masculino
mash *n (crushing injury)* machucón *m*,
machucadura; *vt* machucar

mask *n* máscara, *(surg)* cubre-boca *m*; *(of*
pregnancy) paño; *vt (symptoms)*
enmascarar
masochism *n* masoquismo
masochist *n* masoquista *mf*
mass *n* masa
massage *n* masaje *m*; *vt* masajear, dar
masaje, sobar *(fam)*
MAST *V.* **military anti-shock trousers.**
mastectomy *n (pl* **-mies)** mastectomía
mastitis *n* mastitis *f*
mastoid *adj* mastoideo; —— **process**
apófisis *f* mastoides
masturbate *vi* masturbarse
match *vt (blood, tissue)* ser compatible con
(sangre, tejido); **We need to find out if**
your sister's tissue type matches your
own.. Tenemos que averiguar si el tejido
de su hermana es compatible con el suyo.
material *n* material *m*
maternal *adj* materno; *(motherly)* maternal
maternity *n* maternidad *f*
matter *n* **gray** —— substancia gris; **white**
—— substancia blanca
mattress *n* colchón *m*
mature *adj* maduro; *vi* madurar
maturity *n* madurez *f*
maxilla *n (pl* **-lae)** maxilar *m* (superior)
maxillary *adj* maxilar
maxillofacial *adj* maxilofacial
maximum *adj* & *n (pl* **-ma** *o* **-mums)**
máximo
mayonnaise *n* mayonesa
M.D. *V.* **Doctor of Medicine.**
meal *n* comida; **balanced** —— comida
balanceada
measles *n* sarampión *m;* **German** —— *o*
three-day —— sarampión alemán,
rubeola *or* rubéola *(form)*
measure *n* medida; *vt* medir
measurement *n* medida
measuring tape *n* cinta métrica
meat *n* carne *f;* **organ meats** vísceras; **red**
—— carne roja
meatus *n (pl* **meatus)** meato
mebendazole *n* mebendazol *m*
mechanism *n* mecanismo; **defense** ——
mecanismo de defensa
meconium *n* meconio
medial *adj (anat)* interno
median *adj (anat)* mediano
mediastinum *n* mediastino
medical *adj* médico
medicate *vt* medicar

medication *n* medicamento
medicinal *adj* medicinal
medicine *n* medicina, medicamento; —— **chest** *o* **cabinet** botiquín *m*; —— **dropper** gotero, cuentagotas *m*; **family** —— medicina familiar; **folk** —— curanderismo; **internal** —— medicina interna; **nuclear** —— medicina nuclear; **occupational** —— medicina ocupacional; **preventive** —— medicina preventiva; **socialized** —— medicina socializada; **sports** —— medicina deportiva; **veterinary** —— medicina veterinaria
medicolegal *adj* medicolegal
meditate *vi* meditar
medium *adj* mediano; *n* medio; **contrast** —— medio de contraste
medroxyprogesterone *n* medroxiprogesterona
medulla *n* (*pl* **-lae**) bulbo raquídeo; (*of the adrenal gland*) médula
megacolon *n* megacolon *m*
megadose *n* megadosis *f*
melancholy *adj* melancólico; *n* melancolía
melanin *n* melanina
melanoma *n* melanoma *m*
member *n* miembro
membrane *n* membrana; **mucous** —— membrana mucosa; **tympanic** —— membrana timpánica
memory *n* memoria; **long-term** —— memoria remota; **short-term** —— memoria reciente
men *pl de* **man**
meninges *pl de* **meninx**
meningioma *n* meningioma *m*
meningitis *n* meningitis *f*
meningocele *n* meningocele *m*
meningococcus *n* (*pl* **-ci**) meningococo
meninx *n* (*pl* **meninges**) meninge *f*; (*en inglés se emplea casi siempre la forma plural:* **meninges**)
menopause *n* menopausia, cambio de vida
men's room *n* baño para hombres
menstruate *vi* menstruar, reglar
menstruation *n* menstruación *f*
mental *adj* mental
menthol *n* mentol *m*
meperedine *n* meperedina
mercury *n* mercurio
mercy killing *n* eutanasia, muerte piadosa
mescaline *n* mescalina
mesenteric *adj* mesentérico
mesentery *n* mesenterio
mesh *n* malla
mesothelioma *n* mesotelioma *m*
metabolic *adj* metabólico
metabolism *n* metabolismo
metacarpal *adj* & *n* metacarpiano
metal *n* metal *m*; **heavy** —— metal pesado
metallic *adj* metálico
metaproterenol *n* metaproterenol *m*,

orciprenalina
metastasis *n* (*pl* **-ses**) metástasis *f*
metastasize *vi* dar metástasis
metastatic *adj* metastásico
metatarsal *adj* & *n* metatarsiano
meter *n* metro; (*measuring device*) medidor *m*; —— **squared** *o* **square** —— metro cuadrado
methadone *n* metadona
methane *n* metano
methanol *n* metanol *m*
methaqualone *n* metaqualona
methicillin *n* meticilina
methionine *n* metionina
method *n* método
methotrexate *n* metotrexato
methyl alcohol *n* alcohol metílico
methylcellulose *n* metilcelulosa
methyldopa *n* metildopa
methylphenidate *n* metilfenidato
metoclopramide *n* metoclopramida
metoprolol *n* metoprolol *m*
metric system *n* sistema métrico
metronidazole *n* metronidazol *m*
Mexican *adj* & *n* mexicano -na *mf*
mice *pl de* **mouse**
miconazole *n* miconazol *m*
microbe *n* microbio
microbial *adj* microbiano
microbiology *n* microbiología
microgram *n* microgramo
microorganism *n* microorganismo
microscope *n* microscopio; **electron** —— microscopio electrónico
microscopic *adj* microscópico
microsurgery *n* microcirugía
microwave *n* microonda
midbrain *n* mesencéfalo, cerebro medio
middle *adj* medio; *n* mitad *f*, medio
midget *n* enano -na *mf*
midwife *n* (*pl* **-wives**) partera, (*esp. untrained*) comadrona
migraine *n* migraña, jaqueca
mild *adj* (*soap, etc.*) suave; (*illness, injury*) leve
mildew *n* moho
miliary *adj* miliar
military antishock trousers (MAST) *n* pantalones *mpl* antichoque
milk *n* leche *f*; **breast** —— leche materna; **condensed** —— leche condensada; **cow's** —— leche de vaca; **evaporated** —— leche evaporizada; **goat's** —— leche de cabra; **low fat** —— leche baja en grasa; **pasteurized** —— leche pasteurizada; **powdered** —— leche en polvo; **raw** —— leche sin procesar, leche bronca (*Mex*); **skim** —— leche descremada *or* desnatada; **whole** —— leche entera
milk of magnesia *n* leche *f* de magnesia
milligram *n* miligramo
milliliter *n* mililitro

millimeter *n* milímetro
mind *n* mente *f*; **to lose one's** —— perder la razón, volverse loco
miner *n* minero
mineral *adj* & *n* mineral *m*; —— **oil** aceite *m* mineral; —— **water** agua mineral
minimum *adj* & *n* (*pl* -ma *o* -mums) mínimo
minor *adj* menor; *n* menor *m* (de edad)
minoxidil *n* minoxidil *m*
minute *n* minuto
miracle *n* milagro
mirror *n* espejo
miscarriage *n* aborto (espontáneo *or* natural)
miscarry *vi* abortar (*sin intención*)
mischievous *adj* travieso
miss *vt* (*an appointment*) faltar a, perder; (*dose of medication*) dejar de tomar; (*a loved one, etc.*) extrañar, echar de menos; **Be sure not to miss this appointment, señora**..Esté segura de no faltar a esta cita, señora...**How many doses did you miss?**..¿Cuántas dosis dejó de tomar?...**Do you miss your husband?**..¿Extraña a su esposo?
missing *adj* ausente; **She is missing two fingers**..Le faltan dos dedos.
mite *n* ácaro
mitral *adj* mitral
mix *vt* mezclar
mixture *n* mezcla
moan *n* gemido; *vi* gemir
mobile *adj* móvil
mobilize *vt* movilizar
mobility *n* movilidad *f*
moderate *adj* moderado
moderation *n* moderación *f*
modification *n* modificación *f*
modify *vt* (*pret* & *pp* -fied) modificar
moist *adj* húmedo
moisten *vt* humedecer, mojar un poco
moisture *n* humedad *f*
moisturize *vt* humedecer
moisturizing *adj* hidratante
molar *adj* molar; *n* muela, molar *m* (*form*)
mold *n* (*dent*) molde *m*; (*fungus*) moho
mole *n* lunar *m*; (*obst*) mola; **hidatidiform** —— **mola** hidatidiforme *or* hidatídica
molecule *n* molécula
molluscum contagiosum *n* molusco contagioso
mom *n* mamá
momentary *adj* momentáneo
monitor *n* monitor *m*; **cardiac** —— monitor cardiaco; **fetal heart** —— monitor cardiaco fetal, monitor cardiotocográfico; **Holter** —— monitor Holter, monitor cardiaco portátil; *vt* monitorizar
monitoring *n* monitoreo, monitorización *f*, vigilancia
monoclonal *adj* monoclonal
monogamous *adj* monógamo

mononucleosis *n* mononucleosis *f*
monosodium glutamate (MSG) *n* glutamato monosódico
monster *n* monstruo
month *n* mes *m*
mood *n* estado de ánimo; —— **swing** cambio repentino del estado de ánimo
morbid *adj* (*path*) morboso
morbidity *n* morbilidad *f*
morgue *n* morgue *f*
morning *adj* matutino (*form*), de la mañana; —— **sickness** náuseas *or* vómitos del embarazo; *n* mañana
morphine *n* morfina
morphology *n* morfología
mortal *adj* mortal, fatal
mortality *n* mortalidad *f*
mortuary n funeraria
mosquito *n* (*pl* -toes *o* -tos) mosquito
mother *n* madre *f*
mother-in-law *n* (*pl* mothers-in-law) suegra
motion sickness *n* mareo producido por el movimiento
motivation *n* motivación *f*
motor *adj* motor
motorcycle *n* motocicleta, moto *f* (*fam*)
mountain sickness *n* mal *m* de montaña, soroche *m* (*SA*)
mourn *vt*, *vi* lamentar(se)
mouse *n* (*pl* mice) ratón *m*
moustache *n* bigote *m*
mouth *n* boca; **by** —— por vía bucal, por la boca; **roof of the** —— paladar *m*
mouthful *n* (*pl* -fuls) bocado
mouthpiece *n* boquilla
mouthwash *n* enjuage *m* bucal
move *vt* mover, (*a patient*) trasladar, cambiar; **We have to move you to another room**..Tenemos que trasladarlo a otro cuarto; *vi* moverse; **Don't move**..No se mueva.
movement *n* movimiento; **bowel** —— **(BM)** defecación *f* (*form*), evacuación *f*, deposición *f* (*SA*); **rapid eye movements (REM)** movimientos oculares rápidos (MOR), movimientos rápidos de los ojos
MRI *V.* magnetic resonance imaging.
MSG *V.* monosodium glutamate.
much *adj* & *adv* mucho
mucinous *adj* mucinoso
mucolytic *adj* & *n* mucolítico
mucous *adj* mucoso; —— **membrane** membrana mucosa
mucus *n* mucosidad *f*, moco
multiple *adj* múltiple; —— **myeloma** mieloma *m* múltiple; —— **sclerosis** esclerosis *f* múltiple
multiply *vi* (*pret* & *pp* -plied) multiplicarse
multivitamin *adj* multivitamínico; *n* multivitamina
mumps *n* paperas
murmur *n* (*card*) soplo

muscle *n* músculo; —— **pull** estiramiento (*form*), desgarro leve (muscular)
muscular *adj* muscular; (*person*) musculoso; —— **dystrophe** distrofia muscular progresiva
mushroom *n* hongo
musician *n* músico -ca *mf*
mutation *n* mutación *f*
mute *adj* & *n* mudo -da *mf*
mutism *n* mudez *f*, (*esp. elective*) mutismo
myalgia *n* mialgia
myasthenia gravis *n* miastenia grave *or* gravis
Mycoplasma Mycoplasma

myelin *n* mielina
myelomeningocele *n* mielomeningocele *m*
myocardial *adj* miocárdico
myocarditis *n* miocarditis *f*
myocardium *n* miocardio
myoglobin *n* mioglobina
myoma *n* mioma *m*
myopathy *n* miopatía
myopia *n* miopía
myopic *adj* miope
myositis *n* miositis *f*
myxedema *n* mixedema *m*
myxoma *n* mixoma *m*

N

nail *n* (*anat*) uña; (*carpentry*) clavo; —— **file** lima para las uñas; —— **polish** esmalte *m* para las uñas; **ingrown** —— uña enterrada *or* encarnada, uñero
naked *adj* desnudo
nalidixic acid *n* ácido nalidíxico
naloxone *n* naloxona
nap *n* siesta; **to take a** —— tomar una siesta
napalm *n* napalm *m*
naproxen *n* naproxén *m*
narcissism *n* narcisismo
narcissistic *adj* narcisista
narcolepsy *n* narcolepsia
narcotic *adj* & *n* narcótico
narrow *adj* estrecho
narrowing *n* estrechez *f*
nasal *adj* nasal; (*sound of voice*) gangoso; —— **passage** conducto nasal
nasogastric *adj* nasogástrico
nasopharynx *n* nasofaringe *f*
natural *adj* natural
nature *n* (la) naturaleza
nausea *n* náusea (*often pl*)
nauseated *adj* **to be** —— tener náusea(s); **to make** —— dar náusea(s)
navel *n* ombligo
nearsighted *adj* miope, que tiene dificultad para ver los objetos lejanos
nebulizer *n* nebulizador *m*
neck *n* cuello; **back of the** —— nuca
necrosis *n* necrosis *f*
necrotic *adj* necrótico

needle *n* aguja; **hypodermic** —— aguja hipodérmica
negative *adj* negativo
negativism *n* negativismo
neglect *n* negligencia, descuido; *vt* descuidar, desatender
negligent *adj* negligente, descuidado
neighbor *n* vecino -na *mf*
neighborhood *n* vecindad *f*, barrio
Neisseria Neisseria
neomycin *n* neomicina
neonatology *n* neonatología
neoplasm *n* neoplasia
neoplastic *adj* neoplásico
neostigmine *n* neostigmina
nephew *n* sobrino
nephritis *n* nefritis *f*
nephrologist *n* nefrólogo -ga *mf*
nephrology *n* nefrología
nephrosis *n* nefrosis *f*
nephrotic *adj* nefrótico
nerve *n* nervio; —— **block** bloqueo nervioso; —— **root** raíz nerviosa; **acoustic** —— nervio auditivo *or* acústico; **cranial** —— nervio craneal; **entrapped** —— nervio comprimido *or* atrapado; **facial** —— nervio facial; **femoral** —— nervio femoral; **median** —— nervio mediano; **motor** —— nervio motor; **optic** —— nervio óptico; **parasympathetic** —— nervio parasimpático; **peroneal** —— nervio peroneo *or* peroneal; **phrenic** —— nervio frénico; **pinched** —— nervio

atrapado; **pudendal** —— nervio pudendo; **radial** —— nervio radial; **recurrent laryngeal** —— nervio laríngeo recurrente; **sciatic** —— nervio ciático; **sensory** —— nervio sensorial *or* sensitivo; **spinal** —— nervio raquídeo *or* espinal; **sympathetic** —— nervio simpático; **trigeminal** —— nervio trigémino; **ulnar** —— nervio cubital; **vagus** —— nervio vago

nerves *n* (*anxiety*) nervios

nervous *adj* nervioso; —— **breakdown** choque *or* colapso nervioso, crisis nerviosa

nervousness *n* nerviosismo

nettle *n* ortiga

network *n* red *f*, retículo

neural *adj* neural

neuralgia *n* neuralgia

neurinoma *n* neurinoma *m*

neuritis *n* neuritis *f*

neuroblastoma *n* neuroblastoma *m*

neurofibroma *n* neurofibroma *m*

neurofibromatosis *n* neurofibromatosis *f*

neurogenic *adj* neurogénico *or* neurógeno

neuroleptic *adj* & *n* neuroléptico

neurological, neurologic *adj* neurológico

neurologist *n* neurólogo -ga *mf*

neurology *n* neurología

neuroma *n* neuroma *m*; **acoustic** —— neuroma del acústico

neuromuscular *adj* neuromuscular

neuropathy *n* neuropatía *f*

neurosis *n* (*pl* -ses) neurosis *f*

neurosurgeon *n* neurocirujano -na *mf*

neurosurgery *n* (*pl* -ries) neurocirugía

neurosyphillis *n* neurosífilis *f*

neurotic *adj* & *n* neurótico -ca *mf*

neutral *adj* neutral

neutrophil *n* neutrófilo

nevus *n* (*pl* nevi) nevo

newborn *n* recién nacido -da *mf*, **premature** —— prematuro -ra *mf*

next *adj* próximo, siguiente

niacin *n* niacina

Nicaraguan *adj* & *n* nicaragüense *mf*

nick *n* cortada pequeña, herida pequeña

nickel *n* níquel *m*

niclosamide *n* niclosamida

nicotine *n* nicotina

nicotinic acid *n* ácido nicotínico

niece *n* sobrina

nifedipine *n* nifedipina

night *n* noche *f*; **last** —— anoche

nightmare *n* pesadilla

night-terrors *npl* terrores nocturnos

nipple *n* (*female*) pezón *m*; (*male*) tetilla; (*of a nursing bottle*) mamila, tetera, mamadera; —— **shield** pezonera

nit *n* liendre *f*

nitrate *n* nitrato

nitrite *n* nitrito

nitrofurantoin *n* nitrofurantoína

nitrogen *n* nitrógeno

nitroglycerin *n* nitroglicerina

nitrous oxide *n* óxido nitroso

nocardiosis *n* nocardiosis *f*

nocturnal *adj* nocturno; —— **emission** eyaculación nocturna

node *n* (*card*) nodo; (*lymph*) ganglio; **atrioventricular** —— nodo auriculoventricular; **lymph** —— ganglio linfático; **sinoatrial** —— nodo sinoauricular

nodule *n* nódulo

noise *n* ruido

nonabsorbable *adj* no absorbible

nonflammable *adj* no inflamable, que no se quema

noninvasive *adj* no invasor

nonketotic *adj* no cetónico

nonspecific *adj* inespecífico

nonsteroidal antiinflammatory drug (**NSAID**) *n* antiinflamatorio no esteroide

noon *n* mediodía *m*

norepinephrine *n* norepinefrina

norfloxacin *n* norfloxacina

norm *n* norma

normal *adj* normal

North American *adj* norteamericano -na *mf*

nortriptyline *n* nortriptilina

nose *n* nariz *f*; **to blow one's** —— sonarse la nariz, soplarse la nariz (*Carib*); **to hold one's** —— taparse la nariz; **to pick one's** —— limpiarse la nariz con el dedo, sacarse los mocos con el dedo

nosebleed *n* hemorragia nasal (*form*), sangrado por la nariz; **Have you had any nosebleeds?**..¿Ha sangrado por la nariz?

no-see-um *n* jején *m*

nostril *n* fosa nasal, hoyo de la nariz (*fam*)

notice *vt* notar, fijarse (en); **When did you first notice blood in your stool?**..¿Cuándo fue la primera vez que notó que había sangre en el excremento?

nourishing *adj* nutritivo

nourishment *n* nutrición *f*, alimentación *f*

novacaine *n* novacaína

NSAID *V.* **nonsteroidal antiinflammatory drug.**

nuclear war *n* guerra nuclear

numb *adj* dormido, adormecido; **to become** —— dormirse, adormecerse; *vt* (*también* **to** —— **up**) anestesiar, dormir; **I'm going to numb up your finger**..Le voy a anestesiar el dedo.

number one *n* (*fam, urination*) número uno (*fam*), (el) orinar

number two *n* (*fam, defecation*) número dos (*fam*), (el) defecar

numbness *n* adormecimiento, falta de sensación

nurse *n* enfermera (enfermero *if male*); **charge** —— jefa de turno (jefe *if male*); **head** —— jefa de enfermeras; **home** —— enfermera domiciliaria; **visiting** —— enfermera que visita pacientes a domicilio, enfermera visitadora; *vt* (*to breastfeed*) amamantar (*form*), dar pecho, dar de mamar; (*to care for patients*) cuidar; *vi* (*to suckle*) mamar

nurse-practitioner *n* (*US*) enfermero -ra *mf* que tiene entrenamiento adicional para diagnosticar y tratar padecimientos sencillos

nursery *n* (*pl* -ries) guardería infantil; **newborn** —— sala de cuneros

nursing *n* enfermería; —— **home** asilo de ancianos

nut *n* nuez *f*

nutrition *n* nutrición *f*; **total parenteral** —— **(TPN)** nutrición parenteral total

nutritional *adj* nutricional, alimenticio

nutritious *adj* nutritivo

nylon *n* nilón *m*

nystagmus *n* nistagmo

nystatin *n* nistatina

O

oatmeal *n* avena
obese *adj* obeso
obesity *n* obesidad *f*
obsession *n* obsesión *f*
obsessive-compulsive *adj* obsesivo-compulsivo
obstetrical, obstetric *adj* obstétrico
obstetrician *n* obstetra *mf*
obstetrics *n* obstetricia
obstruct *vt* obstruir, tapar (*fam*)
obstruction *n* obstrucción *f*
obstructive *adj* obstructivo
occipital *adj* occipital
occlusion *n* oclusión *f*
occlusive *adj* oclusivo
occupation *n* ocupación *f*, trabajo
ocular *adj* ocular
oculist *n* (*ant*) oculista *mf*
odor *n* olor *m*
off *prep* (*drugs, a medication, etc.*) ya no usando, ya no tomando (*drogas, un medicamento, etc.*); **How long have you been off heroin?**..¿Desde cuándo no usa heroína?...**Are you off prednisone?**..¿Ya no toma prednisona?
office *n* oficina, (*of a doctor*) consultorio; —— **hours** horas de consulta
often *adv* seguido, muchas veces; **How often do you have chest pain?**..¿Qué tan seguido tiene dolor de pecho?
oil *n* aceite *m*
ointment *n* ungüento, pomada
old *adj* viejo; **How old are you?**..¿Cuántos años tiene? —— **man** viejo, anciano; —— **woman** vieja, anciana; **to grow** —— envejecer(se)
old wives' tale *n* creencia sin base médica
olfactory *adj* olfatorio

olive oil *n* aceite *m* de oliva
olive-skinned *adj* trigueño
on *prep* (*drugs, a medication, etc.*) usando, tomando, bajo el efecto de (*drogas, un medicamento, etc.*); **Are you on lithium?**..¿Está tomando litio?...**Were you on PCP when you kicked the policeman?**..¿Estaba bajo el efecto de la fenciclidina cuando le dio una patada al policía?
onchocerciasis *n* oncocercosis *f*
oncologist *n* oncólogo -ga *mf*
oncology *n* oncología
one-armed *adj* manco
one-eyed *adj* tuerto
one-handed *adj* manco
onset *n* comienzo, principio
opacity *n* opacidad *f*, (*of the eye*) nube *f*
opaque *adj* opaco
open *vt, vi* abrir(se); **Open your mouth, please**..Abra la boca, por favor.
opening *n* abertura
operable *adj* operable
operate *vi* operar; **We need to operate on your leg**..Tenemos que operarle la pierna.
operating room (OR) *n* quirófano, sala de operaciones
operating table *n* mesa de operaciones
operation *n* operación *f*; **to have an** —— operarse; **You need to have an operation**..Tiene que operarse.
ophthalmic *adj* oftálmico
ophthalmologist *n* oftalmólogo -ga *mf*
ophthalmology *n* oftalmología
ophthalmoscope *n* oftalmoscopio
opiate *adj & n* opiáceo
opinion *n* opinión *f*; **second** —— segunda opinión

opium *n* opio
opportunistic *adj* oportunista
optical, optic *adj* óptico
optician *n* óptico
optics *n* óptica
optometrist *n* optometrista *mf*
OR *V.* operating room.
oral *adj* oral, bucal
orange *adj* naranja, de color naranja; *n* (*fruit*) naranja
orbit *n* (*anat*) órbita
orchidectomy *var de* orchiectomy
orchiectomy *n* (*pl* -mies) orquiectomía, orquidectomía
orchitis *n* orquitis *f*
order *n* (*for patient in a hospital*) indicación *f*; *vt* indicar (*form*), recetar, ordenar
orderly *n* (*pl* -lies) asistente *m* de enfermera
organ *n* órgano
organic *adj* orgánico; sembrado sin uso de substancias químicas
organism *n* organismo
organophosphate *n* organofosforado
orgasm *n* orgasmo
orifice *n* orificio
oropharynx *n* orofaringe *f*
orphan *n* huérfano -na *mf*
orphanage *n* orfanatorio, orfelinato
orthodontia, orthodontics *n* ortodoncia
orthodontist *n* ortodoncista *mf*
orthopedic *adj* ortopédico
orthopedics *n* ortopedia
orthopedist *n* ortopedista *mf*
osseous *adj* óseo
ossicle *n* huesecillo, huesillo
osteitis *n* osteítis *f*; —— fibrosa cystica osteítis fibroquística
osteoarthritis *n* osteoartritis *f*
osteogenesis imperfecta *n* osteogénesis *or* osteogenia imperfecta
osteoma *n* osteoma *m*
osteomalacia *n* osteomalacia
osteomyelitis *n* osteomielitis *f*
osteopathy *n* osteopatía
osteophyte *n* osteofito
osteoporosis *n* osteoporosis *f*
osteosarcoma *n* osteosarcoma *m*
otic *adj* ótico
otitis *n* otitis *f*; —— externa otitis externa; —— interna otitis interna; —— media otitis media

otolaryngologist *n* otorrinolaringólogo -ga *mf*
otolaryngology *n* otorrinolaringología
otosclerosis *n* otosclerosis *f*
otoscope *n* otoscopio
ouch *interj* ¡Ay! *or* ¡Ai!
ounce (oz.) *n* onza (onz.)
outbreak *n* brote *m*
outcome *n* resultado
outdated, out of date *adj* (*medication, etc.*) vencido, caducado
outdoors *adv* al aire libre
outer *adj* externo, exterior
outgrow *vt* (*pret* -grew; *pp* -grown) (*a habit*) quitarse, perder; She will outgrow it..Se le quitará.
outlet *n* (*psych*) desahogo, escape *m*; (*electrical*) tomacorriente *f*, enchufe *m*
outlook *n* perspectiva
outpatient *n* paciente *mf* externo -na *or* ambulatorio -ria
outside *adj* exterior, externo; *n* exterior *m*; *prep* fuera de
ova *pl de* ovum
ovarian *adj* ovárico
ovary *n* (*pl* -ries) ovario; polycystic —— ovario poliquístico
overcoat *n* abrigo
overcome *vt* superar
overdo *vt* (*pret* -did; *pp* -done) to —— it esforzarse demasiado, excederse; Don't overdo it..No se esfuerce demasiado..No se exceda.
overdose *n* sobredosis *f*, dosis excesiva
overload *vt* sobrecargar
over-the-counter *adj* que no requiere receta médica
overweight *adj* pasado de peso, que tiene peso excesivo, que tiene sobrepeso
ovulate *vi* ovular
ovulation *n* ovulación *f*
ovum *n* (*pl* ova) óvulo, huevo (*fam*)
oxacillin *n* oxacilina
oxazepam *n* oxacepam *m*
oxide *n* óxido
oxycodone *n* oxicodona
oxygen *n* oxígeno; —— tank tanque *m* de oxígeno
oxytocin *n* oxitocina
oz. *V.* ounce.
ozone *n* ozono

P

PAC *abbr* premature atrial contraction. *V.* contraction.

pace *n* paso; *vi* to —— oneself no excederse

pacemaker *n* marcapaso *m*

pacifier *n* chupón *m*, chupete *m*, entretenedor *m*

pacing *n* (*card*) uso de marcapaso

pack *n* compresa; **ice** —— compresa *or* bolsa de hielo

package insert *n* instructivo

packing *n* material como gasa usado para llenar una cavidad

pad *n* cojín *m*, almohadilla; **alcohol** —— gasita con alcohol; **heating** —— cojín eléctrico

padding *n* (*ortho, surg*) huata

page *n* (*overhead*) llamada por vocina; (*by beeper*) llamada por el bíper; *vt* vocear, llamar por vocina; llamar por el bíper

pager *n* bíper *m* (*Ang*)

pain *n* dolor *m*

painful *adj* doloroso; (*sore*) adolorido *or* dolorido

painkiller *n* (*fam*) medicamento para quitar el dolor

painless *adj* sin dolor, indoloro

palate *n* paladar *m*; **cleft** —— paladar hendido; **hard** —— paladar duro; **soft** —— paladar blando

pale *adj* pálido

paleness, pallor *n* palidez *f*

palliative *adj & n* paliativo

palm *n* (*anat, bot*) palma; —— oil aceite *m* de palma

palmar *adj* palmar

palpate *vt* palpar

palpitate *vi* palpitar

palpitation *n* palpitación *f*, latido rápido o fuerte del corazón

pamphlet *n* folleto

Panamanian *adj & n* panameño -ña *mf*

pancreas *n* (*pl* -creases *o* -creata) páncreas *m*

pancreatic *adj* pancreático

pancreatitis *n* pancreatitis *f*

pang *n* punzada, dolor breve y agudo; **hunger** —— dolor de hambre

panic attack *n* ataque *m* de pánico

pant *vi* jadear

panties *npl* calzón *m* (*often pl*), pantaletas (*Mex*), bloomer *m* (*esp. CA*), panties *mpl* (*Carib*)

pantothenic acid *n* ácido pantoténico

pants *npl* pantalones *mpl*

pantyhose *n* (*pl* -hose) pantimedias

Papanicolaou smear *n* examen *m* de Papanicolaou, examen del cáncer (*fam*)

paper *n* papel *m*

papilla *n* papila

papillary *adj* papilar

papillomavirus *n* papilomavirus *m*

Pap smear *V.* **Papanicolaou smear.**

paracoccidioidomycosis *n* paracoccidioido-micosis *f*

paradoxical *adj* paradójico

paragonimiasis *n* paragonimiasis *f*

Paraguayan *adj & n* paraguayo -ya *mf*

paralysis *n* parálisis *f*

paralyze *vt* paralizar

paramedic *adj* paramédico; *n* paramédico, persona con entrenamiento médico básico encargada de llevar heridos y enfermos al hospital

paranoia *n* paranoia

paranoid *adj* paranoide, paranoico

paraquat *n* paraquat *m*

parasite *n* parásito

parasitic *adj* parasitario

parathion *n* paratión *m*

parathyroid *adj* paratiroideo

paregoric *n* paregórico

parent *n* padre *m*, madre *f*; **parents** padres

parenteral *adj* parenteral

paresis *n* paresia

parietal *adj* parietal

parotid *adj* parotídeo; *n* parótida

parotiditis, parotitis *n* parotiditis *f*

partial *adj* parcial

particle *n* partícula

partner *n* (*marital, sexual*) pareja; (*professional*) socio -cia *mf*

pass *n* paso; *vt* (*parasites, a stone, etc.*) eliminar, expulsar, botar, arrojar (*esp. Mex*), echar; **Have you ever passed a stone?..**¿Ha eliminado alguna vez una piedra (al orinar)? **to** —— **gas** tirar gases *or* vientos, pasar gas; **Are you passing gas yet?..**¿Está tirando gases ya? *vi* **to** —— **out** desmayarse

passive *adj* pasivo

passive-aggressive *adj* pasivo-agresivo

paste *n* pasta

pastime *n* pasatiempo

pat *n* palmada, palmadita; *vt* (*pret & pp* **patted**; *ger* **patting**) dar palmadas, dar palmaditas

patch *n* parche *m*

patella *n* (*pl* -lae) patela, rótula

paternal *adj* paterno

paternity *n* paternidad *f*

pathological, pathologic *adj* patológico
pathologist *n* patólogo -ga *mf*
pathology *n* patología
patient *adj* paciente; *n* paciente *mf*, enfermo -ma *mf*
pattern *n* patrón *m*
paunch *n* panza, barriga
PCP *V.* **phencyclidine.**
PDA *abbr* **patent ductus arteriosus.** *V.* **ductus arteriosus.**
peak *n* punto máximo, pico; *vi* alcanzar el punto máximo, alcanzar el pico
pectoral *adj* pectoral
pediatric *adj* pediátrico
pediatrician *n* pediatra *or* pedíatra *mf*
pediatrics *n* pediatría
pediculosis *n* pediculosis *f*
pedicure *n* pedicure *m*
pee (*esp. ped*) *n* pipí *m*; *vi* hacer pipí
peel *vi* (*skin*) despellejarse, pelarse; **I'm peeling** *o* **My skin is peeling**..Me estoy despellejando.
pellagra *n* pelagra
pelvic *adj* pélvico; *n* (*fam*) examen ginecológico; revisión *f* de (sus) partes (*fam*)
pemphigoid *adj* & *n* penfigoide *m*
pemphigus *n* pénfigo
pending *adj* pendiente
penetrate *vt* penetrar
penetration *n* penetración *f*
penicillamine *n* penicilamina
penicillin *n* penicilina
penis *n* (*pl* **penises** *o* **penes**) pene *m*, miembro (*fam*)
pentamidine *n* pentamidina
pentazocine *n* pentazocina
pepsin *n* pepsina
peptic *adj* péptico; —— **ulcer** úlcera péptica
per *prep* por; **beats per minute**..latidos por minuto; —— **day** por día, al día
percent *n* por ciento
percentage *n* porcentaje *m*
perception *n* percepción *f*; **depth** —— visión profunda, percepción de la profundidad
percutaneous *adj* percutáneo
perforate *vt* perforar
perforation *n* perforación *f*
perform *vt* practicar; **We need to perform more tests**..Tenemos que practicarle más estudios.
performance *n* funcionamiento
perfume *n* perfume *m*
pericardial *adj* pericárdico
pericarditis *n* pericarditis *f*; **constrictive** —— pericarditis constrictiva
pericardium *n* pericardio
perineal *adj* perineal
period *n* periodo *or* período, regla; **Do you still have periods?**..¿Todavía tiene la regla?...**When was your last period?**..

¿Cuándo fue su último periodo?
incubation —— periodo de incubación
peripheral *adj* periférico
periphery *n* periferia
peristalsis *n* peristalsis *f*
peritoneal *adj* peritoneal
peritoneum *n* peritoneo
peritonitis *n* peritonitis *f*
permanent *adj* permanente
permission *n* permiso
peroxide *n* peróxido
persist *vi* persistir
person *n* persona
personal *adj* personal
personality *n* (*pl* **-ties**) personalidad *f*; —— **disorder** trastorno de personalidad; **antisocial** —— personalidad antisocial; **borderline** —— personalidad limítrofe; **cyclothymic** —— personalidad ciclotímica; **histrionic** —— personalidad histriónica; **narcissistic** —— personalidad narcisista; **obsessive-compulsive** —— personalidad obsesivo-compulsiva; **paranoid** —— personalidad paranoide; **passive-aggressive** —— personalidad pasivo-agresiva; **squizoid** —— personalidad esquizoide
perspiration *n* transpiración *f*, sudor *m*
perspire *vi* transpirar, sudar
pertussis *n* pertussis *f*, tos ferina, coqueluche *m&f*
Peruvian *adj* & *n* peruano -na *mf*
pessary *n* pesario
pessimism *n* pesimismo
pest *n* peste *f*
pesticide *n* pesticida *m*
pestilence *n* pestilencia
pet *n* mascota, animal doméstico; **Do you have pets at home?**..¿Tiene animales en la casa?
PET *abbr* **positive emission tomography.** *V.* **tomography.**
petroleum *n* petróleo; —— **distillate** destilado del petróleo; —— **jelly** vaselina
peyote *n* peyote *m*
pH *n* pH *m*
phallic *adj* fálico
phallus *n* (*pl* **-li**) falo
pharmaceutical, pharmaceutic *adj* farmacéutico
pharmacist *n* farmacéutico -ca *mf*, boticario -ria *mf*
pharmacological, pharmacologic *adj* farmacológico
pharmacologist *n* farmacólogo -ga *mf*
pharmacology *n* farmacología
pharmacy *n* (*pl* **-cies**) farmacia, botica
pharyngitis *n* faringitis *f*
pharynx *n* (*pl* **-inges**) faringe *f*
phase *n* fase *f*
phenacetin *n* fenacetina
phencyclidine (PCP) *n* fenciclidina (PCP)

phenobarbital *n* fenobarbital *m*
phenomenon *n* fenómeno; **Raynaud's** ——
  fenómeno de Raynaud
phenothiazine *n* fenotiacina
phenotype *n* fenotipo
phenylalanine *n* fenilalanina
phenylbutazone *n* fenilbutazona
phenylketonuria (PKU) *n* fenilcetonuria
phenytoin *n* fenitoína
pheochromocytoma *n* feocromocitoma *m*
phlebitis *n* flebitis *f*
phlebotomist *n* persona que extrae sangre
phlebotomy *n* extracción *f* de sangre de una
  vena, flebotomía (*Ang*); (*therapeutic*)
  flebotomía, sangría (*fam*)
phlegm *n* flema
phobia *n* fobia, temor morboso y obsesivo
phosphate *n* fosfato
phosphorus *n* fósforo
photosensitive *adj* fotosensible
phototherapy *n* fototerapia
phrenic *adj* frénico
physiatrist *n* médico especializado en
  fisioterapia
physical *adj* físico; *n* (*fam*) examen físico
physician *n* médico, doctor -ra *mf*;
  attending —— médico adscrito; **family**
  —— médico de cabecera *or* de la familia;
  private —— médico privado
physician's assistant *n* (*US*) técnico
  entrenado para asistir al médico
physiological, physiologic *adj* fisiológico
physiologist *n* fisiólogo -ga *mf*
physiology *n* fisiología
physiotherapist *n* fisioterapeuta *mf*,
  fisioterapista *mf*
physiotherapy *n* fisioterapia
physique *n* físico, complexión *f*
physostigmine *n* fisostigmina
pick *vt* (*a scab, etc.*) rascarse; **to —— one's
  nose** limpiarse la nariz con el dedo,
  sacarse los mocos con el dedo
PID *abbr* **pelvic inflammatory disease.** *V.*
  disease.
piece *n* pedacito
pierce *vt* perforar, atravesar, penetrar
piercing *adj* (*pain*) penetrante, punzante
pigeon-toed *adj* con los pies torcidos hacia
  dentro
pigment *n* pigmento
pigmentation *n* pigmentación *f*
piles *npl* (*fam*) hemorroides *fpl*, almorranas
pill *n* (*capsule*) cápsula; (*solid*) píldora,
  pastilla, tableta; **birth control** ——
  píldora anticonceptiva
pillow *n* almohada
pillowcase *n* funda de almohada
pilonidal *adj* pilonidal
pimple *n* (*any cause*) grano, (*due to acne*)
  barro, espinilla
pin *n* alfiler *m*; (*ortho*) clavo
pinch *vt, vi* (*to bind*) apretar

pindolol *n* pindolol *m*
pineal *adj* pineal
pink *adj* rosado
pinkeye *n* ojo enrojecido, ojo rojo,
  conjuntivitis *f* (*form*),
pins and needles *n* (*sensation*) hormigueo
pint *n* pinta
pinta *n* pinta, mal *m* del pinto
pinworm *n* oxiuro
pipe *n* (*for smoking*) pipa
piperacillin *n* piperacilina
pitch *n* (*sound*) tono
pitcher *n* jarra
pituitary *adj* pituitaria
pityriasis *n* pitiriasis *f*; —— **versicolor**
  pitiriasis versicolor
PKU *V.* **phenylketonuria.**
placebo *n* (*pl* **-bos** *o* **-boes**) placebo
placenta *n* (*pl* **-tae** *o* **-tas**) placenta; ——
  abruptio desprendimiento prematuro de
  placenta; —— **previa** placenta previa
plague *n* peste *f*, plaga; **bubonic** —— peste
  bubónica
planned parenthood *n* planificación *f*
  familiar
plant *n* (*bot*) planta
plantar *adj* plantar
plaque *n* (*dent*) placa (bacteriana)
plasma *n* plasma *m*
plasmapheresis *n* plasmaféresis *f*
plaster *n* (*for a cast*) yeso; (*medicinal*)
  cataplasma, emplasto
plastic *adj* & *n* plástico
plate *n* (*dent, surg*) placa
platelet *n* plaqueta
platinum *n* platino
pleasure *n* placer *m*
plethysmography *n* pletismografía
pleura *n* (*pl* **-rae**) pleura
pleural *adj* pleural
pleurisy *n* pleuresía
pleuritic *adj* pleurítico
pleuritis *n* pleuritis *f*
plexus *n* (*pl* **-xuses**) plexo
plunger *n* (*of a syringe*) émbolo
pneumococcus *n* (*pl* **-ci**) neumococo
pneumoconiosis *n* (*pl* **-ses**) neumoconiosis *f*
Pneumocystis carinii Pneumocystis carinii
pneumonia *n* pulmonía, neumonía;
  aspiration —— pulmonía *or* neumonía
  por aspiración
pneumothorax *n* neumotórax *m*
pockmark *n* cicatriz producida por la
  viruela; **to have pockmarks** estar
  cacarizo; **She has pockmarks.**.Está
  cacariza.
podiatrist *n* podíatra *or* podiatra *mf*
podiatry *n* podiatría
podophyllin *n* podofilina
point *n* (*anat*) punto
poison *n* veneno; —— **ivy** hiedra venenosa;
  —— **oak** zumaque venenoso; **ant** ——,

rat ——, etc. veneno para hormiga, veneno para rata *or* raticida *m*, etc.; *vt* envenenar

poisoning *n* envenenamiento, intoxicación *f*

polio *n* polio *f*

poliomyelitis *n* poliomielitis *f*

pollen *n* polen *m*

pollution *n* contaminación *f*, polución *f*; **air** —— contaminación atmosférica *or* del aire

polyarteritis nodosa *n* poliarteritis nudosa

polycystic *adj* poliquístico

polycythemia vera *n* policitemia vera

polymyalgia rheumatica *n* polimialgia reumática

polymyositis *n* polimiositis *f*

polymyxin *n* polimixina

polyp *n* pólipo; **adenomatous** —— pólipo adenomatoso; **juvenile polyps** pólipos juveniles; **nasal** —— pólipo nasal

polyunsaturated *adj* poliinsaturado

pons *n* puente *m*

pool *vi* (*blood*) estancarse (*la sangre*)

poopoo *n* (*ped*) popó *or* pupú *m*, caca (*esp. Carib*)

poorly *adv* mal

popliteal *adj* poplíteo

porcelain *n* porcelana

porcine *adj* porcino

pore *n* poro

pork *n* (carne *f* de) cerdo *or* puerco

porphyria *n* porfiria

portable *adj* portátil

portion *n* porción *f*

port-wine stain *n* mancha de vino oporto

position *n* posición *f*; *vt* poner en posición

positive *adj* positivo

posterior *adj* posterior

postmortem *adj* & *adv* post mortem

postnasal drip *n* secreción *f or* descarga nasal posterior

postnatal *adj* postnatal

postoperative *adj* postoperatorio

postpartum *adj* postparto (*invariant with respect to gender*); **the second week postpartum**..la segunda semana postparto

postpone *vt* aplazar, posponer

postural *adj* postural

posture *n* postura

pot *n* (*fam*) marihuana *or* marijuana

potable *adj* potable

potassium *n* potasio

potbelly *n* panza, barriga

potency *n* (*pl* -cies) potencia

potent *adj* potente

potential *adj* & *n* potencial *m*; **evoked** —— potencial evocado

potion *n* poción *f*, pócima

pouch *n* bolsa

poultry *n* aves *fpl* de corral

pound (lb.) *n* libra (lb.)

powder *n* polvo

powdered *adj* en polvo

powerful *adj* (*medication, etc.*) potente, fuerte

power of attorney *n* (*pl* **powers of attorney**) poder *m* legal

PPD *V.* **purified protein derivative of tuberculin.**

practice *n* práctica; *vt*, *vi* practicar

practitioner *n* médico clínico; **general** —— médico general

praziquantel *n* praziquantel *m*

prazosin *n* prazosina

precaution *n* precaución *f*

precise *adj* preciso

precision *n* precisión *f*

precocious *adj* precoz

precordial thump *n* golpe precordial *or* torácico

predict *vt* predecir, pronosticar

predispose *vt* predisponer

predisposition *n* predisposición *f*

prednisone *n* prednisona

preeclampsia *n* preeclampsia

preemie *n* (*fam*) prematuro -ra *mf*

pregnancy *n* (*pl* -cies) embarazo; **ectopic** —— embarazo ectópico; **tubal** —— embarazo tubárico

pregnant *adj* embarazada, encinta; **You are three months pregnant**..Tiene tres meses de embarazo.

preliminary *adj* preliminar

premature *adj* prematuro, precoz

premedication *n* premedicación *f*

premolar *adj* & *n* premolar *m*

prenatal *adj* prenatal

preoperative *adj* preoperatorio

preparation *n* (*pharm*) preparado, preparación *f*

prepare *vt* preparar

prescribe *vt* recetar, prescribir

prescription *n* receta (médica), prescripción *f*

presentation *n* presentación *f*

preservative *n* preservativo

preserve *vt* preservar

press *vt* (*to apply pressure*) presionar, apretar; **Does it hurt when I press here?**..¿Le duele cuando presiono aquí?

pressure *n* presión *f*; —— **sore** escara de presión, úlcera por presión, llaga (*debida a permanecer mucho tiempo sin cambiar de posición*); **blood** —— presión arterial (*form*), presión (de la sangre) (*fam*); **diastolic** —— presión diastólica; **systolic** —— presión sistólica

preterm *adj* pretérmino (*invariant with respect to gender*)

prevalence *n* prevalencia

prevent *vt* (*disease, etc.*) prevenir, evitar; **Brushing your teeth every day helps prevent cavities**..El cepillarse los dientes todos los días ayuda a prevenir la caries.

preventible *adj* prevenible
prevention *n* prevención *f*
preventive *adj* preventivo
previous *adj* previo, anterior
prick *n* pinchazo, piquete *m* (*esp. Mex*), picadura; *vt* pinchar, picar (*esp. Mex*)
priest *n* sacerdote *m*, padre *m*, cura *m*
primary *adj* primario, del primer nivel
prison *n* cárcel *f*, prisión *f*
privacy *n* privacidad *f*
private *adj* privado, confidencial; —— **doctor** médico privado; —— **parts** (*fam*) genitales *mpl*, partes privadas *or* íntimas, partes (*fam, esp. female*)
probability *n* (*pl* -**ties**) probabilidad *f*
probably *adv* probablemente
probe *n* sonda; *vt* sondear *or* sondar
problem *n* problema *m*
probucol *n* probucol *m*
procainamide *n* procainamida
procaine *n* procaína
procedure *n* procedimiento
process *n* (*anat*) apófisis *f*; **mastoid** —— apófisis mastoides; **xiphoid** —— apófisis xifoides
proctitis *n* proctitis *f*
prodrome *n* pródromo
produce *vt* producir
professional *adj* profesional
profile *n* perfil *m*
progeria *n* progeria
progesterone *n* progesterona
prognosis *n* (*pl* -**ses**) pronóstico
program *n* programa *m*
progress *n* progreso; *vi* progresar
progression *n* progresión *f*
progressive *adj* progresivo; —— **multifocal leukoencephalopathy** encefalopatía multifocal progresiva; —— **systemic sclerosis** esclerosis sistémica progresiva
projectile *n* proyectil *m*
projection *n* proyección *f*
prolactin *n* prolactina
prolactinoma *n* tumor secretor de prolactina, prolactinoma *m*
prolapse *n* prolapso; **mitral valve** —— prolapso valvular mitral
prolapsed *adj* —— **umbilical cord,** —— **uterus, etc.** prolapso del cordón umbilical, prolapso del útero, etc.
proline *n* prolina
prolong *vt* prolongar
prone *adj* prono, acostado boca abajo
proof *n* prueba
prophylactic *adj & n* profiláctico
prophylaxis *n* profilaxis *f*
proportion *n* proporción *f*
propoxyphene *n* propoxifeno
propranolol *n* propranolol *m*
proprioceptive *adj* propioceptivo
proptosis *n* proptosis *f*
propylthiouracil *n* propiltiouracilo

prostaglandin *n* prostaglandina
prostate *n* próstata
prostatitis *n* prostatitis *f*
prosthesis *n* (*pl* -**ses**) prótesis *f*
prosthetic *adj* protésico *or* protético (*form*), postizo
prostitute *n* prostituto -ta *mf*
prostrate *adj* postrado
protect *vt* proteger
protection *n* protección *f*
protective *adj* protector
protein *n* proteína
Proteus Proteus
protocol *n* protocolo
protozoan *adj & n* protozoario
protuberance *n* protuberancia
provide *vt* suministrar, proporcionar
provoke *vt* provocar
pruritis *n* prurito
pseudocyst *n* seudoquiste *m*; **pancreatic** —— seudoquiste pancreático
pseudoephedrine *n* seudoefedrina
pseudogout *n* seudogota
pseudohypoparathyroidism *n* seudohipoparatiroidismo
Pseudomonas Pseudomonas
psilocybin *n* psilocibina
psittacosis *n* psitacosis *f*
psoas *n* psoas *m*
psoriasis *n* psoriasis *f*
psychedelic *adj* psicodélico
psychiatric *adj* psiquiátrico
psychiatrist *n* psiquiatra *mf*
psychiatry *n* psiquiatría
psychoactive *adj* psicoactivo
psychoanalysis *n* psicoanálisis *m*
psychoanalyst *n* psicoanalista *mf*
psychoanalyze *vt* psicoanalizar
psychological *adj* psicológico
psychologist *n* psicólogo -ga *mf*
psychology *n* psicología
psychopath *n* psicópata *mf*
psychosis *n* (*pl* -**ses**) psicosis *f*
psychosomatic *adj* psicosomático
psychotherapist *n* psicoterapista *mf*, psicoterapeuta *mf* (*form*)
psychotherapy *n* psicoterapia
psychotic *adj & n* psicótico -ca *mf*
psychotropic *adj & n* psicotrópico
PTC *abbr* **percutaneous transhepatic cholangiography.** *V.* **cholangiography.**
pterygium *n* pterigión *m*, carnosidad *f*
ptosis *n* ptosis *f*
puberty *n* pubertad *f*
pubic *adj* púbico
public *adj* público
pudendal *adj* pudendo
puerperal *adj* puerperal
puerperium *n* puerperio
Puerto Rican *adj & n* puertorriqueño -ña *mf*
puffy *adj* (*comp* -**fier;** *super* -**fiest**) hinchado
puke (*vulg*) *n* vómito; *vt, vi* arrojar,

devolver, deponer (*Mex*), tener basca, vomitar

pull *n* **muscle** —— estiramiento (*form*), desgarro leve (muscular); *vt* **to** —— **a muscle** estirarse un músculo, desgarrarse un músculo, sufrir un tirón

pulmonary *adj* pulmonar; —— **edema** edema *m* pulmonar; —— **embolism** embolia pulmonar

pulmonic *adj* pulmonar

pulmonologist *n* neumólogo -ga *mf*

pulmonology *n* neumología

pulsation *n* pulsación *f*

pulse *n* pulso; **I'm going to take your pulse.**.Voy a tomarle el pulso.

pumice stone *n* piedra pómez

pump *n* bomba

puncture *n* punción *f* (*form*), pinchazo, piquete *m* (*esp. Mex*), picadura; —— **wound** herida por punción; **lumbar** —— punción lumbar; *vt* puncionar (*form*), hacer una punción, pinchar, picar, penetrar

pupil *n* (*of the eye*) pupila

pure *adj* puro

purgative *adj & n* purgante *m*

purified protein derivative of tuberculin (PPD) *n* proteína purificada derivada de la tuberculina (PPD)

purify *vt* purificar

purine *n* purina

purple *adj* morado

purpura *n* púrpura; **Henoch-Schönlein** —— púrpura de Henoch-Schönlein; **idiopathic thrombocytopenic** —— (**ITP**) púrpura trombocitopénica idiopática; **thrombotic thrombocytopenic** —— (**TTP**) púrpura trombocitopénica trombótica

pus *n* pus *m*

push *vi* (*obst*) pujar; **Take a deep breath and push!**..¡Respire profundo y puje!

pustule *n* pústula

put *vt* (*pret & pp* put; *ger* putting) **to** —— **on** (*clothing, etc.*) ponerse; **Put on this gown.**.Póngase esta bata.

PVC *abbr* **premature ventricular contraction.** *V.* **contraction.**

pyelogram *n* urograma *m*, pielograma *m*; **intravenous** —— (**IVP**) urograma excretorio, pielograma intravenoso

pyelography *n* urografía, pielografía

pyelonephritis *n* pielonefritis *f*

pyloric *adj* pilórico

pyloroplasty *n* (*pl* **-ties**) piloroplastia

pylorus *n* píloro

pyoderma *n* piodermia *m&f*

pyorrhea *n* piorrea

pyrazinamide *n* pirazinamida

pyridoxine *n* piridoxina

Q

quack *n* (*fam*) charlatán -na *mf*; matasanos *m*, medicastro, medicucho, mediquillo

quadrant *n* cuadrante *m*

quadriceps *n* cuádriceps *m*

quadriplegia *n* cuadriplejía

quadriplegic *adj & n* cuadripléjico -ca *mf*

quadruplet *n* cuadrillizo -za *mf*, cuadrupleto -ta *mf*

quality *n* calidad *f*; —— **of life** calidad de vida

quarantine *n* cuarentena; *vt* poner en cuarentena

quart *n* cuarto

queasy *adj* (*comp* **-ier**; *super* **-iest**) con un poco de náusea, que tiene náusea(s); **I feel queasy** *o* **My stomach is queasy.**.Siento un poco de náusea.

questionnaire *n* cuestionario

quickening *n* percepción *f* por la madre de los movimientos fetales

quiet *adj* quieto; *vi* **to** —— **down** calmarse

quinacrine *n* quinacrina

quinidine *n* quinidina

quinine *n* quinina

quintuplet *n* quintillizo -za *mf*, quintupleto -ta *mf*

quit *vt* (*pret & pp* quit; *ger* quitting) dejar de, parar; **You need to quit drinking.**.Tiene que dejar de tomar.

R

rabid *adj* rabioso
rabies *n* rabia
raccoon *n* mapache *m*
race *n* (*of people*) raza; *vi* (*one's heart*) latir rápido
radial *adj* radial
radiation *n* radiación *f*
radical *adj* radical
radiculopathy *n* radiculopatía
radioactive *adj* radiactivo *or* radioactivo
radioactivity *n* radiactividad *or* radioactividad *f*
radiography *n* radiografía
radioisotope *n* radioisótopo
radiologist *n* radiólogo -ga *mf*
radiology *n* radiología
radionuclide *n* radionúclido
radiotherapy *n* radioterapia
radium *n* radio, rádium *m*
radius *n* (*pl* **radii** *o* **radiuses**) radio
radon *n* radón *m*
rage *n* ira, enojo
raise *vt* levantar, elevar; (*a child*) criar; **Raise your leg**..Levante su pierna...**This medicine may raise your sugar**..Esta medicina le puede elevar el azucar.
ran *pret de* **run**
random, at al azar
range *n* rango; —— **of motion** rango de movimiento; —— **of values** rango de valores
ranitidine *n* ranitidina
rape *n* violación *f*; *vt* violar
rare *adj* (*disease, etc.*) raro
rash *n* erupción *f*, rash *m*, (*esp. due to heat or chafing*) salpullido *or* sarpullido
rat *n* rata
rate *n* tasa, frecuencia; **basal metabolic** —— tasa de metabolismo basal; **birth** —— tasa de natalidad; **death** —— tasa de mortalidad; **heart** —— frecuencia cardiaca; **respiratory** —— frecuencia respiratoria
rattlesnake *n* serpiente *f* de cascabel
rave *vi* delirar, desvariar
raw *adj* (*food*) crudo; (*skin, mucous membrane*) pelado
ray *n* rayo
Raynaud's phenomenon *n* fenómeno de Raynaud
razor *n* (*manual*) rastrillo; (*electric*) rasuradora, máquina de afeitar; —— **blade** navaja *or* hoja de afeitar *or* rasurar
RDA *V.* **recommended dietary allowance.**

reach *n* alcance *m*; **out of** —— **of children** fuera del alcance de los niños; *vt, vi* alcanzar
react *vi* reaccionar
reaction *n* reacción *f*; **adverse** —— reacción adversa; **allergic** —— reacción alérgica; **conversion** —— reacción conversiva; **cross** —— reacción cruzada; **delayed** —— reacción tardía
reactive *adj* reactivo
read *vt, vi* (*pret & pp* **read**) leer
reality *n* realidad *f*
rebound *n* rebote *m*
recently *adv* últimamente, recientemente
recessive *adj* recesivo
recombinant *adj* recombinante
recommend *vt* recomendar
recommended dietary allowance (RDA) *n* dosis diaria recomendada
reconstruct *vt* reconstruir
record *n* (*patient chart*) expediente *m*; (*of temperatures, etc.*) registro
recover *vt* recobrar, recuperar; *vi* recuperarse, aliviarse, restablecerse
recovery *n* recuperación *f*, restablecimiento; —— **room** sala de recuperación
recreation *n* recreación *f*, (*esp. during school*) recreo
rectal *adj* rectal
rectum *n* (*pl* **-tums** *o* **-ta**) recto
recuperate *vi* recuperarse
recuperation *n* recuperación *f*
recur *vi* (*pret & pp* **recurred**; *ger* **recurring**) volver (*una enfermedad, condición, etc.*)
recurrence *n* recurrencia
red *adj* (*comp* **redder**; *super* **reddest**) rojo, colorado
Red Cross *n* Cruz Roja
reddish *adj* rojizo
reddening *n* enrojecimiento
redness *n* enrojecimiento
reduce *vt* reducir, disminuir, bajar; (*ortho*) reducir; *vi* (*fam, to lose weight*) rebajar
reduction *n* reducción *f*
reevaluate *vt* reevaluar, revalorar
refill *n* surtido nuevo (*de medicamentos*); *vt* surtir de nuevo
refined *adj* refinado
reflex *n* reflejo; **conditioned** —— reflejo condicionado; **gag** —— reflejo nauseoso; **patellar** —— reflejo patelar *or* rotuliano
reflux *n* reflujo; **esophageal** —— reflujo esofágico

refrigeration *n* refrigeración *f*
refrigerator *n* refrigerador *m*
regain *vt* recuperar; **to —— consciousness** volver en sí
regenerate *vi* regenerarse
regimen *n* régimen *m*
register *n* (*of births, etc.*) registro
regression *n* regresión *f*
regular *adj* regular
regulate *vt* regular
regulator *n* regulador *m*
regurgitate *vt* regurgitar
regurgitation *n* regurgitación *f*; **aortic ——, mitral ——, etc.** regurgitación aórtica, regurgitación mitral, etc.
rehabilitate *vt* rehabilitar
rehabilitation *n* rehabilitación *f*
rehydrate *n* rehidratar
rehydration *n* rehidratación *f*
reinfection *n* reinfección *f*
reinfestation *n* reinfestación *f*
reinforce *vt* reforzar
reinforcement *n* refuerzo
reject *vt* rechazar
rejection *n* rechazo
relapse *n* recaída; *vi* recaer
relation *n* relación *f*
relative *n* familiar *m*, pariente *mf*; **blood ——** pariente consanguíneo, pariente que tiene la misma sangre (*fam*)
relax *vt, vi* relajar(se), aflojar(se); **Relax..Relájese...Relax your leg..**Afloje la pierna.
relaxant *n* relajante *m*
relaxation *n* relajación *f*, (*rest*) descanso
relaxing *adj* relajante
release *n* liberación *f*; **slow ——** liberación prolongada; **sustained ——** liberación sostenida; **timed ——** difusión regulada; *vt* liberar; **copper-releasing, hormone-releasing, etc.** liberador de cobre, liberador de hormona, etc.
reliable *adj* confiable
relief *n* alivio, (*emotional*) desahogo
relieve *vt* aliviar
REM *abbr* **rapid eye movement.** V. **movement.**
remedy *n* (*pl* -dies) remedio; **home ——** remedio casero
remember *vt* recordar, acordarse (de)
remission *n* remisión *f*
removal *n* extracción *f*, (el) quitar, (el) sacar
remove *vt* extraer (*form*), sacar, quitar
renal *adj* renal; **—— failure** insuficiencia renal
renovascular *adj* renovascular
repair *n* reparación *f*; *vt* reparar, arreglar
repeat *vt* repetir
repellant *n* repelente *m*; **insect ——** repelente de insectos
repetitive *adj* repetitivo
replace *vt* reemplazar

replacement *n* reemplazo; **total hip ——** reemplazo total de cadera
repress *vt* reprimir
repression *n* represión *f*
reproduce *vt, vi* reproducir(se)
reproduction *n* reproducción *f*
reproductive *adj* reproductor, reproductivo
rescue *n* rescate *m*, salvamento; *vt* rescatar, salvar
rescuer *n* socorrista *mf*
research *n* investigación *f*
resection *n* resección *f*
reserpine *n* reserpina
reserve *n* reserva
reservoir *n* reservorio
resident *n* (*physician*) residente *mf*
resin *n* resina
resist *vt, vi* resistir(se)
resistance *n* resistencia
resistant *adj* resistente
resolve *vi* resolverse
resorb *vt, vi* reabsorber, resorber
respect *n* respeto
respiration *n* respiración *f*
respirator *n* respirador *m*
respiratory *adj* respiratorio; **—— failure** insuficiencia respiratoria
respire *vt, vi* respirar
respond *vi* responder
response *n* respuesta; **immune ——** respuesta inmune
rest *n* descanso, reposo; **at ——** en reposo; *vt, vi* descansar
restless *adj* inquieto, intranquilo
restore *vt* reponer, restablecer
restrain *vt* sujetar
restraints *npl* sujetadores *mpl*
restrict *vt* restringir
restriction *n* restricción *f*
rest room *n* baño
result *n* resultado
resuscitate *vt* resucitar
resuscitation *n* resucitación *f*, reanimación *f*; **cardiopulmonary —— (CPR)** resucitación *or* reanimación cardiopulmonar (RCP); **mouth-to-mouth ——** resucitación *or* respiración *f* boca-a-boca
retainer *n* (*orthodontia*) arco de Hawley
retardation *n* retardo, retraso; **mental ——** retardo *or* retraso mental
retarded *adj* retardado, retrasado; **mentally ——** retardado *or* retrasado mental
retch *vi* vomitar sin tener nada que expulsar
retention *n* retención *f*
reticulocyte *n* reticulocito
retina *n* (*pl* -nas *o* -nae) retina; **detached ——** retina desprendida
retinopathy *n* retinopatía
retrograde *adj* retrógrado
reusable *adj* para uso repetido, reusable
revaccination *n* revacunación *f*
reversible *adj* reversible

revive *vt, vi* reanimar(se)
rhabdomyolysis *n* rabdomiólisis *f*
rhabdomyosarcoma *n* rabdomiosarcoma *m*
rheumatic *adj* reumático
rheumatoid *adj* reumatoide
rheumatologist *n* reumatólogo -ga *mf*
rheumatology *n* reumatología
Rh factor *n* factor *m* Rh
rhinitis *n* rinitis *f*; **allergic** ——— rinitis alérgica
rhinoplasty *n* (*pl* -**ties**) rinoplastia
rhythm *n* ritmo; ——— **method** método del ritmo
rib *n* costilla; ——— **cage** caja torácica
riboflavin *n* riboflavina
ribonucleic acid *n* ácido ribonucleico
rice *n* arroz *m*
rickets *n* raquitismo
Rickettsia Rickettsia
rifampin *n* rifampicina
right *adj* derecho; *n* (*right-hand side*) derecha; (*legal, moral*) derecho
right-handed *adj* que usa la mano derecha; **Are you right-handed or left-handed?..** ¿Ud. escribe con la derecha o la izquierda?
rigid *adj* rígido
rigor mortis *n* rigor mortis *m*
ring *n* anillo; *vi* (*in one's ears*) zumbar
ringing *n* (*in one's ears*) zumbido
ringworm *n* tiña del cuerpo
rinse *n* enjuague *m*; *vt* enjuagar
ripe *adj* maduro
rise *n* aumento, elevación *f*, subida; *vi* (*pret* **rose**; *pp* **risen**) subir(se), elevar(se); (*to get up*) levantarse; **Your sugar rose..** Le subió el azucar.
risk *n* riesgo; ——— **factor** factor *m* de riesgo; **high** ——— alto riesgo; **to run the** ——— **of** correr el riesgo de; **to take a** ——— arriesgarse; *vt* arriesgar
roasted *adj* asado
rod *n* (*bacteria*) bacilo; (*of the eye*) bastón *m*
rodent *adj* roedor; *n* roedor *m*
role *n* papel *m*; ——— **model** modelo *mf* (a seguir)
roll *vi* **to** ——— **over** voltearse, darse vuelta; **Roll over facing the wall..** Voltéese viendo hacia la pared.
room *n* cuarto, sala; **delivery** ——— sala de

partos; **emergency** ——— (**ER**) sala de emergencia *or* urgencias; **operating** ——— (**OR**) quirófano, sala de operaciones; **recovery** ——— sala de recuperación; **waiting** ——— sala de espera
root raíz *f*; ——— **canal** endodoncia (*form*), tratamiento de nervio (*fam*), curación *f* de nervio (*fam*)
rose *pret de* **rise**
roseola infantum *n* roséola *or* roseola infantil
rot *vt, vi* (*pret & pp* **rotted**; *ger* **rotting**) pudrir(se)
rotten *adj* podrido
rough *adj* áspero
round *adj* redondo
rounds *npl* visitas, rondas (*Ang*); **to make** ——— pasar visita, hacer rondas
roundworm *n* ascáride *m* (*form*), gusano redondo, lombriz *f* (*fam*)
routine *adj* rutinario; *n* rutina
rub *vt* (*pret & pp* **rubbed**; *ger* **rubbing**) (*to massage*) sobar; (*to chafe*) rozar; *vi* rozar
rubber *n* hule *m*, goma; (*fam*) condón *m*, preservativo
rubella *n* rubeola *or* rubéola, sarampión *m* alemán (*fam*)
rubeola *n* (*form*) sarampión *m*
rule *vt* **to** ——— **out** descartar; **Cancer was ruled out..** Se descartó el cáncer.
rum *n* ron *m*
run *n* **to have the runs** (*fam*) tener diarrea; *vt* (*pret* **ran**; *pp* **run**; *ger* **running**) **to** ——— **over** atropellar; *vi* correr; **to** ——— **in one's family** venir de familia; **to** ——— **out** acabarse; **When did your medicine run out?..** ¿Cuándo se le acabó su medicina?
runaway *n* niño -ña *mf* que ha abandonado el hogar
run-down *adj* agotado, exhausto, debilitado, decaído
runny *adj* (*comp* -**nier**; *super* -**niest**) líquido, de consistencia líquida; **to have a** ——— **nose** tener secreciones por la nariz, fluirle la nariz, tener mocosidad, tener moquera (*fam*)
rupture *n* ruptura; **premature** ——— **of membranes** ruptura prematura de membranas; *vt, vi* reventar(se)
rural *adj* rural, del campo

S

S-A *V.* sinoatrial.
saccharin *n* sacarina
sacral *adj* sacro
sacroiliac *adj* sacroiliaco
sacrum *n* (*pl* -cra) sacro
sad *adj* (*comp* sadder; *super* saddest) triste
sadism *n* sadismo
sadist *n* sádico -ca *mf*
sadistic *adj* sádico
safe *adj* seguro
safety *n* seguridad *f*; —— cap tapa de seguridad; —— pin imperdible *m*, alfiler *m* de seguridad, seguro (*Mex*), gancho
safflower oil *n* aceite *m* de cártamo
sag *vi* (*pret & pp* sagged; *ger* sagging) caerse
salbutamol *n* salbutamol *m*
salicylate *n* salicilato
salicylic acid *n* ácido salicílico
saline *adj* salino; normal —— solution solución salina isotónica
saliva *n* saliva
salivary *adj* salival
salivation *n* salivación *f*
Salmonella Salmonella
salmonellosis *n* salmonelosis *f*
salpingitis *n* salpingitis *f*
salt *n* sal *f*; —— substitute substituto de sal; Epsom —— sal de Epsom; smelling salts sales aromáticas
Salvadoran, Salvadorian *adj & n* salvadoreño -ña *mf*
salvage *vt* salvar
salve *n* ungüento, pomada
sample *n* muestra
sanatorium *n* sanatorio
sandfly *n* (*pl* -flies) jején *m*, mosquito, mosquito simúlido
sane *adj* cuerdo
sanitarium *n* centro de recreo para la salud; sanatorio
sanitary *adj* sanitario; —— napkin toalla sanitaria, toalla femenina (*esp. Mex*)
sanitation *n* saneamiento (ambiental), medidas sanitarias
sanity *n* cordura
saphenous *adj* safeno
sarcoidosis *n* sarcoidosis *f*
sarcoma *n* sarcoma *m*; Ewing's —— sarcoma de Ewing; Kaposi's —— sarcoma de Kaposi
sat *pret & pp de* sit
satellite *adj* (*lesion, clinic*) satélite
saturated *adj* saturado

sauna *n* sauna *m*
save *vt* salvar; We want to save your leg..Queremos salvar su pierna.
saw *n* sierra
saw *pret de* see
scab *n* costra
scabies *n* sarna
scald *vt* escaldar
scale *n* (*for weighing*) báscula, balanza; (*piece of skin*) escama; (*of measurement*) escala; sliding —— escala flexible *or* móvil
scalp *n* cuero cabelludo
scalpel *n* escalpelo, bisturí *m*
scaly *adj* (*comp* -ier; *super* -iest) escamoso
scan *n* escán *m* (*Ang*), imagen diagnóstica, (*nuclear*) gammagrama *m*, gammagrafía; bone —— serie ósea; CAT —— tomografía axial computarizada, TAC *m* (*fam*), tomografía (*fam*); CT —— tomografía computada, tomografía (*fam*); gallium —— gammagrama de galio; thallium —— gammagrama de talio
scapula *n* (*pl* -lae *o* -las) escápula (*form*), omóplato, paleta (*fam*)
scar *n* cicatriz *f*
scarce *adj* escaso
scare *n* susto; *vt* to be scared tener miedo; Don't be scared..No tenga miedo.
schedule *n* horario; (*of vaccinations*) esquema
schistosomiasis *n* esquistosomiasis *f*
schizoid *adj* esquizoide
schizophrenia *n* esquizofrenia
schizophrenic *adj & n* esquizofrénico -ca *mf*
school *n* escuela
sciatic *adj* ciático
sciatica *n* ciática
scientific *adj* científico
scientist *n* científico -ca *mf*
scissors *npl* tijeras
sclera *n* (*pl* -rae) esclerótica, esclera
scleroderma *n* esclerodermia
sclerosis *n* esclerosis *f*
sclerotherapy *n* escleroterapia
scoliosis *n* escoliosis *f*
scopolamine *n* escopolamina
scored *adj* (*tablet*) ranurado
scorpion *n* escorpión *m*, alacrán *m*
scrape *n* raspón *m*, raspadura; *vt* raspar(se)
scratch *n* rasguño, raspado, (*with claws*) arañazo; *vt* rasguñar(se), raspar(se), arañar(se); (*an itch, etc.*) rascar(se); How did you scratch yourself?..¿Cómo se

rasguñó?...**You have to quit scratching (yourself)**..Tiene que dejar de rascarse.

screen *n* examen *m* de detección; *vt, vi* practicar exámenes de detección

screening *n* detección *f*, práctica de exámenes de detección; —— **for cancer, glaucoma, etc.** detección del cáncer, glaucoma, etc.

scrofula *n* escrófula

scrotum *n* escroto

scurvy *n* escorbuto

seafood *n* marisco(s); **Are you allergic to seafood?**..¿Es alérgico a los mariscos?

seasickness *n* mareo (en un barco)

season *n* (*winter, spring, etc.*) estación *f*; (*for a disease, rain, etc.*) temporada

seat *n* asiento; —— **belt** cinturón *m* de seguridad

sea urchin *n* erizo de mar

sebaceous *adj* sebáceo

seborrhea *n* seborrea

second *adj* segundo; *n* segundo

secondary *adj* secundario

secretary *n* (*pl* -ries) secretario -ria *mf*

secrete *vt* secretar

secretion *n* secreción *f*

secretory *adj* secretorio

section *n* sección *f*; **frozen** —— corte *m* por congelación

sedate *vt* sedar, dar un sedante

sedative *adj* & *n* sedante *m*, calmante *m*

sedentary *adj* sedentario

sediment *n* sedimento

see *vt, vi* (*pret* **saw**; *pp* **seen**) ver; **When was the last time you saw an eye doctor?**..¿Cuándo fue la última vez que vio a un médico de los ojos?

Seeing Eye dog *n* perro guía

seize *vi* tener una convulsión

seizure *n* crisis (convulsiva *or* epiléptica) (*form*), convulsión *f* (*form*), ataque *m*; **Did you have a seizure?**..¿Tuvo una convulsión?..¿Le dio un ataque?; **absence** —— crisis de ausencia; **complex partial** —— crisis parcial compleja; **focal** —— crisis focal; **generalized** —— crisis generalizada; **gran mal** —— crisis gran mal; **Jacksonian** —— crisis jacksoniana; **partial** —— crisis parcial; **petit mal** —— crisis pequeño mal; **psychomotor** —— crisis psicomotora; **temporal lobe** —— crisis del lóbulo temporal; **tonic-clonic** —— crisis tónico-clónica

selenium *n* selenio

self-centered *adj* egocéntrico

self-confidence *n* confianza en sí mismo

self-conscious *adj* consciente de sí mismo

self-control *n* dominio de sí mismo

self-destructive *adj* autodestructivo

self-discipline *n* autodisciplina

self-esteem *n* autoestima (*form*), amor propio

self-examination *n* autoevaluación *f*, autoexamen *m*

self-limited *adj* autolimitado

self-prescribe *vt* autorrecetarse, autoprescribirse

self-respect *n* respeto de sí mismo, autorrespeto

semen *n* semen *m*

semicircular canal *n* conducto semicircular

seminoma *n* seminoma *m*

senile *adj* senil

senior citizen *n* (*US*) persona anciana

sensation *n* sensación *f*

sense *n* sentido; —— **of hearing** sentido del oído; —— **of sight** sentido de la vista; —— **of smell** sentido del olfato; —— **of taste** sentido del gusto; —— **of touch** sentido del tacto

sensitive *adj* sensible

sensitivity *n* (*pl* -ties) sensibilidad *f*

sensitize *vt* sensibilizar; **to become sensitized** sensibilizarse

sensory *adj* sensorio

sepsis *n* sepsis *f*

septic *adj* séptico

septum *n* (*pl* -ta) tabique *m*; **deviated** —— tabique desviado; **interventricular** —— tabique interventricular; **nasal** —— tabique nasal

sera *pl de* **serum**

serial *adj* seriado

series *n* (*pl* **series**) serie *f*

serine *n* serina

serious *adj* serio, grave

seroconversion *n* seroconversión *f*

serology *n* (*pl* -gies) serología

seronegative *adj* seronegativo

seropositive *adj* seropositivo

serum *adj* sérico; *n* (*pl* **sera** *o* **serums**) suero; —— **sickness** enfermedad *f* del suero

service *n* servicio

set *vt* (*a bone*) reducir (*form*), acomodar

severe *adj* severo

severity *n* gravedad *f*

sew *vt* (*fam, to suture*) suturar, coser (*fam*)

sewage *n* aguas negras

sewer *n* drenaje *m*

sex *n* sexo; —— **life** vida sexual; **oral** —— sexo oral; **to have** —— tener relaciones (sexuales)

sex-linked *adj* ligado al sexo

sexual *adj* sexual

sexuality *n* sexualidad *f*

shake *vi* (*pret* **shook**; *pp* **shaken**) (*to tremble*) temblar; (*to shiver*) estremecerse, tiritar; **Shake well before using.**..Agítese bien antes de usarse.

shame *n* vergüenza

shampoo *n* (*pl* -poos) champú *m*; *vt* (*pret & pp* -pooed) lavarse el pelo *or* la cabeza

shape *n* forma, condición *f*; **in** —— **en** forma

shark *n* tiburón *m*
sharp *adj* (*pain*) agudo; (*instrument*) afilado, filoso
shave *vt*, *vi* afeitar(se), rasurar(se)
shed *vt* (*pret & pp* **shed**; *ger* **shedding**) (*viruses, parasites, etc.*) eliminar, liberar, botar, tirar (*esp. Mex*), echar
sheepskin *n* piel *f* de oveja
sheet *n* (*for a bed*) sábana
shell shock *n* neurosis *f* de guerra
shellfish *n* (*pl* **-fish** *o* **-fishes**) marisco(s)
shelter *n* refugio; **women's ——**, **homeless ——**, etc. refugio para mujeres, refugio para personas sin hogar, etc.
Shigella Shigella
shigellosis *n* shigelosis *f*
shin *n* espinilla, canilla; **—— guard** espinillera; **—— splints** dolor de la pierna debido a ejercicio fuerte
shinbone *n* (*anat*) tibia (*form*), espinilla, canilla
shingles *n* herpes *m* zoster, zona
shirt *n* camisa
shiver *vi* tiritar, estremecerse
shock *n* choque *m*, shock *m* (*Ang*); **anaphylactic ——** choque anafiláctico; **cardiogenic ——** choque cardiogénico *or* cardiógeno; **electric ——** choque eléctrico, descarga eléctrica; **hypovolemic ——** choque hipovolémico; **neurogenic ——** choque neurogénico *or* neurógeno; **septic ——** choque séptico
shoe *n* zapato
shook *pret de* **shake**
shooter *n* (*vulg*) persona que se inyecta drogas
shooting *adj* (*pain*) punzante
short *adj* (*stature*) bajo, chaparro; (*dimension*) corto; (*time*) breve; **—— of breath** V. **breath.**
short-acting *adj* de acción corta
shorten *vt* acortar, hacer más corto
short-term *adj* a corto plazo
shot (*fam*) inyección *f*
shoulder *n* hombro; **—— blade** omóplato, paleta
shower *n* ducha, baño de regadera (*Mex*); **to take a ——** tomar una ducha, ducharse, bañarse (en la ducha)
shrink *n* (*vulg*) psiquiatra *mf*; *vt*, *vi* (*pret* **shrank**; *pp* **shrunk**) (*tumor, etc.*) reducir(se)
shunt *n* (*physio*) cortocircuito; (*surg*) derivación *f*
shy *adj* (*comp* **shyer** *o* **shier**; *super* **shyest** *o* **shiest**) tímido
shyness *n* timidez *f*
Siamese twins *npl* hermanos -nas siameses
sibling *n* hermano -na *mf*; **siblings** hermanos; **—— rivalry** rivalidad *f* entre hermanos
sick *adj* enfermo, malo; **to get ——**

enfermarse, ponerse enfermo
sickly *adj* (*comp* **-lier**; *super* **-liest**) enfermizo
sickness *n* enfermedad *f*, mal *m*; **decompression ——** enfermedad por descompresión; **morning ——** náuseas *or* vómitos del embarazo; **motion ——** mareo (producido por el movimiento); **mountain ——** mal de montaña, soroche *m* (*SA*); **serum ——** enfermedad del suero; **sleeping ——** enfermedad del sueño
side *n* lado, (*anat*) costado; **—— ache** *n* dolor *m* de costado (*esp. al hacer ejercicio después de comer*); **—— rail** (*of a bed*) barandal *m*, baranda
SIDS *abbr* **sudden infant death syndrome.** V. **syndrome.**
sigh *n* suspiro; *vi* suspirar
sight *n* vista, visión *f*
sigmoid *adj* sigmoideo; **—— colon** colon *m* sigmoide
sigmoidoscopy *n* (*pl* **-pies**) sigmoidoscopia *or* (*esp. spoken*) sigmoidoscopía
sign *n* (*of an illness*) signo; **vital signs** signos vitales; **warning ——** signo de advertencia, señal *f* de alarma; *vt*, *vi* (*one's name*) firmar; (*deaf language*) hablar por señas
signature *n* firma
silica *n* sílice *f*
silicone *n* silicona
silicosis *n* silicosis *f*
silk *n* seda
silver *n* plata; **—— nitrate** nitrato de plata
simethicone *n* simeticona
sinoatrial (S-A) *adj* sinoauricular *or* sinoatrial (SA)
sinus *n* seno; **—— tract** fístula
sinusitis *n* sinusitis *f*
sip *n* sorbo; *vt* (*pret & pp* **sipped**; *ger* **sipping**) sorber
sister *n* hermana
sister-in-law *n* (*pl* **sisters-in-law**) cuñada
sit *vi* (*pret & pp* **sat**; *ger* **sitting**) sentarse; **to —— down** sentarse; **to —— up** (*from a supine position*) sentarse
size *n* tamaño, talla, medida, dimensiones *fpl*
skeleton *n* esqueleto
skill *n* destreza, habilidad *f*
skin *n* piel *f*; **—— tag** fibroma *m* pendular (*form*), verruga (*fam*)
skirt *n* falda
skull *n* cráneo
skunk *n* zorrillo
sleep *n* sueño; (*eye secretions*) legaña (*form*), lagaña; **—— apnea** apnea del sueño; **to go to ——** dormirse; **Do you have trouble going to sleep?**..¿Tiene problemas para dormirse?...**Does your arm go to sleep?**..¿Se le duerme el brazo? **to go without ——** desvelarse; **to put to ——**

dormir, anestesiar; **We will put you to sleep for the operation.**.Vamos a dormirlo para la operación; *vi* (*pret & pp* **slept**) dormir

sleeping pill *n* somnífero (*form*), pastilla para dormir

sleeping sickness *n* enfermedad *f* del sueño

sleepless *adj* desvelado

sleepwalk *vi* caminar dormido

sleepwalking *n* sonambulismo (*form*), (el) caminar dormido

sleepy *adj* (*comp* -ier; *super* -iest) **to be** ―― tener sueño; **to make** ―― dar sueño

slept *pret & pp de* **sleep**

sliding scale *n* escala flexible *or* móvil

slight *adj* leve, ligero

sling *n* cabestrillo

slip *n* resbalón *m*; *vi* (*pret & pp* **slipped**; *ger* **slipping**) resbalar(se)

slitlamp *n* lámpara de hendidura

sliver *n* astilla

slouch *vi* sentarse o pararse con mala postura, encorvarse

slough *vi* (*también* **to** ―― **off**) desprenderse, caerse

slur *vi* (*pret & pp* **slurred**; *ger* **slurring**) hablar con la lengua pesada, arrastrar la voz, balbucear

small *adj* pequeño, chico; **to get smaller** ponerse más pequeño, reducir(se), disminuir(se); *n* ―― **of the back** parte baja de la espalda

smallpox *n* viruela

smart *vi* doler de una manera aguda e intensiva

smear *n* (*micro*) frotis *m*; **Papanicolaou** ―― frotis de Papanicolaou

smell *n* olor *m*; *vt, vi* oler; **to** ―― **bad** oler mal; **to** ―― **like** oler a

smile *n* sonrisa; *vi* sonreir(se); **Smile**..Sonría.

smog *n* aire contaminado, esmog *m* (*Ang*)

smoke *n* humo; *vt, vi* fumar

smoking *n* (el) fumar (*tabaco*); **No smoking**..No fumar

smooth *adj* liso, suave

smother *vt, vi* ahogar(se), sofocar(se)

snack *n* bocadillo, refrigerio, botana (*Mex*); *vi* comer entre comidas

snail *n* caracol *m*

snake *n* serpiente *f*, culebra

sneeze *n* estornudo; *vi* estornudar

Snellen chart *n* carta de Snellen, (*pocket size*) tarjeta de Snellen

sniff *vt* (*cocaine, glue, etc.*) inhalar, oler (*cocaína, cemento, etc.*); *vi* aspirar por la nariz

sniffle *n* **to have the sniffles** tener secreciones por la nariz, fluirle la naríz, tener mocosidad, tener moquera (*fam*); *vi* aspirar moco líquido por la nariz

snore *vi* roncar

snort *vt* (*vulg, cocaine*) inhalar, oler (*cocaína*)

snot *n* (*vulg*) moquera, moco

snuff *n* (*tobacco*) rapé *m*

soak *vt* remojar

soap *n* jabón *m*

sober *adj* sobrio, no intoxicado; *vi* **to** ―― **up** desemborracharse, desembriagarse

social service *n* servicio social

social worker *n* trabajador -ra *mf* social

sock *n* calcetín *m*

socket *n* (*of a tooth*) alveolo *or* alvéolo; (*of an eye*) cuenca

sodium *n* sodio; ―― **bicarbonate** bicarbonato de sodio; ―― **chloride** cloruro de sodio; ―― **hydroxide** hidróxido de sodio

soft *adj* blando, suave

soft drink *n* refresco

soften *vt* (*skin*) suavizar

softening *adj* (*lotion, etc.*) suavizador, suavizante

soil *vt* ensuciar; **to** ―― **oneself** ensuciarse

solar *adj* solar

soldier *n* soldado

sole *n* (*of the foot*) planta; (*of a shoe*) suela

soleus *n* sóleo

solid *adj & n* sólido

solution *n* solución *f*; **normal saline** ―― solución salina isotónica

solvent *n* solvente *m*

somatic *adj* somático

son *n* hijo

son-in-law *n* (*pl* **sons-in-law**) yerno

sonogram *n* sonograma *m*

soothe *vt* aliviar, calmar

sorbitol *n* sorbitol *m*

sore *adj* adolorido *or* dolorido; ―― **throat** dolor *m* de garganta; *n* úlcera, llaga; **pressure** ―― escara de presión, úlcera por presión, llaga (*debida a permanecer mucho tiempo sin cambiar de posición*)

sorry *adj* **to be** ―― sentir; **I'm sorry you had to wait so long**..Siento que haya tenido que esperar tanto tiempo...**I'm sorry**..Lo siento.

sound *n* sonido

soup *n* sopa, caldo

sour *adj* agrio

source *n* origen *m*, fuente *f*

South American *adj & n* sudamericano -na *mf*

soybean *n* soya *or* soja

Spaniard *n* español -la *mf*

spasm *n* espasmo

spasmodic *adj* espasmódico

spastic *adj* espástico

spasticity *n* espasticidad *f*

spat *pret & pp de* **spit**

speak *vt, vi* (*pret* **spoke**; *pp* **spoken**) hablar

specialist *n* especialista *mf*

specialty *n* (*pl* -ties) especialidad *f*

species *n* (*pl* -cies) especie *f*
specific *adj* específico
specimen *n* espécimen *m*, muestra
spectacles *npl* anteojos, gafas
spectinomycin *n* espectinomicina
spectrum *n* (*pl* -tra *o* -trums) espectro
speculum *n* (*pl* -la *o* -lums) espéculo
speech *n* habla; —— development
    desarrollo del habla
speed *n* (*vulg*) anfetamina
spell *n* acceso, periodo *or* período (*de
    mareo, tos, etc.*)
sperm *n* (*with semen*) esperma; (*individual
    spermatozoon*) espermatozoide *m*
spermatocidal, spermicidal *adj* espermati-
    cida
spermatocide, spermicide *n* espermaticida
    m
spermatozoon *n* espermatozoide *m*
sphincter *n* esfínter *m*
spicy *adj* (*comp* -ier; *super* -iest) picante
spider *n* araña
spider angioma *n* telangiectasia aracniforme
    (*form*), araña vascular, nevo en araña
spina bifida *n* espina bífida
spinal *adj* espinal, raquídeo; —— column
    columna vertebral, espina dorsal; ——
    cord médula espinal
spine *n* espina dorsal, columna vertebral,
    columna (*fam*); (*thorn*) espina; cervical
    —— columna cervical; lumbar ——
    columna lumbar; sacral —— columna
    sacra; thoracic —— columna torácica *or*
    dorsal
spirochete *n* espiroqueta
spirometer *n* espirómetro
spirometry *n* espirometría; incentive ——
    ejercicio respiratorio postquirúrgico
spironolactone *n* espironolactona
spit *n* saliva; *vt, vi* (*pret & pp* spat *o* spit;
    ger spitting) escupir; to —— up (*fam,
    esp. ped*) vomitar, arrojar, devolver
spleen *n* bazo
splenectomy *n* (*pl* -mies) esplenectomía
splenic *adj* esplénico
splint *n* férula (*form*), tablilla; *vt* colocar una
    férula, entablillar
splinter *n* astilla
split *adj* partido, quebrado; *n* quebradura,
    fisura; *vt, vi* (*pret & pp* split; *ger*
    splitting) partir(se), quebrar(se)
spoil *vi* (*pret & pp* spoiled *o* spoilt) (*food*)
    echarse a perder
spoke *pret de* speak
spoken *pp de* speak
spondylitis *n* espondilitis *f*; ankylosing ——
    espondilitis anquilosante
spondylosis *n* espondilosis *f*
sponge *n* esponja
spontaneous *adj* espontáneo
spoonful *n* cucharada
sporadic *adj* esporádico

spore *n* espora
sporotrichosis *n* esporotricosis *f*
spot *n* mancha
spotting *n* sangrado vaginal ligero (*que deja
    manchas en la ropa interior*)
sprain *n* torcedura; *vt* torcer(se); I sprained
    my wrist..Me torcí la muñeca..Se me
    torció la muñeca.
spray *n* aerosol *m*, rociada, espray *m* (*Ang*);
    vt rociar
spread *n* diseminación *f* (*form*), propagación
    f; *vt, vi* (*pret & pp* spread) diseminar(se)
    (*form*), propagar(se)
spring, springtime *n* primavera
sprue *n* esprue *m&f*; celiac *o* nontropical
    —— esprue celiaco *or* no tropical;
    tropical —— esprue tropical
spur *n* (*ortho*) espolón *m*
sputum *n* esputo (*form*), flema
squamous *adj* escamoso
square *adj* cuadrado; —— meter metro
    cuadrado
squared *adj* cuadrado; meter —— metro
    cuadrado
squat *vi* ponerse en cuclillas
squint *vt* entrecerrar (*los ojos*), medio cerrar
    (*los ojos*); *vi* mirar entrecerrado, fruncir la
    vista
squirrel *n* ardilla
stabbing *adj* (*pain*) punzante
stabilize *vt, vi* estabilizar(se)
stable *adj* estable
stage *n* (*disease, cancer*) estadío *or* (*esp.
    spoken*) estadio, etapa; (*sleep*) etapa
stagger *vi* tambalear(se)
stain *n* mancha; (*micro*) coloración *f*;
    Gram's —— coloración de Gram; port-
    wine —— mancha de vino oporto
stainless steel *n* acero inoxidable
stamina *n* vigor *m*, resistencia
stammer *vi* tartamudear
stanch *vt* restañar
stand *vt* (*pret & pp* stood) (*to endure*)
    tolerar, aguantar; *vi* pararse; (*también* to
    —— up) levantarse, pararse, ponerse de
    pie; Stand here, please..Párese aquí, por
    favor...Now stand..Ahora levántese.
standard *adj* estándar; *n* norma, estándar *m*
staphylococcus *n* estafilococo
Staphylococcus Staphylococcus
staple *n* (*surg*) grapa
starch *n* almidón *m*
stare *vi* fijar la vista; Stare at that point on
    the wall..Fije la vista en ese punto en la
    pared.
starvation *n* inanición *f*
starve *vi* morir de hambre
stasis *n* estasis *f*; venous —— estasis venosa
state *n* estado, condición *f*
station *n* estación *f*; nursing —— estación
    de enfermeras
statistic *n* estadística

status *n* status *m*, estado; —— **asthmaticus** status asthmaticus; —— **epilepticus** status epilepticus

staunch *var de* **stanch**

stay *vi* **to** —— **in bed** guardar cama

STD *abbr* **sexually transmitted disease.** *V.* **disease.**

steady *adj* (*comp* -ier; *super* -iest) (*pain*) constante; (*hands, gait*) firme; (*gaze*) fijo

steam *n* vapor *m*

steamed *adj* (cocido) al vapor

steel *n* acero; **stainless** —— acero inoxidable

stenosis *n* (*pl* -ses) estenosis *f*

stenotic *adj* estenótico

stent *n* férula (*para mantener permeable un conducto*)

step *n* paso; *vi* (*pret & pp* stepped; *ger* stepping) (*también* to take a ——) dar un paso

stepbrother *n* hermanastro

stepchild *n* (*pl* -children) hijastro -tra *mf*

stepdaughter *n* hijastra

stepfather *n* padrastro

stepmother *n* madrastra

stepsister *n* hermanastra

stepson *n* hijastro

sterile *adj* estéril

sterility *n* esterilidad *f*

sterilization *n* esterilización *f*

sterilize *vt* esterilizar

sternum *n* (*pl* -na) esternón *m*

steroid *adj & n* esteroide *m*

stethoscope *n* estetoscopio

stick *n* (*of a needle, cactus spine, etc.*) pinchazo, piquete *m* (*esp Mex*), picadura; **You are going to feel a stick.**.Va a sentir un pinchazo..Va a sentir un piquete; *vt* (*pret & pp* stuck) pinchar(se), picar(se) (*esp. Mex*); **How did you stick yourself?.** ¿Cómo se pinchó? **to** —— **out one's tongue** sacar la lengua..**Stick out your tongue.**.Saque la lengua.

sticker *n* (*bot*) espina, cadillo

sticky *adj* (*comp* -ier; *super* -iest) pegajoso

sties *pl de* **sty**

stiff *adj* rígido, tieso; **Do your hands feel stiff in the morning?.**¿Siente sus manos rígidas en la mañana?

stiffness *n* rigidez *f*

stillbirth *n* nacimiento de un niño muerto

stillborn *adj* nacido muerto

stimulant *n* estimulante *m*

stimulate *vt* estimular

stimulation *n* estimulación *f*

stimulus *n* (*pl* -li) estímulo

sting *n* piquete *m*, picadura; **Did you feel a sting?.**¿Sintió un piquete? **bee** —— picadura de abeja; *vt* (*pret & pp* stung) picar; *vi* arder; **The numbing medication will sting a little bit.**.El anestésico le va a arder un poco.

stingray *n* raya

stirrup *n* estribo

stitch *n* punto (de sutura); *vt* (*también* **to** —— **up**) suturar (*form*), coser

stocking *n* media

stomach *n* estómago; (*fam*) abdomen *m*; **pit of the** —— boca del estómago; **to be sick to one's** —— (*fam*) tener náusea(s)

stomachache *n* dolor *m* de estómago

stomatitis *n* estomatitis *f*

stone *n* cálculo (*form*), piedra; **kidney** —— cálculo renal (*form*), piedra del riñón

stood *pret & pp de* **stand**

stool *n* excremento, popó *or* pupú *m* (*fam*), caca (*esp. Carib, fam*)

stoop *vi* doblarse (hacia adelante), agacharse

stopped up, tapado; **My nose is stopped up.**.Tengo tapada la nariz.

stopper *n* tapón *m*

store *n* reserva, depósito; *vt* almacenar

strabismus *n* estrabismo

straight *adj* derecho, recto

straighten *vt* (*teeth, etc.*) enderezar; (*one's leg, arm*) estirar, extender, poner derecho; **Straighten your leg.**.Estire la pierna; *vi* enderezarse

strain *n* tensión *f*; (*of bacteria, etc.*) cepa; (*muscle, ligament, etc.*) dolor debido a uso excesivo o incorrecto; *vt* lastimar(se) (*un músculo o ligamento*) por uso excesivo o incorrecto; (*one's eyes, one's voice*) forzar (*la vista, la voz*); *vi* (*at stool*) pujar

straitjacket *n* camisa de fuerza

strangle *vt, vi* estrangular(se)

strangulate *vt* estrangular

strangulation *n* estrangulación *f*

strap *n* correa

streak *n* raya, línea

stream *n* (*of urine*) chorro

strength *n* fuerza, potencia; **double** —— fuerza doble; **extra** —— fuerza extra

strengthen *vt* fortalecer, reforzar

strenuous *adj* fuerte, vigoroso; **You should avoid strenuous activity for two weeks.**.Debe evitar actividades fuertes por dos semanas.

streptococcus *n* estreptococo

Streptococcus Streptococcus

streptokinase *n* estreptoquinasa

streptomycin *n* estreptomicina

stress *n* tensión *f*, estrés *m*; **under** —— bajo tensión, presionado

stressed *adj* bajo tensión, presionado

stretch *vt, vi* estirar(se)

stretcher *n* camilla

stretch mark *n* estría

stricture *n* estenosis *f* (*form*), estrechez *f*

strip *V.* **test strip.**

stroke *n* (*blow*) golpe *m*; (*cerebrovascular event*) derrame *m* cerebral, embolia

strong *adj* fuerte, potente

Strongyloides Strongyloides

strongyloidiasis *n* estrongiloidiasis *f*
strychnine *n* estricnina
stuck *pret & pp de* **stick**
student *n* estudiante *mf*
study *n* (*pl* -**dies**) estudio; **double-blind**
—— estudio doble ciego
stuffy, stuffed up *adj* tapado; **I have a**
stuffy nose..Tengo la nariz tapada.
stumble *vi* tropezar, dar un traspié
stump *n* (*anat*) muñón *m*
stun *vt* (*pret & pp* **stunned**; *ger* **stunning**)
atarantar, aturdir; **to become stunned**
atarantarse, aturdirse
stung *pret & pp de* **sting**
stupor *n* estupor *m*
stutter *vi* tartamudear
sty, stye *n* (*pl* **sties, styes**) orzuelo, perrilla
(*Mex, fam*)
subacute *adj* subagudo
subarachnoid *adj* subaracnoideo
subclavian *adj* subclavio
subclinical *adj* subclínico
subconscious *adj* subconsciente; *n* subconsciencia
subconsciousness *n* subconsciencia
subcutaneous *adj* subcutáneo
subdural *adj* subdural
sublimation *n* (*psych*) sublimación *f*
sublingual *adj* sublingual
subluxation *n* subluxación *f*
subspecialty *n* subespecialidad *f*
substance *n* substancia
substitute *n* substituto; *vt* substituir; **You**
can substitute tortillas for bread..Puede
substituir el pan por las tortillas (*Note that*
the two objects tortillas *and* bread *are*
inverted when translating to Spanish.
Observe que los dos objetos pan *y* tortillas
se invierten al traducir al inglés.)
subtract *vt, vi* (*arith*) restar, quitar; **Subtract**
seven from one hundred..Réstele siete a
cien.
suck *vt* chupar, (*at mother's breast*) mamar;
to —— **one's thumb** chuparse el dedo
suckle *vt* amamantar; *vi* mamar
sucralfate *n* sucralfato
suction *n* succión *f*
sudden *adj* repentino, súbito
suddenly *adv* de repente
sue *vt, vi* demandar
suffer *vt, vi* sufrir, padecer
suffering *n* sufrimiento
sufficient *adj* suficiente
suffocate *vt, vi* sofocar(se), asfixiar(se),
ahogar(se)
sugar *n* azúcar *m&f*
sugarless *adj* sin azúcar
suicidal *adj* (*act, idea, etc.*) suicida, (*person*)
con tendencias suicidas
suicide *n* suicidio; —— **attempt** intento de
suicidio; —— **gesture** intento de suicidio
sin mucha posibilidad de lograrlo; **to**

commit —— suicidarse
suit *n* demanda (*legal*)
sulfacetamide *n* sulfacetamida
sulfadiazine *n* sulfadiacina
sulfa drug *n* medicamento a base de sulfas
sulfamethoxazole *n* sulfametoxazol *m*
sulfasalazine *n* salazosulfapiridina
sulfate *n* sulfato
sulfisoxazole *n* sulfisoxazol *m*
sulfonamide *n* sulfonamida
sulfur *n* azufre *m*; —— **dioxide** bióxido *or*
dióxido de azufre
sulindac *n* sulindaco
summer *n* verano
sun *n* sol *m*; —— **lamp** lámpara bronceadora; **to get** —— asolearse, tomar el sol
sunburn *n* quemadura de sol; *vi* (*también* **to**
get sunburned *o* **sunburnt**) quemarse por
el sol; **Do you sunburn easily?**..¿Se
quema facilmente por el sol?
sunglasses *npl* lentes *mpl* para el sol, lentes
or anteojos oscuros, gafas de sol
sunlight *n* luz *f* del sol
sunscreen *n* filtro *or* protector *m* solar
sunstroke *n* insolación *f*
suntan *n* bronceado; **to get a** ——
broncearse
superego *n* (*pl* -**gos**) (*psych*) superego
superficial *adj* superficial
superior *adj* (*anat*) superior
supine *adj* supino, acostado boca arriba
supper *n* cena
supplement *n* suplemento
supplementary, supplemental *adj* suplementario
supply *n* surtido, suministro; *vt* suministrar,
proporcionar
support *n* apoyo; (*physical*) soporte *m*; ——
group grupo de apoyo, amigos y
familiares que apoyan a uno; **arch** ——
soporte para el arco del pie; *vt* apoyar
suppository *n* (*pl* -**ries**) supositorio
suppress *vt* suprimir
suppression *n* supresión *f*
sure *adj* seguro, cierto; **We have to make**
sure you don't have tuberculosis..Tene-
mos que estar seguros que no tiene
tuberculosis.
surface *n* superficie *f*
surfactant *n* surfactante *m*
surgeon *n* cirujano -na *mf*
surgery *n* (*pl* -**ries**) cirugía; **cosmetic** ——
cirugía cosmética *or* estética; **elective**
—— cirugía electiva; **general** ——
cirugía general; **major** —— cirugía
mayor; **minor** —— cirugía menor; **open**
heart —— cirugía de corazón abierto;
oral —— cirugía oral; **orthopedic** ——
cirugía ortopédica; **plastic** —— cirugía
plástica; **radical** —— cirugía radical;
reconstructive —— cirugía reconstructiva
surgical *adj* quirúrgico

surrogate mother n madre subrogada
survive vt, vi sobrevivir
susceptible adj susceptible, sensible
suspend vt suspender
suspension n suspensión f
sustained-release adj (pharm) de liberación sostenida
suture n sutura; vt suturar, coser (fam)
swab n hisopo, aplicador m
swallow vt tragar, pasar (esp. Mex); vi tragar, tragar saliva, pasar saliva; **Swallow, please**..Trague, por favor..Trague saliva, por favor..Pase saliva, por favor.
swam pret de swim
sweat n sudor m; vi (pret & pp **sweat** o **sweated**) sudar
sweater n suéter m
sweet adj dulce; n **sweets** dulces mpl
swell vi (pret **swelled**; pp **swelled** o **swollen**) hincharse; **Do your feet swell?**..¿Se le hinchan los pies?
swelling n hinchazón f
swim vi (pret **swam**; pp **swum**; ger **swimming**) nadar
swimmer's itch n dermatitis f de los bañistas, anquilostomiasis f (form)
swollen (pp de swell) adj hinchado
swum pp de swim
symmetrical, symmetric adj simétrico
symmetry n simetría
sympathectomy n simpatectomía
sympathetic adj compasivo, comprensivo; (neuro) simpático; —— **nervous system** sistema nervioso simpático
sympathy n compasión f
symphysis n (pl -ses) sínfisis f
symptom n síntoma m
synapse n sinapsis f
syncope n síncope m
syndrome n síndrome m; **acquired immunodeficiency** —— **(AIDS)** síndrome de inmunodeficiencia adquirida (SIDA); **adult respiratory distress** —— **(ARDS)** síndrome de insuficiencia respiratoria del adulto; **Asherman's** —— síndrome de Asherman; **attention deficit** —— síndrome del niño hiperactivo; **battered child** —— síndrome del niño maltratado; **carcinoid** —— síndrome carcinoide; **carpal tunnel** —— síndrome del túnel carpiano; **Cushing's** —— síndrome de Cushing; **DiGeorge** —— síndrome de DiGeorge; **Down's** —— síndrome de Down; **Ehlers-Danlos** —— síndrome de Ehlers-Danlos; **Felty's** —— síndrome de Felty; **fetal alcohol** —— síndrome alcohólico fetal; **Gilbert's** —— enfermedad f de Gilbert; **Gilles de la Tourette** —— síndrome de Gilles de la Tourette; **Guillain-Barré** —— síndrome de Guillain-Barré; **hemolytic-uremic** —— síndrome hemolítico-urémico; **hepatorenal**

—— síndrome hepatorrenal; **irritable bowel** —— síndrome del intestino irritable; **Kawasaki's** —— síndrome de Kawasaki; **Klinefelter's** —— síndrome de Klinefelter; **Korsakoff's** —— síndrome de Korsakoff; **malabsorption** —— síndrome de malabsorción; **Mallory-Weiss** —— síndrome de Mallory-Weiss; **Marfan's** —— síndrome de Marfan; **Ménière's** —— síndrome de Ménière; **nephrotic** —— síndrome nefrótico; **organic brain** —— síndrome cerebral orgánico; **Osler-Rendu-Weber** —— síndrome de Osler-Rendu-Weber; **Peutz-Jeghers** —— síndrome de Peutz-Jeghers; **Pickwickian** —— síndrome de Pickwick; **postconcussional** —— síndrome de cefalea postraumática; **premenstrual** —— síndrome premenstrual; **Reiter's** —— síndrome de Reiter; **restless legs** —— síndrome de piernas inquietas; **Reye's** —— síndrome de Reye; **Sheehan's** —— síndrome de Sheehan; **sick sinus** —— síndrome del seno enfermo; **Sjögren's** —— síndrome de Sjögren; **staphylococcal scalded skin** —— síndrome estafilocócico de piel escaldada; **Stevens-Johnson** —— síndrome de Stevens-Johnson; **sudden infant death (SIDS)** síndrome de muerte súbita infantil; **toxic shock** —— síndrome del choque tóxico; **Turner's** —— síndrome de Turner; **von Willebrand's** —— enfermedad f de von Willebrand
synergy n sinergia
synovial adj sinovial
synovitis n sinovitis f
synthesize vt sintetizar
synthetic adj sintético
syphillis n sífilis f
syringe n jeringa, jeringuilla (esp. Carib); **bulb** —— perilla, pera
syringomyelia n siringomielia
syrup n jarabe m; **cough** —— jarabe para la tos
system n sistema m; **autonomic nervous** —— sistema nervioso autónomo; **cardiovascular** —— sistema cardiovascular; **central nervous** —— **(CNS)** sistema nervioso central (SNC); **digestive** —— sistema digestivo; **endocrine** —— sistema endocrino; **musculoskeletal** —— sistema musculoesquelético; **parasympathetic nervous** —— sistema nervioso parasimpático; **peripheral nervous** —— sistema nervioso periférico; **reproductive** —— sistema reproductor; **respiratory** —— sistema respiratorio; **skeletal** —— sistema esquelético; **sympathetic nervous** —— sistema nervioso simpático
systemic adj sistémico
systolic adj sistólico

tab 61 ter

T

table *n* mesa; **examining** —— mesa de exploración *(form)*, mesa de exámenes; **operating** —— mesa de operaciones, mesa de cirugía
tablespoonful *n (pl* **-fuls)** cucharada
tablet *n* tableta
taboo *n (pl* **taboos)** tabú *m*
tachycardia *n* taquicardia
taenia, tenia *n* tenia
tailbone *n (fam)* coccix *m*, colita
take *vt (pret* **took;** *pp* **taken)** tomar; **to** —— **off** *(clothing, etc.)* quitarse; **Take off your shirt.**.Quítese la camisa; **to** —— **out** extraer *(form)*, sacar; **We have to take out your appendix.**.Tenemos que sacarle el apéndice.
talc *n* talco
talcum powder *n* talco, polvos de talco
tall *adj* alto; **How tall are you?.**.¿Qué altura tiene?
tamoxifen *n* tamoxifén *m*
tampon *n* tampón *m*
tamponade *n* taponamiento; **cardiac** —— taponamiento cardiaco
tan *adj & n* bronceado; *vi (pret & pp* **tanned;** *ger* **tanning)** *(también* **to get a** ——**)** broncearse
tantrum *n* berrinche *m*
tap *n (procedure to extract fluid)* punción *f*; **spinal** —— punción lumbar; *vt (pret & pp* **tapped;** *ger* **tapping)** puncionar *(form)*, hacer una punción
tape *n (for dressings)* tela, cinta; —— **measure** *o* **measuring** —— cinta métrica
tapeworm *n* tenia, solitaria
tar *n* alquitrán *m*
tarantula *n* tarántula
tardive dyskinesia *n* discinesia tardía
tarsal *adj* tarsal
tartar *n* tártaro *(form)*, sarro (dental)
tartaric acid *n* ácido tartárico
taste *n* sabor *m*, gusto; —— **bud** papila gustativa; *vt (to try)* probar; **Taste it.**.Pruébelo...**Can you taste all right?.**.¿Distingue bien los sabores? *vi* saber; **This medicine doesn't taste bad.**.Esta medicina no sabe mal; **to** —— **like** saber a
tattoo *n (pl* **-toos)** tatuaje *m*
taught *pret & pp de* **teach**
tea *n* té *m*
teach *vt (pret & pp* **taught)** enseñar
teacher *n* maestro -tra *mf*
team *n (of health workers, etc.)* equipo

tear *n (from crying)* lágrima
tear *n (muscle, ligament, etc.)* desgarro, desgarre *m*, desgarramiento; *vt, vi (pret* **tore;** *pp* **torn)** desgarrar(se)
teaspoonful *n (pl* **-fuls)** cucharadita
technician *n* técnico -ca *mf*
technique *n* técnica, método
technology *n* tecnología
teenager *n* joven *mf* de 13 a 19 años
teeth *pl de* **tooth**
teethe *vi* salirle los dientes; **Is he teething yet?.**.¿Le están saliendo los dientes ya?
teething *n* dentición *f (form)*, salida de los dientes
telangiectasia *n* telangiectasia
telemetry *n* telemetría
telephone *n* teléfono; **to call by** —— llamar por teléfono, telefonear
temperament *n* temperamento
temperature *n* temperatura; *(fam)* fiebre; **Did you take your temperature at home?.**.¿Se tomó la temperatura en la casa? **room** —— temperatura ambiente
temple *n (anat)* sien *f*
temporal *adj* temporal
temporary *adj* temporal, transitorio; **This bandage is only temporary.**.Este vendaje es solo temporal.
temporomandibular *adj* temporomandibular
tendency *n (pl* **-cies)** tendencia
tender *adj (sore, painful)* adolorido *or* dolorido, doloroso
tenderness *n* dolor *m (al tocar)*
tendinitis *n* tendonitis *f*
tendon *n* tendón *m*; **Achilles** —— tendón de Aquiles
tendonitis *var de* **tendinitis**
tennis elbow *n* codo de tenista
tenosynovitis *n* tenosinovitis *f*
tense *adj* tenso; *vt (one's muscles)* poner tenso *(los músculos)*; *vi* **to** —— **up** ponerse tenso; **Try not to tense up, señorita.**.Trate de no ponerse tensa, señorita.
tension *n* tensión *f*; **nervous** —— tensión nerviosa
tent *n* tienda; **oxygen** —— tienda de oxígeno
tepid *adj* tibio
teratoma *n* teratoma *m*
terbutaline *n* terbutalina
term *n* término; **at** —— **a** término
terminal *adj* terminal
tertiary *adj* del tercer nivel

test *n* prueba, examen *m*; **blood** —— prueba de sangre; **exercise stress** —— prueba de esfuerzo; **eye** —— examen de la vista; **glucose tolerance** —— prueba de tolerancia a la glucosa; **hearing** —— prueba de la audición; **patch** —— prueba del parche; **pregnancy** —— prueba de embarazo; **pulmonary function** —— prueba de función pulmonar; **skin** —— prueba cutánea; **TB** —— prueba de la tuberculosis; **urine** —— prueba de la orina; *vt* examinar, probar

test strip *n* tira reactiva

test tube *n* tubo de ensayo

testicle *n* testículo, huevo (*vulg, usually pl*), cojón *m* (*vulg, usually pl*); **undescended** —— testículo no descendido

testosterone *n* testosterona

tetanus *n* tétanos *m*

tetracycline *n* tetraciclina

tetrahydrocannabinol (THC) *n* tetrahidrocanabinol *m*

tetralogy of Fallot *n* tetralogía de Fallot

texture *n* textura

thalamus *n* tálamo

thalassemia *n* talasemia, talasanemia

thallium *n* talio

THC *V.* **tetrahydrocannabinol**.

theophylline *n* teofilina

theory *n* (*pl* -ries) teoría

therapeutic *adj* terapéutico

therapist *n* terapista *mf*, terapeuta *mf* (*form*); (*fam*) psicoterapista *mf*

therapy *n* (*pl* -pies) terapia, terapéutica (*form*); **electroconvulsive** —— (**ECT**) terapia electrochoque *or* electroconvulsiva (**TEC**); **group** —— terapia de grupo; **occupational** —— terapia ocupacional; **physical** —— terapia física; **radiation** —— radioterapia; **respiratory** —— terapia respiratoria; **speech** —— terapia del habla

thermal *adj* termal

thermometer *n* termómetro; **oral** —— termómetro bucal *or* oral; **rectal** —— termómetro rectal

thiabendazole *n* tiabendazol *m*

thiamine *n* tiamina

thick *adj* (*dimension*) grueso; (*consistency*) espeso

thickness *n* (*dimension*) espesor *m*, grosor *m*; (*consistency*) espesura, espesor *m*, viscosidad *f*

thigh *n* muslo

thin *adj* (*comp* **thinner**; *super* **thinnest**) delgado, flaco; (*hair*) ralo, escaso; **to become** —— enflaquecerse

think *vt, vi* (*pret & pp* **thought**) pensar

thinner *n* tíner *m*; **blood** —— (*fam*) anticoagulante *m*

thioridazine *n* tioridacina

thirst *n* sed *f*

thirsty *adj* **to be** —— tener sed

thistle *n* cardo

thoracic *adj* torácico

thoracotomy *n* (*pl* -mies) toracotomía

thorax *n* tórax *m*

thorn *n* espina

thought (*pret & pp de* **think**) *n* pensamiento

three-day measles *n* sarampión *m* alemán, rubeola *or* rubéola (*form*)

threonine *n* treonina

threshold *n* umbral *m*

threw *pret de* **throw**

throat *n* garganta; **sore** —— dolor *m* de garganta

throb *vi* (*pret & pp* **throbbed**; *ger* **throbbing**) latir, pulsar; **Is your head throbbing?**..¿Le late la cabeza?..¿Le pulsa la cabeza?

throbbing (*ger de* **throb**) *adj* pulsante, pulsátil, que late

thrombectomy *n* (*pl* -mies) trombectomía

thrombocytopenia *n* trombocitopenia

thromboembolism *n* (*pl* -li) tromboembolia

thrombophlebitis *n* tromboflebitis *f*

thrombosis *n* (*pl* -ses) trombosis *f*

thrombus *n* (*pl* -bi) trombo

throw *vt, vi* (*pret* **threw**; *pp* **thrown**) **to —— up** arrojar, devolver, deponer (*Mex*), tener basca, vomitar

thrush *n* algodoncillo, sapo (*PR, SD*)

thumb *n* pulgar *m*, dedo gordo

thumbnail *n* uña del pulgar

thump *n* precordial —— golpe precordial *or* torácico

thymoma *n* timoma *m*

thymus *n* (*pl* -muses *o* -mi) timo

thyroglobulin *n* tiroglobulina

thyroid *adj* tiroideo; —— **storm** crisis tiroidea; *n* (*gland*) tiroides *m&f*

thyroidectomy *n* (*pl* -mies) tiroidectomía

thyroiditis *n* tiroiditis *f*; **Hashimoto's** —— tiroiditis de Hashimoto; **subacute** —— tiroiditis subaguda

thyrotoxic *adj* tirotóxico

thyrotoxicosis *n* tirotoxicosis *f*

thyrotropin (TSH) *n* tirotropina

thyroxine *n* tiroxina

tibia *n* tibia

tic *n* tic *m*; —— **douloureux** tic doloroso

tick *n* garrapata

tickle *n* cosquilleo; *vt* causar cosquillas, dar *or* hacer cosquillas; **Am I tickling you?**..¿Le causo cosquillas?

tickling *n* cosquillas, cosquilleo

ticklish *adj* cosquilloso

tight *adj* apretado

time *n* tiempo, vez *f*; (*by the clock*) hora; **all the time** todo el tiempo; **a long** —— mucho tiempo; **a short** —— un rato, poco tiempo; **at times** a veces; **each** —— *o* **every** —— cada vez; **four times a day** cuatro veces al día; **from** —— **to** —— de

vez en cuando; **in** —— (*eventually*) con el tiempo; **one** —— una vez; **next** —— la próxima vez; **partial thromboplastin** —— (PTT) tiempo parcial de tromboplastina; **prothrombin** —— (PT) tiempo de protrombina; **the first** —— la primera vez; **the last** —— la última vez
timed release *n* (*pharm*) difusión regulada
timid *adj* tímido
timolol *n* timolol *m*
tincture *n* tintura
tinea *n* tiña *or* tinea; —— **capitis** tiña de la cabeza; —— **corporis** tiña del cuerpo; —— **cruris** tiña inguinal; —— **pedis** tiña del pie; —— **versicolor** tiña versicolor
tingle *vi* hormiguear
tingling *n* hormigueo
tip *n* (*tongue, finger, etc.*) punta
tire *vt, vi* (*también* **to** —— **out**) cansar(se); **Just walking to the bathroom tires him out**..Con solo caminar al baño se cansa.
tired *adj* (*también* —— **out**) cansado; **to get** —— cansarse
tiredness *n* cansancio, fatiga
tirosine *n* tirosina
tissue *n* tejido; (*for blowing one's nose*) pañuelo de papel; **connective** —— tejido conectivo *or* conjuntivo; **granulation** —— tejido de granulación; **soft** —— tejido blando
tissue plasminogen activator (tPA) *n* activador *m* del plasminógeno tisular
titer *n* título
tobacco *n* (*pl* -cos *o* -coes) tabaco; —— **use** tabaquismo
tocopherol *n* tocoferol *m*
today *adv* hoy
toe *n* dedo (del pie); **big** —— dedo gordo (del pie); **little** —— dedo chico (del pie)
toenail *n* uña (*de un dedo del pie*)
toilet *n* inodoro, excusado; —— **bowl** taza del inodoro *or* excusado; —— **paper** papel sanitario *or* higiénico; —— **training** (*ped*) (el) enseñar a usar el baño
tolbutamide *n* tolbutamida
tolerance *n* tolerancia
tolerate *vt* tolerar, aguantar
toluene *n* tolueno
tomogram *n* tomograma *m*, tomografía
tomography *n* tomografía; **computed** —— (CT) tomografía computada (TC); **computerized axial** —— (CAT) tomografía axial computarizada (TAC); **positron emission** —— (PET) tomografía por emisión de positrones (TEP)
tomorrow *adv* mañana
tone *n* tono; **muscle** —— tono muscular
tongue *n* lengua; —— **depressor** *o* **blade** bajalenguas *m*, depresor *m*, abatelenguas *m* (*Mex*), paleta (*fam*)
tonic *adj & n* tónico
tonsil *n* amígdala, angina (*Mex, fam, usually pl*)

tonsillectomy *n* (*pl* -mies) amigdalectomía
tonsillitis *n* amigdalitis *f*
took *pret de* **take**
tooth *n* (*pl* **teeth**) diente *m*, muela; **baby** —— diente de leche; **back** —— muela; **canine** —— (diente) canino, colmillo (*fam*); **false teeth** dientes postizos, dentaduras postizas; **front** —— diente, diente incisivo (*form*); **set of teeth** dentadura; **wisdom** —— muela del juicio
toothache *n* dolor *m* de muelas, (*front tooth*) dolor de dientes
toothbrush *n* cepillo de dientes
toothpaste *n* pasta dental
tophus *n* (*pl* -phi) tofo
topical *adj* tópico
tore *pret de* **tear**
torn *pp de* **tear**
torsion *n* torsión *f*
torticollis *n* tortícolis *f*
torture *n* tortura; *vt* torturar
torus *n* torus *m*; —— **palatinus** torus palatino
total *adj & n* total *m*
touch *n* (*sense*) tacto; *vt* tocar
tough *adj* duro, correoso
tourniquet *n* torniquete *m*
towel *n* toalla
toxemia *n* toxemia
toxemic *adj* toxémico
toxic *adj* tóxico; —— **epidermal necrolysis** necrólisis tóxica epidérmica
toxicity *n* toxicidad *f*
toxicologist *n* toxicólogo -ga *mf*
toxicology *n* toxicología
toxin *n* toxina
toxocariasis *n* toxocariasis *f*
toxoid *n* toxoide *m*; **diphtheria** —— toxoide diftérico; **tetanus** —— toxoide tetánico
toxoplasmosis *n* toxoplasmosis *f*
tPA *V.* **tissue plasminogen activator.**
TPN *abbr* total parenteral nutrition. *V.* **nutrition.**
trace *n* trazas; **There is a trace of protein in your urine**..Hay trazas de proteína en su orina.
trachea *n* (*pl* -cheae) tráquea
tracheitis *n* traqueítis *f*
tracheobronchitis *n* traqueobronquitis *f*
tracheostomy *n* (*pl* -mies) traqueostomía
tracheotomy *n* (*pl* -mies) traqueotomía
trachoma *n* tracoma *m*
tracing *n* (*EKG, etc.*) trazo, registro
tracks *npl* (*from drug addiction*) marcas
tract *n* tracto, vía, fascículo, haz *m*; **biliary** —— vías biliares; **corticospinal** —— vía corticoespinal; **gastrointestinal** —— tubo digestivo; **pyramidal** —— vía piramidal; **respiratory** —— tracto respiratorio; **spinothalamic** —— vía espinotalámica; **urinary** —— tracto urinario

traction n tracción f
train vt, vi entrenar(se)
training n entrenamiento
trait n característica
trance n trance m
tranquilize vt tranquilizar
tranquilizer n tranquilizante m
transfer vt (a patient) trasladar
transference n (psych) transferencia
transfuse vt hacer una transfusión, poner sangre (fam)
transfusion n transfusión f; **to give a** ⸺ hacer una transfusión, poner sangre (fam); **I need to give you a transfusion**..Tengo que hacerle una transfusión..Tengo que ponerle sangre...**Have you ever had a tranfusion before?**..¿Le han hecho una transfusión alguna vez antes?..¿Le han puesto sangre alguna vez antes?
transient adj transitorio, pasajero
translate vt traducir
translocation n translocación f
transmission n transmisión f
transmit vt (pret & pp -mitted; ger -mitting) transmitir
transparent adj transparente
transplant n trasplante m; vt trasplantar
transport n transporte m; vt transportar
transsexual adj & n transexual mf
transvestite n transvestista mf
trapezius n trapecio
trauma n traumatismo, trauma m; (psych) trauma
traumatic adj traumático
traumatize vt traumatizar
trazodone n trazodona
tray n bandeja, charola (Mex)
treat vt (illness, patient) tratar
treatment n tratamiento
tremble vi temblar
tremor n temblor m
tremulous adj tembloroso
trench mouth n angina or enfermedad f de Vincent
trend n tendencia
treponeme n treponema
tretinoin n tretinoína
triage n evaluación f inicial de pacientes de emergencia para establecer prioridades
trial n ensayo, prueba
triamcinolone n triamcinolona
triamterene n triamtereno
triazolam n triazolam m
triceps n tríceps m
trichinosis n triquinosis f
Trichomonas Trichomonas
trichomoniasis n tricomoniasis f
tricuspid adj tricúspide
tried pret de try
tries pl de try
trifluoperazine n trifluoperacina
trigeminal adj trigémino; ⸺ **neuralgia**

neuralgia del trigémino
trigger vt provocar
trigger finger n dedo de gatillo
trigger point n punto doloroso
triglyceride n triglicérido
trimester n trimestre m
trimethoprim n trimetoprim m
trip vi tropezar, dar un traspié
triplet n trillizo -za mf
trismus n trismo
trisomy n trisomía; ⸺ **21** trisomía 21
trivalent adj trivalente
trochanter n trocánter m
troche n trocisco, pastilla para chupar
tropical adj tropical
trouble n molestia; **Do you have trouble with your back?**..¿Tiene molestias con su espalda?
trousers npl pantalón m (often pl)
trunk n (anat) tronco
truss n faja abdominal
trust n confianza; vt tener confianza en, confiar en
trypanosomiasis n tripanosomiasis f
trypsin n tripsina
tryptophan n triptófano
TSH abbr **thyroid-stimulating hormone.** V. **hormone.**
TTP abbr **thrombotic thrombocytopenic purpura.** V. **purpura.**
tube n tubo, sonda, manguera, trompa, conducto; **auditory** ⸺ conducto auditivo; **drainage** ⸺ tubo de drenaje; **endotracheal** ⸺ tubo endotraqueal; **Eustachian** ⸺ trompa de Eustaquio; **fallopian** ⸺ trompa de Falopio; **feeding** ⸺ sonda para alimentación; **nasogastric** ⸺ sonda nasogástrica; **ventilating** ⸺ tubo de ventilación
tuberculosis n tuberculosis f
tubing n tubería
tubular adj tubular
tubule n túbulo
tularemia n tularemia
tummy n (ped) estómago, barriguita
tumor n tumor m; **Wilms'** ⸺ tumor de Wilms
tuning fork n diapasón m
tunnel n túnel m
turbid adj turbio
turn n vuelta; vi darse vuelta; **to** ⸺ **around** darse (media) vuelta; **to** ⸺ **blue, stiff, numb, etc.** ponerse azul, tieso, dormido, etc.; **Did he turn blue?**..¿Se puso azul? **to** ⸺ **out** resultar, salir; **The tests turned out negative**..Las pruebas resultaron negativas; **to** ⸺ **over** voltearse, darse vuelta; **Turn over faceup**..Voltéese boca arriba.
turpentine n trementina
tweezers npl pinzas
twin adj & n gemelo -la mf, mellizo -za mf;

fraternal twins gemelos fraternos, gemelos que no se parecen; **identical twins** gemelos idénticos; **Siamese twins** hermanos -nas siameses *mf*
twinge *n* punzada, dolor agudo y repentino
twist *vt, vi (one's ankle, etc.)* torcer(se); **Did you twist your neck?**..¿Se le torció el cuello?
twitch *n* contracción espasmódica, sacudida

repentina; *vi* contraer espasmódicamente
tympanic *adj* timpánico; —— **membrane** membrana timpánica
type *n* tipo; **blood** —— grupo sanguíneo *(form)*, tipo de sangre
typhus *n* tifus *m*, tifo
typical *adj* típico
tyramine *n* tiramina
tyrosine *n* tirosina

U

ulcer *n* úlcera, llaga; **decubitus** —— úlcera de decúbito; **duodenal** —— úlcera duodenal; **gastric** —— úlcera gástrica; **stress** —— úlcera de estrés
ulna *n* cúbito
ulnar *adj* cubital
ultrasonography *n* ultrasonografía
ultrasound *n* ultrasonido
ultraviolet *adj* ultravioleta
umbilical cord *n* cordón *m* umbilical
umbilicus *n (pl* **-ci)** ombligo
unable *adj* incapaz
unavoidable *adj* inevitable
unbreakable *adj* irrompible
unbuckle *vt* desabrochar(se), desabotonar(se)
unbutton *vt* desabrochar(se), desabotonar(se); **Unbutton your shirt**..Desabróchese la camisa.
uncle *n* tío
uncomfortable *adj* incómodo
uncommon *adj* poco común
unconscious *adj* inconsciente
underachiever *n* persona que no logra su potencial
underpants *npl (men's)* calzoncillos; *(women's)* calzón *m (often pl)*, pantaletas *(Mex)*, bloomer *m (esp. CA)*, panties *mpl (esp. Carib)*
undershirt *n* camiseta
underwear *n* ropa interior
undifferentiated *adj* indiferenciado
uneasy *adj (comp* **-ier**; *super* **-iest)** inquieto
unexpected *adj* inesperado
unhappy *adj* infeliz
uniform *adj* uniforme; *n* uniforme *m*
unit *n* unidad *f*; **coronary care** —— unidad de cuidado coronario; **intensive care** —— **(ICU)** unidad de cuidados intensivos **(UCI)**, unidad de terapia intensiva;

international —— unidad internacional
unpleasant *adj* desagradable
unresponsive *adj* que no responde
unsaturated *adj* no saturado, insaturado
unstable *adj* inestable
unusual *adj* raro, extraño
upper *adj (anat)* superior, de arriba
upset *adj* alterado, trastornado; *(stomach)* revuelto; **I have an upset stomach**..Tengo revuelto el estómago; **to become** —— alterarse, trastornarse; *vt (pret & pp* **upset**; *ger* **upsetting)** alterar, trastornar
upward *adv* hacia arriba
urban *adj* urbano
urea *n* urea
uremia *n* uremia
uremic *adj* urémico
ureter *n* uréter *m*
urethra *n* uretra
urethritis *n* uretritis *f*; **non-gonococcal** —— uretritis no gonocócica
urgent *adj* urgente
uric acid *n* ácido úrico
urinal *n (hand-held)* orinal *m*, pato
urinalysis *n (pl* **-ses)** examen *m* general de orina, prueba de la orina
urinary *adj* urinario
urinate *vi* orinar, *(ped)* hacer pipí
urine *n* orina
urodynamics *n* urodinámica
urogenital *adj* urogenital
urogram *n* urograma *m*, urografía
urography *n* urografía; **excretory** —— urografía excretoria; **retrograde** —— urografía retrógrada
urokinase *n* urokinasa
urologist *n* urólogo -ga *mf*
urology *n* urología
urosepsis *n* urosepsis *f*

urticaria *n* urticaria
Uruguayan *adj & n* uruguayo -ya *mf*
use *n* uso; *vt* usar; to —— up usar todo,
agotar
useless *adj* inútil
user *n* usuario -ria *mf*
usual *adj* usual; as —— como de
costumbre, como siempre; **Are you taking
your insulin as usual?**..¿Está tomando su

insulina como de costumbre? **than** ——
que de costumbre; **Are you drinking
more liquids than usual?**..¿Está tomando
más líquidos que de costumbre?
uterus *n* (*pl* -ri) útero, matriz *f*
uvea *n* úvea
uveitis *n* uveítis *f*
uvula *n* (*pl* -las *o* -lae) úvula, campanilla

V

vaccinate *vt* vacunar
vaccination *n* vacunación *f*
vaccine *n* vacuna; **BCG** ——, **DPT** ——,
Salk ——, etc. vacuna BCG, vacuna
DPT, vacuna Salk, etc.; **mumps** ——,
rabies ——, etc. vacuna contra las
paperas, vacuna contra la rabia, etc.
vacuum *n* vacío
vagal *adj* vagal
vagina *n* vagina
vaginal *adj* vaginal
vaginitis *n* vaginitis *f*
vagotomy *n* (*pl* -mies) vagotomía; **selective**
—— vagotomía selectiva
vagus *n* (*pl* vagi) vago
valgus *adj* valgus, valgo
valine *n* valina
valproic acid *n* ácido valpróico
value *n* valor *m*
valve *n* válvula; **aortic** —— válvula aórtica;
mitral —— válvula mitral; **pulmonic**
—— válvula pulmonar; **pyloric** ——
válvula pilórica; **tricuspid** —— válvula
tricúspide
valvuloplasty *n* (*pl* -ties) valvuloplastia *or*
(*esp. spoken*) valvuloplastía
vancomycin *n* vancomicina
vapor *n* vapor *m*
vaporizer *n* vaporizador *m*
variable *adj & n* variable *f*
variant *adj & n* variante *f*
variation *n* variación *f*
varicella *n* varicela
varices *pl de* varix
varicose vein *n* vena varicosa
varix *n* (*pl* -ices) várice *f* (*en inglés se
emplea casi siempre la forma plural:*
varices)
varus *adj* varus, varo
vary *vi* variar

vascular *adj* vascular
vasculitis *n* vasculitis *f*; **hypersensitivity**
—— vasculitis por hipersensibilidad;
necrotizing —— vasculitis necrosante
vas deferens *n* conducto deferente
vasectomy *n* (*pl* -mies) vasectomía
vasoconstriction *n* vasoconstricción *f*
vasoconstrictor *n* vasoconstrictor *m*
vasodilation *n* vasodilatación *f*
vasodilator *n* vasodilatador *m*
vasopressin *n* vasopresina
vasospasm *n* vasospasmo *or* vasoespasmo
vasovagal *adj* vasovagal
VD *abbr* venereal disease. *V.* disease.
VDRL *n* VDRL *m*
vector *n* vector *m*
vegetable *n* vegetal *m*, verdura; —— **oil**
aceite *m* de vegetal
vegetarian *adj & n* vegetariano -na *mf*
vegetarianism *n* vegetarianismo
vegetation *n* vegetación *f*
vegetative *adj* vegetativo
vehicle *n* vehículo
vein *n* vena; **antecubital** —— vena
antecubital; **external jugular** —— vena
yugular externa; **femoral** —— vena
femoral; **internal jugular** —— vena
yugular interna; **portal** —— vena porta;
saphenous —— vena safena; **subclavian**
—— vena subclavia; **varicose** —— vena
varicosa
vein stripping *n* extracción *f* de várices *or*
venas varicosas
vena cava *n* vena cava; **inferior** —— ——
vena cava inferior; **superior** —— ——
vena cava superior
venereal *adj* (*ant*) venéreo
Venezuelan *adj & n* venezolano -na *mf*
venogram *n* flebografía, flebograma *m*,
venograma *m*

venography n flebografía
venom n veneno
venous adj venoso
ventilation n ventilación f
ventilator n ventilador m
ventral adj ventral
ventricle n ventrículo
venule n vénula
verapamil n verapamil m
vermicide n vermicida m
vernix caseosa n vérnix caseosa
vertebra n (pl -brae o -bras) vértebra
vertebral column n columna vertebral, columna (fam)
vertigo n vértigo
vesicle n vesícula
vessel n vaso; **blood** —— vaso sanguíneo
veterinarian n veterinario -ria mf
veterinary adj veterinario
viable adj viable
vibration n vibración f
vice n vicio
victim n víctima
vigorous adj vigoroso
vinblastine n vinblastina
vincristine n vincristina
vinegar n vinagre m
violence n violencia
violent adj violento
violet adj violeta
viper n víbora
viral adj viral, vírico
virgin adj & n virgen mf
virginity n virginidad f
virilization n virilización f
virology n virología
virulence n virulencia
virulent adj virulento
virus n (pl **viruses**) virus m; **Epstein-Barr** —— (EBV) virus de Epstein-Barr; **human immunodeficiency** —— (HIV) virus de inmunodeficiencia humana (VIH)

visceral adj visceral
viscosity n viscosidad f
viscous adj viscoso
visible adj visible
vision n vista, visión f; **blurred** —— vista empañada, visión borrosa; **double** —— visión or vista doble; **nocturnal** o **night** —— vista or visión nocturna; **peripheral** —— visión periférica; **tunnel** —— visión en túnel
visit n visita; vt, vi visitar
visiting hours npl horas de visita
visitor n visita, visitante mf
visual adj visual
visualize vt formar una imagen mental
visualization n formación f de una imagen mental
vital adj vital
vitamin adj vitamínico; n vitamina; —— **A, B₁₂, etc.** vitamina A, B₁₂, etc.; **fat-soluble** —— vitamina liposoluble; **water-soluble** —— vitamina hidrosoluble
vitiligo n vitíligo
vocal adj vocal; —— **cord** cuerda vocal
voice n voz f
void vi vaciar la vejiga, orinar
volt n voltio
volume n volumen m
voluntary adj voluntario
volunteer n voluntario -ria mf
volvulus n vólvulo
vomit n vómito; vt, vi vomitar, arrojar (fam), devolver (fam), deponer (Mex, fam), tener basca (fam); **Did you vomit blood?**..¿Vomitó sangre?
voodoo n vudú m
voyeurism n voyeurismo
VSD abbr **ventricular septal defect.** V. defect.
vulnerable adj vulnerable
vulva n (pl -vae) vulva

W

waist *n* cintura
wait *vi* esperar; **to** —— **for** esperar
waiting list *n* lista de espera
waiting room *n* sala de espera
wake *vt, vi (pret* **waked** *o* **woke;** *pp* **waked)**
    (también **to** —— **up)** despertar(se)
walk *vi* caminar, andar; **to** —— **in one's**
    sleep caminar dormido
walker *n* andadera
war *n* guerra; **nuclear** —— guerra nuclear
ward *n (of a hospital)* sala; —— **clerk**
    secretaria de sala
warfarin *n* warfarina
warm *adj* caliente; **to be** *o* **feel** —— tener
    or sentir calor; *vt, vi (también* **to** —— **up)**
    calentar(se); **to** —— **up** *(before*
    exercising) hacer calentamiento
warmth *n* calor *m*
warmup *n* calentamiento
wart *n* verruga; **genital** —— verruga
    genital; **plantar** —— verruga plantar
wash *vt* lavar; *(to bathe)* bañar; **to** ——
    one's hair, face, hands, etc. lavarse la
    cabeza *or* el pelo, la cara, las manos, etc.;
    vi bañarse
washable *adj* lavable
wasp *n* avispa
wastes *npl* desechos, desperdicios;
    hazardous —— desechos peligrosos;
    metabolic —— desechos metabólicos
water *n* agua; —— **on the lung, knee, etc.**
    agua en el pulmón, la rodilla, etc.;
    distilled —— agua destilada; **fresh** ——
    agua dulce; **hard** —— agua con alto
    contenido de minerales; **mineral** ——
    agua mineral; **purified** —— agua
    purificada; **running** —— agua corriente;
    salt —— agua salada; **soft** —— agua con
    escaso contenido de minerales; **tap** ——
    agua de la llave *or* del grifo
water-borne *adj* transmitido por el agua
wave *n* onda; **brain** —— onda cerebral
wavelength *n* longitud *f* de onda
wax *n* cera
weak *adj* débil
weaken *vt, vi* debilitar(se)
weakening *n* debilitación *f*, decaimiento
weakness *n* debilidad *f*
wean *vt* destetar
weaning *n* destete *m*
weapon *n* arma; **sharp** —— arma blanca
wear *vt (pret* **wore;** *pp* **worn)** llevar; *vi* **to**
    —— **off** pasar; **The numbness will wear**
    off in a couple hours.. Lo dormido se le

va a pasar en un par de horas.
weather *n* tiempo, clima *m*
web *n* membrana; **esophageal** ——
    membrana esofágica
week *n* semana
weekend *n* fin *m* de semana
weigh *vt, vi* pesar; **How much did you**
    weigh six months ago?..¿Cuánto pesaba
    hace seis meses?...¿**Did the nurse weigh**
    you?..¿Lo pesó la enfermera?
weight *n* peso; **birth** —— peso al
    nacimiento, peso al nacer; **excess** ——
    sobrepeso
welfare *n* bienestar *m*, bien *m*; asistencia
    social, asistencia pública
well *adj & adv (comp* **better;** *super* **best)**
    bien; **to get** —— aliviarse, curarse
wellbeing *n* bienestar *m*
wet *adj (comp* **wetter;** *super* **wettest)**
    mojado; **to get** —— mojarse; *vt (pret &*
    pp **wet** *o* **wetted;** *ger* **wetting)** mojar; **to**
    —— **the bed** orinarse en la cama
wet dream *n* sueño húmedo *or* mojado
wet nurse *n* nodriza
wheal *n* roncha
wheat *n* trigo
wheelchair *n* silla de ruedas
wheeze *n* sibilancia *(form)*, chillido, silbido;
    vi chillarle *or* silbarle el pecho, tener
    chillidos *or* silbidos; **Are you**
    wheezing?..¿Le chilla el pecho?..¿Tiene
    silbidos?
whiplash *n* lesión *f* por latigazo
whipworm *n* tricocéfalo
whiskers *npl* pelitos de la cara del hombre
    que no se ha afeitado
white *adj* blanco; *n (of an egg)* clara *(del*
    huevo)
whitlow *n* panadizo
whole *adj* entero; —— **wheat** trigo integral
    or entero
whooping cough *n* tos ferina, coqueluche
    m&f
wick *n* mecha
wide *adj* ancho
widen *vt* ensanchar, hacer más ancho
widow *n* viuda
widowed *adj* viudo
widower *n* viudo
wife *n (pl* **wives)** esposa, señora
wig *n* peluca
wiggle *vt, vi* mover(se); **Wiggle your**
    toes.. Mueva los dedos del pie.
will *n* voluntad *f*; —— **power** fuerza de

voluntad; **against one's** —— contra la voluntad de uno; **of one's own free** —— por voluntad propia

wind *n* viento

windburn *n* resequedad de la piel debida al viento

windpipe *n* gaznate *m*, tráquea

winter *n* invierno

wipe *vt* enjugar; **to** —— *(oneself)* *(after moving bowels)* limpiarse, asearse; **You should wipe from front to back**..Debe limpiarse de adelante hacia atrás.

wire *n* alambre *m*

wired *adj (vulg)* acelerado

witch hazel *n* agua de hamamelis

witchcraft *n* brujería

withdrawal *n* síndrome *m* de abstinencia *(form)*, síntomas sufridos por el adicto al suspender drogas o alcohol

wives *pl de* **wife**

woman *n (pl* **women**) mujer *f*

womb *n* matriz *f*, útero

women's room *n* baño para mujeres

wood alcohol *n* alcohol *m* de madera

wool *n* lana

wore *pret de* **wear**

work *n* trabajo; *vi* trabajar; **to** —— **out** hacer ejercicio, levantar pesas

worker *n* obrero -ra *mf*, trabajador -ra *mf*

worm *n* gusano; *(intestinal)* lombriz *f*

worn *pp de* **wear**

worry *vi (pret & pp* **worried**) preocuparse; **Don't worry so much**..No se preocupe tanto.

worse *adj & adv (comp de* **bad** *y* **poorly**) peor; **to get** —— empeorar(se), agravarse, ponerse peor; **to make** —— agravar, empeorar; **Is there anything that makes the pain worse?**..¿Hay algo que le agrave el dolor?

worsening *n* empeoramiento

wound *n* herida; **gunshot** —— balazo, herida de bala; **knife** —— cuchillada; **puncture** —— herida por punción; **stab** —— puñalada; *vt* herir

wounded *adj* herido

wrinkle *n* arruga; *vt, vi* arrugar(se)

wrist *n* muñeca; —— **drop** mano péndula

writer's cramp *n* calambre *m* del escritor

writhe *vi* retorcerse

X

xanthoma *n* xantoma *m*

xiphoid process *n* apófisis *f* xifoides

X-linked *adj* ligado al cromosoma X, ligado al X

x-ray *n (single ray)* rayo X, *(in general)* rayos X; *(film)* radiografía, rayos X *(fam)*; *vt* tomar una radiografía (de); tratar con rayos X

Y

yawn *n* bostezo; *vi* bostezar
yaws *n* pián *m*, frambesia
year *n* año
yeast *n* (clase *f* de) hongo, hongos (*fam*)
yellow *adj* amarillo
yellow jacket *n* (especie *f* de) avispa

yesterday *adv* ayer
yoga *n* yoga
yogurt *n* yogurt *m*
yolk *n* yema; egg —— yema del huevo
young *adj* joven
youth *n* juventud *f*

Z

zidovudine *n* zidovudina
zinc *n* cinc *or* zinc *m*; —— oxide óxido de
  cinc

zip code *n* código postal
zipper *n* cierre *m*
zone *n* zona

ESPAÑOL-INGLÉS

SPANISH-ENGLISH

A

abajo *adv* de —— lower
abandonar *vt* (*un tratamiento, una dieta, etc.*) to give up on
abanico *m* fan
abatelenguas *m* (*Mex*) tongue depressor *o* blade
abatido -da *adj* depressed
abdomen *m* abdomen, belly, stomach (*fam*)
abeja *f* bee; —— **africana** *or* **asesina** Africanized *or* killer bee
abertura *f* opening
abierto -ta (*pp of* **abrir**) *adj* open
abortar *vt* to abort; *vi* (*con intención*) to have an abortion; (*sin intención*) to miscarry, to have a miscarriage
aborto *m* (*inducido*) abortion; (*espontáneo*) miscarriage; —— **accidental** accidental abortion; —— **espontáneo** spontaneous abortion; —— **habitual** *or* **de repetición** habitual abortion; —— **incompleto** incomplete abortion; —— **terapéutico** therapeutic abortion; **amenaza de** —— threatened abortion
abotagado -da *adj* bloated
abotonar *vt, vr* to button (up)
abrasión *f* abrasion
abrasivo -va *adj* & *m* abrasive
abrazar *vt* to embrace, hug
abrazo *m* embrace, hug
abrigo *m* coat, overcoat
abrir *vt, vr* (*pp* **abierto**) to open, (*un absceso, con bisturí*) to lance
abrochar *vt, vr* to button (up), buckle
absceso *m* abscess
absorbente *adj* absorbent
absorber *vt* to absorb
absorbible *adj* absorbable; **no** —— nonabsorbable
absorción *f* absorption
abstinencia *f* abstinence
abuelo -la *m* grandfather, grandparent; *f* grandmother
abuso *m* abuse; —— **de substancias intoxicantes** substance abuse; —— **infantil** child abuse
acabarse *vr* to run out; **Se me acabaron las pastillas..My** pills ran out.
acalasia *f* achalasia
acalenturado -da *adj* feverish

ácaro *m* mite
acaso, por si just in case
acatarrado -da *adj* (*fam*) having a cold; **Estoy acatarrado..I** have a cold.
acceso *m* attack, fit, spell; access; —— **para sillas de rueda** wheelchair access
accidentarse *vr* to have an accident
accidente *m* accident
acción *f* action; **de** —— **corta** short-acting; **de** —— **prolongada** long-acting; **de** —— **rápida** fast-acting, (*insulina*) regular
acedía *f* heartburn
aceite *m* oil; —— **de cártamo** safflower oil; —— **de coco** coconut oil; —— **de hígado de bacalao** cod-liver oil; —— **de maíz** corn oil; —— **de oliva** olive oil; —— **de palma** palm oil; —— **de ricino** castor oil; —— **mineral** mineral oil; —— **vegetal** vegetable oil
acelerado -da *adj* nervously energetic
acero *m* steel; —— **inoxidable** stainless steel
acetaminofén *m* acetaminophen
acético -ca *adj* acetic
acetona *f* acetone
aciclovir *m* acyclovir
acidez *f* acidity; (*estomacal*) heartburn
ácido -da *adj* & *m* acid; —— **acético** acetic acid; —— **ascórbico** ascorbic acid; —— **bórico** boric acid; —— **clorhídrico** hydrochloric acid; —— **desoxirribonucleico** (ADN *or* DNA) deoxyribonucleic acid (DNA); —— **fólico** folic acid; —— **gástrico** gastric acid; —— **glutámico** glutamic acid; —— **graso** fatty acid; —— **láctico** lactic acid; —— **linoleico** linoleic acid; —— **nalidíxico** nalidixic acid; —— **nicotínico** nicotinic acid; —— **pantoténico** pantothenic acid; —— **ribonucleico** ribonucleic acid; —— **salicílico** salicylic acid; —— **tartárico** tartaric acid; —— **úrico** uric acid; —— **valproico** valproic acid
acné *f* acne
acomodar *vt* (*los huesos*) to set (*a bone*), to reduce (*a fracture or dislocation*), to adjust, perform an adjustment
acondroplasia *f* achondroplasia
acordarse *vr* (*also* —— **de**) to remember

acortar *vt* to shorten
acostarse *vr* to lie down; to go to bed
acrocordón *m* (*form*) skin tag
acromegalia *f* acromegaly
acta de nacimiento *f* birth certificate
actinomicosis *f* actinomycosis
activador del plasminógeno tisular *m* tissue plasminogen activator (tPA)
activar *vt* to activate
actividad *f* activity; —— fuerte strenuous activity, exertion
activo -va *adj* active
acto *m* act; —— sexual sexual intercourse, intercourse; durante el acto sexual..during sexual intercourse
acumulación *f* buildup
acumular *vt, vr* to accumulate, build up
acumulativo -va *adj* cumulative
acuoso -sa *adj* aqueous
acupuntura *f* acupuncture
acústico -ca *adj* acoustic
achacoso -sa *adj* sickly, having many ailments
achaque *m* mild illness, ailment, affliction
adaptación *f* adaptation
adaptar *vt, vr* to adapt
adecuado -da *adj* adequate; appropriate
adelante *adv* hacia —— forward
adenitis *f* adenitis
adenocarcinoma *m* adenocarcinoma
adenoidectomía *f* adenoidectomy
adenoiditis *f* adenoiditis
adenoma *m* adenoma; —— velloso villous adenoma
adentro *adv* inside
adherencia *f* adhesion
adhesivo -va *adj* adhesive; cinta *or* tela adhesiva adhesive tape
adicción *f* addiction
adictivo -va *adj* addictive
adicto -ta *mf* addict
aditivo -va *adj* & *m* additive
administración *f* administration
admisión *f* (*al hospital*) admission
Admisión *f* Admissions
admitir *vt* (*al hospital*) to admit
ADN *abbr* ácido desoxirribonucleico. *See* ácido.
adolescencia *f* adolescence
adolescente *adj* & *mf* adolescent
adolorido -da *adj* sore, painful, tender
adopción *f* adoption
adoptar *vt* to adopt
adormecer *vt* to numb (up); *vr* to become numb, to go to sleep (*fam*)
adormecido -da *adj* numb, asleep (*fam*)
adormecimiento *m* numbness
adormilado -da *adj* drowsy
adquirido -da *adj* acquired
adquirir *vt* to acquire
adrenal *adj* adrenal; *f* adrenal gland
adrenalina *f* adrenaline

adulto -ta *adj* & *mf* adult
adyuvante *adj* (*quimioterapia*) adjuvant
aeróbicos *mpl* aerobics
aerobics *mpl* (*Ang*) aerobics
aerosol *m* aerosol, inhaler, spray; —— dosificador metered dose inhaler; en —— aerosolized
afasia *f* aphasia
afectar *vt* to affect
afecto *m* affection; (*psych*) affect
afectuoso -sa *adj* affectionate
afeitar *vt, vr* to shave
afeminado -da *adj* effeminate
afilado -da *adj* sharp
afinidad *f* affinity
aflicción *f* grief, distress
afligirse *vr* to grieve
aflojar *vt* to loosen; (*fam*) to relax; Afloje la pierna..Relax your leg; *vr* to relax
afrecho *m* bran
afta *f* canker sore; thrush
agachar *vt* (*la cabeza*) to bend down (*one's head*); Agache la cabeza..Bend your head down; *vr* to bend over, bend down, stoop; to squat
agammaglobulinemia, agamaglobulinemia *f* agammaglobulinemia
agarrar *vt* to grasp, grip; (*una enfermedad*) to catch; —— aire to catch one's breath
agarrotarse *var of* engarrotarse
agencia *f* agency
agente *m* (*pharm*) agent
agitar *vt* to agitate; Agítese bien antes de usarse..Shake well before using; *vr* to become agitated
agorafobia *f* agoraphobia
agotado -da *adj* exhausted, run-down; depleted, used up
agotar *vt* to deplete, use up; *vr* to become fatigued; to become depleted
agrandar *vt* to enlarge
agravar *vt* to aggravate, make worse; *vr* to get worse; Se agravó..He got worse.
agresión *f* aggression
agresivo -va *adj* aggressive
agrietarse *vr* to crack, to chap, get chapped
agrio -ria *adj* sour
agruras *fpl* heartburn
agua *f* water; —— con alto contenido de minerales *or* —— dura hard water; —— con escaso contenido de minerales soft water; —— corriente running water; —— de hamamelis witch hazel; —— de la llave *or* del grifo tap water; —— destilada distilled water; —— dulce fresh water; —— en el pulmón, la rodilla, etc. water on the lung, the knee, etc.; —— mineral mineral water; aguas negras sewage; —— oxigenada hydrogen peroxide; —— purificada purified water; —— salada salt water; aguas termales hot springs

aguamala *f* jellyfish
aguantar *vt* to tolerate, endure, stand, bear; —— la respiración *or* el resuello to hold one's breath; **Aguante la respiración..**Hold your breath.
agudeza *f* acuity; —— visual visual acuity
agudo -da *adj* (*enfermedad*) acute; (*dolor*) sharp; (*tono*) high-pitched
agüita *f* (*esp. Mex, CA*) serum, body fluid
aguja *f* needle; —— hipodérmica hypodermic needle
agujero *m* hole
ahogar *vt, vr* to suffocate, smother; to drown; **¿Siente que se ahoga?..**Do you feel as though you are suffocating?..Do you feel short of breath?
ahogo *m* choking sensation, shortness of breath
ahorcar *vt* to hang (*by the neck*); *vr* to hang oneself
ai *interj* Ouch!
aire *m* air; —— acondicionado air conditioning; —— contaminado air pollution, smog; al —— libre outdoors; tener —— (*en el pecho, abdomen, etc.*) to have air (*in one's chest, abdomen, etc.*) (*refers to a popular belief that pain in the chest or abdomen may be due to trapped air*)
aislado -da *adj* isolated; (*emocionalmente*) alienated
aislamiento *m* isolation
aislar *vt* to isolate
ajustable *adj* adjustable
ajustador *m* (*Carib*) brassiere
ajustar *vt* to adjust, correct, to fit
ajuste *m* adjustment, correction
alacrán *m* scorpion
alambre *m* wire
alanina *f* alanine
albinismo *m* albinism
albino -na *adj & mf* albino
albúmina *f* albumin
albuterol *m* albuterol
álcali *m* alkali
alcalino -na *adj* alkaline
alcalosis *f* alkalosis
alcance *m* reach; fuera del —— de los niños out of reach of children
alcanfor *m* camphor
alcanzar *vt, vi* to reach
alcaptonuria *f* alkaptonuria
alcohol *m* alcohol, liquor; —— de madera wood alcohol; —— desnaturalizado denatured alcohol; —— etílico ethyl alcohol; —— metílico methyl alcohol; —— para fricciones rubbing alcohol
alcohólico -ca *adj & mf* alcoholic
Alcohólicos Anónimos *m* Alcoholics Anonymous (AA)
alcoholismo *m* alcoholism
aldosterona *f* aldosterone

aldosteronismo *m* aldosteronism
alegre *adj* cheerful
alergia *f* allergy
alérgico -ca *adj* allergic; **¿Es Ud. alérgico a la penicilina?..**Are you allergic to penicillin?
alerta *adj* alert
aleteo *m* flutter; —— auricular atrial flutter
alfa *f* alpha; —— feto proteína alpha fetoprotein
alfiler *m* pin, safety pin; —— de seguridad safety pin
algas *fpl* algae
algodón *m* cotton
algodoncillo *m* thrush
alguate *m* (*Mex*) fine cactus spine
aliento *m* breath; mal —— bad breath
alimentación *f* feeding, nourishment
alimentar *vt* to feed
alimentario -ria *adj* alimentary
alimenticio -cia *adj* nutritional
alimento *m* (*often pl*) food; alimentos enlatados canned food; alimentos procesados processed food
alineamiento *m* alignment
alinear *vt, vr* to align, line up
aliviar *vt* to alleviate, soothe, relieve; *vr* to recover, get well; (*Mex, fam*) to give birth, deliver
alivio *m* relief
almacén *m* store
almacenar *vt* to store
almidón *m* starch
almohada *f* pillow, cushion
almohadilla *f* small pillow, small cushion, pad
almorrana *f* hemorrhoid
almorzar *vi* to have lunch
almuerzo *m* lunch
áloe *m* aloe
alojarse *vr* to lodge
alopurinol *m* allopurinol
alprazolam *m* alprazolam
alquitrán *m* tar; —— de hulla coal tar
alteración *f* disturbance
alterado -da *adj* upset
alterar *vt* to upset; *vr* to become upset
alternar *vt, vi* to alternate
alterno -na *adj* alternate; días alternos alternate days
altitud *f* altitude
alto -ta *adj* high, tall; **Su glucosa está muy alta..**Your glucose is very high...**¿Es muy alto su papá?..**Is your father very tall?
altura *f* height; altitude, elevation; **¿Qué altura tiene Ud.?..**How tall are you?
alucinación *f* hallucination
alumbramiento *m* (*form*) delivery of the placenta; (*fam*) childbirth
alumbrar *vi* to give birth
aluminio *m* aluminum
alveolo, alvéolo *m* alveolus; (*dent*) socket

ama de casa *f* housewife, homemaker
amalgama *f* (*dent*) amalgam
amamantar *vt* (*form*) to breast-feed, to nurse
Amanita Amanita
amantadina *f* amantadine
amar *vt, vi* to love
amargo -ga *adj* bitter
amarillo -lla *adj* yellow
ambiental *adj* environmental
ambulancia *f* ambulance
ambulatorio -ria *adj* ambulatory
ameba *var de* amiba
amebiasis *var de* amibiasis
amenorrea *f* amenorrhea
americano -na *adj & mf* American
amiba *f* ameba
amibiano -na *adj* amebic
amibiasis *f* amebiasis
amígdala *f* tonsil
amigdalectomía *f* tonsillectomy
amigdalitis *f* tonsillitis
amilasa *f* amylase
amiloidosis *f* amyloidosis
amilorida *f* amiloride
aminoácido *m* amino acid
aminofilina *f* aminophylline
aminoglucósido *m* aminoglycoside
aminorar *vt, vr* to diminish, reduce
amitriptilina *f* amitriptyline
amnesia *f* amnesia
amniocentesis *f* (*pl* -sis) amniocentesis
amnionitis *f* amnionitis
amodorrado -da *adj* drowsy
amoniaco, amoníaco *m* ammonia
amontonamiento *m* buildup
amor *m* love; —— **propio** self-esteem
amoratado -da *adj* bruised, black-and-blue;
   cyanotic
amortiguado -da *adj* buffered
amortiguador *m* buffer; **solución
   amortiguadora** buffer solution
amoxacilina *f* amoxacillin
ampicilina *f* ampicillin
ampolla *f* blister
ampolleta *f* ampule
ámpula *f* ampule
amputación *f* amputation
amputar *vt* to amputate
anabólico -ca *adj* anabolic
anaerobio -bia *adj* anaerobic
anafiláctico -ca *adj* anaphylactic
anafilaxis *f* anaphylaxis
anal *adj* anal
analfabetismo *m* illiteracy
analfabeto -ta *adj* illiterate
analgesia *f* analgesia
analgésico -ca *adj & m* analgesic
análisis *m* (*pl* -sis) analysis, test
analizar *vt* to analyze
anatomía *f* anatomy
anatómico -ca *adj* anatomical, anatomic
anciano -na *adj* old, elderly; *m* old man, old

person; *f* old woman
ancho -cha *adj* wide
andadera *f* walker
andar *vi* to walk
andrógeno *m* androgen
anemia *f* anemia; —— **aplásica** aplastic
   anemia; —— **de células falciformes** *or*
   —— **drepanocítica** sickle cell anemia;
   —— **ferropriva, ferropénica,** *or* **por
   deficiencia de hierro** iron deficiency
   anemia; —— **hemolítica** hemolytic
   anemia; —— **perniciosa** pernicious
   anemia; —— **sideroblástica** sideroblastic
   anemia
anémico -ca *adj* anemic
anencefalia *f* anencephaly
anergia *f* anergy
anestesia *f* anesthesia; —— **general** general
   anesthesia; —— **local** local anesthesia;
   —— **regional** regional anesthesia
anestesiar *vt* to anesthetize, numb up, put to
   sleep (*fam*)
anestésico -ca *adj & m* anesthetic
anestesiología *f* anesthesiology
anestesiólogo -ga *mf* anesthesiologist
anestesista *mf* anesthetist
aneurisma *m* aneurysm; —— **disecante**
   dissecting aneurysm; —— **micótico**
   mycotic aneurysm
anfetamina *f* amphetamine
anfiteatro *m* (*esp. Mex*) morgue
anfotericina B *f* amphotericin B
angina *f* (de pecho) angina; **anginas** (*esp.
   Mex, fam*) tonsils; —— **de Prinzmetal**
   Prinzmetal's angina; —— **de Vincent**
   Vincent's angina, trench mouth; ——
   inestable unstable angina; **tener anginas**
   (*Mex, fam*) to have tonsillitis
angiodisplasia *f* angiodysplasia
angiografía *f* angiography; angiogram
angiograma *m* angiogram
angioma *m* angioma
angioplastia *f* angioplasty; —— **transluminal percutánea coronaria** percutaneous
   transluminal coronary angioplasty
angiosarcoma *m* angiosarcoma
ángulo *m* angle, bend; —— **del ojo** angle *o*
   corner of the eye
angustia *f* anxiety
anilina *f* aniline
anillo *m* ring
animal *m* animal; —— **doméstico** pet
animalito (*fam*) *m* bug, insect; parasite
ano *m* anus
anoche *adv* last night
anomalía *f* anomaly
anorexia *f* anorexia; —— **nerviosa** anorexia
   nervosa
anormal *adj* abnormal
anormalidad *f* abnormality
anovulación *f* anovulation
anovulatorio -ria *adj* anovulatory

anquilosis *f* ankylosis
anquilostomiasis *f* ancylostomiasis
ansia *f* (*often pl*) anxiety; (*fam*) asthma, shortness of breath
ansiedad *f* anxiety
ansioso -sa *adj* anxious
anteanoche *adv* night before last
anteayer *adv* the day before yesterday
antebrazo *m* forearm
anteojos *mpl* glasses, eyeglasses; —— oscuros sunglasses
antepasado *m* ancestor
anterior *adj* anterior; previous
antiácido -da *adj & m* antacid
antiarrítmico -ca *adj & m* antiarrhythmic
antibacteriano -na *adj* antibacterial
antibiótico -ca *adj & m* antibiotic; —— de amplio espectro broad spectrum antibiotic
anticoagulante *adj & m* anticoagulant
anticoagular *vt* to anticoagulate
anticolinérgico -ca *adj* anticholinergic
anticoncepción *f* contraception
anticonceptivo -va *adj & m* contraceptive
anticongelante *m* antifreeze
anticonvulsivante *adj & m* anticonvulsant
anticonvulsivo -va *adj & m* anticonvulsant
anticuerpo *m* antibody
antidepresivo -va *adj & m* antidepressant; —— tricíclico tricyclic antidepressant
antídoto *m* antidote
antiemético -ca *adj & m* antiemetic
antier *var of* anteayer
antiespasmódico -ca *adj & m* antispasmodic
antiespástico -ca *adj & m* antispasmodic
antígeno *m* antigen; —— carcinoembriónico carcinoembryonic antigen
antihelmíntico -ca *adj & m* anthelminthic
antihipertensivo -va *adj* antihypertensive
antihistamínico *m* antihistamine
antiinflamatorio -ria *adj* antiinflammatory; *m* antiinflammatory agent; —— no esteroide nonsteroidal antiinflammatory drug (NSAID)
antimicrobiano -na *adj & m* antimicrobial
antiperspirante *adj & m* antiperspirant
antipirético -ca *adj & m* antipyretic
antipsicótico -ca *adj & m* antipsychotic
antiséptico -ca *adj & m* antiseptic
antisocial *adj* antisocial
antisuero *m* antiserum
antitoxina *f* antitoxin
antitranspirante *m* antiperspirant, deodorant
antojo *m* (*obst*) craving
ántrax *m* anthrax
anual *adj* annual
anular *adj* annular
anzuelo *m* fishhook
año *m* year; ¿Cuántos años tiene Ud.?..How old are you?
aorta *f* aorta
aórtico -ca *adj* aortic
aparato *m* apparatus, device; (*cardiovas-*

cular, etc.) system; (*fam, obst*) intrauterine device (IUD); —— ortopédico brace
apariencia *f* appearance
apatía *f* apathy
apático -ca *adj* apathetic
apenarse *vr* to grieve
apéndice *m* appendix
apendicectomía *f* appendectomy
apendicitis *f* appendicitis
apetito *m* appetite
aplastante *adj* (*sensación, dolor*) crushing
aplastar *vt* to crush
aplazar *vt* to postpone
aplicador *m* applicator, swab
apnea *f* apnea; —— del sueño sleep apnea
apófisis *f* (*pl* -sis) (*anat*) process; —— mastoides mastoid process; —— xifoides xiphoid process
apósito *m* large gauze dressing, dressing
apoyar *vt* to support
apoyo *m* support; grupo de —— support group
apraxia *f* apraxia
aprendizaje *m* learning; dificultad *f or* problema *m* del —— learning disability
apretado -da *adj* tight; (*el pecho*) tight (*as with asthma*)
apretar *vt* to press; to constrict; (*ropa, calzado*) to pinch, to be too tight for; —— la mano to make a fist; —— los dientes to bite down; *vi* (*ropa, calzado*) to bind, to be too tight
apropiado -da *adj* appropriate
aproximadamente *adv* approximately
aptitud *f* aptitude
aquejar *vt* to bother; Me aqueja un dolor de rodilla..A pain in my knee is bothering me.
araña *f* spider; —— vascular spider angioma
arañar *vt* to scratch (*esp. with claws*)
arañazo *m* scratch (*esp. by claws*)
arco *m* arch; —— de Hawley (*orthodontia*) retainer; —— del pie arch of the foot
arder *vi* to burn; Esto le va a arder un poco..This will burn a little bit.
ardiente *adj* burning
ardilla *f* squirrel
ardor *m* (*sensación*) burning, burning sensation; Siento ardor en el pecho..I feel burning in my chest.
área *f* area
arete *m* earring
argentino -na *adj & mf* Argentine *o* Argentinean
arginina *f* arginine
arma *f* weapon; —— blanca sharp weapon
arqueo *m* (*form*) retching, doubling over
arrastrar *vt* —— la voz *or* la lengua to slur
arrebatado -da *adj* (*vulg*) high (*on drugs*)
arreglar *vt* to repair, fix

arriba *adv* **de** —— upper; **hacia** —— upward

arriesgar *vt* to risk; *vr* to take a risk

arritmia *f* arrhythmia

arrojar *vt* to throw up, to vomit; (*esp. Mex, fam*) to cough up; (*Mex*) to pass, to shed; —— **gases** *or* **vientos** to pass gas; —— **una piedra** (*Mex*) to pass a stone; *vi* to throw up, to vomit

arrollar *vt* (*con un vehículo*) to run over

arroz *m* rice

arruga *f* wrinkle

arrugar *vt, vr* to wrinkle

arrullar *vi* to coo

arsénico *m* arsenic

arteria *f* artery; —— **braquial** brachial artery; —— **carótida** carotid artery; —— **coronaria** coronary artery; —— **femoral** femoral artery; —— **ilíaca** iliac artery; —— **radial** radial artery; —— **subclavia** subclavian artery

arteriosclerosis *f* arteriosclerosis

arteriovenoso -sa *adj* arteriovenous

arteritis *f* arteritis; —— **temporal** temporal arteritis

articulación *f* joint; —— **de la cadera** hip-joint

artificial *adj* artificial

artrítico -ca *adj* arthritic

artritis *f* arthritis; —— **juvenil** juvenile arthritis; —— **reumatoide** rheumatoid arthritis

artrografía *f* arthrography; arthrogram

artrograma *m* arthrogram

artroscopia, artroscopía *f* arthroscopy

asado -da *adj* roasted; —— **a la parilla** grilled, broiled

asaltar *vt* to assault

asalto *m* assault

asbesto *m* asbestos

ascariasis, ascaridiasis *f* ascariasis

ascáride *m* roundworm

Ascaris Ascaris

ascendente *adj* ascending

ascitis *f* ascites

asco *m* (*Mex, CA*) nausea; **dar** —— to make nauseated; **tener** —— to be nauseated

ascórbico -ca *adj* ascorbic

asearse *vr* (*después de defecar*) to wipe (oneself)

aseo *m* hygiene; —— **oral** *or* **bucal** oral hygiene

aséptico -ca *adj* aseptic

asfixia *f* asphyxia

asfixiar *vt, vr* to asphyxiate, suffocate

asiento *m* seat

asilo *m* asylum, nursing home; —— **de ancianos** nursing home

asistencia *f* assistence; —— **social** *or* **pública** welfare

asistente *mf* assistant, aide; —— **de enfermera** nursing assistant, nurse's aide

asistir *vt* to assist, aid; (*una clínica, clase, etc.*) to attend

asma *f* asthma

asmático -ca *adj & mf* asthmatic

asociación *f* association

asolearse *vr* to get sun

asparagina *f* asparagine

aspecto *m* appearance

aspergilosis *f* aspergillosis

áspero -ra *adj* rough, harsh

aspiración *f* aspiration; —— **articular** joint aspiration; —— **con aguja** needle aspiration

aspirar *vt* to aspirate, to inhale

aspirina *f* aspirin

astigmatismo *m* astigmatism

astilla *f* sliver, splinter, chip, fragment

astillar *vt, vr* to chip

astringente *adj & m* astringent

atacar *vt* to attack

ataque *m* attack, fit, convulsion, seizure; —— **cardiaco** *or* **al corazón** heart attack; —— **de nervios** (*fam*) anxiety attack, panic attack; —— **de pánico** panic attack; **darle** *or* **pegarle un** —— to have an attack, to have a seizure

atarantado -da *adj* dazed, in a daze, stunned

atarantar *vt* to daze, stun; *vr* to become dazed, to become stunned

ataxia *f* ataxia

atáxico -ca *adj* ataxic

atención *f* attention; —— **del tercer nivel** tertiary care; —— **médica** healthcare; —— **prenatal** prenatal care; —— **primaria** *or* **del primer nivel** primary care

atender *vt* (*un paciente*) to take care of, to treat; (*un parto*) to deliver; **La Dra. Ng atendió seis partos anoche..**Dr. Ng delivered six babies last night...**Atendió a la señora Reid..**She delivered Mrs. Reid...**Atendió a los gemelos..**She delivered the twins.

atenolol *m* atenolol

atenuado -da *adj* attenuated

aterosclerosis *f* atherosclerosis

atípico -ca *adj* atypical

atleta *mf* athlete; **pie** *m* **de** —— athlete's foot

atmósfera *f* atmosphere

atorar *vr* to stick, get stuck; **¿Siente que se le atora la comida?..**Does it feel as though food sticks in your throat?

atragantarse *vr* —— **con** to choke on

atrás *adv* **de** —— back; **hacia** —— backward; **la parte de** —— the back part

atravesar *vt* to pierce

atrioventricular (AV) *adj* atrioventricular (A-V)

atrofia *f* atrophy

atrofiarse *vr* to atrophy

atropellar *vt* to run over
atropina *f* atropine
aturdido -da *adj* dazed, in a daze
aturdir *vt* to stun, daze, make dizzy; *vr* to become stunned, dazed, dizzy
audición *f* hearing, sense of hearing
audífono *m* hearing aid
audiograma *m* audiogram
audiología *f* audiology
audiólogo -ga *mf* audiologist
audiometría *f* audiometry
audiómetro *m* audiometer
auditivo -va *adj* auditory
aumentar *vt, vi* to increase, enlarge, (*de peso*) to gain (*weight*); —— **las defensas** to build up (*one's*) resistance
aumento *m* increase, gain, rise
aura *m* aura
aurícula *f* (*del corazón*) atrium
auricular *adj* atrial
auriculoventricular **(AV)** *adj* atrioventricular (A-V)
ausencia *f* absence
ausente *adj* absent
autismo *m* autism
autista *mf* autistic
autístico -ca *adj* autistic
autoclave *m* autoclave
autodestructivo -va *adj* self-destructive
autodisciplina *f* self-discipline
autoestima *f* self-esteem
autoevaluación *f* self-examination
autoexamen *m* self-examination
autoinmune *adj* autoimmune
autoinmunidad *f* autoimmunity
autolimitado -da *adj* self-limited

autólogo -ga *adj* autologous
automóvil *m* automobile, car
autoprescribirse *vr* (*pp* **-scrito**) to self-prescribe
autopsia *f* autopsy
autorrecetarse *vr* to self-prescribe
autorrespeto *m* self-respect
autosómico -ca *adj* autosomal
auxiliar *mf* assistant, aide
auxilio *interj* Help! *m* help, aid; **primeros auxilios** first aid
AV *See* **auriculoventricular** *or* **atrioventricular.**
avance *m* advance, progress
avena *f* oatmeal
aversión *f* aversion
aves de corral *fpl* poultry
avispa *f* wasp, yellow jacket
avispón *m* hornet
axila *f* axilla, armpit (*fam*)
axilar *adj* axillary
ay *interj* Ouch!
ayer *adv* yesterday
ayuda *f* help, aid, assistance
ayudante *mf* assistant, aide
ayudar *vt, vi* to help, aid, assist
ayunar *vi* to fast
ayunas, en fasting; **glucosa en ayunas** fasting glucose
ayuno *m* fast, fasting; **glucosa en** —— fasting glucose
azar, al randomly, at random
azatioprina *f* azathioprine
azúcar *m&f* sugar; **sin** —— sugarless
azufre *m* sulfur
azul *adj* blue

B

baba *f* drool
babear *vi* to drool
bacilo *m* bacillus, rod; —— **de Calmette-Guérin (BCG)** Calmette-Guérin bacillus (BCG)
bacín *m* basin
bacinica *f* bedpan
bacinilla *f* bedpan
bacteria *f* bacterium (*en inglés se emplea casi siempre la forma plural*: bacteria)
bacteriano -na *adj* bacterial
Bacteroides Bacteroides
baja *f* fall, drop

bajalenguas *m* tongue depressor *o* blade
bajar *vt* to lower; *vi* to go down, fall, drop; **Le bajó el potasio..**Your potassium went down; —— **de peso** to lose weight; **bajarle la regla** (*fam*) to have one's period
bajo -ja *adj* low; (*anat*) lower; (*de estatura*) short; **Su potasio está bajo..**Your potassium is low...**la parte baja..**the lower part
bala *f* bullet
balanza *f* balance scale, scale
balazo *m* gunshot wound

balbucear *vi* to slur; *(ped)* to babble
balbuceo *m* slurring; *(ped)* babble
balón *m (de una sonda Foley, etc.*) balloon
bálsamo *m* balm
banco de sangre *m* blood bank
bandeja *f* tray
bañadera *f (Cub)* bathtub
bañar *vt* to wash, bathe; *vr* wash oneself, bathe, take a bath; to go swimming
bañera *f* bathtub
baño *m* bath; bathroom, rest room; —— **de asiento** sitz bath; —— **de regadera** *(Mex)* shower; —— **de vapor** steam bath; —— **para hombres** men's room; —— **para mujeres** women's room; **hacer del** —— *(Mex, fam)* to have a bowel movement; **ir al** —— to go to the bathroom
baranda *f* bedrail, side rail
barandal *m* bedrail, side rail
barba *f* beard, whiskers; chin
barbero *m* barber
barbitúrico *m* barbiturate
bario *m* barium
barrera *f* barrier
barriga *f* belly, stomach *(fam)*
barriguita *f (ped)* tummy
barril *m (de una jeringa)* barrel
barrio *m* neighborhood
barro *m* pimple *(due to acne)*
basal *adj* baseline
basca *f (often pl)* nausea, vomiting; vomit; **dar** —— to make sick *o* nauseated; **tener** —— to be nauseated, to vomit
báscula *f* scale *(for weighing)*
base *f (chem, pharm)* base; —— **libre de cocaína** freebase; **a** —— **de aceite** oil-based; **a** —— **de agua** water-based
básico -ca *adj* basic
basquear *vi (esp. Mex)* to vomit
bastón *m* cane; *(del ojo)* rod
bata *f* gown
batata *f (PR, SD; fam)* calf
baumanómetro *m* blood pressure cuff
bazo *m* spleen
BCG *abbr* **bacilo de Calmette-Guérin.** *See* **bacilo.**
bebé *m (pl* **bebés)** baby
bebedero *m* drinking fountain
bebedor -ra *mf* drinker
beber *vt, vi* to drink
bebida *f* drink
beclometasona *f* beclomethasone
belladona *f* belladonna
bencedrina *f* benzedrine
benceno *m* benzene
beneficio *m* benefit; **por su** —— for your benefit
benéfico -ca *adj* beneficial
benigno -na *adj* benign
benzodiacepina *f* benzodiazepine
beriberi *m* beriberi
berrinche *m* tantrum

besar *vt* to kiss
beso *m* kiss
beta *f* beta; —— **bloqueador** *m* beta blocker
betahemolítico -ca *adj* beta hemolytic
biberón *m* nursing bottle, baby's bottle
bicarbonato *m* bicarbonate; —— **de sodio** sodium bicarbonate
bíceps *m (pl* **bíceps)** biceps
bicicleta *f* bicycle
bicúspide *adj & m* bicuspid
bicho *m* bug
bien *adj & adv* well; **Estoy bien**..I'm well...**Estoy comiendo bien**..I'm eating well; —— **parecido** good-looking; *m* good, welfare, benefit; **por su** —— for your benefit; **por su propio** —— for your own good
bienestar *m* wellbeing, welfare
bifocales *mpl* bifocals
bigote *m* moustache
biliar *adj* biliary
bilingüe *adj* bilingual
bilirrubina *f* bilirubin
bilis *f* bile
biodegradable *adj* biodegradable
bioestadística *f* biostatistics
biología *f* biology
biológico -ca *adj* biological, biologic
biometría hemática *f* blood count
biopsia *f* biopsy; —— **abierta** open biopsy; —— **con aguja** needle biopsy
bioquímico -ca *adj* biochemical; *f* biochemistry
biorretroalimentación *f* biofeedback
bióxido *m* dioxide; —— **de azufre** sulfur dioxide; —— **de carbono** carbon dioxide
bíper *m (Ang)* beeper, pager
bipolar *adj* bipolar
bisexual *adj* bisexual
bismuto *m* bismuth
bisturí *m (pl* **-ríes)** scalpel
bizco -ca *adj* cross-eyed; *mf* cross-eyed person
blanco -ca *adj* white, *(tez)* fair
blando -da *adj* soft
blanqueador *m* bleach
blanquillo *m (Mex, fam)* egg
bleomicina *f* bleomycin
bloomer *m (esp. CA)* panties, (women's) underpants
bloqueador *m* blocker; —— **de los canales de calcio** calcium channel blocker; —— **de los receptores H₂** H_2-blocker; **beta** —— beta blocker
bloquear *vt (pharm, physio)* to block
bloqueo *m* block; obstruction, blockage; —— **cardiaco** heart block; —— **de rama** bundle branch block; —— **nervioso** nerve block
blusa *f* blouse
bobito *m* gnat
bobo *m (PR)* pacifier

boca *f* mouth; —— abajo facedown; ——
    arriba faceup; —— del estómago pit of
    the stomach; por la —— by mouth
bocadillo *m* snack
bocado *m* mouthful
bocio *m* goiter
bochorno *m* flush, hot flash
bola *f* lump, bump
bolita *f* small lump *o* bump
boliviano -na *adj* & *mf* Bolivian
bolsa *f* pouch; bursa; bag; bolsas bajo los
    ojos bags under one's eyes; —— de agua
    caliente hot-water bottle *o* bag; —— de
    hielo ice pack; —— de las aguas bag of
    waters
bomba *f* pump; bomb; (*esp. CA, fam*)
    blister; —— atómica atomic bomb
bombero *m* fireman
boquera *f* dryness and fissures at the corners
    of the mouth; cold sore, fever blister
boquilla *f* mouthpiece
borde *m* border, edge, margin
bordón *m* cane
bórico -ca *adj* boric
borrachera *f* binge
borracho -cha *adj* & *mf* drunk
borrarse *vr* (*la vista*) to blur; Se me borra
    la vista..My vision blurs.
borroso -sa *adj* blurred; visión borrosa
    blurred vision
bostezar *vi* to yawn
bostezo *m* yawn
bota *f* boot
botana *f* (*Mex*) snack
botanear *vi* (*Mex*) to snack
botánica *f* herb shop
botar *vt* to eliminate, expel, pass, shed; ——
    aire to breathe out; —— una piedra (*al
    orinar*) to pass a stone
bote *m* can
botella *f* bottle
botica *f* pharmacy, drugstore
boticario -ria *mf* pharmacist, druggist
botiquín *m* medicine chest *o* cabinet; ——
    de primeros auxilios first-aid kit
botulismo *m* botulism
bovino -va *adj* bovine
bradicardia *f* bradycardia
braguero *m* truss
bragueta *f* fly (*of trousers*)

Braille *m* Braille
brasileño -ña *adj* & *mf* Brazilian
brassiere *m* brassiere
brazalete de identificación *m* identification
    bracelet
brazo *m* arm
breve *adj* brief, short
brincar *vi* to hop
brinco *m* hop
bromocriptina *f* bromocriptine
bronceado -da *adj* tan; *m* suntan, tan
broncearse *vr* to tan, to get a suntan
broncodilatador *m* bronchodilator
broncogénico -ca, broncógeno -na *adj*
    bronchogenic
bronconeumonía *f* bronchopneumonia
broncoscopia, broncoscopía *f* broncho-
    scopy
broncospasmo, broncoespasmo *m* broncho-
    spasm
bronquial *adj* bronchial
bronquiectasia *f* bronchiectasis
bronquio *m* bronchus
bronquiolitis *f* bronchiolitis
bronquiolo *m* bronchiole
bronquitis *f* bronchitis
brotar *vi* brotarle los dientes (*esp. Mex*) to
    teethe; brotarle granos (*esp. Mex*) to
    break out (*one's skin*); Le brotaron
    granos..His skin broke out.
brote *m* outbreak
brucelosis *f* brucellosis
brujería *f* witchcraft
bubón *m* bubo
bubónico -ca *adj* bubonic
bucal *adj* oral; por vía —— by mouth
buen *See* bueno.
bueno -na *adj* (buen *before masculine
    singular nouns*) good; un buen médico..a
    good doctor
buffer *m* buffer
bulbo raquídeo *m* medulla
bulimia *f* bulimia
bulímico -ca *adj* bulimic
bulto *m* large lump *o* bump
burbuja *f* bubble
bursitis *f* bursitis
busto *m* bust, female breast
busulfán *m* busulfan
bypass *m* (*Ang*) bypass

C

cabecera *f* head (*of a bed*)
cabello *m* hair (*head only*)
cabestrillo *m* sling
cabeza *f* head; ——— *or* cabecita de vena (*fam*) spider angioma
cabra *f* goat
caca *f* (*fam, esp. Carib*) stool, (*ped*) poopoo
cacarizo -za *adj* having pockmarks
cacto *m* cactus
cadáver *m* cadaver
cadera *f* hip
cadillo *m* (*bot*) burr, sticker
cadmio *m* cadmium
caducado -da *adj* outdated, out of date
caerse *vr* to fall, fall down, collapse; (*los párpados, etc.*) to droop, sag; (*una costra, tejido necrótico, etc.*) to slough
café *adj* brown; *m* (*pl* cafés) coffee
cafeína *f* caffeine
caída *f* fall; ——— del pelo hair loss; ——— de mollera (*Mex, CA*) sunken fontanel; pediatric folk illness manifest by a sunken fontanel and other signs and symptoms of dehydration, believed to be caused by improper handling of the infant and said to be cured by massage of the upper palate
caja *f* ——— de dientes (*esp. Carib*) denture; ——— torácica *or* de las costillas rib cage
calambre *m* cramp; ——— del escritor writer's cramp
calamina *f* calamine
calcetín *m* sock
calcificar *vt, vr* to calcify
calcio *m* calcium
calcitonina *f* calcitonin
cálculo *m* stone; ——— biliar gallstone; ——— renal *or* del riñón kidney stone
caldo *m* broth, soup
calefacción *f* heating
calentador *m* heater
calentamiento *m* warmup; hacer ——— to warm up (*before exercising*)
calentar *vt, vr* to warm (up), to heat (up)
calentura *f* fever
calibrar *vt* to calibrate
calidad *f* quality; ——— de vida quality of life
caliente *adj* warm, hot
calistenia *f* calisthenics
calma *f* calm
calmante *adj* & *m* sedative
calmar *vt* to calm, soothe; *vr* to calm down, quiet down

calomel *m* calomel
calor *m* heat, warmth; hot flash; tener *or* sentir ——— to be *o* feel hot; Tengo mucho calor..I'm really hot.
caloría *f* calorie
calostro *m* colostrum
calvicie *f* baldness
calvo -va *adj* bald
calzado *m* footwear; ——— ortopédico orthopedic shoes
calzón *m* (*often pl*) panties, (women's) underpants
calzoncillos *mpl* (men's) underpants
callejero -ra *adj* pertaining to the street, street; droga callejera street drug
callo *m* callus
callosidad *f* callus, hardened skin
cama *f* bed
cámara *f* chamber; ——— hiperbárica hyperbaric chamber
cambiar *vt, vi* to change
cambio *m* change; ——— de vida change of life
camilla *f* stretcher, litter
caminar *vi* to walk; ——— dormido to sleepwalk, walk in one's sleep
camisa *f* shirt; ——— de fuerza straitjacket
camiseta *f* undershirt
camisón *m* gown
campaña *f* campaign
campanilla *f* uvula
campo *m* field; rural area, country; ——— visual visual field
Campylobacter Campylobacter
cana *f* gray hair
canal *m* canal; ——— auditivo auditory tube *o* canal; ——— del parto birth canal
cancelar *vt* to cancel
cáncer *m* cancer; ——— de la mama, del seno *or* del pecho breast cancer; ——— del pulmón, de la próstata, etc. lung cancer, prostate cancer, etc.
cancerología *f* oncology, study of cancer
cancerólogo -ga *mf* oncologist, cancer specialist
canceroso -sa *adj* cancerous
Candida Candida
candidiasis *f* candidiasis
canilla *f* shin, leg, thin leg, calf
canino *m* (*diente*) cuspid, canine tooth
cansado -da *adj* tired
cansancio *m* tiredness, fatigue; ——— visual eyestrain
cansar *vt* to tire (out), make tired; *vr* to tire

(out), get tired
canto negro *m* (*PR, fam*) bruise
canturrear *vt, vi* to hum (*a note*)
cánula *f* cannula; —— **nasal** nasal cannula
capa *f* coating, layer, film
capacidad *f* ability, capacity
capar *vt* (*fam*) to castrate
capaz *adj* (*pl* **capaces**) capable
capilar *m* capillary
cápsula *f* capsule
captopril *m* captopril
capuchón cervical *m* cervical cap
cara *f* face
caracol *m* snail
característico **-ca** *adj* characteristic; *f* characteristic, trait
carbamazepina *f* carbamazepine
carbidopa *f* carbidopa
carbohidrato *m* carbohydrate
carbón *m* coal, charcoal; —— **activado** activated charcoal
carbonato *m* carbonate; —— **de calcio** calcium carbonate
carbono *m* carbon (*element*)
carbunco *m* carbuncle
cárcel *f* jail; prison
carcinoide *adj & m* carcinoid
carcinoma *m* carcinoma; —— **basocelular** basal cell carcinoma; —— **de células en avena** oat cell carcinoma; —— **de células pequeñas** small cell carcinoma; —— **espinocelular** *or* **de células escamosas** squamous cell carcinoma
cardiaco -ca, cardíaco -ca *adj* cardiac
cardiogénico -ca, cardiógeno -na *adj* cardiogenic
cardiología *f* cardiology
cardiólogo -ga *mf* cardiologist
cardiomiopatía *f* cardiomyopathy; —— **dilatada** dilated cardiomyopathy; —— **hipertrófica** hypertrophic cardiomyopathy; —— **restrictiva** restrictive cardiomyopathy
cardiopatía *f* cardiopathy; —— **reumática** rheumatic heart disease
cardiovascular *adj* cardiovascular
cardioversión *f* cardioversion
carditis *f* carditis
cardo *m* thistle
carencia *f* lack, deficiency
caries *f* caries, tooth decay
cariño *m* affection, love
cariñoso -sa *adj* affectionate, loving
carne *f* flesh; meat; —— **de cerdo** pork; —— **de cordero** lamb; —— **de puerco** pork; —— **de res** beef
carnicero -ra *mf* butcher
carnosidad *f* pterygium (*form*), benign growth on the eye
carótido -da *adj* carotid
carpiano -na *adj* carpal
carpintero -ra *mf* carpenter

carraspear *vi* to clear one's throat
carraspera *f* irritation of the throat
carro *m* car, automobile
carta *f* chart; —— **del examen visual** eye chart; —— **de Snellen** Snellen chart
cartílago *m* cartilage
casa *f* home; —— **de cuna** orphanage; **en** —— at home
casco *m* helmet
caso *m* case; **en nueve de diez casos**..in nine out of ten cases
caspa *f* dandruff
castañetear *vi* (*los dientes*) to chatter
castración *f* castration
castrar *vt* to castrate
cataplasma *f* plaster (*medicinal*)
catarata *f* cataract
catarro *m* cold
catatonía *f* catatonia
catéter *m* catheter; —— **central** central line; —— **Foley** Foley catheter; —— **Hickman** Hickman catheter; —— **Tenckhoff** Tenckhoff catheter
cateterismo *m* catheterization; —— **cardiaco** cardiac catheterization
catgut *m* catgut
causa *f* cause
causalgia *f* causalgia
causar *vt* to cause
cáustico -ca *adj* caustic
cauterizar *vt* to cauterize
cavidad *f* cavity
cc. *abbr* **centímetro cúbico.** *See* **centímetro.**
célula *f* cell; —— **B** B cell; —— **plasmática** plasma cell; —— **T** T cell
cecear *vi* to lisp
ceceo *m* lisp
cefaclor *m* cefaclor
cefalea *f* (*form*) headache; —— **en grupos** cluster headache; —— **por tensión** *or* **tensional** tension headache; —— **postraumática** postconcussional syndrome; —— **vascular** vascular headache
cefálico -ca *adj* cephalic
cefalosporina *f* cephalosporin
cefalotina *f* cephalothin
cefotaxima *f* cefotaxime
ceftriaxona *f* ceftriaxone
ceguera *f* blindness; —— **nocturna** night blindness
ceja *f* eyebrow
celiaco -ca, celíaco -ca *adj* celiac
celulitis *f* cellulitis; (*depósitos de grasa debajo de la piel*) cellulite
cena *f* dinner, supper
centígrado -da *adj* centigrade
centímetro (cm.) *m* centimeter (cm.); —— **cúbico (cc.)** centimeter cubed *o* cubic centimeter (cc.)
central *adj* central
centro *m* center; —— **de salud** healthcare center

cepa f strain (of bacteria, etc.)
cepillado m brushing
cepillar vt to brush; vr **cepillarse el pelo** to brush one's hair; **cepillarse los dientes** to brush one's teeth
cepillo m brush; —— **de dientes** toothbrush
cera f wax
cerclaje m cerclage
cerdo m pork
cereal m cereal, grain
cerebelo m cerebellum
cerebral adj cerebral
cerebro m cerebrum (form), brain; (fam) back of head or neck; —— **medio** midbrain
cerebrovascular adj cerebrovascular
cerilla f earwax
cerrar vt to close; —— **la mano** to make a fist; vi, vr to close
certificado m certificate; —— **de defunción** death certificate; —— **de nacimiento** birth certificate; —— **para no trabajar** work excuse
cerveza f beer
cervical adj cervical
cervicitis f cervicitis
cérvix f (pl -**vix**) cervix
cetoacidosis f ketoacidosis
cetona f ketone
cetónico -ca adj ketotic; **no** —— nonketotic
CIA abbr **comunicación interauricular**. See **comunicación**.
cianosis f cyanosis
cianótico -ca adj cyanotic
cianuro m cyanide
ciático -ca adj sciatic; f sciatica
cicatriz f (pl -**trices**) scar; **dejar** —— **to** leave a scar
cicatrizar vt, vr to heal (a wound)
ciclamato m cyclamate
cíclico -ca adj cyclic
ciclo m cycle; —— **anovulatorio** anovulatory cycle; —— **menstrual** menstrual cycle; —— **ovulatorio** ovulatory cycle; —— **reproductor** reproductive cycle
ciclofosfamida f cyclophosphamide
ciego -ga adj blind; mf blind person; m cecum
ciempiés m (pl -**piés**) centipede
científico -ca adj scientific; mf scientist
cierre m zipper
cierto -ta adj sure
cifoscoliosis f kyphoscoliosis
cifosis f kyphosis
cigarrillo m cigarette
cigarro m cigarette, cigar
cilindro urinario m urinary cast
cimetidina f cimetidine
cinc m zinc; **óxido de** —— zinc oxide
cincho m belt
cinta f tape; —— **adhesiva** adhesive tape; —— **métrica** measuring tape; —— **reactiva** test strip, dipstick
cinto m belt
cintura f waist
cinturón m belt, wide belt, (para prevenir hernias) abdominal supporter, kidney belt; —— **de seguridad** seat belt
ciprofloxacina f ciprofloxacin
circulación f circulation; —— **colateral** collateral circulation; —— **fetal** fetal circulation; —— **pulmonar** pulmonary circulation; —— **sistémica** or **mayor** systemic circulation
circulatorio -ria adj circulatory
círculo m circle
circuncidar vt (pp -**ciso**) to circumcise
circuncisión f circumcision
circunciso -sa (pp of **circuncidar**) adj circumcised
cirrosis f cirrhosis
cirrótico -ca adj & mf cirrhotic
cirugía f surgery; —— **cosmética** or **estética** cosmetic surgery; —— **de corazón abierto** open heart surgery; —— **electiva** elective surgery; —— **general** general surgery; —— **mayor** major surgery; —— **menor** minor surgery; —— **oral** oral surgery; —— **ortopédica** orthopedic surgery; —— **plástica** plastic surgery; —— **radical** radical surgery; —— **reconstructiva** reconstructive surgery
cirujano -na mf surgeon
cisplatin m cisplatin
cistectomía f cystectomy
cisteina f cysteine
cisticercosis f cysticercosis
cístico -ca adj cystic (duct, artery)
cistinuria f cystinuria
cistitis f cystitis
cistocele m cystocele
cistoscopia, cistoscopía f cystoscopy
cita f appointment
citología f (exfoliativa) Papanicolaou smear
citomegalovirus m cytomegalovirus
citotóxico -ca adj cytotoxic
citrato m citrate
CIV abbr **comunicación interventricular**. See **comunicación**.
claro -ra adj clear; f (de huevo) white (of an egg)
clase f class
clásico -ca adj classic
claudicación f claudication; —— **intermitente** intermittent claudication
claustrofobia f claustrophobia
clavícula f clavicle
clavo m nail; (ortho) pin
clima m climate, weather
clindamicina f clindamycin
clínico -ca adj clinical; m clinician; f clinic; **clínica de urgencias** urgent care clinic

clítoris *m* clitoris
clofazimina *f* clofazamine
clofibrato *m* clofibrate
clomifén *m* clomiphene
clona *f* clone
clonacepam *m* clonazepam
clónico -ca *adj* clonic
clonidina *f* clonidine
clonus, clono *m* clonus
cloración *f* chlorination
clorado -da *adj* chlorinated
clorambucilo *m* chlorambucil
cloranfenicol, cloramfenicol *m* chloramphenicol
clordano *m* chlordane
clorhídrico -ca *adj* hydrochloric
cloro *m* chlorine
cloroformo *m* chloroform
cloropromacina *f* chlorpromazine
clorpropamida *f* chlorpropamide
cloruro *m* chloride; —— **de sodio** sodium chloride
Clostridium Clostridium
clotrimazol *m* clotrimazole
cm. *See* **centímetro.**
coagulación *f* coagulation; —— **intravascular diseminada** disseminated intravascular coagulation (DIC)
coagular *vt, vr* to clot, coagulate
coágulo *m* clot
coagulopatía *f* coagulopathy
coartación *f* coarctation
cobalto *m* cobalt
cobayo *m* guinea pig
cobertor *m* bedspread; —— **eléctrico** electric blanket
cobertura *f* (*seguros*) coverage
cobija *f* (*esp. Mex*) blanket; —— **eléctrica** electric blanket
cobre *m* copper
cobro *m* bill, charge
coca *f* (*bot*) coca; (*fam*) cocaine, coke (*fam*); —— **en pasta** free base (cocaine)
cocaína *f* cocaine
cocainómano -na *mf* cocaine addict
coccidioidomicosis *f* coccidioidomycosis
cóccix *m* coccyx
cocer *vt, vi* (*carne*) to boil (*meat*)
cocido -da *adj* cooked, boiled; —— **al horno** baked; —— **al vapor** steamed
cociente de inteligencia (CI) *m* intelligence quotient (IQ)
cocinar *vt, vi* to cook
cocinero -ra *mf* cook
cóclea *f* cochlea
coco *m* (*micro*) coccus; (*bot*) coconut
coche *m* automobile, car
codeína *f* codeine
código postal *m* zip code
codo *m* elbow; —— **de tenista** tennis elbow
coger *vt* to grasp, grip; (*una enfermedad*) to catch

cohibición *f* inhibition
cohibido -da *adj* inhibited
coito *m* coitus; —— **bucal** *or* **oral** fellatio; —— **interrumpido** coitus interruptus
cojear *vi* to limp
cojín *m* cushion, pad; —— **eléctrico** heating pad
cojincillo *m* small cushion, pad
cojo -ja *adj* lame, crippled; *mf* lame person, crippled person
cojones *mpl* (*vulg*) testicles, balls (*vulg*)
colágeno, colágena *m* collagen
colangiocarcinoma *m* cholangiocarcinoma
colangiografía *f* cholangiography; cholangiogram; —— **transhepática percutánea** percutaneous transhepatic cholangiography (PTC)
colangiograma *m* cholangiogram
colangiopancreatografía retrógrada endoscópica *f* endoscopic retrograde cholangiopancreatography (ERCP)
colangitis *f* cholangitis
colapso *m* collapse, breakdown; —— **nervioso** nervous breakdown; **sufrir un** —— to collapse
colateral *adj* collateral
colcha *f* blanket
colchicina *f* colchicine
colchón *m* mattress
colecistectomía *f* cholecystectomy
colecistitis *f* cholecystitis
colectomía *f* colectomy
cólera *m* cholera; *f* anger, rage
colesterol *m* cholesterol
colestiramina *f* cholestyramine
colgajo *m* (*surg*) flap
colgar *vt* to hang, to dangle
cólico -ca *adj* pertaining to the colon, (*anat*) colic; *m* colic; —— **menstrual** menstrual cramp
colirio *m* eyewash
colitis *f* colitis; —— **seudomembranosa** pseudomembranous colitis; —— **ulcerosa** ulcerative colitis
colmillo *m* cuspid, canine tooth, fang
coloide *m* colloid
colombiano -na *adj & mf* Colombian
colon *m* colon; —— **sigmoide** sigmoid colon
colónico -ca *adj* colonic, pertaining to the colon
colonización *f* colonization
colonoscopia, colonoscopía *f* colonoscopy
color *m* color
coloración *f* (*micro*) stain; —— **de Gram** Gram's stain
colorado -da *adj* red
colorante *m* dye
colostomía *f* colostomy
colposcopia, colposcopía *f* colposcopy
colquicina *f* colchicine
columna *f* backbone, spine; —— **cervical**

cervical spine; —— **lumbar** lumbar spine; —— **sacra** sacral spine; —— **torácica** *or* **dorsal** thoracic spine; —— **vertebral** spinal column

collar cervical *m* (*rígido o blando*) cervical collar (*hard or soft*)

collarín *m* (*rígido o blando*) cervical collar (*hard or soft*)

coma *m* coma; **en** —— in a coma

comadrona *f* midwife (*esp. without training*)

comatoso -sa *adj* comatose

combinación *f* combination

combustible *m* fuel

comer *vt, vi* to eat; (*Mex*) to have lunch; **dar de** —— to feed; *vr* **comerse las uñas** to bite *o* chew one's nails

comezón *f* itching, itch; **tener** —— to itch

comida *f* food, meal; (*Mex*) lunch; —— **balanceada** balanced meal; —— **para niños** baby food

comienzo *m* onset, beginning

comodidad *f* comfort

cómodo -da *adj* comfortable; *m* (*Mex*) bedpan

compasión *f* compassion, sympathy

compasivo -va *adj* sympathetic

compatible *adj* compatible

compensar *vt, vi* to compensate

complejo *m* complex; —— **de Edipo** Oedipal complex; —— **relacionado con el SIDA** AIDS-related complex (ARC)

complemento *m* complement

completo -ta *adj* complete

complexión *f* build, physique

complicación *f* complication

componer *vt* (*pp* **-puesto**) to fix; *vr* (*fam*) to get well

comportamiento *m* behavior

comportarse *vr* to behave

comprensivo -va *adj* understanding, sympathetic

compresa *f* compress, pack; —— **de hielo** ice pack

compresión *f* compression, (*de un nervio*) entrapment; **compresiones torácicas** chest compressions

comprimido *m* tablet

comprimir *vt* to compress

comprometer *vt* to compromise

compuesto *pp* of **componer**

compuesto *m* compound

compulsión *f* compulsion

compulsivo -va *adj* compulsive

computadora *f* computer

común *adj* common; **poco** —— uncommon

comunicación *f* communication; —— **interauricular (CIA)** atrial septal defect (ASD); —— **interventricular (CIV)** ventricular septal defect (VSD)

comunidad *f* community

comunitario -ria *adj* community

cóncavo -va *adj* concave

concebir *vi* to conceive

concentración *f* concentration

concentrado -da *adj* concentrated; *m* (*pharm*) concentrate

concentrar *vt, vr* to concentrate

concepción *f* conception

conciencia *f* consciousness; conscience; —— **culpable** guilty conscience; **perder la** —— to lose consciousness

concusión *f* concussion

condado *m* county (*US*)

condición *f* condition

condicionado -da *adj* conditioned

condón *m* condom, rubber (*fam*)

condrosarcoma *m* chondrosarcoma

conducir *vt* (*un vehículo*) to drive

conducta *f* behavior; **modificación** *f* **de la** —— behavior modification

conducto *m* duct; canal; —— **arterioso persistente** patent ductus arteriosus (PDA); —— **de Eustaquio** Eustachian tube; —— **deferente** *or* —— **excretorio del testículo** vas deferens; —— **semicircular** semicircular canal

conejillo de Indias *m* guinea pig (*esp. fig*)

confabulación *f* confabulation

confiable *adj* reliable

confianza *f* confidence, trust; —— **en sí mismo** self-confidence; **tener** —— **(en)** to trust

confiar *vi* to trust; **Confío en Ud...**I trust you.

confidencial *adj* confidential, private

conflicto *m* conflict

confort *m* comfort

confortar *vt* to comfort

confundir *vt* to confuse; *vr* to become confused

confusión *f* confusion

congelación *f* freezing; (*path*) frostbite

congelar *vt, vr* to freeze

congénito -ta *adj* congenital

congestión *f* congestion

congestionado -da *adj* congested

congestivo -va *adj* congestive

conjugado -da *adj* conjugated

conjuntiva *f* conjunctiva

conjuntivitis *f* conjunctivitis, pinkeye (*fam*)

conmoción *f* concussion

cono *m* cone

conocimiento *m* consciousness; **perder el** —— to lose consciousness

consciente *adj* conscious; —— **de sí mismo** self-conscious

consecuencia *f* consequence

consecutivo -va *adj* consecutive

consejero -ra *mf* counselor

consejo *m* counseling

consentimiento *m* consent

consentir *vi* to consent; —— **en** to consent to

conservador -ra *adj* (*medidas, etc.*)

conservative
consistencia f consistency
consolador m (fam) dildo
consomé m consommé, broth
constante adj constant, (dolor) steady
constipación f (del intestino) constipation; (esp. Mex, CA; de la nariz) congestion; nasal congestion
constipado -da adj (del intestino) constipated; (esp. Mex, CA; de la nariz) congested, having nasal congestion
constipar vt to constipate; vr to become constipated; (esp. Mex, CA; de la nariz) to become congested
constitución f constitution
consulta f consultation; **horas de** —— office hours
consultar vt to consult
consultorio m office (of a doctor)
consumo m consumption
contacto m contact
contador m meter, measuring device
contagiar vt (una enfermedad) to give, to spread; **Me contagió la gripe..**He gave me the flu; vr to catch, to become infected; **Me contagié con la gripe..**I caught the flu...**Podría contagiarse..**You could become infected.
contagioso -sa adj contagious, catching (fam)
contaminación f contamination, pollution; —— **atmosférica** or **del aire** air pollution, smog
contaminar vt to contaminate; vr to become contaminated
contar vt, vi to count
contenido m content(s)
contento -ta adj happy
continuo -nua adj continual
contorno m contour
contracción f contraction; —— **auricular prematura** premature atrial contraction (PAC); —— **ventricular prematura** premature ventricular contraction (PVC)
contracepción f contraception
contraceptivo -va adj & m contraceptive
contractura f contracture
contraer vt, vr to contract
contraindicación f contraindication
contrarrestar vt to counteract
control m control; —— **de la natalidad** birth control; **fuera de** —— out of control
controlar vt to control
contusión f contusion
convalecencia f convalescence
convalecerse vr to convalesce
convaleciente adj convalescent
conversión f conversion; **reacción** f **de** —— conversion reaction
convexo -xa adj convex
convulsión f convulsion, seizure
cooperar vi to cooperate

cooperativo -va adj cooperative
coordinación f coordination
coprocultivo m stool culture
coqueluche m&f whooping cough
coraje m rage
coral m coral
corazón m heart; core; **ataque** m **al** —— heart attack; **enfermedad** f **del** —— heart disease
corcova f hump
corcovado -da mf humpback
cordal See **muela cordal**.
cordero m lamb
cordón m cord; —— **umbilical** umbilical cord
cordura f sanity
corea f chorea; —— **de Huntington** Huntington's chorea
coriorretinitis f chorioretinitis
córnea f cornea
corona f (anat, dent) crown
coronario -ria adj coronary
corpúsculo m corpuscle
correa f strap
corrección f correction, adjustment
correctivo -va adj corrective
correcto -ta adj correct
corredor m hall, hallway
corregir vt to correct; vi (Cub) to have a bowel movement
correlación f correlation
correoso -sa adj tough, leathery
correr vi to run
corrosivo -va adj corrosive
corsé m (pl -sés) girdle; truss
cortada f cut
cortadura f cut
cortar vt to cut; vr to cut oneself; **Me corté..**I cut myself...**Me corté la mano..**I cut my hand; **cortarse el pelo** to get a haircut; **cortarse las uñas** to cut one's nails
corte m cut; —— **de pelo** haircut; —— **por congelación** frozen section
corteza f cortex
cortical adj cortical
corticosteroide m corticosteroid
cortisol m cortisol
cortisona f cortisone
corto -ta adj short; **a** —— **plazo** short-term; **hacer más** —— to shorten
cortocircuito m shunt (physiological)
corva f back of the knee; **tendón** m **de la** —— hamstring
coser vt (una herida) to sew, stitch (up)
cosmético -ca adj & m cosmetic
cosquillas fpl tickling; **¿Siente cosquillas?..**Do you feel tickling?..Does that tickle?...**¿Le causo cosquillas?..**Am I tickling you?
cosquilleo m tickle, tickling
cosquilloso -sa adj ticklish

costado *m* (*anat*) side
costarricense *adj* & *mf* Costa Rican
costilla *f* rib
costo *m* charge, cost
costocondritis *f* costochondritis
costra *f* scab, crust
costumbre *f* habit; como de —— as usual; ¿Está comiendo tanto como de costumbre?..Are you eating as much as usual; que de —— than usual; ¿Está orinando más que de costumbre?..Are you urinating more than usual?
coyuntura *f* joint
crack *m* (*Ang*) crack (*cocaine*)
craneal *adj* cranial
craneano -na *adj* cranial
cráneo *m* cranium (*form*), skull
craneofaringioma *m* craniopharyngioma
creatinina *f* creatinine
crecer *vi* to grow, to get bigger; to grow up
crecimiento *m* growth
creencia *f* belief
crema *f* cream; —— dental toothpaste; —— limpiadora cold cream; —— para el sol suntan lotion, —— para los labios lip balm
cresa *f* maggot
cresta *f* (*Mex*) genital wart
cretinismo *m* cretinism
cretino -na *mf* cretin
criar *vt* to raise (*a child, animal, etc.*)
criatura *f* infant, baby
crioterapia *f* cryotherapy
criptorquidia *f* cryptorchidism
crisis *f* (*pl* -sis) crisis; (convulsiva *or* epiléptica) seizure; —— blástica blast crisis; —— de ausencia absence seizure; —— de identidad identity crisis; —— de la edad madura midlife crisis; —— del lóbulo temporal temporal lobe seizure; —— focal focal seizure; —— generalizada generalized seizure; —— gran mal gran mal seizure; —— jacksoniana Jacksonian seizure; —— nerviosa nervous breakdown; —— parcial compleja complex partial seizure; —— pequeño mal petit mal seizure; —— psicomotora psychomotor seizure; —— tiroidea thyroid storm; —— tónico-clónica tonic-clonic seizure
cristal *m* crystal
cristalino *m* lens (*of the eye*)
crítico -ca *adj* critical
cromo *m* chromium
cromoglicato de sodio *m* cromolyn sodium
cromosoma *m* chromosome
crónico -ca *adj* chronic
crudo -da *adj* raw; (*Mex*) hungover; *f* (*Mex*) hangover; tener una cruda to have a hangover, to be hungover
crup *m* croup
cruzar *vt* (*la sangre*) to crossmatch (*blood*);

—— los brazos to fold one's arms
Cruz Roja *f* Red Cross
Cryptococcus Cryptococcus
cuadrado -da *adj* square, squared; metro —— meter squared *o* square meter
cuadrante *m* quadrant
cuádriceps *m* (*pl* -ceps) quadriceps
cuadrillizo -za *mf* quadruplet
cuadriplejía *f* quadriplegia
cuadripléjico -ca *adj* & *mf* quadriplegic
cuadrupleto -ta *mf* quadruplet
cuajarón *m* (*Mex, fam*) clot, large clot
cuarentena *f* quarantine; (*Mex, CA*) forty days following childbirth; poner en —— to quarantine
cuarto *m* room, bedroom; (*de galón*) quart; —— de baño bathroom
cuasiorcor *m* kwashiorkor
cuate -ta *mf* (*Mex, fam*) twin
cubano -na *adj* & *mf* Cuban
cubierto *pp* of cubrir
cubital *adj* ulnar
cúbito *m* ulna
cubre-boca *m* (*surg, etc.*) mask
cubrir *vt* (*pp* cubierto) to cover; (*el estómago, etc.*) to coat
cucaracha *f* cockroach
cuclillas, en squatting
cucharada *f* spoonful, tablespoonful
cucharadita *f* teaspoonful
cuchillada *f* knife wound, gash
cuchillo *m* knife
cuello *m* neck; collar; —— uterino *or* de la matriz cervix
cuenca *f* (*del ojo*) socket
cuenta *f* bill, charges
cuentagotas *m* medicine dropper, eyedropper
cuerda *f* cord; —— vocal vocal cord
cuerdo -da *adj* sane
cuero cabelludo *m* scalp
cuerpo *m* body; —— de bomberos fire department; —— extraño foreign body
cuestionario *m* questionnaire
cuidado *m* care; —— del primer nivel primary care; —— del tercer nivel tertiary care; cuidados intensivos intensive care; tener —— to be careful; Tenga cuidado con este medicamento..Be careful with this medication.
cuidador -ra *mf* caregiver, caretaker
cuidar *vt* to care for, take care of; ¿Quién cuida a su abuelo en casa?..Who cares for your grandfather at home? *vr* to take care of oneself; (*fam*) to use birth control; Tiene que cuidarse si no quiere quedarse embarasada..You have to use birth control if you don't want to end up pregnant.
culdocentesis *f* (*pl* -sis) culdocentesis
culdoscopia, culdoscopía *f* culdoscopy
culebra *f* snake
culebrilla *f* (*esp. Carib*) shingles

culero *m* (*Carib*) diaper
culpa *f* guilt; **sentimientos de** —— guilt feelings
cultivar *vt* (*micro*) to culture
cultivo *m* (*micro*) culture
cultura *f* culture
cumarina *f* coumarin
cumpleaños *m* birthday; ¡**Feliz cumpleaños!**..Happy birthday!
cuna *f* cradle, crib
cuñada *f* sister-in-law
cuñado *m* brother-in-law
cunilinguo *m* cunnilingus
cura *m* priest; *f* cure
curable *adj* curable
curación *f* cure, treatment; —— de nervio

(*dent, fam*) root canal
curanderismo *m* folk medicine, faith healing
curandero -ra *mf* folk healer, faith healer
curar *vt* to cure, heal, treat; *vr* to be cured, heal, get well
curativo -va *adj* curative
curetaje *m* curettage
Curita *m&f* Band-Aid (*Los dos términos son marcas. Both terms are trademarks.*)
curso *m* course
curva *f* curve, bend; —— **de crecimiento** growth curve
cutáneo -a *adj* cutaneous
cutícula *f* cuticle
cutis *m* complexion

Ch

chalazión *m* chalazion
chamaco -ca *m* boy, child; *f* girl
chamarra *f* (*Mex*) jacket
chamorro *m* (*Mex, fam*) calf (*of leg*)
champú *m* (*pl* -púes) shampoo
chancro *m* chancre; —— **blando** soft chancre
chancroide *f* chancroid
chaparro -ra *adj* short (*stature*)
chaqueta *f* jacket; (*dent*) cap
charlatán -na *mf* charlatan, quack
charola *f* (*Mex*) tray
chasquido *m* (*card*) click
chata *f* bedpan
chato *m* (*Mex, fam*) crab louse, crab (*fam*)
chequeo *m* checkup
chicle *m* chewing gum
chico -ca *adj* small, little; *m* boy, child; *f* girl
chichi, chiche, chicha *f* (*vulg*) breast
chichón *m* lump, bump (*due to trauma, esp. about the head*)
chiflar *vi* **chiflarle el pecho** to wheeze
chiflido *m* wheeze
chileno -na *adj & mf* Chilean
chillar *vi* **chillarle el pecho** to wheeze; **Me chilla el pecho**..I am wheezing.
chillido *m* wheeze; **Tengo chillidos**..I have wheezing.

chimpinilla *f* (*CA, fam*) shin
china *f* (*PR, fam*) orange
chinche *f* bedbug; (*vector de la enfermedad de Chagas*) kissing bug
chipote *m* (*Mex, CA; fam*) lump, bump (*due to trauma*)
chiva *f* (*Mex, vulg*) heroin; (*PR, fam*) jaw
chivola *f* (*ES*) bump, lump
Chlamydia Chlamydia
chocolate *m* chocolate
choque *m* shock; automobile accident; —— **anafiláctico** anaphylactic shock; —— **cardiogénico** *or* **cardiógeno** cardiogenic shock; —— **eléctrico** electric shock; —— **hipovolémico** hypovolemic shock; —— **nervioso** nervous breakdown; —— **neurogénico** *or* **neurógeno** neurogenic shock; —— **séptico** septic shock
choquezuela *f* kneecap
chorro *m* (*de la orina*) stream; (*Mex, CA; fam*) diarrhea
choyarse *vr* (*Nic*) to graze (*oneself*)
choyón *m* (*Nic*) graze
chueco -ca *adj* (*Mex*) crooked
chupar *vt* to suck; **chuparse el dedo** to suck one's thumb
chupete *m* pacifier; hickey
chupón *m* pacifier; hickey

D

dacriocistitis *f* dacryocystitis
daltoniano -na *adj* color-blind
daltonismo *m* color blindness
danazol *m* danazol
dañado -da *adj* damaged, impaired
dañar *vt* to damage, harm
dañino -na *adj* harmful; **no** —— harmless
daño *m* damage, harm; **hacer** —— to hurt,
    damage, harm; to be bad for (*one*), to
    make (*one*) sick; **No le hizo ningún daño
    la caída.**.The fall didn't hurt him at
    all...**¿Le hace daño la medicina?**..Is the
    medicine making you sick?
dapsona *f* dapsone
dar *vt* —— **a luz** to give birth to, deliver;
    **La señora Ruiz dio a luz una niña
    ayer.**.Mrs. Ruiz gave birth to a baby girl
    yesterday; —— **de alta** to discharge (*from
    the hospital*); **Voy a darlo de alta
    mañana.**.I am going to discharge you
    tomorrow; —— **de comer** to feed; ——
    del cuerpo (*Carib, fam*) to have a bowel
    movement; **darle** (*a uno*) to have, to get,
    to catch; **Le dieron vómitos.**.He had
    vomiting...**Me dio un catarro.**.I got a
    cold; —— **pecho,** —— **seno,** *or* —— **de
    mamar** to breast-feed, to nurse; **¿Le va a
    dar pecho?**..Are you going to breast-feed
    him? *vi* —— **a luz** to give birth, to
    deliver; *vr* **darse vuelta** to turn around, to
    turn over, roll over
datos *mpl* data *n o npl*
DDT *See* **diclorodifeniltricloroetano.**
debido -da a, due to
débil *adj* weak, (*el pulso*) faint
debilidad *f* weakness
debilitación *f* debilitation, weakening
debilitado -da *adj* debilitated, run-down
debilitante *adj* debilitating
debilitar *vt* to weaken, make weak; *vr* to
    weaken, become weak
decaer *vi* to weaken, to get worse; to
    become depressed
decaído -da *adj* weak, run-down, debilitated;
    depressed
decaimiento *m* weakening, weakness,
    debilitation; depression
decibel *m* decibel
decidir *vt, vr* to decide
decilitro *m* deciliter
decisión *f* decision
dedo *m* (*de la mano*) finger; (*del pie*) toe;
    —— **anular** ring finger; —— **chico** (*del
    pie*) little toe; —— **de gatillo** trigger

finger; —— **de hule** finger cot; —— **del
    corazón** middle finger; —— **gordo** (*de la
    mano*) thumb, (*del pie*) big toe; **dedos
    hipocráticos** *or* **en palillo de tambor**
    clubbing, clubbed fingers; —— **índice**
    index finger; —— **medio** middle finger;
    —— **meñique** little finger
defecación *f* bowel movement (BM)
defecar *vi* to defecate, to have a bowel
    movement
defecto *m* defect; —— **del tubo neural**
    neural tube defect; —— **de nacimiento**
    birth defect
deficiencia *f* deficiency, lack
deficiente *adj* deficient
déficit *m* (*pl* **déficits**) deficit
definitivo -va *adj* definitive
deforme *adj* deformed
deformidad *f* deformity
degenerar *vi* to degenerate
degenerativo -va *adj* degenerative
deglutir *vi* to swallow
dejar *vi* —— **de** to quit, give up; **¿Cuándo
    dejó de comer?**..When did you quit
    eating?...**Debe dejar de fumar.**.You
    should give up smoking
delantal *m* apron
deleción *f* deletion
delgado -da *adj* thin
delicado -da *adj* frail, sickly, delicate; ill,
    seriously ill; (*condición*) serious
delirante *adj* delirious
delirar *vi* to be delirious, to rave; **Está
    delirando.**.He is delirious.
delirio *m* delirium
delirium tremens *m* delirium tremens, the
    d.t.'s (*fam*)
delta *f* delta
deltoides *m* (*pl* **-des**) deltoid
demacrado -da *adj* emaciated
demandar *vt* to sue
demencia *f* dementia
demente *adj* demented
demostrar *vt* to demonstrate
dengue *m* dengue fever, dengue
dentadura *f* teeth, set of teeth; denture;
    —— **postiza** denture, false teeth (*fam*)
dental *adj* dental
dentario -ria *adj* dental
dentición *f* (*form*) teething
dentista *mf* dentist
dentro *adv* inside; —— **de su cuerpo.**.in-
    side your body
departamento *m* department; —— **de salud**

Health Department
dependencia *f* dependence
dependiente *adj* dependent
depilatorio -ria *adj & m* depilatory
deponer *vt, vi* (*pp* **depuesto**) (*Mex, fam*) to throw up, vomit
deposición *f* (*SA*) bowel movement (BM)
depositar *vt, vr* to deposit
depósito *m* deposit, buildup; store; **de ——** (*pharm*) depot
depresión *f* depression
depresivo -va *adj* depressive
depresor -ra *adj* (*pharm, physio*) depressant; *m* depressant; tongue depressor *o* blade
deprimido -da *adj* depressed
deprimirse *vr* to get depressed
depuesto *pp of* **deponer**
derecho -cha *adj* straight; right; right-handed; *m* right (*legal, moral*); *f* right, right-hand side
derivación *f* (*surg*) shunt
dermatitis *f* dermatitis; **—— de los bañistas** swimmer's itch; **—— por contacto** contact dermatitis; **—— por pañal** diaper rash
dermatología *f* dermatology
dermatólogo -ga *mf* dermatologist
dermatomiositis *f* dermatomyositis
derrame *m* effusion, bleed; **—— cerebral** cerebral hemorrhage, hemorrhagic stroke, (*fam*) stroke (*of any type*); **—— pericárdico** *or* **pericardiaco** pericardial effusion; **—— pleural** pleural effusion
DES *See* **dietilestilbestrol.**
desabotonar *vt, vr* to unbutton
desabrochar *vt, vr* to unbutton, to unbuckle
desagradable *adj* unpleasant
desahogo *m* (*psych*) relief, outlet
desalentado -da *adj* despondent, discouraged
desalentar *vt* to discourage; *vr* to become discouraged
desanimado -da *adj* despondent, discouraged
desanimar *vt* to discourage; *vr* to become discouraged
desaparecerse *vr* to disappear
desagüe *m* sewer
desarrollar *vt, vr* to develop
desarrollo *m* development
desatender *vt* to neglect
desayunarse *vr* to have breakfast
desayuno *m* breakfast
desbaratar *vt* (*una tableta, etc.*) to crush
desbridamiento *m* debridement
descalabrar *vt* to injure the head of (*someone*); **Lo descalabraron.**.They injured his head; *vr* to injure (*one's*) head; **Me descalabré.**.I injured my head.
descalzo -za *adj* barefoot
descamarse *vr* (*form*) to peel, flake
descansar *vt, vr* to rest
descanso *m* rest

descarga *f* discharge; **—— eléctrica** electric shock; **—— nasal posterior** postnasal drip
descartar *vt* to rule out; **Tenemos que descartar el cáncer.**.We need to rule out cancer.
descendente *adj* descending
descendiente *mf* descendant
descongestionante *adj & m* decongestant
descongestivo -va *adj & m* decongestant
descontinuar *vt* to discontinue
describir *vt* to describe
descuidado -da *adj* careless; neglected
descuidar *vt* to neglect
descuido *m* neglect, carelessness
desde *prep* ¿**Desde cuándo tiene diabetes?**.. How long have you had diabetes?
desear *vt* to desire
desecante *adj & m* desiccant
desechable *adj* disposable
desecho *m* (*often pl*) waste; (*Mex, fam*) vaginal discharge; **desechos metabólicos** metabolic wastes; **desechos peligrosos** hazardous wastes
desemborracharse *vr* to sober up
desembriagarse *vr* to sober up
desensibilización *f* desensitization
desensibilizar *vt* to desensitize
deseo *m* desire; **—— sexual** sexual desire, libido
desequilibrio *m* imbalance
desesperación *f* desperate feeling, severe anxiety
desesperado -da *adj* hopeless, desperate
desesperarse *vr* to lose hope; to become desperate
desfibrilación *f* defibrillation
desfibrilar *vt* to defibrillate
desgarradura *f* (*de un músculo, ligamento, etc.*) tear
desgarramiento *m* (*de un músculo, ligamento, etc.*) tear
desgarrar *vt, vr* (*un músculo, ligamento, etc.*) to tear; (*flema*) to cough up; **Se me desgarró el músculo.**.I tore my muscle... ¿**Está desgarrando flema?**..Are you coughing up phlegm?
desgarre *m* (*de un músculo, ligamento, etc.*) tear
desgarro *m* (*de un músculo, ligamento, etc.*) tear
desguanzado -da *adj* (*Mex, fam*) tired, run-down, lightheaded
desguanzarse *vr* (*Mex, fam*) to become tired, to become run-down, to feel faint
deshidratación *f* dehydration
deshidratado -da *adj* dehydrated
deshidrogenasa láctica *f* lactic dehydrogenase
deshumanizante *adj* dehumanizing
desinfectante *adj & m* disinfectant
desinfectar *vt* to disinfect

desintoxicación *f* detoxification
desmayarse *vr* to faint, pass out
desmayo *m* faint, blackout
desmielinizante *adj* demyelinating
desmoralizar *vt* to demoralize; *vr* to become demoralized
desnudo -da *adj* naked
desnutrición *f* malnutrition
desnutrido -da *adj* malnourished
desodorante *m* deodorant
desorden *m* disorder
desorientado -da *adj* disoriented
despellejarse *vr* (*fam*) to peel
desperdicios *mpl* wastes
despersonalización *f* (*psych*) depersonalization
despertar *vt* (*pp* -tado *or* -pierto) to wake (up), arouse; *vr* to wake up
despierto -ta (*pp of* despertar) *adj* awake
despigmentación *f* depigmentation
desplomarse *vr* to collapse
desprenderse *vr* to slough (off)
destetar *vt* to wean
destete *m* weaning
destilado -da *adj* distilled
destreza *f* skill
destructivo -va *adj* destructive
destruir *vt* to destroy
desvanecerse *vr* to faint
desvariar *vi* to rave, talk nonsense
desvelado -da *adj* sleepless, lacking sleep
desvelarse *vr* to go without sleep
desventaja *f* disadvantage
detección *f* screening, detection
detectar *vt* to detect
detener *vt* —— la respiración *or* el resuello to hold one's breath; Detenga la respiración..Hold your breath.
detergente *adj* & *m* detergent
deteriorarse *vr* to deteriorate
deterioro *m* deterioration
devolver *vt*, *vi* (*pp* devuelto) to throw up, vomit
dexametasona *f* dexamethasone
día *m* day; cada dos días every other day; el —— anterior the day before; el —— siguiente the day after, the following day; todos los días every day
diabetes *f* diabetes; —— insípida diabetes insipidus; —— mellitus diabetes mellitus
diabético -ca *adj* & *mf* diabetic
diacepam *var of* diazepam
diafragma *m* (*anat*, *gyn*) diaphragm
diagnosis *f* (*pl* -sis) diagnosis
diagnosticar *vt* to diagnose
diagnóstico -ca *adj* diagnostic; *m* diagnosis
diagrama *m* diagram
diálisis *f* dialysis; —— peritoneal peritoneal dialysis
diámetro *m* diameter
diapasón *m* tuning fork
diarrea *f* diarrhea; —— del viajero

traveler's diarrhea
diastólico -ca *adj* diastolic
diazepam *m* diazepam
diclorodifeniltricloroetano (DDT) *m* dichlorodiphenyltrichloroethane (DDT)
dicloxacilina *f* dicloxacillin
dieldrín *m* dieldrin
diente *m* tooth, front tooth; —— canino canine tooth, cuspid; —— de leche baby tooth; —— incisivo incisor, front tooth; —— molar molar; —— picado decayed tooth, tooth with a cavity; Tiene un diente picado..You have a cavity; dientes postizos false teeth; dientes salidos buckteeth
dieta *f* diet; estar a —— to be on a diet, to diet
dietético -ca *adj* dietary
dietilamida del ácido lisérgico (LSD) *f* lysergic acid diethylamide (LSD)
dietilestilbestrol (DES) *m* diethylstilbestrol (DES)
dietista *mf* dietician
difenhidramina *f* diphenhydramine
difteria *f* diphtheria
difunto -ta *adj* & *mf* deceased
difusión *f* diffusion; de —— regulada (*pharm*) timed-release
digerible *adj* digestible
digerir *vt* to digest
digestión *f* digestion
digestivo -va *adj* digestive
digital *adj* digital; *f* (*pharm*) digitalis
digoxina *f* digoxin
dilatación *f* dilation
dilatador *m* dilator
dilatar *vt*, *vr* to dilate
diltiazem *m* diltiazem
diluido -da *adj* dilute
diluir *vt* to dilute
diluvio *m* flood
dimensión *f* dimension
dimetilsulfóxido *m* dimethyl sulfoxide (DMSO)
dimetiltriptamina (DMT) *f* dimethyltryptamine (DMT)
dinitrato de isosorbide *m* isosorbide dinitrate
dióxido *m* dioxide; —— de azufre sulfur dioxide; —— de carbono carbon dioxide
diplococo *m* diplococcus
dirección *f* direction; address
discinesia tardía *f* tardive dyskinesia
disco *m* disk; —— desplazado slipped disk; —— herniado herniated disk
discrasia *f* dyscrasia; —— sanguínea blood dyscrasia
diseminación *f* spread
diseminado -da *adj* disseminated
diseminar *vt*, *vr* to disseminate, spread
disentería *f* dysentery
disfasia *f* dysphasia

disfunción f dysfunction
disgregación f (psych) disintegration
dislexia f dyslexia
dislocación f dislocation
dislocar vt, vr to dislocate, to become dislocated; ¿Se le había dislocado el hombro antes?..Had you dislocated your shoulder before?
disminución f decrease
disminuir vt to reduce, decrease; vi, vr to decrease, to get smaller
disociación f (psych) dissociation
disolvente m solvent
disolver vt, vr (pp disuelto) to dissolve
disopiramida f disopyramide
dispensar vt (pharm) to dispense
displasia f dysplasia
disponible adj available
dispositivo m device; —— **intrauterino** (DIU) intrauterine device (IUD)
distender vt to distend; vi, vr to become distended; **distendérsele el estómago** to get bloated; **Se me distiende el estómago**..My stomach gets bloated.
distinguir vt to distinguish
distraído -da adj absent-minded
distrofia muscular progresiva f muscular dystrophe
disuelto pp of **disolver**
disulfiramo m disulfiram
disvariar var of **desvariar**
DIU abbr **dispositivo intrauterino**. See **dispositivo**.
diuresis f diuresis
diurético -ca adj & m diuretic
diván m (psych) couch
diverticulitis f diverticulitis
divertículo m diverticulum
diverticulosis f diverticulosis
divorciar vt, vr to divorce
divorcio m divorce
DMT See **dimetiltriptamina**.
doblar vt to bend, flex; to double; **Doble la pierna**..Bend your leg; vr to bend, bend over, bend down; to sprain, twist; **Dóblese**..Bend over...**Me doblé el tobillo**.. I sprained my ankle.
doble adj & adv double
doctor -ra mf doctor, physician
dolencia f ache, pain, ailment
doler vi to hurt; ¿Le duele?..Does it hurt?...¿Le duele el pie?..Does your foot hurt?...¿Dónde le duele?..Where does it hurt?...El procedimiento no duele..The procedure doesn't hurt.
dolor m pain, ache; —— **de barriga** bellyache; —— **de cabeza** headache; —— **de dientes** toothache; —— **de espalda** backache; —— **de estómago** stomachache; —— **de garganta** sore throat; —— **de hambre** hunger pang o

pain; —— **del parto** labor pain, contraction; —— **de muelas** toothache; —— **de oído** earache; —— **menstrual** menstrual cramp; **sin** —— painless
dolorido -da adj sore, tender
doloroso -sa adj painful, sore, tender
domicilio m home; address
dominante adj dominant
dominicano -na adj & mf Dominican
dominio de sí mismo m self-control
donado -da adj donated, donor; **sangre donada** donated blood, donor blood
donador -ra mf donor
donante mf donor
donar vt to donate
Doppler m Doppler
dormido -da adj asleep; (adormecido) numb, asleep; **Tengo dormido el brazo**..My arm is numb..My arm is asleep.
dormir vt to put to sleep; to numb (up); ¿Me van a dormir el pie?..Are you going to numb up my foot? vi to sleep; ¿Duerme bien?..Do you sleep well? vr to go to sleep, to fall asleep; (adormecerse) to become numb, to go to sleep, to fall asleep; **Se me duerme el brazo**..My arm gets numb.
dormitorio m bedroom
dorsal adj dorsal
dorso m (de la mano) back (of the hand)
dosificación f dosage
dosis f (pl dosis) dose; —— **excesiva** overdose
doxiciclina f doxycycline
dren m drain
drenaje m drain, drainage; sewer
drenar vt, vr to drain
drepanocitemia f sickle cell disease
droga f drug
drogadicto -ta mf drug addict
drogado -da adj drugged, high (fam)
drogar vt to drug; vr to take drugs, to become intoxicated
ducha f shower; douche; **darse** or **tomarse una** —— to take a shower
ducharse vr to take a shower; to douche
duela f fluke
dulce adj sweet; m piece of candy; **dulces** candy, sweets
duodenal adj duodenal
duodenitis f duodenitis
duodeno m duodenum
duración f duration
duradero -ra adj durable
durar vi to last; **Los vómitos me duraron toda la noche**..The vomiting lasted all night.
duro -ra adj hard, tough; stiff; **Se me puso duro el brazo**..My arm got stiff;—— **de oído** hard of hearing

E

eccema *m&f* eczema
ECG *See* **electrocardiograma.**
eclampsia *f* eclampsia
ecocardiografía *f* echocardiography; echocardiogram
ecocardiograma *m* echocardiogram
ectópico -ca *adj* ectopic
ecuatoriano -na *adj* & *mf* Ecuadoran
echar *vt* to pass, to shed; —— de menos to miss; ¿Echa de menos a su hija?..Do you miss your daughter? *vr* echarse a perder to spoil (*food, etc.*); echarse vientos *or* gases to pass gas
Echinococcus Echinococcus
edad *f* age; —— madura *or* mediana middle age; —— ósea bone age
edema *m* edema; —— pulmonar pulmonary edema
educación *f* education
educar *vt* to educate
EEG *See* **electroencefalograma.**
efecto *m* effect; —— adverso adverse effect; —— colateral *or* secundario side effect; hacer —— to take effect
efedrina *f* ephedrine
eficaz *adj* (*pl* -caces) effective
eficiente *adj* efficient
ego *m* (*psych*) ego
egocéntrico -ca *adj* self-centered, egocentric
ejercicio *m* exercise; hacer —— to exercise
elástico -ca *adj* & *m* elastic
eléctrico -ca *adj* electric, electrical
electrocardiografía *f* electrocardiography; electrocardiogram (ECG *o* EKG)
electrocardiograma (ECG) *m* electrocardiogram (ECG *o* EKG)
electrocutar *vt* to electrocute
electroencefalograma (EEG) *m* electroencephalogram (EEG)
electroforesis *f* electrophoresis
electrolítico -ca *adj* pertaining to electrolytes, electrolyte
electrólito, electrolito *m* electrolyte
electromiografía (EMG) *f* electromyography (EMG)
elefantiasis *f* elephantiasis
elegible *adj* eligible
elemento *m* element
elevación *f* elevation, rise
elevar *vt* to elevate, raise; *vi, vr* to rise
eliminar *vt* to eliminate, (*parásitos, una piedra, etc.*) to pass
emaciado -da *adj* emaciated
embarado -da *adj* (*fam*) bloated

embarazada *adj* pregnant
embarazo *m* pregnancy; Tengo cuatro meses de embarazo..I'm four months pregnant; —— ectópico ectopic pregnancy; —— tubárico tubal pregnancy
embolectomía *f* embolectomy
embolia *f* embolism, (*fam*) stroke; —— pulmonar pulmonary embolism
embolio (*Mex*) *var of* embolia
émbolo *m* embolus; (*de una jeringa*) plunger
emborracharse *vr* to get drunk
embriagarse *vr* to get drunk
embriología *f* embryology
embrión *m* embryo
emergencia *f* emergency; sala de —— emergency room (ER)
emético -ca *adj* & *m* emetic
EMG *See* **electromiografía.**
emoción *f* emotion, feeling
emocional *adj* emotional
emotivo -va *adj* emotional (*said of a person*)
empacharse *vr* to develop indigestion, to get a stomach ache. *See* empacho.
empacho *m* indigestion, folk illness manifest by abdominal bloating and other gastrointestinal complaints and believed due to food sticking to the sides of the intestine
empañado -da *adj* blurred; vista empañada blurred vision
empañarse *vr* (*la vista*) to blur, to become blurred; Me empaña la vista..My vision blurs..My vision gets blurred.
empastar *vt* (*dent*) to fill (*a tooth*)
empaste *m* (*dent*) filling
empatía *f* empathy
empeine *m* instep; groin; ringworm
empeoramiento *m* worsening
empeorar *vt* to make worse; *vi, vr* to get worse, deteriorate
empiema *m* empyema
emplasto *m* plaster (*medicinal*)
empleador -ra *mf* employer
empleo *m* employment, occupation, job
enalapril *m* enalapril
enanismo *m* dwarfism
enano -na *mf* dwarf, midget
encamado -da *adj* in bed, in a bed; *mf* patient in a bed
encefalitis *f* encephalitis
encefalomielitis *f* encephalomyelitis
encefalopatía *f* encephalopathy; —— de Wernicke Wernicke's encephalopathy
encía *f* (*anat*) gum

encinta *adj* pregnant
encoger *vt* (*la pierna, el brazo*) to bend; *vi* to get smaller; *vr* to get smaller; (*fam*) to get stiff, to cramp (up), to become contracted
enconarse *vr* to fester
encorvarse *vr* to bend down, stoop
enchufe *m* electrical outlet
endarterectomía *f* endarterectomy
endémico -ca *adj* endemic
enderezar *vt, vr* (*los dientes, un hueso, etc.*) to straighten
endocardio *m* endocardium
endocarditis *f* endocarditis
endocrino -na *adj* endocrine
endocrinología f endocrinology
endocrinólogo -ga *mf* endocrinologist
endodoncia *f* root canal
endometrio *m* endometrium
endometriosis *f* endometriosis
endometritis *f* endometritis
endorfina *f* endorphin
endoscopia, endoscopía *f* endoscopy
endotraqueal *adj* endotracheal
endovenoso -sa *adj* intravenous (IV)
enema *m&f* enema; —— **de bario** barium enema
energía *f* energy
enérgico -ca *adj* energetic
enfermarse *vr* to get sick
enfermedad *f* disease, sickness, illness; —— **articular degenerativa** degenerative joint disease; —— **celiaca** celiac disease; —— **colágeno-vascular** *or* **del colágeno** collagen-vascular disease; —— **de Addison** Addison's disease; —— **de almacenamiento de glucógeno** glycogen storage disease; —— **de Alzheimer** Alzheimer's disease; —— **de células falciformes** *or* **drepanocíticas** sickle cell disease; —— **de Crohn** Crohn's disease; —— **de Cushing** Cushing's disease; —— **de Chagas** Chagas' disease; —— **de Gaucher** Gaucher's disease; —— **de Gilbert** Gilbert's disease *o* syndrome; —— **de Gilles de la Tourette** Gilles de la Tourette syndrome; —— **de Graves** Graves' disease; —— **de Hansen** Hansen's disease; —— **de Hirschsprung** Hirschsprung's disease; —— **de Hodgkin** Hodgkin's disease; —— **de Huntington** Huntington's disease; —— **de Kawasaki** Kawasaki's disease; —— **de lesiones mínimas** minimal change disease; —— **del injerto contra el huésped** graft-versus-host disease; —— **de los legionarios** Legionnaire's disease; —— **del sueño** sleeping sickness; —— **del suero** serum sickness; —— **del tejido conectivo** *or* **conjuntivo** connective tissue disease; —— **de Lyme** Lyme disease; —— **de mano, pie y boca** hand-foot-and-

mouth disease; —— **de membrana hialina** hyaline membrane disease; —— **de Paget** Paget's disease; —— **de Parkinson** Parkinson's disease; —— **de Pott** Pott's disease; —— **de transmisión sexual** sexually transmitted disease (STD); —— **de Vincent** Vincent's angina, trench mouth; —— **de von Willebrand** von Willebrand's disease *o* syndrome; —— **de Whipple** Whipple's disease; —— **de Wilson** Wilson's disease; —— **fibroquística** fibrocystic disease; —— **inflamatoria pélvica** pelvic inflammatory disease (PID); —— **intersticial pulmonar** interstitial lung disease; —— **mamaria benigna** benign breast disease; —— **mental** mental illness; —— **por arañazo de gato** cat-scratch disease; —— **por descompresión** decompression sickness, the bends; —— **pulmonar de los granjeros** farmer's lung; —— **pulmonar obstructiva crónica** (**EPOC**) chronic obstructive pulmonary disease (COPD); —— **vascular periférica** peripheral vascular disease; —— **venérea** sexually transmitted disease (STD); **quinta** —— fifth disease
enfermera *f* nurse; —— **domiciliaria** home nurse; —— **visitadora** visiting nurse
enfermería *f* nursing; infirmary
enfermero *m* male nurse
enfermizo -za *adj* sickly
enfermo -ma *adj* sick, ill; *mf* sick person, patient
enfisema *m* emphysema
enflaquecerse *vr* to become thin
enfocar *vt* to focus
enfrentarse *vr* —— **a** to cope with
enfrente *adv* **de** —— front; **la parte de enfrente de**..the front of
engarrotado -da *adj* stiff
engarrotarse *vr* to become stiff
engarruñarse *vr* (*esp. Mex*) to become stiff, contracted
engordar *vi* to get fat
enjuagar *vt* to rinse
enjuage *m* rinse; —— **bucal** mouthwash
enjugar *vt* to wipe
enlace *m* (*psych, obst*) bond
enlazamiento *m* (*psych, obst*) bonding
enloquecerse *vr* to go crazy
enmascarar *vt* (*síntomas, etc.*) to mask
enojado -da *adj* angry, mad
enojarse *vr* to get angry *o* mad
enojo *m* rage, anger
enriquecido -da *adj* enriched
enrojecimiento *m* redness, reddening
ensayo *m* trial
enseñar *vt* to teach
ensuciar *vt* to soil, to get (*something*) dirty; *vr* to soil oneself, to get dirty
entablillar *vt* to splint

entérico -ca *adj* enteric
enteritis *f* enteritis; —— **regional** regional enteritis
entero -ra *adj* whole
enterococo *m* enterococcus
enterocolitis *f* enterocolitis
enteropatía *f* enteropathy; —— **con pérdida de proteínas** protein-losing enteropathy
enterotoxina *f* enterotoxin
entrada *f* entrance
entrecejo *m* space between eyebrows
entrecerrar *vt* —— **los ojos** to squint
entrenamiento *m* training
entrenar *vt, vr* to train
entrepiernas, entrepierna *f* crotch
entretenedor *m* pacifier
entuertos *mpl* postpartum cramps
entumecerse *vr* to become numb, to become numb and stiff
entumecido -da *adj* numb, numb and stiff
entumecimiento *m* numbness, numbness and stiffness
entumido -da *adj* numb, numb and stiff
entumirse *vr* to become numb, to become numb and stiff
enuresis *f* (*form*) bed-wetting
envejecer *vi, vr* to grow old
envejecimiento *m* aging
envenenamiento *m* poisoning; —— **de la sangre** blood poisoning
envenenar *vt* to poison
enviciar *vt* to addict; *vr* to become addicted
enzima *f* enzyme
eosinófilo *m* eosinophil
epidemia *f* epidemic
epidémico -ca *adj* epidemic
epidemiología *f* epidemiology
epididimitis *f* epididymitis
epidídimo *m* epididymis
epidural *adj* epidural
epiglotis *f* epiglottis
epiglotitis *f* epiglottitis
epilepsia *f* epilepsy
epinefrina *f* epinephrine
episiotomía *f* episiotomy
episodio *m* episode
epispadias *m* epispadias
EPOC *abbr* **enfermedad pulmonar obstructiva crónica.** *See* **enfermedad.**
épulis *m* epulis
equilibrio *m* equilibrium, balance
equipo *m* (*de profesionales de la salud*) team; —— **de urgencia** first aid kit
erección *f* erection
erecto -ta *adj* erect
ergocalciferol *m* ergocalciferol
ergotamina *f* ergotamine
erisipela *f* erysipelas
eritema *m* erythema; —— **infeccioso** erythema infectiosum; —— **multiforme** erythema multiforme; —— **nodoso** erythema nodosum

eritrocito *m* erythrocyte
eritromicina *f* erythromycin
erizarse *vr* —— **la piel** *or* **el pelo** to have goose pimples
erizo de mar *m* sea urchin
erógeno -na *adj* erogenous
erosión *f* erosion
erosionar *vt, vr* to erode
erótico -ca *adj* erotic
erradicar *vt* to eradicate
eructar *vi* to burp, belch; **hacer** —— (*a un bebé*) to burp (*a baby*)
erupción *f* eruption, rash
escala *f* scale (*of measurement*); —— **móvil** *or* **flexible** sliding scale
escaldar *vt* to scald
escalofrío *m* chill
escalpelo *m* scalpel
escama *f* (*de la piel*) scale, flake
escamoso -sa *adj* squamous; flaky, scaly
escán *m* (*Ang*) scan
escape *m* (*psych*) outlet
escápula *f* scapula
escara *f* (*form*) scab, crust; —— **de presión** pressure sore
escaso -sa *adj* scarce, (*el pelo*) thin
esclera *f* sclera
esclerodermia, escleroderma *f* scleroderma
esclerosis *f* sclerosis; —— **lateral amiotrófica** amyotrophic lateral sclerosis; —— **múltiple** multiple sclerosis; —— **sistémica progresiva** progressive systemic sclerosis
escleroterapia *f* sclerotherapy
esclerótica *f* sclera
escocer *vi* to itch; to burn, sting, smart
escoliosis *f* scoliosis
escopolamina *f* scopolamine
escorbuto *m* scurvy
escorpión *m* scorpion
escozor *m* itching; smarting, stinging, burning
escritura *f* handwriting
escrófula *f* scrofula
escroto *m* scrotum
escuchar *vt* to listen to; *vi* to listen
escuela *f* school
escupidera *f* emesis basin
escupir *vt, vi* to spit
escupitajo *m* (*fam*) spit, gob of phlegm
escurrir *vi* **escurrirle la nariz** (*fam*) to have a runny nose
Escherichia coli Escherichia coli
esencial *adj* essential
esfigmomanómetro *m* blood pressure cuff
esfínter *m* sphincter
esforzarse *vr* to exert oneself; **No se esfuerce demasiado..**Don't overdo it.
esfuerzo *m* effort, exertion
esguince *m* (*form*) sprain, twist
esmalte *m* enamel; —— **para las uñas** nail polish

esmog *m* (*Ang*) smog
esofagitis *f* esophagitis; —— por reflujo reflux esophagitis
esófago *m* esophagus
espalda *f* back; parte baja de la —— lower back
español -la *adj* Spanish; *mf* Spaniard
espasmo *m* spasm
espasmódico -ca *adj* spasmodic
espasticidad *f* spasticity
espástico -ca *adj* spastic
especialidad *f* specialty
especialista *mf* specialist
especie *f* species
específico -ca *adj* specific
espécimen *m* (*pl* -címenes) specimen
espectinomicina *f* spectinomycin
espectro *m* spectrum
espéculo *m* speculum
espejo *m* mirror
espejuelos *mpl* (*esp. Carib*) eyeglasses, glasses
esperanza *f* hope; —— de vida life expectancy
esperar *vt* to hope for; to wait for; to expect; *vi* to hope; to wait
esperma *f* sperm, semen
espermaticida *adj* spermatocidal, spermicidal; *m* spermatocide, spermicide
espermatozoide *m* sperm, spermatozoon
espeso -sa *adj* thick
espesor *m* thickness
espesura *f* thickness
espina *f* (*anat*) spine; (*bot*) thorn, spine, burr; (*de un pescado*) fish bone; —— bífida spina bifida; —— dorsal spinal column
espinal *adj* spinal
espinarse *vr* to prick oneself (*with a thorn, etc.*)
espinazo *m* (*fam*) backbone, spine
espinilla *f* (*anat*) shin; (*derm*) blackhead, (*con pus*) pimple
espinillera *f* shin guard
espirar *vt*, *vi* to expire, exhale
espirometría *f* spirometry
espirómetro *m* spirometer
espironolactona *f* spironolactone
espiroqueta *f* spirochete
esplenectomía *f* splenectomy
esplénico -ca *adj* splenic
espolón *m* (*ortho*) spur, bone spur
espondilitis *f* spondylitis; —— anquilosante ankylosing spondylitis
espondilosis *f* spondylosis
esponja *f* sponge
espontáneo -a *adj* spontaneous
espora *f* spore
esporádico -ca *adj* sporadic
esporotricosis *f* sporotrichosis
esposa *f* wife
esposo *m* husband

espray *m* (*Ang*) spray
esprue *m&f* sprue; —— celiaco *or* no tropical celiac *o* nontropical sprue; —— tropical tropical sprue
espuma *f* foam
espumoso -sa *adj* foamy, frothy
esputo *m* sputum
esqueleto *m* skeleton
esquema *f* (*de vacunas, etc.*) schedule
esquistosomiasis *f* schistosomiasis
esquizofrenia *f* schizophrenia
esquizofrénico -ca *adj* & *mf* schizophrenic
esquizoide *adj* schizoid
estabilizar *vt*, *vr* to stabilize
estable *adj* stable
estación *f* station; (*invierno, etc.*) season; —— de enfermeras nursing station
estadío, estadio *m* (*de una enfermedad, del cáncer, etc.*) stage
estadística *f* (*dato*) statistic
estado *m* status, state, condition; —— de ánimo mood; en —— (*fam*) pregnant
estadounidense *adj* American, of the United States
estafilococo *m* staphylococcus
estancarse *vr* (*la sangre*) to pool
estándar *adj* & *m* standard
estasis *f* stasis; —— venosa venous stasis
estenosis *f* stenosis (*form*), stricture
estenótico -ca *adj* stenotic
estéril *adj* sterile, infertile
esterilidad *f* sterility, infertility
esterilización *f* sterilization
esterilizar *vt* to sterilize
esternón *m* sternum, breastbone (*fam*)
esteroide *adj* & *m* steroid
estetoscopio *m* stethoscope
estilo de vida *m* lifestyle
estimulación *f* stimulation
estimulante *m* stimulant
estimular *vt* to stimulate
estímulo *m* stimulus
estiramiento *m* (*form*) muscle pull
estirar *vt* to stretch; (*enderezar*) to straighten; *vi*, *vr* to stretch; estirar(se) un músculo to pull a muscle
estítico -ca *adj* (*esp. ES*) constipated
estitiquez *f* (*esp. ES*) constipation
estomacal *adj* pertaining to the stomach
estómago *m* stomach; (*fam*) abdomen, belly; boca del —— pit of the stomach; dolor *m* de —— stomachache; tener el —— revuelto to have an upset stomach
estomatitis *f* stomatitis
estornudar *vi* to sneeze
estornudo *m* sneeze
estrabismo *m* strabismus
estradiol *m* estradiol
estrangulación *f* strangulation
estrangular *vt* to strangle, choke; (*una hernia*) to strangulate; *vr* to strangle, choke; to become strangulated

estrechez *f* stricture, narrowing
estrecho -cha *adj* narrow
estrellita *f* (*visual*) floater
estremecerse *vr* to shake, to shiver
estreñimiento *m* constipation
estreñir *vt* to constipate; *vr* to become constipated
estreptococo *m* streptococcus
estreptomicina *f* streptomycin
estreptoquinasa *f* streptokinase
estrés *m* (*pl* estreses) stress
estría *f* stretch mark
estribo *m* stirrup
estricnina *f* strychnine
estriol *m* estriol
estrógeno *m* estrogen
estrongiloidiasis *f* strongyloidiasis
estuche *m* kit
estudiante *mf* student
estudio *m* study; —— doble ciego double-blind study
estupor *m* stupor
etambutol *m* ethambutol
etanol *m* ethanol
etapa *f* (*del sueño*) stage
éter *m* ether
ético -ca *adj* ethical
etilenglicol *m* ethylene glycol
etilo *m* ethyl
etionamida *f* ethionamide
etiqueta *f* label
étnico -ca *adj* ethnic
etosuximida *f* ethosuximide
euforia *f* euphoria
eunuco *m* eunuch
eutanasia *f* euthanasia, mercy killing
evacuación *f* bowel movement (BM)
evacuar *vt* to evacuate; *vi* to have a bowel movement
evaluación *f* evaluation
evaluar *vt* to evaluate
evaporación *f* evaporation
evaporarse *vr* to evaporate
evitar *vt* to avoid, prevent; Evite comer comidas grasosas..Avoid eating fatty foods.
evolución *f* evolution
exactitud *f* accuracy
exacto -ta *adj* exact, accurate
examen *m* examination, exam (*fam*), test; —— de la vista eye test; —— de los senos breast examination; —— de Papanicolaou *or* —— del cáncer (*fam*) Papanicolaou smear, Pap smear (*fam*); —— físico physical examination, physical (*fam*); —— general de orina urinalysis; —— ginecológico pelvic examination, pelvic (*fam*); —— visual eye examination, eye test
examinar *vt* to examine, to test

exantema súbito *m* exanthem subitum
excederse *vr* to overdo it; Puede caminar, pero no se exceda..You can walk, but don't overdo it.
excesivo -va *adj* excessive
exceso *m* excess
excitar *vt* to arouse, excite, stimulate; *vr* to become excited, to become aroused
excremento *m* stool
excusa *f* excuse
excusado *m* bathroom, toilet (*esp. rural*)
exhalar *vt, vi* to exhale
exhausto -ta *adj* exhausted, run-down
expectativa de vida *f* life expectancy
expectorante *adj* & *m* expectorant
expectorar *vt* to cough up and spit (out)
expediente *m* chart, medical record, file
expeler *vt* to expel
experimental *adj* experimental
experimentar *vi* to experiment
experimento *m* experiment
experto -ta *adj* & *mf* expert
expirar *vi* to expire, die
explorador -ra *adj* (*surg*) exploratory
explorar *vt* (*form*) to examine; (*surg*) to explore
exploratorio -ria *adj* (*surg*) exploratory
exponer *vt* (*pp* expuesto) to expose; *vr* to be exposed, expose oneself
exposición *f* exposure
expuesto -ta (*pp of* exponer) *adj* exposed
expulsar *vt* to expel, (*parásitos, una piedra, etc.*) to pass; —— el aire to exhale, breathe out
expulsión *f* expulsion
extender *vt, vr* to extend, (*la pierna, el brazo*) to straighten
extensión *f* extension
extenso -sa *adj* extensive
extenuado -da *adj* debilitated, weak, exhausted
exterior *adj* outer, exterior, outside; *m* exterior, outside
externo -na *adj* external, outer, outside
extinguidor *m* fire extinguisher
extra *adj* extra
extracción *f* extraction, removal
extracto *m* (*pharm*) extract
extraer *vt* to extract, remove, take out
extrañar *vt* to miss; ¿Extraña a su hijo?..Do you miss your son?
extraño -ña *adj* unusual
extremidad *f* extremity
extrovertido -da *adj* extroverted; *mf* extrovert
eyaculación *f* ejaculation; —— nocturna nocturnal emission; —— precoz premature ejaculation
eyacular *vi* to ejaculate

F

facciones *fpl* features
facial *adj* facial
factor *m* factor; —— **de riesgo** risk factor; —— **intrínseco** intrinsic factor; —— **Rh** Rh factor
Fahrenheit *adj* Fahrenheit
faja *f* girdle, wide belt, *(para prevenir hernias)* truss, abdominal supporter, kidney belt
falda *f* skirt
fálico -ca *adj* phallic
falo *m* phallus
falsearse *vr (Mex)* to sprain, twist; Me falseé la muñeca..I sprained my wrist.
falseo *m (Mex)* sprain
falso -sa *adj* false
falta *f* lack, absence; —— **de(l) aire** shortness of breath
faltar *vi* to be low; Le falta potasio..Your potassium is low; —— **a** *(una cita)* to miss *(an appointment)*; faltarle (el) aire to be short of breath; ¿Le falta el aire?..Are you short of breath?
falla *f (cardiaca, etc.)* failure
fallar *vi* to fail
fallecer *vi* to expire, die
familia *f* family
familiar *adj* familial, family; *m* relative, family member; —— **consanguíneo** blood relative
famotidina *f* famotidine
fantasía *f* fantasy
farfallota *f (Carib)* mumps
faringe *f* pharynx
faringitis *f* pharyngitis
farmaceútico -ca *adj* pharmaceutical; *mf* pharmacist
farmacia *f* pharmacy, drugstore
fármaco *m (form)* medication
farmacodependencia *f* drug dependence, dependency
farmacodependiente *mf* person dependent on drugs, drug addict
farmacología *f* pharmacology
farmacológico -ca *adj* pharmacological, pharmacologic
farmacólogo -ga *mf* pharmacologist
fascia *f* fascia
fascículo *m* tract
fascioliasis *f* fascioliasis
fasciotomía *f* fasciotomy
fascitis *f* fasciitis
fase *f* phase
fastidioso -sa *adj* annoying, irritating

fatal *adj* fatal
fatiga *f* fatigue, tiredness; *(fam)* asthma, shortness of breath
fatigar *vt* to tire, tire out; *vr* to tire, get tired, tire out
febril *adj* febrile
fecundación *f* fertilization
fecundar *vt* to fertilize
fecha *f* date; —— **de caducidad** expiration date
felación *f* fellatio
felicidad *f* happiness; *(obst, etc.)* ¡Felicidades!..Congratulations!
feliz *(pl felices)* *adj* happy
feminización *f* feminization
femoral *adj* femoral
fémur *m* femur
fenacetina *f* phenacetin
fenciclidina (PCP) *f* phencyclidine (PCP)
fenilalanina *f* phenylalanine
fenilbutazona *f* phenylbutazone
fenilcetonuria *f* phenylketonuria (PKU)
fenitoína *f* phenytoin
fenobarbital *m* phenobarbital
fenómeno *m* phenomenon; —— **de Raynaud** Raynaud's phenomenon
fenotiacina *f* phenothiazine
fenotipo *m* phenotype
fentanil *m* fentanyl
feocromocitoma *m* pheochromocytoma
férrico -ca *adj* ferric
fértil *adj* fertile
fertilización *f* fertilization
férula *f* splint; *(sonda para mantener permeable un conducto)* stent
fetal *adj* fetal
fetiche *m* fetish
fetichismo *m* fetishism
feto *m* fetus
fibra *f* fiber; —— **muscular** muscle fiber; —— **nerviosa** nerve fiber; **de** —— **óptica** fiberoptic
fibrilación *f* fibrillation; —— **auricular** atrial fibrillation; —— **ventricular** ventricular fibrillation
fibrinógeno *m* fibrinogen
fibroadenoma *m* fibroadenoma
fibroma *m* fibroma; —— **pendular** skin tag
fibromioma *m* fibromyoma; —— **uterino** uterine fibromyoma, fibroid *(fam)*
fibroquístico -ca *adj* fibrocystic
fibrosis *f* fibrosis; —— **quística** cystic fibrosis
fibrositis *f* fibrositis

fibrótico -ca *adj* fibrotic
fiebre *f* fever, temperature *(fam)*; —— **amarilla** yellow fever; —— **de las trincheras** trench fever; —— **del heno** hay fever; —— **escarlatina** scarlet fever; —— **manchada de las Montañas Rocosas** Rocky Mountain spotted fever; —— **paratifoidea** paratyphoid fever; —— **Q** Q fever; —— **recurrente** relapsing fever; —— **reumática** rheumatic fever; —— **rompehuesos** breakbone fever, dengue; —— **tifoidea** typhoid fever
figura *f (de una persona)* figure
fijación *f* fixation
fijar *vt (la vista)* to stare; *vr* to notice; **No me he fijado..**I haven't noticed.
fijo -ja *adj (mirada, etc.)* steady
filariasis *f* filariasis
filoso -sa *adj* sharp
filtración *f* filtration
filtrar *vt, vr* to filter
filtro *m* filter; —— **solar** sunscreen
fin *m* end; —— **de semana** weekend
final *adj* final
firma *f* signature
firmar *vt, vi* to sign
firme *adj* firm, steady
físico -ca *adj* physical; *m* physique, build, physical appearance
fisicoculturista *mf* bodybuilder
fisiología *f* physiology
fisiológico -ca *adj* physiological, physiologic
fisiólogo -ga *mf* physiologist
fisioterapeuta *mf* physical therapist, physiotherapist
fisioterapia *f* physical therapy, physiotherapy
fisioterapista *mf* physical therapist, physiotherapist
fisostigmina *f* physostigmine
fístula *f* fistula, sinus tract
fisura *f* fissure, crack, hairline fracture
fláccido -da *adj* flaccid, flabby
flaco -ca *adj (fam)* thin, lean
flanco *m* flank
flatulencia *f* flatulence
flebitis *f* phlebitis
flebografía *f* venography; venogram
flebograma *m* venogram
flebotomía *(terapeútica)* phlebotomy; *(Ang, el sacar sangre)* phlebotomy, blood drawing
flema *f* mucus, phlegm
flexible *adj* flexible
flexionar *vt, vr* to flex
flojo -ja *adj (suelto)* loose; *(relajado)* relaxed, limp; *(fláccido)* flabby
flora *f* flora
fluctuar *vi* to fluctuate
flufenacina *f* fluphenazine
fluido *m* fluid
fluir *vi* to flow; **fluirle la nariz** to have a runny nose; **Me fluye la nariz..**I have a runny nose.
flujo *m* flow; *(fam)* vaginal discharge; —— **menstrual** menstrual flow; —— **sanguíneo** blood flow
fluoración *f* fluoridation
fluorescente *adj* fluorescent
fluoridación *f* fluoridation
fluorización *f* fluoridation
fluoroscopia, fluoroscopía *f* fluoroscopy
fluorouracilo *m* fluorouracil
fluoruro *m* fluoride
flurazepam, fluracepam *m* flurazepam
fobia *f* phobia
focal *adj* focal
foco *m* focus
fogaje *m (Carib, fam)* hot flash, flush
fólico -ca *adj* folic
foliculitis *f* folliculitis
folículo *m* follicle; —— **ovárico** ovarian follicle; —— **piloso** hair follicle
folleto *m* booklet, pamphlet
fomento *m* compress; —— **caliente** hot compress
fontanela *f* fontanel *o* fontanelle
fórceps *m (pl -ceps) (obst)* forceps
forense *adj* forensic
forma *f* form, shape; —— **de andar** gait; **en —— ** fit, in shape
formación *f* formation
formaldehído *m* formaldehyde
formar *vt, vr* to form
fórmula *f* formula
formulario *m* formulary; *(papel)* form
fornido -da *adj* heavyset
fortalecer *vt* to strengthen, build up, to fortify; *vr* to become strong
fortificar *vt* to fortify
forzar *vt* —— **la vista** to strain one's eyes; —— **la voz** to strain one's voice
fosa *f* fossa; —— **nasal** nostril
fosfatasa alcalina *f* alkaline phosphatase
fosfato *m* phosphate
fósforo *m* phosphorus
fotocoagulación *f* photocoagulation
fotosensible *adj* photosensitive
fototerapia *f* phototherapy
fracasar *vi* to fail
fracaso *m* failure
fractura *f* fracture, break; —— **abierta** open fracture; —— **cerrada** closed fracture; —— **conminuta** comminuted fracture; —— **del cráneo** cranial *o* skull fracture; —— **en espiral** *or* **espiroidea** spiral fracture; —— **expuesta** open fracture; —— **por compresión** compression fracture; —— **por esfuerzo** stress fracture
fracturar *vt, vr* to fracture, break
frágil *adj* fragile, frail, delicate
fragmento *m* fragment
frambesia *f* frambesia, yaws

frasco *m* bottle, pill bottle
fraterno -na *adj* fraternal
frazada *f* blanket; —— **eléctrica** electric blanket
frecuencia *f* frequency, rate; —— **cardiaca** heart rate; —— **respiratoria** respiratory rate
freir *vt* to fry
frénico -ca *adj* phrenic
frenillos *mpl* bands, braces
frenos *mpl* bands, braces
frente *f* forehead, brow; **hacer** —— **a** to cope with
fresco -ca *adj* fresh; cool
fricción *f* friction
frijoles *mpl* beans
frío -a *adj* cold; *m* cold; **hacer** —— to be cold (*the weather*); **Me duele más cuando hace frío**..It hurts more when the weather is cold; **tener** *or* **sentir** —— to be *o* feel cold; **Tengo frío**..I'm cold.
friolento -ta *adj* sensitive to cold
frito -ta *adj* fried
friza *f* (*PR, SD*) blanket
frontal *adj* frontal
frotis *m* (*pl* **-tis**) (*micro*) smear; —— **de Papanicolaou** Papanicolaou smear
fructosa *f* fructose
fruncir *vt* —— **el ceño** *or* **el entrecejo** to frown; —— **la vista** *or* **los ojos** to squint
fruta *f* fruit; —— **cítrica** *or* **ágria** citrus fruit
fuego *m* fire; (*úlcera en los labios*) cold sore, fever blister
fuente *f* source; (*obst*) bag of waters; —— **para beber** drinking fountain
fuera de, outside, outside of
fuerte *adj* strong, powerful; (*un resfriado, etc.*) bad; (*actividad*) strenuous
fuerza *f* strength, force; —— **de voluntad** will power; **de** —— **doble** double-strength; **de** —— **extra** extra-strength
fugaz *adj* (*pl* **fugaces**) (*dolor, etc.*) fleeting
fumar *vt, vi* to smoke; **No fumar**..No smoking
fumigar *vt* fumigate; —— **con avioneta** to crop-dust
función *f* function
funcionamiento *m* performance
funda de almohada *f* pillowcase
funeraria *f* funeral home, mortuary
furia *f* rage
furosemida *f* furosemide
furúnculo *m* furuncle (*form*), boil
fusil *m* rifle, gun
fusión *f* fusion
fusionar *vi, vr* (*ortho*) to fuse

G

gabinete *m* department, laboratory, office; —— **de fisioterapia, de rayos X, etc.** physical therapy department, x-ray department, etc.
gafas *fpl* spectacles, eyeglasses; —— **de sol** sunglasses
gago -ga *mf* (*esp. Carib, fam*) stammerer, stutterer
gaguear *vi* (*esp. Carib, fam*) to stammer, stutter
galactosa *f* galactose
galactosemia *f* galactosemia
galio *m* gallium
galope *m* (*card*) gallop
galleta *f* cracker, cookie
gamma *f* gamma
gammagrafía *f* nuclear scanning; nuclear scan
gammagrama *m* nuclear scan; —— **de galio** gallium scan; —— **de talio** thallium scan
ganancia *f* gain
ganciclovir *m* gancyclovir
gancho *m* (*de pañal*) safety pin
ganglio *m* node; ganglion; **ganglios basales** basal ganglia; —— **linfático** lymph node
ganglioneuroma *m* ganglioneuroma
gangoso -sa *adj* (*la voz*) nasal
gangrena *f* gangrene; —— **gaseosa** gas gangrene; —— **seca** dry gangrene
Gardnerella vaginalis Gardnerella vaginalis
gargajear *vi* (*fam*) to cough up and spit out phlegm, to spit phlegm
gargajo *m* (*fam*) gob of phlegm
garganta *f* throat
gárgaras *fpl* **hacer** —— to gargle
garrapata *f* tick
garraspear *vi* to clear one's throat
garraspera *f* irritation of the throat
gas *m* (*pl* **gases**) gas; fumes; **gases**

arteriales arterial blood gas; ——
hilarante or **de la risa** laughing gas; ——
lacrimógeno tear gas; —— **natural**
natural gas; **pasar** —— to pass gas; **tener**
—— to have gas; **tirar gases** to pass gas
gasa f gauze; —— or **gasita con alcohol**
alcohol pad
gasolina f gasoline, gas (fam)
gasometría f arterial blood gas
gastrectomía f gastrectomy
gástrico -ca adj gastric
gastrina f gastrin
gastrinoma m gastrinoma
gastritis f gastritis
gastrocnemio m gastrocnemius
gastroenteritis f gastroenteritis
gastroenterología f gastroenterology
gastroenterólogo -ga mf gastroenterologist
gastrointestinal adj gastrointestinal (GI)
gatear vi (ped) to crawl
gato m cat
gaznate m (fam) windpipe
gel m gel
gelatina f gelatin
gemelo -la adj & mf twin; —— **dicigótico**
or **fraterno** fraternal twin; ——
monocigótico or **idéntico** identical twin
gemfibrosilo, gemfibrozil m gemfibrozil
gemido m groan, moan
gemir vi to groan, moan
gen m gene
genérico -ca adj generic
género m gender
genético -ca adj genetic; f genetics
genio m genius
genital adj genital; m **genitales** genitals,
private parts (fam)
gentamicina f gentamicin
geriatra, geríatra mf geriatrician
geriatría f geriatrics
germen m germ
gerontología f gerontology
gerontólogo -ga mf gerontologist
gestación f gestation
gestacional adj gestational
Giardia Giardia
giardiasis f giardiasis
gigantismo m gigantism
ginecología f gynecology
ginecólogo -ga mf gynecologist
gingiva f gingiva
gingivitis f gingivitis; —— **ulcerosa**
necrosante aguda acute necrotizing
ulcerative gingivitis
glándula f gland; —— **endocrina** endocrine
gland; —— **paratiroides** parathyroid
gland; —— **parótida** parotid gland; ——
pineal pineal gland; —— **pituitaria**
pituitary gland; —— **salival** salivary
gland; —— **suprarrenal** adrenal gland;
—— **tiroides** thyroid gland
glaucoma m glaucoma

gliburida f glyburide
glicerina f glycerin, glycerol
glicerol m glycerol
glicina f glycine
glioblastoma m glioblastoma
glioma m glioma
glipizida, glipicida f glipizide
globo m —— **ocular** or **del ojo** eyeball
globulina f globulin; —— **gamma** gamma
globulin; —— **inmune** immune globulin
glóbulo m —— **blanco** white blood cell;
—— **rojo** red blood cell
glomerulonefritis f glomerulonephritis
glositis f glossitis
glotis f glottis
glucagón m glucagon
gluconato m gluconate; —— **de calcio**
calcium gluconate
glucosa f glucose
glutamato monosódico m monosodium
glutamate (MSG)
glutámico -ca adj glutamic
glutamina f glutamine
gluten m gluten
glúteo m buttock
golpe m blow, stroke; —— **de calor**
heatstroke; —— **precordial** or **torácico**
precordial thump
golpecito m pat; **dar golpecitos** to pat
goma m gumma; f rubber; gum; (CA)
hangover; —— **de mascar** chewing gum;
estar de —— (CA) to have a hangover
gónada f gonad
gonadotropina f gonadotropin; ——
coriónica humana human chorionic
gonadotropin (HCG)
gonococo m gonococcus
gonorrea f gonorrhea
gordo -da adj fat
gorgotear vi to gurgle
gorgoteo m gurgle, gurgling
gorro m (para cirugía) cap
gota f drop; (enfermedad) gout
gotear vi to drip
gotero m medicine dropper, eyedropper
gotoso -sa adj gouty
grado m degree; grade
gráfica f graph
gragea f coated pill
gramnegativo -va adj Gram-negative
gramo m gram
grampositivo -va adj Gram-positive
gran See **grande**.
grande adj (**gran** before singular nouns)
big, large; **ponerse más** —— to get
bigger; **¿Qué tan grande era?**..How big
was it?
grandioso -sa adj grandiose
granito m small pimple; **granitos** rash, fine
rash
grano m grain, cereal; (pharm) grain; (derm)
pimple; —— **enterrado** deep pimple

granulación *f* granulation
granulocito *m* granulocyte
granuloma *m* granuloma
granulomatosis *f* granulomatosis; —— de Wegener Wegener's granulomatosis
grapa *f* (*surg*) staple
grasa *f* grease, fat; —— de animal animal fat
grasiento -ta *adj* greasy (*esp. skin*)
grasoso -sa *adj* greasy, fatty
gratificación *f* gratification
grave *adj* serious, seriously ill, (*condición*) grave; (*tono*) low-pitched; **Ella está grave**..She is seriously ill.
gravedad *f* severity
grieta *f* crack
gripa *var of* **gripe**
gripe *f* influenza, flu; —— asiática Asian flu
gris *adj* gray
griseofulvina *f* griseofulvin
gritar *vi* to cry, to cry out
grito *m* cry

grosor *m* thickness
grueso -sa *adj* thick
gruñido *m* grunt
gruñir *vi* to grunt; (*esp. Mex, las tripas*) to growl (*one's stomach*)
grupo *m* group; —— de apoyo support group; —— sanguíneo blood type
guabucho *m* (*PR, SD; fam*) lump, bump (*due to trauma*)
guante *m* glove
guapo -pa *adj* good-looking
guardar *vt* —— cama to stay in bed
guardería infantil *f* nursery, day care center
guardia, de on call
guatemalteco -ca *adj & mf* Guatemalan
güero -ra (*Mex*) *adj* blond; *m* blond; *f* blonde
guerra *f* war; —— nuclear nuclear war
guía *f* (*manual*) guide
guineo *m* (*variety of*) banana
gusano *m* worm; maggot; —— plano flatworm; —— redondo roundworm
gusto *m* taste, flavor

H

habilidad *f* skill, ability
habitación *f* room, bedroom
hábito *m* habit
habituación *f* habituation
habla *f* speech; **desarrollo del** —— speech development
hablar *vt, vi* to speak; —— con la lengua *or* voz pesada to slur; —— por señas to sign
hacer *vi* ¿**Hace cuánto que tiene artritis?**..How long have you had arthritis? —— del baño (*Mex, fam*) to have a bowel movement; —— del cuerpo (*Carib, fam*) to have a bowel movement
hachís *m* hashish
Haemophilus Haemophilus
halitosis *f* halitosis
haloperidol *m* haloperidol
halotano *m* halothane
hallazgo *m* finding
hamartoma *m* hamartoma
hambre *f* hunger; **tener** —— to be hungry; ¿**Tiene hambre?**..Are you hungry?
harina *f* flour
haz *m* (*pl* haces) tract; —— espinotalámico spinothalamic tract

hebilla *f* buckle
heces *fpl* (*also* —— fecales) feces
helado *m* ice cream
helio *m* helium
hemangioma *m* hemangioma; —— cavernoso cavernous hemangioma
hematócrito *m* hematocrit
hematología *f* hematology
hematólogo -ga *mf* hematologist
hematoma *m* hematoma; —— subdural subdural hematoma
hembra *adj & f* female
hemiplejía *f* hemiplegia
hemisferio *m* hemisphere
hemocromatosis *f* hemochromatosis
hemocultivo *m* blood culture
hemodiálisis *f* hemodialysis
hemofilia *f* hemophilia
hemoglobina *f* hemoglobin
hemolítico -ca *adj* hemolytic
hemorragia *f* hemorrhage, bleeding; —— nasal nosebleed; —— subaracnoidea subarachnoid hemorrhage
hemorrágico -ca *adj* hemorrhagic
hemorroide *f* hemorrhoid
hemosiderosis *f* hemosiderosis

heno *m* hay
heparina *f* heparin
hepático -ca *adj* hepatic
hepatitis *f* hepatitis; —— A, B, no A no B,
etc. hepatitis A; B; non-A, non-B; etc.
hepatoma *m* hepatoma
hepatorrenal *adj* hepatorenal
herbario -ria *adj* herbal
herbicida *m* herbicide
heredado -da *adj* inherited
heredar *vt* to inherit
hereditario -ria *adj* hereditary
herencia *f* heredity
herido -da *adj* injured, hurt, wounded; *mf*
wounded person; *f* injury, wound, cut,
incision, abrasion; **herida de bala** gunshot
wound; **herida por punción** puncture
wound
herir *vt* to injure, hurt, wound
hermafrodita *adj* & *mf* hermaphrodite
hermanastra *f* stepsister
hermanastro *m* stepbrother
hermano -na *m* brother, sibling; *f* sister;
hermanos -nas siameses Siamese twins
hernia *f* hernia; —— **estrangulada**
strangulated hernia; —— **hiatal** hiatal
hernia; —— **incarcerada** incarcerated
hernia; —— **inguinal** inguinal hernia;
—— **umbilical** umbilical hernia
heroína *f* heroin
herpangina *f* herpangina
herpes *m* herpes; —— **simple** herpes
simplex; —— **zoster** herpes zoster,
shingles
herpético -ca *adj* herpetic
hervir *vt* (*also* **hacer** ——) to boil; *vi* to
boil; **hervirle el pecho** (*fam*) to breathe
noisily (*as with bronchitis or asthma*), to
be congested in the chest, to wheeze
hervor *m* (*fam, del pecho*) congestion of the
chest, wheezing
heterosexual *adj* & *mf* heterosexual
hidatídico -ca *adj* hydatid
hidatiforme *adj* hydatidiform
hidralacina *f* hydralazine
hidratante *adj* moisturizing
hidrato de cloral *m* chloral hydrate
hidrocarburo *m* hydrocarbon
hidrocefalia *f* hydrocephaly
hidrocéfalo *m* hydrocephalus
hidrocele *m* hydrocele
hidroclorotiazida *f* hydrochlorothiazide
hidrocortisona *f* hydrocortisone
hidrofobia *f* hydrophobia
hidronefrosis *f* hydronephrosis
hidroterapia *f* hydrotherapy
hidróxido de sodio *m* sodium hydroxide
hiedra venenosa *f* poison ivy
hielo *m* ice; **bolsa con** —— ice pack
hierba *f* grass; herb
hierbería *f* herb shop
hierbero -ra *mf* herbalist

hierro *m* iron
hígado *m* liver; **enfermedad** *f* **del** ——
liver disease
higiene *f* hygiene
higiénico -ca *adj* hygienic
higienista *mf* hygienist
hijastro -tra *m* stepson, stepchild; *f*
stepdaughter
hijo -ja *m* son, child; *f* daughter
hilo dental *m* dental floss
himen *m* hymen
hinchado -da *adj* swollen, puffy; —— **del**
estómago bloated
hincharse *vr* to swell, swell up; —— **el**
estómago to become bloated
hinchazón *f* swelling
hioides *m* hyoid bone
hiperactividad *f* hyperactivity
hiperactivo -va *adj* hyperactive
hiperalimentación *f* hyperalimentation
hiperbárico -ca *adj* hyperbaric
hipercalcemia *f* hypercalcemia
hiperextensible *adj* double-jointed
hiperglucemia *f* hyperglycemia
hiperlipemia, hiperlipidemia *f* hyperlipidemia
hiperlipoproteinemia *f* hyperlipoproteinemia
hipermétrope *adj* farsighted
hiperosmolar *adj* hyperosmolar
hiperparatiroideo -a *adj* hyperparathyroid
hiperparatiroidismo *m* hyperparathyroidism
hiperplasia *f* hyperplasia
hipersensibilidad *f* hypersensitivity
hipersensible *adj* hypersensitive
hipertensión *f* hypertension; —— **maligna**
malignant hypertension; —— **portal**
portal hypertension; —— **pulmonar**
pulmonary hypertension
hipertermia *f* hyperthermia
hipertiroideo -a *adj* hyperthyroid
hipertiroidismo *m* hyperthyroidism
hipertrofia *f* hypertrophy; —— **prostática**
benigna benign prostatic hypertrophy
hipnosis *f* hypnosis
hipnótico -ca *adj* & *m* hypnotic
hipnotismo *m* hypnotism
hipnotizador -ra *mf* hypnotist
hipnotizar *vt* to hypnotize
hipo *m* hiccup; **tener** —— to have the
hiccups, to hiccup
hipoalergénico -ca *adj* hypoallergenic
hipocondríaco -ca, hipocondriaco -ca *adj*
& *mf* hypochondriac
hipodérmico -ca *adj* hypodermic
hipoglucemia *f* hypoglycemia
hipoglucemiante *m* hypoglycemic agent;
—— **oral** oral hypoglycemic agent
hipoglucémico -ca *adj* hypoglycemic
hipoparatiroideo -a *adj* hypoparathyroid
hipoparatiroidismo *m* hypoparathyroidism
hipospadias *m* hypospadias

hipotálamo *m* hypothalamus
hipotensión *f* hypotension
hipotermia *f* hypothermia
hipotiroideo -a *adj* hypothyroid
hipotiroidismo *m* hypothyroidism
hisopo *m* swab
histamina *f* histamine
histerectomía *f* hysterectomy; ——
abdominal abdominal hysterectomy; ——
vaginal vaginal hysterectomy
histeria *f* hysteria
histérico -ca *adj* hysterical
histidina *f* histidine
histiocitosis X *f* histiocytosis X
histología *f* histology
histoplasmosis *f* histoplasmosis
historia clínica *f* history, clinical history
histriónico -ca *adj* histrionic
hogar *m* home; sin —— homeless
hoja *f* (*de cuchillo, etc.*) blade; —— de
afeitar *or* rasurar razor blade
hombre *m* man
hombro *m* shoulder
homeópata *mf* homeopath
homeopatía *f* homeopathy
homosexual *adj & mf* homosexual
hondo -da *adj* deep
hondureño -ña *adj & mf* Honduran
hongo *m* fungus, mushroom; **hongos** (*fam*)
yeast (infection)
honorarios *mpl* fee
hora *f* hour, time; ¿A qué hora
comió?..What time did you eat?..When
did you eat? **horas de consulta** *or* **oficina**
office hours; **horas de visita** visiting
hours
horario *m* schedule
hormiga *f* ant
hormiguear *vi* to tingle
hormigueo *m* tingling
hormona *f* hormone; —— adrenocorticotrópica adrenocortical hormone (ACTH);
—— del crecimiento growth hormone
(GH); —— estimulante del folículo
follicle-stimulating hormone (FSH); ——
estimulante del tiroides thyroid-
stimulating hormone (TSH); —— liberadora de gonadotropinas gonadotropin-
releasing hormone (GnRH); —— luteini-

zante luteinizing hormone (LH); ——
paratiroidea parathyroid hormone (PTH);
—— tiroidea thyroid hormone; ——
tirotrópica thyroid-stimulating hormone
(TSH)
hormonal *adj* hormonal
horneado -da *adj* baked
horno, al baked
hospital *m* hospital; —— de la comunidad
community hospital; —— del condado
county hospital (*US*); —— general
general hospital; —— para veteranos
Veterans Administration (VA) hospital;
—— privado private hospital; ——
psiquiátrico mental hospital; ——
público public hospital; **administración** *f*
del —— hospital administration
hospitalario -ria *adj* pertaining to a hospital,
hospital
hospitalizar *vt* to hospitalize
hostil *adj* hostile
hostilidad *f* hostility
hoy *adv* today
hoyo *m* hole; —— de la nariz (*fam*) nostril
hoyuelo *m* dimple
huata *f* (*ortho, surg*) padding
huellas *fpl* traces
huérfano -na *mf* orphan
huesecillo, huesillo *m* ossicle
hueso *m* bone; **huesos** (*esp. Mex, CA; fam*)
joints; Se me hinchan los huesos..My
joints swell; —— de la cadera hipbone;
—— del pecho breastbone; —— del
tobillo anklebone; —— iliaco ilium
huevecillo *m* small egg (*of a parasite, etc.*)
huevo *m* egg; (*fam*) ovum, egg (*fam*);
huevos (*vulg*) testicles, balls (*vulg*)
hule *m* rubber
humanitario -ria *adj* humanitarian
humano -na *adj & m* human; ser humano
human being
humedad *f* humidity, dampness, moisture
humedecedor *m* humidifier
humedecer *vt* to humidify, moisturize,
moisten
húmedo -da *adj* damp, moist, humid
húmero *m* humerus
humo *m* smoke, fumes
huracán *m* hurricane

I

ibuprofén, ibuprofeno *m* ibuprofen
id *m* (*psych*) id
ideal *adj* ideal
identidad *f* identity
identificación *f* identification
identificar *vt* to identify; *vr* (*psych*)
   identificarse con to identify with
idiopático -ca *adj* idiopathic
ilegal *adj* illegal
íleo *m* ileus
íleon *m* ileum
iliaco -ca *adj* iliac
ilusión *f* illusion
imagen *f* image; —— corporal body image;
   —— diagnóstica diagnostic imaging,
   X-ray, scan; imágenes por resonancia
   magnética magnetic resonance imaging
   (MRI)
imipenem *m* imipenem
imipramina *f* imipramine
impacción *f* impaction
impactación *f* impaction
impactado -da *adj* impacted
imperdible *m* safety pin
imperforado -da *adj* imperforate
impétigo *m* impetigo
implantación *f* implantation
implantar *vt* to implant
implante *m* implant
impotencia *f* impotence
impotente *adj* impotent
impulsivo -va *adj* impulsive
impureza *f* impurity
impuro -ra *adj* impure
inactividad *f* inactivity
inactivo -va *adj* inactive
inanición *f* starvation
inapropiado -da *adj* inappropriate
incapacidad *f* disability; —— de trabajo
   (*Mex*) work excuse, certificate of disability
incapacitado -da *adj* disabled
incapacitante *adj* incapacitating
incapaz *adj* (*pl* -paces) incapable, unable
incendio *m* fire
incesto *m* incest
incidencia *f* incidence
incisión *f* incision
inclinar *vt* to bend, bend down; Incline la
   cabeza..Bend your head down...Incline la
   cabeza a la izquierda..Bend your head to
   the left; *vr* to lean, lean forward, stoop;
   Inclínese..Lean forward.
incoherente *adj* incoherent
incómodo -da *adj* uncomfortable

incompatible *adj* incompatible
incompetente *adj* incompetent
incompleto -ta *adj* incomplete
inconsciente *adj* unconscious
incontinencia *f* incontinence; —— de
   esfuerzo stress incontinence
incontinente *adj* incontinent
incordio *m* bubo, enlarged inguinal node
incrustación *f* (*dent*) inlay
incubadora *f* incubator
incurable *adj* incurable
independiente *adj* independent
indicación *f* indication; (*en el expediente*)
   order; (*instrucción*) instruction; poner
   indicaciones to order
índice *adj* (*dedo*) index; *m* index; ——
   Apgar Apgar score
indiferencia *f* indifference, apathy
indiferenciado -da *adj* undifferentiated
indigestión *f* indigestion
indisposición *f* indisposition, slight illness
indistinto -ta *adj* indistinct, dim
indoloro -ra *adj* painless
indometacina *f* indomethacin
inducir *vt* to induce
ineficaz *adj* (*pl* -caces) ineffective
inelegible *adj* ineligible
inespecífico -ca *adj* nonspecific
inesperado -da *adj* unexpected
inestable *adj* unstable
inevitable *adj* unavoidable
infante *m* infant
infantil *adj* infantile
infarto *m* infarct, infarction; —— de
   miocardio myocardial infarction
infección *f* infection; —— del tracto
   urinario urinary tract infection (UTI);
   —— pélvica pelvic inflammatory disease
   (PID)
infeccioso -sa *adj* infectious
infectar *vt* to infect; *vr* to become infected
infeliz *adj* (*pl* -lices) unhappy
inferior *adj* (*anat*) inferior, lower
infertilidad *f* infertility
infestación *f* infestation
infestar *vt* to infest
infiltrar *vt*, *vr* to infiltrate
inflado -da *adj* (*del estómago*) bloated
inflamable *adj* flammable, inflammable; no
   —— nonflammable
inflamación *f* inflammation
inflamado -da *adj* inflamed
inflamarse *vr* to become inflamed
inflarse *vr* —— el estómago to become

bloated
influenza f influenza, flu
información f information, data
infrarrojo -ja adj infrared
infundir vt to infuse
infusión f infusion
ingeniería genética f genetic engineering
ingerir vt to ingest
ingle f groin
ingrediente m ingredient
ingresar vt to admit (to the hospital); vr to
be admitted
ingreso m admission; **Ingresos** Admitting
inguinal adj inguinal
inhabilitado -da adj disabled
inhalador m inhaler
inhalar vt, vi to inhale, breathe in; (cocaína,
cemento, etc.) to sniff (cocaine, glue, etc.)
inhibición f inhibition
inhibido -da adj inhibited
inhibir vt to inhibit
inicial adj initial; f initial
injertar vt (pp -tado or injerto) to graft
injerto (pp of **injertar**) m graft; ——
cutáneo skin graft
inmaduro -ra adj immature
inmediatamente adv immediately
inmediato -ta adj immediate
inmóvil adj immobile
inmovilización f immobilization
inmovilizar vt to immobilize
inmune adj immune
inmunidad f immunity
inmunización f immunization
inmunizar vt to immunize
inmunocompetente adj immunocompetent
inmunocomprometido -da adj immunocompromised
inmunodeficiencia f immunodeficiency
inmunodepresión f immunodepression
inmunodeprimido -da adj immunodepressed
inmunoglobulina f immunoglobulin
inmunología f immunology
inmunológico -ca adj immunological
inmunólogo -ga mf immunologist
inmunosupresor -ra adj immunosuppressive; m immunosuppressant
inmunoterapia f immunotherapy
inocular vt to inoculate
inodoro m toilet; **taza del** —— toilet bowl
inofensivo -va adj harmless
inoperable adj inoperable
inorgánico -ca adj inorganic
inquieto -ta adj restless, uneasy
insaturado -da adj unsaturated
insecticida m insecticide
insecto m insect
inseguridad f insecurity
inseguro -ra adj insecure
inseminación f insemination; —— **artificial**
artificial insemination
inseminar vt to inseminate

insolación f sunstroke, heatstroke
insomnio m insomnia
inspirar vt, vi to inspire, inhale
instinto m drive, instinct
instrucción f instruction
instructivo m package insert
instrumento m instrument
insuficiencia f insufficiency, failure; ——
aórtica, mitral, etc. aortic insufficiency,
mitral insufficiency, etc.; —— **cardiaca**
congestiva congestive heart failure; ——
hepática hepatic insufficiency, liver
failure; —— **renal** renal insufficiency o
failure; —— **respiratoria** respiratory
failure; —— **venosa** venous insufficiency
insulina f insulin; —— **de acción rápida**
regular insulin; —— **lenta** lente insulin;
—— **NPH** or **de acción intermedia** NPH
insulin; —— **semilenta** semilente insulin;
—— **ultralenta** ultralente insulin
intacto -ta adj intact
intelecto m intellect
intelectual adj intellectual
inteligencia f intelligence; **cociente de** ——
(**CI**) intelligence quotient (IQ)
intensivo -va adj intensive
intenso -sa adj intense
interacción f interaction
interactuar vi to interact
interferón m interferon
interior adj & m interior
intermedio -dia adj intermediate
intermitente adj intermittent
internar vt to admit (to the hospital), to
hospitalize; vr to be admitted o hospitalized; **¿Ha estado internado aquí**
antes?..Have you been hospitalized here
before?
internista mf internist
interno -na adj internal, inner, inside; (anat)
medial; mf intern
interpersonal adj interpersonal
interpretar vt, vi to interpret
intérprete mf interpreter
intersticial adj interstitial
intervalo m interval
intestinal adj intestinal
intestino m intestine, bowel, gut; ——
delgado small intestine o bowel; ——
grueso large intestine o bowel
intolerancia f intolerance
intoxicación f poisoning, intoxication; ——
alimenticia or **alimentaria** food poisoning
intraarticular adj intraarticular
intracraneal adj intracranial
intramuscular adj intramuscular
intranquilo -la adj restless
intraocular adj intraocular
intravenoso -sa (IV) adj intravenous (IV)
introducir vt to insert
introvertido -da adj introverted; mf introvert
intubación f intubation

intubar *vt* to intubate
intususcepción *f* intussusception
inundación *f* flood
inútil *adj* useless
inválido -da *adj* disabled; *mf* disabled person
invasivo -va *adj* invasive; **no ——** noninvasive
invasor -ra *adj* invasive; **no ——** noninvasive
investigación *f* research; **en ——** (*medicamento, etc.*) investigational
invierno *m* winter
involuntario -ria *adj* involuntary
inyección *f* injection, shot (*fam*); ¿Me van a poner una inyección?..Are you going to give me an injection?
inyectable *adj* injectable
inyectar *vt* to inject, to give (*someone*) an injection; ¿Me va a inyectar?..Are you going to give me an injection? *vr* to inject oneself, give oneself an injection
ipecacuana *f* ipecac
ir *vi* **—— y venir** to come and go; El dolor me va y me viene..The pain comes and goes.
ira *f* anger, rage
iris *m* (*pl* iris) iris
iritis *f* iritis
irradiar *vt* to irradiate
irregular *adj* irregular
irreversible *adj* irreversible
irrigar *vt* to irrigate
irritabilidad *f* irritability
irritable *adj* irritable
irritación *f* irritation
irritante *adj* irritating; *m* irritant
irritar *vt* to irritate; *vr* to become irritated
irrompible *adj* unbreakable
isoetarina *f* isoetharine
isoleucina *f* isoleucine
isoniacida *f* isoniazid (INH)
isquemia *f* ischemia; **—— cerebral transitoria** transient ischemic attack
isquémico -ca *adj* ischemic
IV *See* **intravenoso.**
izquierdo -da *adj* left; left-handed; *f* left, left-hand side

J

jabón *m* soap
jadear *vi* to pant
jalar *vt* **—— aire** to gasp
jalea *f* jelly
jamón *m* ham
jaqueca *f* migraine, severe headache
jarabe *m* syrup; **—— para la tos** cough syrup
jardinero -ra *mf* gardener
jarra *f* pitcher
jefe -fa *mf* employer; **—— de enfermeras** head nurse; **—— de turno** charge nurse
jején *m* gnat, no-see-um, sandfly
jeringa *f* syringe
jeringuilla *f* (*esp. Carib*) syringe
jimagua *mf* (*Cub*) twin
jiricua *f* (*Mex, fam*) vitiligo
joroba *f* hump
jorobado -da *mf* humpback
joven *adj* young; *m* young man, young person; *f* young woman
juanete *m* bunion
jugo *m* juice; **—— de fruta, naranja, tomate, etc.** fruit juice, orange juice, tomato juice, etc.
juntar *vt, vr* (*dos objetos*) to join
juramento hipocrático *m* Hippocratic Oath
juvenil *adj* juvenile
juventud *f* youth

K

ketoconazol *m* ketoconazole
kilo *See* kilogramo.
kilogramo *m* kilogram

Klebsiella Klebsiella
kwashiorkor *m* kwashiorkor

L

laberintitis *f* labyrinthitis
laberinto *m* labyrinth
labetolol *m* labetolol
labio *m* lip; (*genital*) labium (*form*), lip
laboratorio *m* laboratory
laceración *f* laceration
lacrimógeno *m* tear gas
lactancia *f* lactation; —— materna breast-
   feeding
lactante *mf* nursing infant, breast-fed infant
lactar *vi* to lactate
lactasa *f* lactase
láctico -ca *adj* lactic
lactosa *f* lactose
lactulosa *f* lactulose
ladilla *f* crab louse, crab (*fam*)
lado *m* side
lagaña *f* sleep (*eye secretions*)
lágrima *f* tear
laguna mental *f* blackout, lapse of memory
lamentar *vt, vr* to mourn
lamer *vt* to lick
lámpara *f* lamp; —— bronceadora sun
   lamp; —— de hendidura slitlamp
lana *f* wool
lanceta *f* lancet
lanolina *f* lanolin
lanugo *m* lanugo
laparoscopia, laparoscopía *f* laparoscopy
laparotomía *f* laparotomy
lapso *m* lapse
largo -ga *adj* long; a —— plazo long-term;
   hacer más —— to lengthen; *m* length
laringe *f* larynx
laringectomía *f* laryngectomy
laríngeo -a *adj* laryngeal
laringitis *f* laryngitis
laringoscopia, laringoscopía *f* laryngoscopy

larva *f* larva; —— migrans larva migrans
láser *m* laser
lastimadura *f* sprain, dislocation, muscle
   pull, bruise, minor injury (*in which skin
   remains intact*)
lastimar *vt, vr* to hurt, injure, to get hurt, to
   hurt oneself; ¿Se lastimó?..Did you hurt
   yourself?
lata *f* can
latente *adj* latent
lateral *adj* lateral
látex *m* latex
latido *m* beat; —— del corazón heartbeat
latir *vi* (*el corazón*) to beat; (*un dolor*) to
   throb
lavable *adj* washable
lavado *m* lavage; (*intestinal*) enema; ——
   broncoalveolar bronchoalveolar lavage;
   —— gástrico gastric lavage; ——
   peritoneal peritoneal lavage
lavar *vt* to wash; *vr* lavarse la cabeza *or* el
   pelo to wash one's hair; lavarse las
   manos, la cara, etc. to wash one's hands,
   one's face, etc.
lavativa *f* enema
lavatorio *m* lavatory
laxante *adj & m* laxative
lazo *m* loop
lb. *See* libra.
lecitina *f* lecithin
leche *f* milk; —— baja en grasas low fat
   milk; —— bronca (*Mex*) raw milk; ——
   condensada condensed milk; —— de
   cabra goat's milk; —— descremada *or*
   desnatada skim milk; —— de vaca
   cow's milk; (*fam*) raw milk; —— en
   polvo powdered milk; —— entera whole
   milk; —— evaporizada evaporated milk;

—— **materna** breast milk; ——
pasteurizada pasteurized milk; —— **sin**
procesar raw milk
leche de magnesia *f* milk of magnesia
lecho *m* bed, sickbed, deathbed; ——
vascular vascular bed
leer *vt, vi* to read; —— **los labios** to lipread
legaña *f* sleep (*eye secretions*)
lego -ga *adj* lay (*opinion, etc.*)
legrado *m* (*fam*) curettage
legumbre *f* legume; (*vegetal*) vegetable
leiomioma *m* leiomyoma
leiomiosarcoma *m* leiomyosarcoma
leishmaniasis *f* leishmaniasis
lejía *f* lye
lengua *f* tongue; —— **saburral** coated
tongue; **sacar la** —— to stick out one's
tongue; **Saque la lengua**..Stick out your
tongue.
lenguaje *m* language (*referring to structure
and development*)
lente *m&f* lens; —— **de contacto** (*duro o
blando*) contact lens (*hard or soft*)
lentes *mpl* eyeglasses, glasses; —— **para el
sol** *or* **oscuros** sunglasses; —— **protectores** protective eyewear, goggles
lepra *f* leprosy
leptospirosis *f* leptospirosis
lesbiana *f* lesbian
lesión *f* lesion, injury; —— **por latigazo**
whiplash
letal *adj* lethal
letargo *m* lethargy
letra *f* handwriting
letrina *f* latrine
leucemia *f* leukemia; —— **granulocítica**
granulocytic leukemia; —— **linfoblástica**
lymphoblastic leukemia; —— **linfocítica
aguda** acute lymphocytic leukemia; ——
mielógena crónica chronic myelogenous
leukemia; —— **mieloide** myeloid
leukemia
leucina *f* leucine
leucocito *m* leukocyte
leucoencefalopatía multifocal progresiva *f*
progressive multifocal leukoencephalopathy
levantar *vt* to raise, to lift; **Levante la
pierna**..Raise your leg; —— **pesas** to lift
weights, to work out; *vr* to get up, to
stand (up)
leve *adj* slight, light, mild
liberación *f* release; **de** —— **prolongada**
slow-release; **de** —— **sostenida**
sustained-release
liberador -ra *adj* releasing; —— **de cobre,
—— de hormona, etc.** copper-releasing,
hormone-releasing, etc.
liberar *vt* to release; (*virus, etc.*) to shed
libido *f* libido
libra (lb.) *f* pound (lb.)
libre *adj* free, loose

licor *m* liquor
lidocaína *f* lidocaine
liendre *f* nit
lienzo *m* cloth, towel
ligado -da *adj* —— **al cromosoma X** *or*
—— **al X** X-linked; —— **al sexo**
sex-linked
ligadura *f* ligation; —— **de las trompas** *or*
tubárica tubal ligation
ligamento *m* ligament
ligar *vt* to join (*two objects*)
ligero -ra *adj* light, slight; gentle
lima *f* file; —— **para las uñas** nail file
limar *vt* to file
limitar *vt* to limit
límite *m* limit; —— **inferior normal** lower
limit of normal; —— **superior normal**
upper limit of normal
limpia *f* (*Mex, CA; fam*) healing ritual
limpiador -ra de casa *mf* housecleaner
limpiar *vt* to clean; *vr* (*después de defecar*)
to wipe (oneself)
limpieza *f* cleaning; cleanliness; (*fam*)
healing ritual
limpio -pia *adj* clean
lindano *m* lindane
línea *f* line, streak
linfa *f* lymph
linfadenitis *f* lymphadenitis
linfangitis *f* lymphangitis
linfático -ca *adj* lymphatic
linfocito *m* lymphocyte; —— **B** B
lymphocyte; —— **T ayudante** helper T
lymphocyte; —— **T supresor** suppressor
T lymphocyte
linfogranuloma venéreo *or* **inguinal** *m*
lymphogranuloma venereum (LGV)
linfoide *adj* lymphoid
linfoma *m* lymphoma; —— **no Hodgkin**
non-Hodgkin's lymphoma
linimento *m* liniment
linoleico -ca *adj* linoleic
liofilizado-da *adj* lyophilized
liomioma *m* leiomyoma
liomiosarcoma *m* leiomyosarcoma
lipasa *f* lipase
lípido *m* lipid
lipoma *m* lipoma
lipoproteína *f* lipoprotein; —— **de alta
densidad (LAD)** high density lipoprotein
(HDL); —— **de baja densidad (LBD)**
low density lipoprotein (LDL); —— **de
muy baja densidad (LMBD)** very low
density lipoprotein (VLDL)
liposucción *f* liposuction
liquen plano *m* lichen planus
líquido -da *adj* liquid, runny; *m* liquid, fluid;
—— **amniótico** amniotic fluid; ——
cefalorraquídeo (LCR) cerebrospinal
fluid (CSF); —— **pleural** pleural fluid;
—— **seminal** seminal fluid; —— **sinovial**
synovial fluid

lisiado -da *adj* crippled; *mf* crippled person
lisiar *vt* to cripple
lisina *f* lysine
lisinopril *m* lisinopril
liso -sa *adj* smooth, even
lista de espera *f* waiting list
listeriosis *f* listeriosis
litio *m* lithium
litotripsia *f* lithotripsy
litro *m* liter
liviano -na *adj* light (*weight*)
lobar *adj* lobar
lobectomía *f* lobectomy
lóbulo *m* lobe; (*del oído*) earlobe
local *adj* local
loción *f* lotion; —— **bronceadora** suntan lotion
loco -ca *adj* crazy, insane; **volver** —— (*a alguien*) to drive (*someone*) crazy; **volverse** —— to go crazy, lose one's mind; *mf* crazy person
locura *f* insanity, craziness
lombriz *f* (*pl* **-brices**) worm, intestinal worm
longevidad *f* longevity
longitud *f* length; —— **de onda** wavelength

loperamida *f* loperamide
loracepam *m* lorazepam
lordosis *f* lordosis
lordótico -ca *adj* lordotic
lote *m* (*pharm*) lot
lovastatina *f* lovastatin
LSD *See* **dietilamida del ácido lisérgico.**
lubricante *adj & m* lubricant
lubricar *vt* to lubricate
lucecita *f* (*visual*) floater
lumbar *adj* lumbar
lumpectomía *f* (*Ang*) lumpectomy
lunar *m* mole, birthmark
lupa *f* magnifying glass
lupus *m* lupus; —— **eritematoso generalizado** *or* **sistémico** systemic lupus erythematosus (SLE)
luteínico -ca *adj* luteal
lúteo -a *adj* luteal
luxación *f* dislocation
luxar *vt, vr* to dislocate, to become dislocated; **Me luxé el hombro..**I dislocated my shoulder...**Se me luxó el hombro..**My shoulder became dislocated.
luz *f* (*pl* **luces**) light; —— **del sol** sunlight

Ll

llaga *f* ulcer, sore
llamada *f* page; —— **por el bíper** page by beeper; —— **por vocina** overhead page
llamar *vt* (*por vocina, por bíper*) to page
llanto *m* cry, crying
llenar *vt* to fill

lleno -na *adj* full; ¿**Está lleno?**..Are you full?
llenura *f* fullness
llevar *vt* (*ropa, etc.*) to wear
llorar *vt* to mourn; *vi* to cry

M

macrobiótico -ca *adj* macrobiotic
machucadura *f* mash, mild crush injury
machucar *vt* to mash, crush
machucón *m* mash, mild crush injury
madrastra *f* stepmother
madre *f* mother; —— **subrogada** surrogate
mother
madrugada *f* early morning (*before dawn*)
madurar *vi* to mature; (*un absceso*) to come
to a head, to secrete pus
madurez *f* maturity
maduro -ra *adj* mature; (*fruta*) ripe
maestro -tra *mf* teacher
magnesio *m* magnesium
magro -gra *adj* (*persona*) lean, thin; (*carne*)
lean
magullado -da *adj* bruised, sore
magulladura *f* bruise
magullar *vt* to bruise; *vr* to bruise, get
bruised
maíz *m* corn
mal *adj* See **malo**; *m* illness, sickness,
ailment, disease; —— **del pinto** pinta,
mal del pinto; —— **de montaña** mountain
sickness; —— **de ojo** (*fam*) eye infection,
conjunctivitis; evil eye, pediatric folk
illness believed to occur when a person
with magical powers eyes an infant with
ill intent; —— **de orín** (*fam*) urinary tract
infection
malabsorción *f* malabsorption
malaria *f* malaria
malatión *m* malathion
malestar *m* malaise
maletín *m* (*médico*) doctor's bag
malformación *f* malformation
malignidad *f* malignancy
maligno -na *adj* malignant
malo -la *adj* (**mal** *before masculine singular
nouns*) bad; sick, ill; **¿Está mala ella?..**Is
she sick?
malparir *vi* to have complications at
childbirth
malparto *m* childbirth with complications
malla *f* mesh
mallugar *var of* **magullar**
mama *f* breast
mamá *f* (*pl* **mamás**) mom
mamadera *f* nursing bottle, baby's bottle;
nipple of nursing bottle
mamar *vi* to nurse, suck (*at mother's
breast*); (*vulg*) to perform fellatio
mamario -ria *adj* mammary
mamila *f* nipple (*of a nursing bottle*)

mamografía *f* mammography; mammogram
mamograma *m* mammogram
manco -ca *adj* one-handed, one-armed
mancha *f* spot, stain; —— **de vino oporto**
port-wine stain
mandíbula *f* jaw, lower jaw, jawbone
manejar *vt* to manage; (*un vehículo*) to
drive
manejo *m* management
manguera *f* hose, tube
manía *f* mania
maniacodepresivo -va *adj* manic-depressive
manicomio *m* insane asylum
manicura *f* manicure
manifestación *f* manifestation
maniobra *f* maneuver
maniobrar *vt, vi* to maneuver
manipular *vt* to manipulate
mano *f* hand; —— **péndula** wrist drop
manometría *f* manometry
manta *f* blanket, light blanket; ——
eléctrica electric blanket
manteca *f* lard, fat, cooking grease; —— **de
cacao** cocoa butter
mantener *vt* to maintain; —— **la
respiración** *or* **el resuello** to hold one's
breath; **Mantenga la respiración..**Hold
your breath.
mantenimiento *m* maintenance
mantequilla *f* butter
manual *adj* manual, hand-held; *m* manual,
booklet
manzana *f* apple; —— **de Adán** Adam's
apple
mañana *adv* tomorrow; **pasado** —— the
day after tomorrow; *f* morning; **inyección
de la mañana..**morning injection
mapache *m* raccoon
maquillaje *m* make-up, cosmetics
máquina de afeitar *f* electric razor
marca *f* mark; brand; **marcas** (*de los
drogadictos*) tracks; —— **de nacimiento**
birthmark
marcapaso *m* pacemaker
marcha *f* gait
mareado -da *adj* dizzy, lightheaded, faint
mareo *m* dizziness, lightheadedness, (*en
avión*) airsickness, (*en un barco*)
seasickness, (*en un vehículo*) carsickness,
(*debido al movimiento en general*) motion
sickness; **dar** —— to make dizzy; **tener**
—— to feel dizzy, to feel lightheaded
margarina *f* margarine
margen *m* margin, border, edge

marido *m* husband
marihuana, marijuana *f* marijuana, grass (*fam*), pot (*fam*)
marisco *m* (*often pl*) shellfish, seafood
martillo *m* hammer
masa *f* mass, lump
masaje *m* massage; —— cardiaco externo (MCE) chest compressions; dar —— to massage
masajear *vt* to massage
mascar *vt, vi* to chew
máscara *f* mask
mascota *f* pet
masculino -na *adj* masculine, male
masoquista *mf* masochist
masoquismo *m* masochism
mastectomía *f* mastectomy
masticable *adj* chewable
masticar *vt, vi* to chew
mastitis *f* mastitis
mastoideo -a *adj* mastoid
masturbarse *vr* to masturbate
matar *vt* to kill
matasanos *m* quack
material *m* material
maternal *adj* maternal, motherly
maternidad *f* maternity
materno -na *adj* maternal
matrimonio *m* married couple
matriz *f* (*pl* -trices) uterus, womb
matutino -na *adj* (*form*) pertaining to morning, morning
maxilar *adj* maxillary; *m* jaw, jawbone; —— inferior lower jaw; —— superior maxilla, upper jaw
maxilofacial *adj* maxillofacial
máximo -ma *adj* & *m* maximum
mayonesa *f* mayonnaise
mayor *adj* (*comp of* grande) bigger, larger; older; (*anat, surg*) major
MCE *abbr* masaje cardiaco externo. *See* masaje.
meato *m* meatus
mebendazol *m* mebendazole
mecanismo *m* mechanism; —— de defensa defense mechanism
meconio *m* meconium
mecha *f* wick, packing
media *f* hose, stocking
mediano -na *adj* medium; (*anat*) median
mediastino *m* mediastinum
medicamento *m* medication, medicine, drug; —— a base de sulfas sulfa drug
medicar *vt* to medicate
medicastro *m* quack
medicina *f* medicine; —— del primer nivel primary care; —— del tercer nivel tertiary care; —— deportiva sports medicine; —— familiar family medicine, family practice; —— interna internal medicine; —— nuclear nuclear medicine; —— ocupacional occupational medicine;

—— preventiva preventive medicine; —— socializada socialized medicine; —— veterinaria veterinary medicine
medicinal *adj* medicinal
médico -ca *adj* medical; *m* doctor, physician; —— adscrito attending physician; —— clínico clinician, practitioner; —— de cabecera *or* de la familia family doctor, family physician; —— forense coroner; —— general general practitioner; —— interno intern; —— privado private doctor, private physician; —— residente resident (physician)
medicolegal *adj* medicolegal
medicucho *m* quack
medida *f* measurement, size; measure; medidas sanitarias sanitation, sanitary measures
medidor *m* meter, measuring device
medio -dia *adj* half, half a, a half; middle; —— dormido half asleep; media hermana half sister; —— hermano half brother; media pastilla half a pill; *m* middle; medium; —— ambiente environment; —— de contraste contrast medium
mediodía *m* noon
mediquillo *m* quack
medir *vt* to measure
meditar *vi* to meditate
medroxiprogesterona *f* medroxiprogesterone
médula *f* medulla; marrow; —— espinal spinal cord; —— ósea bone marrow
medusa *f* jellyfish
megacolon *m* megacolon
megadosis *f* megadose
mejilla *f* cheek
mejor *adj* & *adv* (*comp of* bueno *and* bien) better
mejorar *vt* to improve; *vr* to improve, get better
mejoría *f* improvement
melancolía *f* melancholy
melancólico -ca *adj* melancholy
melanina *f* melanin
melanoma *m* melanoma
mellizo -za *adj* & *mf* twin
membrana *f* membrane, web; —— esofágica esophageal web; —— mucosa mucous membrane; —— timpánica tympanic membrane
memoria *f* memory; —— reciente short-term memory; —— remota long-term memory
meninge *f* meninx (*en inglés se emplea casi siempre la forma plural*: meninges)
meningioma *m* meningioma
meningitis *f* meningitis
meningocele *m* meningocele
meningococo *m* meningococcus
menopausia *f* menopause

menor *adj* (*comp of* **pequeño**) smaller; younger; (*anat, surg*) minor; *m* (*de edad*) minor
menstruación *f* menstruation
menstruar *vi* to menstruate
mental *adj* mental
mente *f* mind
mentol *m* menthol
mentón *m* chin
menudo, a often
meperedina *f* meperedine
mercurio *m* mercury
mes *m* (*pl* **meses**) month
mesa *f* table; —— **de cirugía** operating table; —— **de exploración** (*form*) *or* **de exámenes** examining table; —— **de operaciones** operating table
mescalina *f* mescaline
mesencéfalo *m* midbrain
mesentérico -ca *adj* mesenteric
mesenterio *m* mesentery
mesotelioma *m* mesothelioma
meta *f* goal
metabólico -ca *adj* metabolic
metabolismo *m* metabolism
metacarpiano -na *adj & m* metacarpal
metadona *f* methadone
metal *m* metal; —— **pesado** heavy metal
metálico -ca *adj* metallic
metano *m* methane
metanol *m* methanol
metaproterenol *m* metaproterenol
metaqualona *f* methaqualone
metastásico -ca *adj* metastatic
metástasis *f* (*pl* **-sis**) metastasis; **dar** —— to metastasize
metatarsiano -na *adj & m* metatarsal
meter *vt* to insert; —— **aire** (*Mex, fam*) to breathe in, inhale
meticilina *f* methicillin
metilcelulosa *f* methylcellulose
metildopa *f* methyldopa
metilfenidato *m* methylphenidate
metionina *f* methionine
metoclopramida *f* metoclopramide
método *m* method, technique; —— **del ritmo** rhythm method
metoprolol *m* metoprolol
metotrexato *m* methotrexate
metro *m* meter; —— **cuadrado** meter squared *o* square meter
metronidazol *m* metronidazole
mexicano -na *adj & mf* Mexican
mezcla *f* mixture
mezclar *vt* to mix
mezquino *m* (*Mex, CA*) wart
mialgia *f* myalgia
miastenia grave *or* **gravis** *f* myasthenia gravis
miconazol *m* miconazole
microbiano -na *adj* microbial
microbio *m* microbe

microbiología *f* microbiology
microcirugía *f* microsurgery
microgramo *m* microgram
microonda *f* microwave
microorganismo *m* microorganism
microscópico -ca *adj* microscopic
microscopio *m* microscope; —— **electrónico** electron microscope
miedo *m* fear; **tener** —— to be afraid *o* scared
mielina *f* myelin
mieloma múltiple *m* multiple myeloma
mielomeningocele *m* myelomeningocele
miembro *m* member; (*brazo o pierna*) limb; (*fam*) penis, member (*fam*)
migraña *f* migraine headache, migraine
milagro *m* miracle
miliar *adj* miliary
miligramo *m* milligram
mililitro *m* milliliter
milímetro *m* millimeter
mineral *adj & m* mineral
minero *m* miner
mínimo -ma *adj & m* minimum
minoxidil *m* minoxidil
minuto *m* minute
miocárdico -ca *adj* myocardial
miocardio *m* myocardium
miocarditis *f* myocarditis
mioglobina *f* myoglobin
mioma *m* myoma; —— **uterino** uterine leiomyoma, fibroid (*fam*)
miopatía *f* myopathy
miope *adj* myopic, nearsighted
miopía *f* myopia
miositis *f* myositis
mirada *f* gaze
mirar *vi* to look; **Mire arriba..Look upward.**
mitad *f* half; middle; **Tome la mitad de una pastilla..Take half a pill.**
mitral *adj* mitral
mixedema *m* myxedema
mixoma *m* myxoma
moco *m* mucus
mocosidad *f* (*fam*) mucus; **tener** —— to have a runny nose, to have the sniffles
mocoso -sa *adj* **estar** —— (*vulg*) to have a runny nose
mochar *vt* (*vulg*) to cut off
modelo *mf* (*a seguir*) role model
moderación *f* moderation
moderado -da *adj* moderate
modificación *f* modification, adjustment
modificar *vt* to modify, adjust
modo de vida *m* lifestyle
moho *m* mold, mildew
moisés *m* cradle, bassinet
mojado -da *adj* wet, damp
mojar *vt* to wet; *vr* to get wet
mola *f* (*obst*) mole; —— **hidatiforme** *or* **hidatídica** hydatidiform mole

molar *adj* (*obst, dent*) molar; *m* (*dent*) molar
molde *m* (*dent, etc.*) mold
molécula *f* molecule
moler *vt* to grind, crush
molestar *vt* to bother; **Me molesta el brazo**..My arm is bothering me.
molestia *f* discomfort, trouble; **Tengo una molestia en la espalda**..I have back trouble.
molesto -ta *adj* annoying, irritating
molusco contagioso *m* molluscum contagiosum
mollera *f* fontanel *o* fontanelle
momentáneo -a *adj* fleeting, momentary
monitor *m* monitor; —— **cardiaco** cardiac monitor; —— **cardiaco fetal** *or* —— **cardiotocográfico** fetal heart monitor; —— **cardiaco portátil** *or* **Holter** Holter monitor
monitoreo *m* monitoring
monitorización *f* monitoring
monitorizar *vt* to monitor
monoclonal *adj* monoclonal
monógamo -ma *adj* monogamous
mononucleosis *f* mononucleosis
monóxido de carbono *m* carbon monoxide
monstruo *m* monster; —— **de Gila** Gila monster
moquear *vi* (*fam*) to run (*one's nose*); **Me moquea la nariz**..My nose is running..I have a runny nose.
moquera *f* (*fam*) nasal secretions, mucus; **tener** —— to have a runny nose, to have the sniffles
morado -da *adj* purple; cyanotic; bruised; *m* (*esp. Carib*) bruise
morbilidad *f* morbidity
morboso -sa *adj* morbid
mordedura *f* bite
morder *vt, vi* to bite
mordida *f* bite
moreno -na *adj* dark-skinned; *mf* dark-skinned person, black, black person
morete *m* bruise; **hacerse** *or* **salirle moretes** to bruise, get bruises, get bruised
moreteado -da *adj* bruised (*all over*), black-and-blue
moretón *m* bruise; **hacerse** *or* **salirle moretones** to bruise, get bruises, get bruised
morfina *f* morphine
morfología *f* morphology
morgue *f* morgue
morir *vi, vr* (*pp* **muerto**) to die, expire; —— **de hambre** to starve
mormado -da *adj* (*Mex, fam*) congested, having nasal congestion
mortal *adj* fatal
mortalidad *f* mortality

mosca *f* fly; —— **doméstica** housefly
mosquito *m* mosquito, gnat; —— **simúlido** sandfly
mota *f* (*Mex*) grass, pot, marijuana
motivación *f* motivation
moto *See* **motocicleta.**
motocicleta *f* motorcycle
motor -ra *adj* motor
mover *vi, vr* to move, to wiggle; **No se mueva**..Don't move...**Mueva los dedos del pie**..Wiggle your toes.
móvil *adj* mobile
movilidad *f* mobility
movilizar *vt* to mobilize
movimiento *m* movement; **movimientos oculares rápidos (MOR)** *or* **movimientos rápidos de los ojos** rapid eye movements (REM)
mucinoso -sa *adj* mucinous
mucolítico -ca *adj & m* mucolytic
mucosidad *f* mucus; **tener** —— to have a runny nose, to have the sniffles
mucoso -sa *adj* mucous
muchacho -cha *m* boy, child; *f* girl
mucho -cha *adj* a lot of, much; **mucho vómito**..a lot of vomiting...**no mucho dolor**..not much pain; **muchos** -chas a lot of, many; **muchos granos**..a lot of pimples..many pimples; *adv* much, a lot; **mucho peor**..much worse..a lot worse
mudez *f* mutism
mudo -da *adj & mf* mute
muela *f* molar, back tooth (*fam*); —— **del juicio** *or* **cordal** wisdom tooth
muerte *f* death; —— **cerebral** brain death; —— **piadosa** mercy killing
muerto -ta (*pp* *of* **morir**) *adj* dead, deceased; *mf* dead person, corpse
muestra *f* sample, specimen
mujer *f* woman, wife
muleta *f* crutch
múltiple *adj* multiple
multiplicarse *vr* to multiply
multivitamina *f* multivitamin
multivitamínico -ca *adj* pertaining to multivitamins, multivitamin
muñeca *f* wrist
muñón *m* (*anat*) stump
murciélago *m* (*zool*) bat
muscular *adj* muscular
músculo *m* muscle
musculoso -sa *adj* muscular (*said of a person*)
músico -ca *mf* musician
muslo *m* thigh
mutación *f* mutation
mutismo *m* mutism (*esp. elective*)
Mycoplasma Mycoplasma

N

nacer *vi* to be born
nacido -da *adj* born; —— **muerto** stillborn; **recien** —— newborn; *m* (*esp. Carib*) boil
nacimiento *m* birth
nadar *vi* to swim
nalga *f* (*fam*) buttock; **nalgas** bottom
nalidíxico -ca *adj* nalidixic
naloxona *f* naloxone
napalm *m* napalm
naproxén *m* naproxen
naranja *adj* orange; *f* (*fruta*) orange
narcisismo *m* narcissism
narcisista *adj* narcissistic
narcolepsia *f* narcolepsy
narcótico -ca *adj & m* narcotic
nariz *f* (*pl* **narices**) nose; nostril
nasal *adj* nasal
nasofaringe *f* nasopharynx
nasogástrico -ca *adj* nasogastric
natural *adj* natural
naturaleza *f* nature
náusea *f* (*often pl*) nausea; **náuseas del embarazo** morning sickness; **dar** —— to make nauseated, to make gag; **sentir** *or* **tener** —— to feel *o* be nauseated, to gag
navaja *f* (*de afeitar or rasurar*) razor blade
nebulizador *m* nebulizer, inhaler
necrólisis tóxica epidérmica *f* toxic epidermal necrolysis
necrosis *f* necrosis
necrótico -ca *adj* necrotic
nefritis *f* nephritis
nefrología *f* nephrology
nefrólogo -ga *mf* nephrologist
nefrosis *f* nephrosis
nefrótico -ca *adj* nephrotic
negación *f* denial
negativismo *m* negativism
negativo -va *adj* negative
negligencia *f* neglect; —— **médica** malpractice
negligente *adj* negligent
negro -gra *adj* black; *mf* (*persona*) black, black person
Neisseria Neisseria
nene -na *mf* (*fam*) baby
neomicina *f* neomycin
neonatología *f* neonatology
neoplasia *f* neoplasm
neoplásico -ca *adj* neoplastic
neostigmina *f* neostigmine
nervio *m* nerve; —— **atrapado** pinched nerve; —— **auditivo** *or* **acústico** acoustic nerve; —— **ciático** sciatic nerve; ——

comprimido entrapped nerve, pinched nerve (*fam*); —— **craneal** cranial nerve; —— **cubital** ulnar nerve; —— **espinal** spinal nerve; —— **facial** facial nerve; —— **femoral** femoral nerve; —— **frénico** phrenic nerve; —— **laríngeo recurrente** recurrent laryngeal nerve; —— **mediano** median nerve; —— **motor** motor nerve; —— **óptico** optic nerve; —— **parasimpático** parasympathetic nerve; —— **peroneo** *or* **peroneal** peroneal nerve; —— **pudendo** pudendal nerve; —— **radial** radial nerve; —— **raquídeo** spinal nerve; —— **sensorial** *or* **sensitivo** sensory nerve; —— **simpático** sympathetic nerve; —— **trigémino** trigeminal nerve; —— **vago** vagus nerve
nervios *mpl* (*esp. Mex, CA*) nerves, anxiety
nerviosidad *f* nervousness
nerviosismo *m* nervousness
nervioso -sa *adj* nervous
neumococo *m* pneumococcus
neumoconiosis *f* pneumoconiosis
neumología *f* pulmonology
neumólogo -ga *mf* pulmonologist
neumonía *f* pneumonia; —— **por aspiración** aspiration pneumonia
neumotórax *m* pneumothorax
neural *adj* neural
neuralgia *f* neuralgia; —— **del trigémino** trigeminal neuralgia
neurinoma *m* neurinoma
neuritis *f* neuritis
neuroblastoma *m* neuroblastoma
neurocirugía *f* neurosurgery
neurocirujano -na *mf* neurosurgeon
neurofibroma *m* neurofibroma
neurofibromatosis *f* neurofibromatosis
neurogénico -ca, neurógeno -na *adj* neurogenic
neuroléptico -ca *adj & m* neuroleptic
neurología *f* neurology
neurológico -ca *adj* neurological, neurologic
neurólogo -ga *mf* neurologist
neuroma *m* neuroma; —— **del acústico** acoustic neuroma
neuromuscular *adj* neuromuscular
neuropatía *f* neuropathy
neurosífilis *f* neurosyphillis
neurosis *f* (*pl* -sis) neurosis; —— **de guerra** shell shock; —— **postraumática** posttraumatic stress disorder
neurótico -ca *adj & mf* neurotic
neutral *adj* neutral

neutrófilo *m* neutrophil
nevo *m* nevus, birthmark; —— **en araña** spider angioma
niacina *f* niacin
nica *f* (*Mex, CA*) bedpan, chamber pot, portable commode
nicaragüense *adj* & *mf* Nicaraguan
niclosamida *f* niclosamide
nicotina *f* nicotine
nicotínico -ca *adj* nicotinic
nieto -ta *m* grandson, grandchild; *f* granddaughter
nifedipina *f* nifedipine
nigua *f* chigger, jigger
nilón *m* nylon
niñera *f* baby sitter
niñez *f* childhood
niño -ña *m* boy, child; *f* girl
níquel *m* nickel
nistagmo *m* nystagmus
nistatina *f* nystatin
nitrato *m* nitrate; —— **de plata** silver nitrate
nitrito *m* nitrite
nitrofurantoína *f* nitrofurantoin
nitrógeno *m* nitrogen
nitroglicerina *f* nitroglycerin
nivel *m* level; **del primer** —— primary; **del tercer** —— tertiary
nocardiosis *f* nocardiosis
nocivo -va *adj* harmful; —— **para la salud** bad for one's health
nocturno -na *adj* nocturnal
noche *f* night, (late) evening
nodo *m* (*card*) node; —— **auriculoventricular** atrioventricular node; —— **sino-auricular** sinoatrial node
nodriza *f* wet nurse
nódulo *m* nodule
norepinefrina *f* norepinephrine
norfloxacina *f* norfloxacin
norma *f* norm, standard
normal *adj* normal
norteamericano -na *adj* & *mf* North American, American
nortriptilina *f* nortriptyline
nostalgia *f* homesickness; **sentir** —— to be homesick
notar *vt* to notice; **¿Ha notado sangre en el excremento?**..Have you noticed blood in your stool?
novacaína *f* novacaine
novia *f* fiancée, girl friend
novio *m* fiancé, boy friend
nube *f* (*del ojo*) cataract, opacity, cloudy spot
nublado -da *adj* blurred, cloudy
nublarse *vr* (*la vista, etc.*) to cloud (up), become blurred
nubosidad *f* (*en el ojo*) cloudy spot, cataract
nuca *f* back of the neck
nudillo *m* knuckle
nuera *f* daughter-in-law
nuez *f* (*pl* **nueces**) nut; —— **de Adán** Adam's apple
número dos *m* (*el defecar*) number two
número uno *m* (*el orinar*) number one
nutrición *f* nutrition; —— **parenteral total** total parenteral nutrition (TPN)
nutricional *adj* nutritional
nutritivo -va *adj* nutritious, nourishing

O

obesidad *f* obesity
obeso -sa *adj* obese
obrar *vi* (*Mex, CA*) to have a bowel movement
obrero -ra *mf* worker
obsesión *f* obsession
obsesivo-compulsivo -va *adj* obsessive-compulsive
obstetra *mf* obstetrician
obstetricia *f* obstetrics
obstétrico -ca *adj* obstetrical, obstetric
obstrucción *f* obstruction, blockage
obstructivo -va *adj* obstructive
obstruir *vt* to obstruct, block; *vr* to become obstructed *o* blocked
occipital *adj* occipital
oclusión *f* occlusion
oclusivo -va *adj* occlusive
ocular *adj* ocular
oculista *mf* ophthalmologist, eye doctor
ocupación *f* occupation
odiar *vt* to hate
odio *m* hate
odontología *f* dentistry
odontólogo -ga *mf* dentist, oral surgeon
oficina *f* office

oftálmico -ca *adj* ophthalmic
oftalmología *f* ophthalmology
oftalmólogo -ga *mf* ophthalmologist
oftalmoscopio *m* ophthalmoscope
oído *m* ear; hearing, sense of hearing; —— externo external ear; —— interno internal *o* inner ear; —— medio middle ear; oídos, nariz, y garganta ear, nose, and throat (ENT)
oír *vt, vi* to hear; ¿Cómo oye Ud.?..How is your hearing?
ojera *f* dark circle under one's eye
ojo *m* eye; —— de pescado *(fam)* wart, plantar wart; —— morado black eye; —— rojo *or* enrojecido pinkeye, conjunctivitis
oleada *f* wave; —— de calor hot flash
oler *vt, vi* to smell; *(cocaína, cemento, etc.)* to sniff *(cocaine, glue, etc.)* ; —— a to smell like; —— mal to smell bad
olfatorio -ria *adj* olfactory
oligoelemento *m* trace element
olor *m* odor, smell
olvidadizo -za *adj* absent-minded
ombligo *m* umbilicus *(form)*, navel, belly-button *(fam)*
omóplato *m* scapula, shoulder blade *(fam)*
oncocerciasis *f* onchocerciasis
oncocercosis *f* onchocerciasis
oncología *f* oncology
oncólogo -ga *mf* oncologist
onda *f* wave; —— cerebral brain wave
onza (onz.) *f* ounce (oz.)
opacidad *f* opacity
opaco -ca *adj* opaque
operable *adj* operable
operación *f* operation; —— cesárea cesarean section; sala de operaciones operating room (OR)
operar *vt* to operate on; Tenemos que operarle la pierna..We need to operate on your leg; *vi* to operate; *vr* to have an operation; Ud. tiene que operarse..You need to have an operation.
opiáceo -a *adj & m* opiate
opinión *f* opinion
opio *m* opium
oportunista *adj* opportunistic
opresivo -va *adj (dolor)* crushing
óptico -ca *adj* optical, optic; *m* optician; *f* optics
optometrista *mf* optometrist
oral *adj* oral
órbita *f (anat)* orbit
orciprenalina *f* metaproterenol
orden *f (en el expediente)* order
ordenar *vt* to order
oreja *f* ear
orfanatorio *m* orphanage
orfelinato *m* orphanage
orgánico -ca *adj* organic
organismo *m* body, organism; No descuide

su organismo..Don't neglect your body.
órgano *m* organ
organofosfato *m* organophosphate
organofosforado *m* organophosphate
orgasmo *m* orgasm, climax
orificio *m* orifice
origen *m* source
orín *m (often pl)* urine
orina *f* urine
orinal *m* urinal
orinar *vi* to urinate; *vr* orinarse en la cama to wet the bed
oro *m* gold
orofaringe *f* oropharynx
orquiectomía, orquidectomía *f* orchiectomy
orquitis *f* orchitis
ortiga *f* nettle
ortodoncia *f* orthodontia, orthodontics
ortodoncista, ortodontista *mf* orthodontist
ortopedia *f* orthopedics
ortopedista *mf* orthopedist
orzuelo *m* sty *o* stye
oscuro -ra *adj* dark, dim
óseo -a *adj* osseous, pertaining to bone, bone; médula ósea bone marrow
osteítis *f* osteitis; —— fibroquística osteitis fibrosa cystica
osteoartritis *f* osteoarthritis
osteofito *m* osteophyte
osteogénesis *or* osteogenia imperfecta *f* osteogenesis imperfecta
osteoma *m* osteoma
osteomalacia *f* osteomalacia
osteomielitis *f* osteomyelitis
osteopatía *f* osteopathy
osteoporosis *f* osteoporosis
osteosarcoma *m* osteosarcoma
ótico -ca *adj* otic
otitis *f* otitis; —— externa otitis externa; —— interna otitis interna; —— media otitis media
otolaringología *f* otolaryngology
otolaringólogo -ga *mf* otolaryngologist
otoño *m* fall, autumn
otorrinolaringología *f* otolaryngology
otorrinolaringólogo -ga *mf* otolaryngologist
otosclerosis *f* otosclerosis
otoscopio *m* otoscope
ovárico -ca *adj* ovarian
ovario *m* ovary; —— poliquístico polycystic ovary
ovulación *f* ovulation
ovular *vi* to ovulate
óvulo *m* ovum, egg *(fam)*; vaginal suppository
oxacepam *m* oxazepam
oxacilina *f* oxacillin
oxicodona *f* oxycodone
óxido *m* oxide; —— de cinc zinc oxide; —— nitroso nitrous oxide
oxígeno *m* oxygen
oxitocina *f* oxytocin

P

pabellón *m* (*de un hospital*) ward
paciente *adj* patient; *mf* patient; ——
  externo *or* ambulatorio outpatient
pacha *f* (*CA*) nursing bottle, baby's bottle
padecer *vi* to suffer; **Padezco de artritis..I**
  suffer from arthritis..I have arthritis.
padecimiento *m* ailment
padrastro *m* stepfather; hangnail
padre *m* father, parent; priest
país *m* (*pl* países) country
pájaro *m* bird
paladar *m* palate; —— **blando** soft palate;
  —— **duro** hard palate; —— **hendido**
  cleft palate
palangana *f* basin
paleta *f* shoulder blade; (*fam*) tongue blade
paliativo -va *adj* & *m* palliative
palidez *f* paleness, pallor
pálido -da *adj* pale
palma *f* (*anat, bot*) palm
palmada, palmadita *f* pat
palmar *adj* palmar
palomita *f* (*ped*) penis
palpar *vt* to palpate
palpitación *f* palpitation
palpitante *adj* throbbing
palpitar *vi* to palpitate; to beat
paludismo *m* malaria
pan *m* bread; —— **integral** whole wheat
  bread
panadero -ra *mf* baker
panadizo *m* felon, whitlow
panameño -ña *adj* & *mf* Panamanian
páncreas *m* (*pl* -as) pancreas
pancreático -ca *adj* pancreatic
pancreatitis *f* pancreatitis
pantaletas *fpl* (*Mex*) panties, (women's)
  underpants
pantalón *m* (*often pl*) pants, trousers;
  pantalones antichoque military antishock
  trousers (MAST)
panties *mpl* (*esp. Carib*) panties, (women's)
  underpants
pantimedias *fpl* pantyhose
pantorrilla *f* (*anat*) calf
pantoténico -ca *adj* pantothenic
panza *f* paunch, belly
pañal *m* diaper

pañalitis *f* (*fam*) diaper rash
paño *m* cloth, towel, compress; mask of
  pregnancy
pañuelo *m* handkerchief; —— **de papel**
  tissue
papá *m* (*pl* papás) dad
papada *f* double chin
Papanicolaou *m* (*fam*) Pap smear
papel *m* role; paper; —— **sanitario,**
  higiénico, *or* **de baño** toilet paper
paperas *fpl* mumps
papila *f* papilla; —— **gustativa** taste bud
papilar *adj* papillary
papilomavirus *m* papillomavirus
paracoccidioidomicosis *f* paracoccidioidomycosis
paradójico -ca *adj* paradoxical
paragonimiasis *f* paragonimiasis
paraguayo -ya *adj* & *mf* Paraguayan
parálisis *f* paralysis; —— **cerebral** cerebral
  palsy; —— **de Bell** *or* **facial** Bell's palsy
paralizar *vt* to paralyze
paramédico -ca *adj* & *m* paramedic
paranoia *f* paranoia
paranoico -ca *adj* paranoid
paranoide *adj* paranoid
paraquat *m* paraquat
parar *vi* to quit; *vr* to stand, to stand up
parasitario -ria *adj* parasitic
parásito *m* parasite
paratión *m* parathion
paratiroideo -a *adj* parathyroid
parcial *adj* partial
parche *m* patch
paregórico *m* paregoric
parejo -ja *adj* even; *f* partner; couple
parenteral *adj* parenteral
parentérico -ca *adj* parenteral
paresia, paresis *f* paresis
pariente *mf* relative; —— **consanguíneo**
  blood relative
parietal *adj* parietal
parir *vt* (*esp. Carib, fam*) to bear (*a child*)
paro *m* arrest; —— **cardiaco** cardiac arrest;
  —— **respiratorio** respiratory arrest
parotiditis *f* parotiditis, parotitis
parótido -da *adj* parotid; *f* parotid gland
parpadear *vi* to blink

parpadeo *m* blinking, blink
párpado *m* eyelid
partera *f* midwife
partero *m* general practitioner who attends deliveries; male midwife
partes *fpl* private parts, genitals (*esp. female*); —— **privadas** *or* **íntimas** private parts, genitals (*esp. female*)
partícula *f* particle
partida *f* certificate
partidura *f* (*Cub*) fracture, break
partir *vt, vr* to split, (*los labios*) to chap; (*Cub, un hueso*) to break
parto *m* birth, childbirth; delivery; —— **natural** natural childbirth; **dolor** *m* **del** —— labor pain, contraction; **estar de trabajo de** —— to be in labor; **sala de partos** delivery room; **trabajo de** —— labor
pasado -da de peso *adj* overweight
pasajero -ra *adj* fleeting, transient
pasar *vt* to pass; (*esp. Mex*) to swallow; —— **gas** to pass gas; —— **saliva** (*esp. Mex*) to swallow; **Pase saliva, por favor**..Swallow, please; *vi* to wear off; **El dolor se le va a pasar**..The pain will wear off.
pasatiempo *m* pastime, hobby
pasillo *m* hall, hallway
pasivo -va *adj* passive
pasivo-agresivo -va *adj* passive-aggressive
paso *m* step, pace; pass; **dar un** —— to step, take a step
pasta *f* paste; —— **dental** *or* **dentífrica** toothpaste
pastilla *f* pill; —— **para dormir** sleeping pill
patela *f* patella, kneecap
paternidad *f* paternity
paterno -na *adj* paternal
patizambo -ba *adj* knock-kneed
pato *m* urinal (*hand-held*); bedpan
patología *f* pathology
patológico -ca *adj* pathological, pathologic
patólogo -ga *mf* pathologist
patrón -na *mf* employer; *m* pattern
pauta *f* guideline
PCP *See* **fenciclidina.**
peca *f* freckle
pectoral *adj* pectoral
pecho *m* chest, breast
pedacito *m* chip, fragment, piece; **pedacitos de hielo** ice chips
pediatra, pediatra *mf* pediatrician
pediatría *f* pediatrics
pediátrico -ca *adj* pediatric
pediculosis *f* pediculosis
pedicure *m* pedicure
pedicuro -ra *mf* podiatrist
pegadizo -za *adj* (*Mex, fam*) catching
pegajoso -sa *adj* sticky
pegar *vt* to strike; **pegarle** (*una enfermedad*)

to catch, get; to give; **Me pegó la gripe**..I caught the flu...¡**Ud. me la pegó!**..You gave it to me!
peinar *vt* to comb; *vr* to comb one's hair
peine *m* comb
pelado -da *adj* (*la piel*) raw, chapped
pelagra *f* pellagra
pelarse *vr* to peel
peligro *m* danger, hazard
peligroso -sa *adj* dangerous, hazardous
pelo *m* hair
pelota *f* (*fam*) bump, lump
peluca *f* wig
peluquero -ra *mf* haircutter; *m* barber
pélvico -ca *adj* pelvic
pellejo *m* (*fam*) skin
pena *f* grief
pendiente *adj* pending
pene *m* penis
penetración *f* penetration
penetrante *adj* piercing
penetrar *vt* to penetrate, pierce, to puncture
pénfigo *m* pemphigus
penfigoide *adj & m* pemphigoid
penicilamina *f* penicillamine
penicilina *f* penicillin
pensamiento *m* thought
pensar *vt, vi* to think
pentamidina *f* pentamidine
pentazocina *f* pentazocine
peor *adj & adv* (*comp of* **malo** *and* **mal**) worse; **ponerse** —— to get worse
pepe *m* (*Guat*) pacifier
pepsina *f* pepsin
péptico -ca *adj* peptic
pequeño -ña *adj* small, little
percepción *f* perception; —— **de la profundidad** depth perception
perceptible *adj* detectable
percutáneo -a *adj* percutaneous
perder *vt* to lose; (*una cita*) to miss; (*un hábito*) to outgrow, grow out of; —— **el conocimiento** *or* **la conciencia** to lose consciousness, to black out; —— **peso** to lose weight
pérdida *f* loss; —— **de la audición** hearing loss
perfil *m* profile
perforación *f* perforation
perforar *vt* to perforate
perfume *m* perfume
periarteritis nodosa *f* polyarteritis nodosa
pericárdico -ca, pericardiaco -ca *adj* pericardial
pericardio *m* pericardium
pericarditis *f* pericarditis; —— **constrictiva** constrictive pericarditis
periferia *f* periphery
periférico -ca *adj* peripheral
perilla *f* bulb syringe
perinatología *f* neonatology, study of human development and disease at or near the

time of birth
perineal *adj* perineal
periodo, período *m* period; —— **de**
incubación incubation period
peristalsis *f* peristalsis
peritoneal *adj* peritoneal
peritoneo *m* peritoneum
peritonitis *f* peritonitis
permanente *adj* permanent
permiso *m* permission, consent
peroné *m* fibula
peroneal *adj* peroneal
peroneo -a *adj* peroneal
peróxido *m* peroxide; —— **de benzoílo**
benzoyl peroxide; —— **de hidrógeno**
hydrogen peroxide
perrilla *f* (*Mex, fam*) sty *o* stye
perro *m* dog; —— **guía** guide dog, Seeing
Eye dog
persistir *vi* to persist
persona *f* person
personal *adj* personal
personalidad *f* personality; —— **antisocial**
antisocial personality; —— **ciclotímica**
cyclothymic personality; —— **esquizoide**
squizoid personality; —— **histriónica**
histrionic personality; —— **limítrofe**
borderline personality; —— **narcisista**
narcissistic personality; —— **obsesivo-**
compulsiva obsessive-compulsive
personality; —— **paranoide** paranoid
personality; —— **pasivo-agresiva**
passive-aggressive personality
perspectiva *f* outlook
pertussis *f* pertussis
peruano -na *adj* & *mf* Peruvian
pesadez *f* heaviness
pesadilla *f* nightmare
pesado -da *adj* heavy
pesar *m* grief; *vt, vi* to weigh; ¿Cuánto pesa
Ud.?..How much do you weigh?...Tene-
mos que pesarlo..We have to weigh you.
pesario *m* pessary
pescado *m* fish
pescador -ra *mf* fisherman
pescar *vt* (*fam, una enfermedad*) to catch
pesimismo *m* pessimism
peso *m* weight; —— **al nacer** *or* **al**
nacimiento birth weight; **bajar de** ——
to lose weight; **ganar** —— to gain
weight; **perder** —— to lose weight; **tener**
—— **excesivo** to be overweight
pestaña *f* eyelash
peste *f* pest, plague; —— **bubónica** bubonic
plague
pesticida *m* pesticide
pestilencia *f* pestilence
petróleo *m* petroleum; **destilado del** ——
petroleum distillate
peyote *m* peyote
pez *m* (*pl* **peces**) fish
pezón *m* nipple (*female*)

pezonera *f* nipple shield
pH *m* pH
pián *m* yaws
picada *f* (*de insecto*) sting, bite
picadura *f* prick, stick, puncture; (*de*
insecto) bite, sting
picante *adj* hot, spicy
picar *vt* (*insecto*) to bite, to sting; (*esp. Mex*)
to stick, prick; *vi* to itch; ¿Le pica el
brazo?..Does your arm itch?
picazón *f* itch, itching; **tener** —— to itch
pico *m* peak; **alcanzar el** —— to peak
pie *m* foot; —— **caído** foot drop; ——
atleta athlete's foot; —— **deforme**
congénito clubfoot; —— **péndulo** foot
drop; —— **plano** flatfoot; **de** ——
standing
piedra *f* stone; —— **de la vesícula**
gallstone; —— **del riñón** kidney stone;
—— **pómez** pumice stone
piel *f* skin; —— **de gallina** goose pimples;
—— **de oveja** sheepskin
pielografía *f* pyelography; pyelogram
pielograma *m* pyelogram
pielonefritis *f* pyelonephritis
pierna *f* leg
pigmentación *f* pigmentation
pigmento *m* pigment
píldora *f* pill; —— **anticonceptiva** birth
control pill
pilonidal *adj* pilonidal
pilórico -ca *adj* pyloric
píloro *m* pylorus
piloroplastia *f* pyloroplasty
pinchar *vt* to puncture, prick, stick
pinchazo *m* puncture, prick, stick; —— **del**
dedo fingerstick
pindolol *m* pindolol
pineal *adj* pineal
pinta *f* pint; pinta, mal del pinto
pinza *f* clamp, clip; **pinzas** tweezers, clamp,
forceps
pinzar *vt* to clamp, to clip
piodermia, pioderma *m&f* pyoderma
piojo *m* louse
piorrea *f* pyorrhea
pipa *f* pipe (*for smoking*)
piperacilina *f* piperacillin
pipí (*ped*) *m* pee; penis; **hacer** —— to pee
piquete *m* (*dolor*) stabbing pain, sharp pain;
(*de insecto*) bite, sting; (*esp. Mex, de*
aguja o espina) prick, stick; —— **del**
dedo fingerstick
pirazinamida *f* pyrazinamide
piridoxina *f* pyridoxine
pispelo *m* (*ES*) sty *o* stye
pistola *f* gun
pitar *vi* pitarle el pecho (*esp. PR*) to
wheeze
pitiriasis *f* pityriasis; —— **versicolor**
pityriasis versicolor
pituitario -ria *adj* pituitary

placa f (dent, bacteriana) plaque; (dent, surg) plate; (rayos X) film, x-ray; —— de Hawley (orthodontia) retainer
placebo m placebo
placenta f placenta, afterbirth (fam); —— previa placenta previa; **desprendimiento prematuro de** —— placenta abruptio
placer m pleasure
plaga f plague
planificación familiar f family planning, planned parenthood
plano -na adj even, flat
planta f (del pie) sole; (bot) plant
plantar adj plantar
plantilla f insole, footpad (fam)
plaqueta f platelet
plasma m plasma
plasmaféresis f plasmapheresis
plástico -ca adj & m plastic
plata f silver
platelminto m flatworm
platino m platinum
plato hondo m bowl
plazo m a corto —— short-term; a largo —— long-term
pleito m suit, lawsuit; **poner** —— to sue
plenitud f fullness
pletismografía f plethysmography
pleura f pleura
pleural adj pleural
pleuresía f pleurisy
pleurítico -ca adj pleuritic
pleuritis f pleuritis
plexo m plexus
pliegue m fold; —— cutáneo skin fold
plomo m lead
Pneumocystis carinii Pneumocystis carinii
pócima f potion
poción f potion
poco -ca adj little, not much; **poca náusea..** little nausea..not much nausea; **pocos -cas** few, not many; **unas pocas veces..**a few times...**Quedan pocas manchas..**Not many spots are left; adv little, not much; **Come poco...**He doesn't eat much; —— a —— little by little, gradually
poder legal m power of attorney
poderoso -sa adj powerful
podíatra, podiatra mf podiatrist
podiatría f podiatry
podiatrista mf podiatrist
podofilina f podophyllin
podrido -da (pp of **pudrir**) adj rotten
polen m pollen
poliarteritis nudosa f polyarteritis nodosa
policitemia f polycythemia; —— vera polycythemia vera
poliinsaturado -da adj polyunsaturated
polimialgia reumática f polymyalgia rheumatica
polimiositis f polymyositis
polimixina f polymyxin

polio f polio
poliomielitis f poliomyelitis
pólipo m polyp; —— adenomatoso adenomatous polyp; **pólipos juveniles** juvenile polyps; —— **nasal** nasal polyp
poliquístico -ca adj polycystic
polivitamínico -ca adj & m multivitamin
polución f pollution; —— nocturna nocturnal emission
polvo m dust, powder; —— de angel (Ang) angel dust, PCP; **polvos de talco** talcum powder; **en** —— powdered
pollo m chicken
pomada f ointment, salve
pomo m small bottle
pomposo -sa adj grandiose
pómulo m cheekbone
ponerse vr (pp **puesto**) (ropa, etc.) to put on; **Póngase esta bata..**Put on this gown; —— **azul, dormido, pálido, etc.** to turn o become blue, numb, pale, etc. ¿**Se le ponen blancos los dedos cuando hace frío?..**Do your fingers turn white when it gets cold? —— **de pie** to stand (up)
poplíteo -a adj popliteal
popó m (fam) stool, (ped) poopoo; **hacer** —— to have a bowel movement
por prep per; **respiraciones por minuto..**respirations per minute; —— **ciento** percent
porcelana f porcelain
porcentaje m percentage
porcino -na adj porcine
porción f portion
porfiria f porphyria
poro m pore
portador -ra mf carrier
portar vt (una enfermedad) to carry
portátil adj portable
posición f position
positivo -va adj positive
posos del café m coffee grounds
posponer vt (pp **-puesto**) to postpone
pospuesto pp of **posponer**
postemilla f (Mex, CA; fam, dent) abscess
posterior adj posterior
postizo -za adj prosthetic (form), artificial, false
post mortem adj & adv postmortem
postnatal adj postnatal
postoperatorio -ria adj postoperative
postparto adj postpartum
postrado -da adj prostrate (form), exhausted, debilitated
postre m dessert
postura f posture
postural adj postural
potable adj potable
potasio m potassium
potencia f potency, strength
potencial adj & m potential; —— **evocado** evoked potential

potente *adj* potent, strong, powerful
PPD *abbr* **proteína purificada derivada de la tuberculina.** *See* **proteína.**
práctica *f* practice
practicar *vt* to practice; (*un estudio, etc.*) to perform
praziquantel *m* praziquantel
prazosina *f* prazosin
precaución *f* precaution; **por —— just in case**
precisión *f* precision, accuracy
preciso -sa *adj* precise, exact
precoz *adj* (*pl* -coces) precocious; premature
predecir *vt* (*pp* -dicho) to predict
predicho *pp of* **predecir**
predisponer *vt* (*pp* -puesto) to predispose
predisposición *f* predisposition
predispuesto *pp of* **predisponer**
prednisona *f* prednisone
preeclampsia *f* preeclampsia
preliminar *adj* preliminary
prematuro -ra *adj* premature; *mf* premature newborn, preemie (*fam*)
premedicación *f* premedication
premolar *adj & m* premolar
prenatal *adj* prenatal
prendido -da *adj* (*esp. Mex*) hooked (*on drugs, etc.*)
prensión *f* grip, grasp
preñada *adj* (*fam*) pregnant
preñez *f* (*fam*) pregnancy
preocuparse *vr* to worry; **¿Está preocupado?..Are you worried?...No se preocupe..Don't worry.**
preoperatorio -ria *adj* preoperative
preparación *f* preparation
preparado *m* (*pharm*) preparation
preparar *vt* (*una prescripción*) to prepare, to fill
prepucio *m* foreskin
prescribir *vt* (*pp* -scrito) to prescribe, order
prescripción *f* prescription
prescrito *pp of* **prescribir**
presentación *f* presentation; **—— pélvica** *or* **de nalgas** breech presentation
preservar *vt* to preserve
preservativo *m* preservative; condom, rubber (*fam*)
presión *f* pressure; (*fam*) blood pressure; **—— alta** (*fam*) high blood pressure; **——arterial** *or* **sanguínea** blood pressure; **—— diastólica** diastolic pressure; **——sistólica** systolic pressure
presionado -da *adj* stressed, under stress
presionar *vt* to press; **No le voy a presionar fuerte..I won't press hard.**
pretérmino *adj* preterm
prevalencia *f* prevalence
prevención *f* prevention
prevenible *adj* preventible
prevenir *vt* to prevent
preventivo -va *adj* preventive

previo -via *adj* previous
primario -ria *adj* primary
primavera *f* spring, springtime
primer *See* **primero.**
primero -ra *adj* (**primer** *before masculine singular nouns*) first; **primeros auxilios** first aid
primo -ma *mf* cousin
principio *m* beginning, onset
prisión *f* prison
privacía *f* privacy
privacidad *f* privacy
privado -da *adj* private
probabilidad *f* probability
probablemente *adv* probably
probar *vt* to test; (*comida, etc.*) to taste
problema *m* problem
probucol *m* probucol
procaína *f* procaine
procainamida *f* procainamide
procedimiento *m* procedure
proctitis *f* proctitis
pródromo *m* prodrome
producir *vt* to produce
profesional *adj* professional
profiláctico -ca *adj & m* prophylactic
profilaxis *f* prophylaxis
profundidad *f* depth
profundo -da *adj* deep
progeria *f* progeria
progesterona *f* progesterone
programa *m* program
progresar *vi* to progress
progresión *f* progression
progresivo -va *adj* progressive
progreso *m* progress
prolactina *f* prolactin
prolactinoma *m* prolactinoma
prolapso *m* prolapse; **—— del cordón umbilical, del útero, de la vejiga, etc.** prolapsed umbilical cord, uterus, bladder, etc.; **—— valvular mitral** mitral valve prolapse
prolina *f* proline
prolongación *f* extension
prolongar *vt* to prolong, extend
promedio *adj* average; **altura promedio** average height; *m* average
prono -na *adj* prone
pronosticar *vt* to predict, to make a prognosis
pronóstico *m* prognosis
propagación *f* spread
propagar *vt, vr* to spread
propiltiouracilo *m* propylthiouracil
propioceptivo -va *adj* proprioceptive
proporción *f* proportion
proporcionar *vt* to provide, supply
propoxifeno *m* propoxyphene
propranolol *m* propranolol
proptosis *f* proptosis
prostaglandina *f* prostaglandin

próstata *f* prostate
prostatitis *f* prostatitis
prostituto -ta *mf* prostitute
protección *f* protection
protector -ra *adj* protective; *m* guard, *(para una aguja)* cap, needle cap; —— **solar** sunscreen
proteger *vt* to protect
proteína *f* protein; —— **purificada derivada de la tuberculina (PPD)** purified protein derivative of tuberculin (PPD)
protésico -ca, protético -ca *adj* prosthetic
prótesis *f (pl -sis)* prosthesis
Proteus Proteus
protocolo *m* protocol
protozoario -ria *adj & m* protozoan
protuberancia *f* protuberance, bump
provocar *vt* to bring on, trigger, provoke; **¿Hay algo en particular que le provoca los dolores?..**Is there anything in particular that brings on the pains?
próximo -ma *adj* next
proyección *f* projection
proyectil *m* projectile
prueba *f* test, trial; proof; —— **cruzada** crossmatch; —— **cutánea** skin test; —— **de embarazo** pregnancy test; —— **de esfuerzo** exercise stress test; —— **de función pulmonar** pulmonary function test; —— **de la audición** hearing test; —— **de la orina** urine test, urinalysis; —— **de la tuberculosis** TB test; —— **del parche** patch test; —— **de sangre** blood test; —— **de tolerancia a la glucosa** glucose tolerance test; —— **VDRL** VDRL; a —— **de agua,** a —— **de niños,** etc. waterproof, childproof, etc.
prurito *m* pruritis
Pseudomonas Pseudomonas
psicoactivo -va *adj* psychoactive
psicoanálisis *m* psychoanalysis
psicoanalista *mf* psychoanalyst, analyst *(fam)*
psicoanalizar *vt* to psychoanalyze
psicodélico -ca *adj* psychedelic
psicología *f* psychology
psicológico -ca *adj* psychological
psicólogo -ga *mf* psychologist
psicópata *mf* psychopath
psicosis *f* psychosis
psicosomático -ca *adj* psychosomatic
psicoterapeuta *mf* psychotherapist, therapist *(fam)*
psicoterapia *f* psychotherapy
psicoterapista *mf* psychotherapist, therapist *(fam)*
psicótico -ca *adj & mf* psychotic
psicotrópico -ca *adj & m* psychotropic
psilocibina *f* psilocybin
psiquiatra, psiquiátra *mf* psychiatrist
psiquiatría *f* psychiatry

psiquiátrico -ca *adj* psychiatric
psitacosis *f* psittacosis
psoas *m (pl -as)* psoas
psoriasis *f* psoriasis
pterigión *m* pterygium
ptosis *f* ptosis
pubertad *f* puberty
pubiano -na *adj* pubic
púbico -ca *adj* pubic
público -ca *adj* public
pudendo -da *adj* pudendal
pudrir *vt, vr (pp* **podrido)** to rot
puente *m (dent)* bridge; *(anat)* pons; *(card)* bypass; —— **coronario** coronary bypass
puerco *m* pork
puerperal *adj* puerperal
puerperio *m* puerperium
puertorriqueño -ña *adj & mf* Puerto Rican
puesto *pp of* poner
pujar *vi* to bear down, to strain *(at stool)*; *(obst)* to push; **¿Tiene que pujar para defecar?..**Do you have to strain to have a bowel movement?...**Respire profundo y puje..**Take a deep breath and push.
pujo *m* straining, straining at stool
pulga *f* flea
pulgada *f* inch
pulgar *m* thumb
pulmón *m* lung
pulmonar *adj* pulmonary, pulmonic
pulmonía *f* pneumonia; —— **por aspiración** aspiration pneumonia
pulpejo *m* earlobe
pulsación *f* pulsation
pulsante *adj* throbbing
pulsar *vi (un dolor)* to throb
pulsátil *adj* throbbing
pulso *m* pulse; **Quisiera tomarle el pulso..**I would like to take your pulse.
punción *f* puncture, tap; —— **digital** fingerstick; —— **lumbar** lumbar puncture, spinal tap; **herida por** —— puncture wound
puncionar *vt (form)* to puncture, tap
punta *f* tip; —— **del dedo** fingertip
puntada *f* stitch, suture
punteagudo -da *adj* pointed, sharp
punto *m* point; *(de sutura)* stitch; —— **doloroso** trigger point; —— **máximo** peak; **alcanzar el** —— **máximo** to peak; **poner puntos** to suture, stitch
punzada *f* prick, stick; *(de dolor)* shooting pain, pang, twinge; **dar punzadas** to give sudden, sharp pains
punzante *adj (dolor)* sharp, stabbing, shooting, throbbing
punzar *vt* to prick, stick; *vi* to give sudden sharp pains
puñalada *f* stab wound
puño *m* fist; **apretar** *or* **cerrar el** —— to make a fist
pupila *f* pupil *(of the eye)*

pupú *m* (*fam*) stool, (*ped*) poopoo; **hacer**
—— to have a bowel movement
purgación *f* purge; (*fam*) gonorrhea, the clap
(*vulg*)
purgante *adj* & *m* purgative
purgativo -va *adj* & *m* purgative
purificar *vt* to purify
purina *f* purine
puro -ra *adj* pure; *m* cigar

púrpura *f* purpura; —— **de Henoch-**
Schönlein Henoch-Schönlein purpura;
—— **trombocitopénica idiopática**
idiopathic thrombocytopenic purpura
(ITP); —— **trombocitopénica trombó-**
tica thrombotic thrombocytopenic purpura
(TTP)
pus *m* pus
pústula *f* pustule

Q

quebradizo -za *adj* fragile
quebrado -da *adj* broken, chipped, split
quebradura *f* break, split
quebrar *vt, vr* to break, fracture, chip, split;
¿**Cuándo se quebró la pierna?**..When
did you break your leg?
quedarse *vr* —— **en cama** to stay in bed
queja *f* complaint
quejarse *vr* to complain
queloide *m* keloid
quemadura *f* burn; —— **de sol** sunburn
quemante *adj* burning
quemar *vt* to burn; *vr* to burn oneself, to get
burned; ¿**Se quemó?**..Did you burn
yourself?...¿**Se quemó la mano?**..Did you
burn your hand? **quemarse por el sol** to
get sunburned
queratotomía *f* keratotomy
querer *vt, vi* to love
queso *m* cheese
quieto -ta *adj* quiet, calm
quijada *f* jawbone, jaw
quilate *m* carat; **oro de 24 quilates** 24 carat
gold
químico -ca *adj* chemical; *f* chemistry
quimioterapia *f* chemotherapy
quinacrina *f* quinacrine

quinidina *f* quinidine
quinina *f* quinine
quinta enfermedad *f* fifth disease
quintillizo -za *mf* quintuplet
quintupleto -ta *mf* quintuplet
quirófano *m* operating room (OR)
quiropodista *mf* podiatrist
quiropráctico -ca *mf* chiropractor; *f*
chiropractic
quirúrgico -ca *adj* surgical
quiste *m* cyst; —— **de Baker** Baker's cyst;
—— **de Bartholin** Bartholin's cyst;
del conducto tirogloso thyroglossal duct
cyst; —— **dermoide** dermoid cyst;
hidatídico hydatid cyst; —— **ovárico**
ovarian cyst; —— **pilonidal** pilonidal
cyst; —— **poplíteo** popliteal cyst; ——
sebáceo sebaceous cyst
quístico -ca *adj* cystic
quitar *vt* to remove; (*arith*) to subtract;
Quítele siete a cien..Subtract seven from
one hundred; *vr* (*ropa*) to take off; (*dolor*)
to go away; (*un hábito*) to outgrow, grow
out of; **Quítese la blusa**..Take off your
blouse...**Se me quitó el dolor**..The pain
went away...¿**Se le quitará el**
hábito?..Will he outgrow the habit?

R

rabadilla *f* tailbone, area around tailbone
rabdomiólisis *f* rhabdomyolysis
rabdomiosarcoma *m* rhabdomyosarcoma
rabia *f* rabies; rage
rabioso -sa *adj* rabid
radiación *f* radiation
radiactividad *f* radioactivity
radiactivo -va *adj* radioactive
radial *adj* radial
radical *adj* radical
radiculopatía *f* radiculopathy
radio *m* (*anat*) radius; (*chem*) radium
radioactividad *f* radioactivity
radioactivo -va *adj* radioactive
radiografía *f* x-ray (*film*); radiography
radioisótopo *m* radioisotope
radiología *f* radiology
radiólogo -ga *mf* radiologist
radionúclido *m* radionuclide
radioterapia *f* radiotherapy, radiation therapy
rádium *m* radium
radón *m* radon
raíz *f* (*pl* raíces) root; —— **nerviosa** nerve root
rajado -da *adj* (*piel, labios*) chapped, cracked, split
rajar *vt* (*fam*) to cut, to split, (*la cabeza*) to crack
ralo -la *adj* thin (*hair*)
rango *m* range; —— **de movimiento** range of motion; —— **de valores** range of values
ranitidina *f* ranitidine
ranurado -da *adj* (*tableta*) scored
rapé *m* (*tabaco*) snuff
raquídeo -a *adj* spinal
raquitismo *m* rickets
raro -ra *adj* rare, unusual
rascacio *m* stonefish
rascar *vt* to scratch; *vr* to scratch (*oneself*); **Procure no rascarse**..Try not to scratch (yourself).
rasgos *mpl* features
rasguñar *vt* to scratch
rasguño *m* scratch
rash *m* rash
raspadita *f* small scrape, abrasion
raspado *m* (*fam*) curettage
raspadura *f* scrape, abrasion
raspar *vt* to scrape, to scratch
raspón *m* scrape, abrasion
rasquera *f* (*fam*) itching
rasquiña *f* (*esp. Carib, fam*) itching

rastrillo *m* razor (*manual*)
rasuradora *f* razor (*electric*)
rasurar *vt, vr* to shave
rata *f* rat
raticida *m* rat poison
rato *m* short time
ratón *m* mouse
raya *f* streak; (*zool*) stingray
rayo *m* ray, beam; —— **láser** laser, laser beam; **rayos X** x-ray; **los rayos X del señor Peck**..Mr. Peck's x-ray...**el departamento de rayos X**..the x-ray department
raza *f* race (*of people*)
razón *f* **perder la** —— to lose one's mind, go crazy
RCP *abbr* **resucitación cardiopulmonar.** See **resucitación.**
reabsorber *vt, vi* to resorb
reacción *f* reaction; —— **adversa** adverse reaction; —— **alérgica** allergic reaction; —— **conversiva** conversion reaction; —— **cruzada** cross reaction; —— **del injerto contra el huésped** graft-versus-host reaction *o* disease; —— **tardía** delayed reaction
reaccionar *vi* to react
reactivo -va *adj* reactive
realidad *f* reality
reanimación *f* resuscitation; —— **cardiopulmonar (RCP)** cardiopulmonary resuscitation (CPR)
reanimar *vt, vr* to revive
rebaba *f* burr (*metal*)
rebajar *vi* to reduce, lose weight
rebote *m* rebound
recaer *vi* to relapse
recaída *f* relapse
recámara *f* bedroom
recesivo -va *adj* recessive
receta *f* (*médica*) prescription, order
recetar *vt* to prescribe, to order
recién nacido -da *mf* newborn
recientemente *adv* recently
recipiente *m* container
recobrar *vt, vr* to recover
recombinante *adj* recombinant
recomendar *vt* to recommend
reconstruir *vt* to reconstruct
recordar *vt* to remember
recreación *f* recreation
recreo *m* recreation
rectal *adj* rectal
recto -ta *adj* straight; *m* rectum
recubrimiento *m* coating

recubrir *vt* (*el estómago, etc.*) to coat
recuento *m* count; —— **de glóbulos blancos** white blood cell count; —— **sanguíneo** blood count
recuperación *f* recuperation, recovery; **sala de** —— recovery room
recuperar *vt* to regain, recover; —— **el aire** to catch one's breath; *vr* to recuperate, recover
recurrencia *f* recurrence
rechazar *vt* to reject
rechazo *m* rejection
rechinar *vt* —— **los dientes** to grit one's teeth
red *f* mesh, network
redondo -da *adj* round
reducción *f* reduction
reducir *vt* to reduce; (*ortho*) to reduce, set; *vr* to get smaller, shrink
reemplazar *vt* to replace
reemplazo *m* replacement; —— **total de cadera** total hip replacement
reevaluar *vt* to reevaluate
refinado -da *adj* refined
reflejo *m* reflex; —— **condicionado** conditioned reflex; —— **nauseoso** gag reflex; —— **patelar** *or* **rotuliano** patellar reflex, knee jerk (*fam*)
reflujo *m* reflux; —— **esofágico** esophageal reflux
reforzar *vt* to reinforce, strengthen
refresco *m* soft drink
refrigeración *f* refrigeration; **en** —— refrigerated
refrigerador *m* refrigerator
refrigerio *m* snack
refuerzo *m* reinforcement; **dosis** *f* **de** —— booster dose
refugio *m* shelter; —— **para mujeres, para personas sin hogar, etc.** women's shelter, homeless shelter, etc.
regaderazo *m* (*Mex, fam*) shower
regarse *vr* (*fam, dolor*) to spread; **El dolor se me riega por todo el brazo..**The pain spreads through my whole arm.
regazo *m* lap (*of a person*)
regenerarse *vr* to regenerate
régimen *m* (*pl* **regímenes**) regimen; diet
registro *m* (*de un monitor, ECG, etc.*) tracing; (*de signos vitales, etc.*) record; (*de nacimientos, etc.*) register
regla *f* (*periodo menstrual*) period; **bajarle la** —— (*fam*) to have one's period
reglar *vi* to menstruate
regresión *f* regression
regulador *m* regulator
regular *adj* regular; *vt* to regulate
regurgitación *f* regurgitation; —— **aórtica, mitral, etc.** aortic regurgitation, mitral regurgitation, etc.
regurgitar *vt* to regurgitate
rehabilitación *f* rehabilitation

rehabilitar *vt* to rehabilitate
rehidratación *f* rehydration
rehidratar *vt* to rehydrate
reinfección *f* reinfection
reinfestación *f* reinfestation
reir *vi, vr* to laugh
relación *f* relation; —— **sexual** sexual intercourse; **¿Cuándo fue la última vez que tuvo relación sexual?..**When was the last time you had sexual intercourse?
relajación *f* relaxation
relajante *adj* relaxing; *m* relaxant
relajar *vt, vr* to relax; **Relaje la pierna..**Relax your leg...**Relájese..**Relax.
relámpago *m* lightning
rellenar *vt* (*un diente*) to fill (*a tooth*)
relleno *m* (*Mex, CA; dent*) filling
remedio *m* remedy, cure; —— **casero** home remedy
remisión *f* remission
remojar *vt* to soak
renal *adj* renal
renovascular *adj* renovascular
renquear *vi* to limp
reparación *f* repair
reparar *vt* to repair, fix
repelente *m* repellant; —— **de insectos** insect repellant
repente, de suddenly
repentino -na *adj* sudden
repetir *vt* to repeat; *vi* (*Mex, fam*) to burp
repetitivo -va *adj* repetitive
reponer *vt* to replace, restore
reposo *m* rest; **en** —— at rest
represión *f* repression
reprimir *vt* to repress
reproducción *f* reproduction
reproducir *vt, vr* to reproduce
reproductivo -va *adj* reproductive
reproductor -ra *adj* reproductive
requesón *m* cottage cheese
res *f* beef
resaca *f* hangover; **tener una** —— to have a hangover, to be hungover
resbalar *vi, vr* to slip
resbalón *m* slip
rescatar *vt* to rescue
rescate *m* rescue
resecar *vi* to get dry, dry out
resección *f* resection
reseco -ca *adj* dry, dried, dried out
resequedad *f* dryness; —— **de boca** dry mouth
reserpina *f* reserpine
reserva *f* reserve, store
reservorio *m* reservoir
resfriado *m* cold
residente *mf* (*médico*) resident
resina *f* resin
resistencia *f* resistence; stamina
resistente *adj* resistant
resistir *vt, vr* to resist

resolverse *vr* (*pp* **resuelto**) to resolve, clear up
resonancia magnética nuclear *f* magnetic resonance imaging (MRI)
resorber *vt, vi* to resorb
respaldo *m* backup
respeto *m* respect; —— **de sí mismo** self-esteem
respiración *f* respiration, breath; **Tome una respiración profunda**..Take a deep breath; —— **boca-a-boca** mouth-to-mouth respiration *o* resuscitation; **falta de la** —— shortness of breath; **faltarle la** —— to be short of breath; **¿Le faltaba la respiración?**..Were you short of breath?
respirador *m* respirator
respirar *vt, vi* to breathe; **Respire profundo**..Breathe deeply..Take a deep breath.
respiratorio -ria *adj* respiratory
responder *vi* to respond
respuesta *f* response; —— **inmune** immune response
restablecer *vt* to restore; *vr* (*de una enfermedad*) to recover
restablecimiento *m* recovery
restañar *vt* to stanch
restar *vt, vi* (*arith*) to subtract; **Réstele siete a cien**..Subtract seven from one hundred.
restaurar *vt* to restore
restricción *f* restriction
restringir *vt* to restrict
resucitación *f* resuscitation; —— **boca-a-boca** mouth-to-mouth resuscitation; —— **cardiopulmonar (RCP)** cardiopulmonary resuscitation (CPR)
resucitar *vt* to resuscitate
resuelto *pp of* **resolver**
resultado *m* result, outcome
resultar *vi* to turn out; **¿Y si resulta positivo?**..And if it turns out positive?
retardado -da *adj* retarded, delayed; —— **mental** mentally retarded
retardar *vt* to delay
retardo *m* retardation; delay; —— **mental** mental retardation
retención *f* retention
retenedor *m* (*orthodontia*) retainer
retículo *m* network
reticulocito *m* reticulocyte
retina *f* retina; —— **desprendida** detached retina
retinopatía *f* retinopathy
retorcerse *vr* to writhe; (*el estómago*) to cramp; **Se me retuerce el estómago**..My stomach is cramping..I have stomach cramps.
retorcijón, retortijón *m* abdominal cramp
retrasado -da *adj* retarded, delayed; —— **mental** mentally retarded
retrasar *vt* (*desarrollo, etc.*) to delay; *vr* to lag

retraso *m* retardation; delay; lag; —— **mental** mental retardation
retroalimentación *f* feedback
retrógrado -da *adj* retrograde
reuma *f* (*fam, often pl*) joint pain, arthritis
reumático -ca *adj* rheumatic
reumatoide *adj* rheumatoid
reumatología *f* rheumatology
reumatólogo -ga *mf* rheumatologist
revacunación *f* booster shot, revaccination
revalorar *vt* to reevaluate
reventar *vt, vr* to rupture, burst
reversible *adj* reversible
revestido -da *adj* lined, coated
revestimiento *m* (*del estómago, etc.*) lining, coating
revestir *vt* to line, to coat; **Células mucosas revisten el intestino**..Mucous cells line the intestine...**Este medicamento reviste la pared interna de su estómago**..This medicine coats the walls of your stomach.
revisar *vt* to examine
revisión *f* examination
riboflavina *f* riboflavin
Rickettsia Rickettsia
riesgo *m* risk; **alto** —— high risk; **correr el** —— **de** to run the risk of; **factor de** —— risk factor
rifampicina *f* rifampin
rigidez *f* stiffness
rígido -da *adj* rigid, stiff
rigor mortis *m* rigor mortis
rinitis *f* rhinitis; —— **alérgica** allergic rhinitis
rinoplastia *f* rhinoplasty
riñón *m* kidney; **emesis basin**; —— **poliquístico** polycystic kidney
riñonera *f* emesis basin
risa *f* laugh
ritmo *m* rhythm; —— **biológico** biorhythm; **método del** —— rhythm method
rivalidad *f* rivalry; —— **entre hermanos** sibling rivalry
robusto -ta *adj* heavyset
rociada *f* spray
rociador *m* sprayer
rociar *vt* to spray
rodilla *f* knee
rodillera *f* kneepad
roedor -ra *adj* rodent; *m* rodent
rojizo -za *adj* reddish
rojo -ja *adj* red
romper *vt, vr* (*pp* **roto**) to break
rompimiento *m* break
ron *m* rum
roncar *vi* to snore; **roncarle el pecho** to breathe noisily (*as with asthma or bronchitis*), to wheeze
ronco -ca *adj* hoarse
roncha *f* wheal; **ronchas** hives, (*fam*) rash
ronchitas *fpl* (*fam*) fine rash
rondas *fpl* (*Ang, de los médicos*) rounds;

hacer —— to make rounds
ronquera *f* hoarseness
roña *f* (*esp. Mex, fam*) scabies
ropa *f* clothes, clothing; —— **de cama** bedclothes, bedding; —— **interior** underwear
rosado -da *adj* pink
roséola *or* **roseola infantil** *f* roseola infantum
roto -ta (*pp of* romper) *adj* broken
rótula *f* patella, kneecap
rotura *f* rupture; (*muscular*) tear
rozadura *f* chafe, scrape
rozar *vt, vi* to graze, chafe, rub; ¿**Le roza el pañal?**..Does the diaper chafe him? *vr* to

graze (*oneself*); **Me rocé el brazo**..I grazed my arm.
rozón *m* graze
rubeola, rubéola *f* rubella, German measles (*fam*), three-day measles (*fam*)
rubio -bia *adj* blond; *m* blond; *f* blonde
rubor *m* (*physio*) flush, redness
ruborizarse *vr* (*physio*) to flush
ruido *m* noise
ruptura *f* rupture; —— **prematura de membranas** premature rupture of membranes
rural *adj* rural
rutina *f* routine
rutinario -ria *adj* routine

S

SA *See* **sinoauricular** *or* **sinoatrial**.
sábana *f* sheet, bedsheet
saber *vi* to taste; —— **a** to taste like; —— **mal** to taste bad
sabor *m* flavor, taste; **con** —— **a cereza, con** —— **a plátano, etc.** cherry-flavored, banana-flavored, etc.
sacaleche *m* breast pump
sacar *vt* to remove, take out; (*sangre*) to draw; ¿**Me van a sacar sangre?**..Are you going to draw blood? —— **aire** (*esp. Mex, CA*) to breathe out; —— **la lengua** to stick out one's tongue; **Saque la lengua**..Stick out your tongue; **sacarle el aire** *or* **los gases** (*a un bebé*) to burp (*a baby*); **Debe sacarle el aire**..You should burp him.
sacarina *f* saccharin
sacerdote *m* priest
sacro -cra *adj* sacral; *m* sacrum
sacroiliaco -ca *adj* sacroiliac
sacudida eléctrica *f* electric shock
sacudirse *vr* —— **la nariz** (*esp. Carib*) to blow one's nose
sádico -ca *adj* sadistic; *mf* sadist
sadismo *m* sadism
safeno -na *adj* saphenous
sal *f* salt; **sales aromáticas** smelling salts; —— **de Epsom** Epsom salt; **substituto de** —— salt substitute
sala *f* room, ward; —— **de cuneros** newborn nursery; —— **de emergencia** emergency room (ER); —— **de espera** waiting room; —— **de operaciones**

operating room (OR); —— **de partos** delivery room; —— **de recuperación** recovery room; —— **de urgencias** emergency room (ER)
salazosulfapiridina *f* sulfasalazine
salbutamol *m* salbutamol
salicilato *m* salicylate
salicílico -ca *adj* salicylic
salida *f* exit
salino -na *adj* saline; **solución salina isotónica** normal saline solution
salir *vi* to turn out; to drain; **El estudio salió positivo**..The test turned out positive...¿**Le sale pus?**..Is it draining pus? **salirle agua de la nariz** (*Carib*) to have a runny nose; **salirle granos** to break out (*one's skin*); **Le están saliendo granos**..He's breaking out..His skin is breaking out; **salirle leche** to lactate (*form*), to produce milk; **salirle los dientes** to teethe, to come in (*one's teeth*); ¿**Le están saliendo los dientes?**..Is he teething?..Are his teeth coming in? **salirle sangre** to bleed; ¿**Le salió sangre?**..Did you bleed? **salirle una piedra** (*al orinar*) to pass a stone
saliva *f* saliva, spit
salivación *f* salivation
salival *adj* salivary
salmonelosis *f* salmonellosis
Salmonella Salmonella
salpingitis *f* salpingitis
salpullido *m* rash (*esp. due to heat or chafing*), diaper rash
saltar *vi* to hop

salto *m* hop
salubridad *f* health
salud *f* health; —— **mental** mental health;
—— **pública** public health
saludable *adj* healthy
salvado *m* bran
salvadoreño -ña *adj* & *mf* Salvadoran,
Salvadorian
salvamento *m* rescue
salvar *vt* to save, rescue, to salvage
sanar *vt* to heal, cure; *vi* to heal, become
cured; (*Mex, fam*) to give birth
sanatorio *m* sanatorium
saneamiento *m* (*ambiental*) sanitation
sangrado *m* bleeding; —— **menstrual**
menstrual bleeding, menstrual flow; ——
por la nariz nosebleed
sangrante *adj* bleeding; **úlcera** ——
bleeding ulcer
sangrar *vi* to bleed
sangre *f* blood; **poner** —— to give a
transfusion, to transfuse; **¿Me van a
poner sangre?**..Are you going to give me
a transfusion?
sangría *f* phlebotomy (*therapeutic*); **hacer**
—— to phlebotomize, remove blood from
sangriento -ta *adj* bloody
sanguijuela *f* leech
sanitario -ria *adj* sanitary; *m* rest room
sano -na *adj* healthy
santero -ra *mf* (*Carib*) faith healer, witch
doctor
santos óleos *mpl* last rites, extreme unction,
anointing of the sick
sarampión *m* measles; —— **alemán**
German measles, rubella
sarcoidosis *f* sarcoidosis
sarcoma *m* sarcoma; —— **de Ewing**
Ewing's sarcoma; —— **de Kaposi**
Kaposi's sarcoma
sarna *f* scabies
sarpullido *m* rash (*esp. due to heat or
chafing*), diaper rash
sarro dental *m* tartar
satélite *adj* (*clínica, lesión*) satellite
saturado -da *adj* saturated; **no** ——
unsaturated
sauna *m* sauna
sebáceo -a *adj* sebaceous
seborrea *f* seborrhea
seca *f* (*fam*) enlarged lymph node
secar *vt* to dry; *vr* to dry, to dry out
sección *f* section
seco -ca *adj* dry
secreción *f* secretion, discharge; —— **nasal
posterior** postnasal drip
secretar *vt* to secrete
secretario -ria *mf* secretary; —— **de sala**
ward clerk
secretorio -ria *adj* secretory
secundario -ria *adj* secondary
secundinas *fpl* afterbirth

sed *f* thirst; **tener** —— to be thirsty; **¿Tiene
sed?**..Are you thirsty?
seda *f* silk
sedante *adj* & *m* sedative
sedar *vt* to sedate
sedentario -ria *adj* sedentary
sedimento *m* sediment, deposit
seguido *adv* often; **¿Qué tan seguido le dan
los dolores (del parto)?**..How often are
the contractions coming?
seguimiento *m* follow-up
segundo -da *adj* second; *m* second
seguridad *f* safety
seguro -ra *adj* safe, sure; **para estar** ——
just in case, to be sure; *m* (*Mex*) safety
pin; **seguros** insurance
selenio *m* selenium
semana *f* week
semen *m* semen
seminoma *m* seminoma
senil *adj* senile
seno *m* sinus; (*pecho*) breast
sensación *f* sensation, feeling
sensibilidad *f* sensitivity
sensibilizar *vt* to sensitize; *vr* to become
sensitized
sensible *adj* sensitive, susceptible
sensorio -ria *adj* sensory
sentaderas *fpl* bottom, buttocks (*form*)
sentarse *vr* to sit, sit down, (*cuando está
acostado*) to sit up
sentido *m* sense; —— **de la vista** sense of
sight; —— **del gusto** sense of taste; ——
del oído sense of hearing; —— **del olfato**
sense of smell; —— **del tacto** sense of
touch
sentimiento *m* feeling, emotion
sentir *vt* to feel; to be sorry; **Va a sentir
algo de dolor**..You're going to feel some
pain...**Lo siento**..I'm sorry; *vr* to feel;
¿Cómo se siente?..How do you feel?...**¿Se
siente cansado?**..Do you feel tired?...**¿Se
siente mal?**..Do you feel sick?
seña *f* sign; **hablar por señas** (*comunicar
con sordomudos*) to sign
señal *f* sign; —— **de advertencia** *or* **alarma**
warning sign
señora *f* wife
sepsis *f* sepsis
séptico -ca *adj* septic
sequedad *f* dryness; —— **de boca** dry
mouth
ser *m* —— **amado** loved one; —— **humano**
human being
seriado -da *adj* serial
sérico -ca *adj* pertaining to serum, serum
serie *f* series; —— **ósea** bone scan
serina *f* serine
serio -ria *adj* serious
seroconversión *f* seroconversion
serología *f* serology
seronegativo -va *adj* seronegative

seropositivo -va *adj* seropositive
serpiente *f* snake; —— de cascabel rattlesnake
servicio *m* service; (*fam, often pl*) restroom; —— social social service
seudoefedrina *f* pseudoephedrine
seudogota *f* pseudogout
seudohipoparatiroidismo *m* pseudohypoparathyroidism
seudoquiste *m* pseudocyst —— pancreático pancreatic pseudocyst
seudosuicidio *m* staged suicide; suicide gesture
severo -ra *adj* severe
sexo *m* sex; —— oral oral sex; ligado al —— sex-linked
sexual *adj* sexual
sexualidad *f* sexuality
shigelosis *f* shigellosis
Shigella Shigella
shock *m* (*Ang*) shock
sibilancia *f* (*form*) wheeze
SIDA *abbr* síndrome de inmunodeficiencia adquirida. *See* síndrome.
siempre *adv* como —— as usual
sien *f* (*anat*) temple
sierra *f* saw
siesta *f* nap; tomar una —— to take a nap
sietemesino -na *mf* baby born at seven months
sífilis *f* syphillis
sigmoideo -a *adj* sigmoid
sigmoidoscopía, sigmoidoscopía *f* sigmoidoscopy
signo *m* (*de una enfermedad*) sign; —— de advertencia *or* alarma warning sign; signos vitales vital signs
siguiente *adj* next
silbar *vi* silbarle el pecho to wheeze
silbido *m* wheeze; tener silbidos to have wheezing, to wheeze; Tengo silbidos..I have wheezing.
sílice *f* silica
silicona *f* silicone
silicosis *f* silicosis
silla *f* chair; —— de ruedas wheelchair
simeticona *f* simethicone
simetría *f* symmetry
simétrico -ca *adj* symmetrical, symmetric
simpatectomía *f* sympathectomy
simpático -ca *adj* (*neuro*) sympathetic
sinapsis *f* synapse
síncope *m* syncope (*form*), faint
síndrome *m* syndrome; —— alcohólico fetal fetal alcohol syndrome; —— carcinoide carcinoid syndrome; —— cerebral orgánico organic brain syndrome; —— de abstinencia withdrawal; —— de Asherman Asherman's syndrome; —— de cefalea postraumática postconcussional syndrome; —— de Cushing Cushing's syndrome; ——

de DiGeorge DiGeorge syndrome; —— de Down Down's syndrome; —— de Ehlers-Danlos Ehlers-Danlos syndrome; —— de Felty Felty's syndrome; —— de Gilles de la Tourette Gilles de la Tourette syndrome; —— de Guillain-Barré Guillain-Barré syndrome; —— de inmunodeficiencia adquirida (SIDA) acquired immunodeficiency syndrome (AIDS); —— de insuficiencia respiratoria del adulto adult respiratory distress syndrome (ARDS); —— de Kawasaki Kawasaki's syndrome; —— de Klinefelter Klinefelter's syndrome; —— de Korsakoff Korsakoff's syndrome; —— del choque tóxico toxic shock syndrome; —— del intestino irritable irritable bowel syndrome; —— del niño hiperactivo attention deficit syndrome; —— del niño maltratado battered child syndrome; —— del seno enfermo sick sinus syndrome; —— del túnel carpiano carpal tunnel syndrome; —— de malabsorción malabsorption syndrome; —— de Mallory-Weiss Mallory-Weiss syndrome; —— de Marfan Marfan's syndrome; —— de Ménière Ménière's syndrome; —— de muerte súbita infantil sudden infant death syndrome (SIDS); —— de Osler-Rendu-Weber Osler-Rendu-Weber syndrome; —— de Peutz-Jeghers Peutz-Jeghers syndrome; —— de Pickwick Pickwickian syndrome; —— de piernas inquietas restless legs syndrome; —— de Reiter Reiter's syndrome; —— de Reye Reye's syndrome; —— de Sheehan Sheehan's syndrome; —— de Sjögren Sjögren's syndrome; —— de Stevens-Johnson Stevens-Johnson syndrome; —— de Turner Turner's syndrome; —— estafilococo de piel escaldada staphylococcal scalded skin syndrome; —— hemolítico-urémico hemolytic-uremic syndrome; —— hepatorrenal hepatorenal syndrome; —— nefrótico nephrotic syndrome; —— posconmocional postconcussional syndrome; —— premenstrual premenstrual syndrome;
sinergia *f* synergy
sínfisis *f* symphysis
sinoauricular, sinoatrial (SA) *adj* sinoatrial (S-A)
sinovial *adj* synovial
sinovitis *f* synovitis
sintético -ca *adj* synthetic
sintetizar *vt* to synthesize
síntoma *m* symptom
sinusitis *f* sinusitis
siringomielia *f* syringomyelia
sirviente -ta *mf* housecleaner
sismo *m* earthquake
sistema *m* system; —— cardiovascular

cardiovascular system; —— **digestivo** digestive system; —— **endocrino** endocrine system; —— **esquelético** skeletal system; —— **métrico** metric system; —— **musculoesquelético** musculoskeletal system; —— **nervioso autónomo** autonomic nervous system; —— **nervioso central (SNC)** central nervous system (CNS); —— **nervioso parasimpático** parasympathetic nervous system; —— **nervioso periférico** peripheral nervous system; —— **nervioso simpático** sympathetic nervous system; —— **reproductor** reproductive system; —— **respiratorio** respiratory system

sistémico -ca adj systemic

sistólico -ca adj systolic

SNC abbr **sistema nerviosa central.** See **sistema.**

sobaco m (fam) armpit

sobador -ra mf folk healer who uses massage

sobar vt to rub, massage; (fam, los huesos) to reduce (a dislocation or fracture)

sobrecargar vt to overload

sobredosis f (pl -sis) overdose

sobrepeso m excess weight

sobrevivir vt, vi to survive

sobrina f niece

sobrino m nephew

sobrio -ria adj sober

socio -cia mf partner, associate

socorrista mf rescuer

socorro interj Help! m help

sodio m sodium

sofocar vt, vr to suffocate, smother

sol m sun

solar adj solar

soldado m soldier

soldar vi (ortho) to fuse, knit

sóleo m soleus

sólido -da adj & m solid

solitaria f tapeworm

soltar vt (pp **suelto**) to loosen, free, (fam) to relax; **Suelte el cinturón..**Loosen your belt...**Suelte la pierna..**Relax your leg.

soltura f (Mex, fam) diarrhea, loose bowels

solución f solution; —— **amortiguadora** buffer solution; —— **salina isotónica** normal saline solution

solvente m solvent

somático -ca adj somatic

sombrero m hat

somnífero m sleeping pill

somnoliento -ta adj sleepy, drowsy

sonambulismo m sleepwalking

sonar vi (las tripas) to growl (one's stomach); vr **sonarse la nariz** to blow one's nose

sonda f catheter, tube; probe; —— **Foley** Foley catheter; —— **nasogástrica** nasogastric tube; —— **para alimentación** feeding tube

sondear, sondar vt to probe

sonido m sound

sonograma m sonogram

sonreír vi, vr to smile

sonrisa f smile

sonrojarse vr (physio) to flush

soñar vt, vi to dream; —— **con** to dream of o about; —— **despierto** to daydream

soñoliento -ta adj sleepy, drowsy

sopa f soup

soplar vi to blow; **Sople lo más fuerte que pueda..**Blow as hard as you can; vr **soplarse la nariz** (Carib) to blow one's nose

soplo m (cardiaco) murmur, heart murmur

soporte m support (physical); —— **para el arco del pie** arch support

sorber vt to sip; —— **los mocos** (fam) to sniffle

sorbitol m sorbitol

sorbo m sip

sordera f deafness

sordo -da adj deaf; (dolor) dull; **medio** —— hard of hearing; mf deaf person

sordomudez f deafmutism

sordomudo -da adj deaf and mute; mf deaf-mute

soroche m (SA) mountain sickness

sostén m brassiere

sostener vt —— **la respiración** or **el resuello** to hold one's breath; **Sostenga la respiración..**Hold your breath.

soya, soja f soybean

Staphylococcus Staphylococcus

status m status; —— **asthmaticus** status asthmaticus; —— **epilepticus** status epilepticus

Streptococcus Streptococcus

Strongyloides Strongyloides

suave adj soft, smooth, gentle, mild

suavizador -ra adj (una loción) softening

suavizante adj (una loción) softening

suavizar vt (la piel) to soften

subagudo -da adj subacute

subaracnoideo -a adj subarachnoid

subclavio -via adj subclavian

subclínico -ca adj subclinical

subconciencia f subconscious, subconsciousness

subconsciente adj subconscious

subcutáneo -a adj subcutaneous

subdural adj subdural

subespecialidad f subspecialty

subida f rise

subir vi to rise, go up; **Le subió el azucar..** Your sugar rose.

súbito -ta adj sudden

sublimación f (psych) sublimation

sublingual adj sublingual

subluxación f subluxation

substancia f substance; —— **blanca** white

matter; —— **gris** gray matter; ——
química chemical
substituir *vt* to substitute; **Ud. puede**
substituir huevos por pescado..You can
substitute fish for eggs (*Observe que los*
dos objetos huevos y pescado *se invierten*
al traducir al inglés. Note that the two
objects fish *and* eggs *are inverted on*
translating to Spanish.)
substituto *m* substitute
succión *f* suction
suciedad *f* dirt
sucio -cia *adj* dirty
sucralfato *m* sucralfate
sudamericano -na *adj & mf* South
American
sudar *vi* to sweat, perspire
sudor *m* sweat, perspiration
suegra *f* mother-in-law
suegro *m* father-in-law
suela *f* sole (*of a shoe*)
suelto -ta (*pp of* **soltar**) *adj* loose, free,
relaxed; **estar** —— **del estómago** (*fam*) to
have diarrhea
sueño *m* sleep; dream; —— **húmedo** *or*
mojado wet dream; **dar** —— to make
sleepy; **tener** —— to be sleepy
suero *m* serum; electrolyte solution, IV
fluids; **¿Me van a poner suero?**..Are you
going to give me IV fluids?
suéter *m* sweater
suficiente *adj* sufficient
sufrimiento *m* suffering
sufrir *vt, vi* to suffer
suicida *adj* suicidal
suicidarse *vr* to commit suicide
suicidio *m* suicide; **intento de** —— suicide
attempt
sujetadores *mpl* restraints
sujetar *vt* to restrain
sulfacetamida *f* sulfacetamide
sulfadiacina *f* sulfadiazine

sulfametoxazol *m* sulfamethoxazole
sulfas *fpl* sulfa drugs
sulfato *m* sulfate; —— **de cobre** copper
sulfate; —— **de magnesio** magnesium
sulfate; —— **ferroso** ferrous sulfate
sulfisoxazol *m* sulfisoxazole
sulfonamida *f* sulfonamide
sulfonilurea *f* sulfonylurea
sulindaco *m* sulindac
sumar *vt* (*arith*) to add; **¿Cuánto es ocho y**
nueve?..How much is eight and nine?
suministrar *vt* to supply, provide
suministro *m* supply
superar *vt* to overcome
superego *m* superego
superficial *adj* superficial
superficie *f* surface
superior *adj* (*anat*) superior, upper
supino -na *adj* supine
suplementario -ria *adj* supplementary,
supplemental
suplemento *m* supplement
supositorio *m* suppository
supresión *f* suppression
suprimir *vt* to suppress; (*una medicina, etc.*)
to eliminate, quit taking
supuración *f* discharge
supurar *vi* to form pus, to drain pus
suramericano -na *var of* **sudamericano -na**
surfactante *m* surfactant
surtir *vt* (*una prescripción*) to fill; —— **de**
nuevo to refill
susceptible *adj* susceptible
suspender *vt* to suspend
suspensión *f* suspension
suspensorio *m* athletic supporter, jockstrap
(*fam*)
suspirar *vi* to sigh
suspiro *m* sigh
susto *m* scare
sutura *f* suture
suturar *vt* to suture, to stitch (up)

tab 134 ten

T

tabaco *m* tobacco
tábano *m* horsefly
tabaquismo *m* tabacco use
tabique *m* septum; —— desviado deviated septum; —— interventricular interventricular septum; —— nasal nasal septum
tabla *f* (*de datos*) chart
tableta *f* tablet
tablilla *f* splint
tabú *m* (*pl* -búes) taboo
TAC *m* CAT scan. *See* tomografía.
tacón *m* heel (*of a shoe*); de —— alto high-heeled
tacto *m* touch, sense of touch; —— rectal rectal examination
tajo *m* cut, gash
taladrar *vt* (*dent*) to drill
taladro *m* (*dent*) drill
tálamo *m* thalamus
talasemia, talasanemia *f* thalassemia
talco *m* talcum powder, talc
talio *m* thallium
talón *m* (*anat*) heel
talla *f* height, size
tallo cerebral *m* brainstem
tamaño *m* size
tambalear *vi*, *vr* to stagger
tamoxifén, tamoxifeno *m* tamoxifen
tampón *m* tampon; (*chem*) buffer
tanque *m* tank; —— de oxígeno oxygen tank
tapa *f* (*de una botella*) cap; —— de seguridad safety cap
tapado -da *adj* (*de la nariz*) congested; (*Mex, del intestino*) constipated, obstructed
tapar *vt* to cover; (*anat, surg*) to block; (*dent*) to fill; *vr* to become blocked; taparse el ojo to cover one's eye; taparse la nariz to hold one's nose
tapón *m* stopper
taponamiento *m* tamponade; —— cardiaco cardiac tamponade
taquicardia *f* tachycardia
taranta *f* dizziness, lightheadedness, dizzy spell
tarántula *f* tarantula
tarde *f* afternoon, early evening
tardío -a *adj* late, delayed
tarjeta *f* (*del hospital, del negocio*) card
tarsal *adj* tarsal
tartamudear *vi* to stutter, stammer
tartárico -ca *adj* tartaric
tártaro *m* tartar
tasa *f* rate; —— de metabolismo basal

basal metabolic rate; —— de mortalidad death rate; —— de natalidad birth rate
tatuaje *m* tattoo
taza *f* cup, cupful
TC *abbr* tomografía computada. *See* tomografía.
té *m* (*pl* tes) tea
TEC *abbr* terapia electrochoque *or* electroconvulsiva. *See* terapia.
tecato -ta *mf* (*PR*) junkie, person who injects drugs
técnico -ca *mf* technician; *f* technique
tecnología *f* technology
techo *m* —— de la boca roof of the mouth
tejido *m* tissue; —— blando soft tissue; —— conectivo *or* conjuntivo connective tissue; —— de granulación granulation tissue
tela *f* tape; film; —— adhesiva adhesive tape
telangiectasia *f* telangiectasia; —— aracniforme spider angioma
telefonear *vt*, *vi* to call (*by telephone*)
teléfono *m* telephone
telemetría *f* telemetry
temblar *vi* to tremble, shake; ¿Le tiemblan las manos?..Do your hands shake?
temblor *m* tremor; earthquake
tembloroso -sa *adj* tremulous
temor *m* fear
temperamento *m* temperament
temperatura *f* temperature; (*fam*) fever; —— ambiente room temperature; tomarse la —— to take one's temperature
temporada *f* season, time of year; —— de la gripe..flu season
temporal *adj* temporary; (*anat*) temporal; Este vendaje es solo temporal..This bandage is only temporary.
temporomandibular *adj* temporomandibular
tendencia *f* tendency; trend
tendón *m* tendon; —— de Aquiles Achilles tendon; —— de la corva hamstring
tendonitis *f* tendinitis
tenia *f* taenia *o* tenia, tapeworm
tenosinovitis *f* tenosynovitis
tensiómetro *m* blood pressure cuff
tensión *f* tension, stress, strain; —— nerviosa nervous tension; bajo —— stressed, under stress
tenso -sa *adj* tense; poner —— (*el brazo, etc.*) to tense; ponerse —— to tense up; Procure de no ponerse tenso..Try not to tense up.

teofilina *f* theophylline
teoría *f* theory
TEP *abbr* **tomografía por emisión de positrones.** *See* **tomografía.**
terapeuta *mf* therapist
terapéutico -ca *adj* therapeutic; *f* therapy
terapia *f* therapy; —— **de grupo** group therapy; —— **del habla** speech therapy; —— **electrochoque** *or* **electroconvulsiva (TEC)** electroconvulsive therapy (ECT); —— **física** physical therapy; —— **intensiva** intensive care; —— **ocupacional** occupational therapy; —— **respiratoria** respiratory therapy
terapista *mf* therapist; —— **del habla** speech therapist; —— **físico** physical therapist; —— **ocupacional** occupational therapist
teratoma *m* teratoma
terbutalina *f* terbutaline
termal *adj* thermal
terminal *adj* terminal
término *m* term; **a** —— at term
termómetro *m* thermometer; —— **oral** *or* **bucal** oral thermometer; —— **rectal** rectal thermometer
terremoto *m* earthquake (*severe*)
terrores nocturnos *mpl* night-terrors
testículo *m* testicle; —— **no descendido** undescended testicle
Testigos de Jehová *mpl* Jehovah's Witnesses
testosterona *f* testosterone
tétanos *m* tetanus
tetera *f* nipple (*of nursing bottle*)
tetilla *f* nipple (*of a male*)
tetraciclina *f* tetracycline
tetracloruro de carbono *m* carbon tetrachloride
tetrahidrocanabinol *m* tetrahydrocannabinol (THC)
tetralogía de Fallot *f* tetralogy of Fallot
textura *f* texture
tez *f* complexion
tía *f* aunt
tiabendazol *m* thiabendazole
tiamina *f* thiamine
tibia *f* tibia, shinbone (*fam*)
tibio -bia *adj* lukewarm, tepid
tiburón *m* shark
tic *m* tic; —— **doloroso** tic douloureux
tiempo *m* time; weather; **¿Cuánto tiempo estuvo inconsciente?**..How long were you unconscious? —— **de protrombina (TP)** prothrombin time (PT); —— **parcial de tromboplastina (TPT)** partial thromboplastin time (PTT); **con el** —— eventually, in time; **mucho** —— a long time; **poco** —— a short time; **todo el** —— all the time
tienda *f* tent; —— **de oxígeno** oxygen tent
tieso -sa *adj* stiff, rigid

tifo *m* typhus
tifus *m* typhus
tijeras *fpl* scissors
timidez *f* shyness
tímido -da *adj* timid, shy, bashful
timo *m* thymus
timolol *m* timolol
timoma *m* thymoma
timpánico -ca *adj* tympanic
tímpano *m* eardrum
tina *f* (*de baño*) bathtub
tiner *m* thinner
tintura *f* tincture
tiña, tinea *f* tinea; —— **corporal** *or* **del cuerpo** tinea corporis, ringworm (*fam*) ; —— **crural** *or* **inguinal** tinea cruris; —— **de la cabeza** tinea capitis; —— **del pie** tinea pedis, athlete's foot (*fam*)
tío *m* uncle
tioridacina *f* thioridazine
típico -ca *adj* typical
tipo *m* type; —— **de sangre** blood type
tiraleche *m* breast pump
tiramina *f* tyramine
tirar *vt* (*esp. Mex*) *vt* to pass, to shed; —— **gases** *or* **vientos** to pass gas
tira reactiva *f* test strip, dipstick
tiritar *vi* to shiver
tiroglobulina *f* thyroglobulin
tiroidectomía *f* thyroidectomy
tiroideo -a *adj* thyroid
tiroides *m&f* (*pl* **-des**) thyroid, thyroid gland
tiroiditis *f* thyroiditis; —— **de Hashimoto** Hashimoto's thyroiditis; —— **subaguda** subacute thyroiditis
tirón *m* muscle pull; **sufrir un** —— to pull a muscle
tirosina *f* tyrosine
tirotóxico -ca *adj* thyrotoxic
tirotoxicosis *f* thyrotoxicosis
tirotropina *f* thyrotropin (TSH)
tiroxina *f* thyroxine
título *m* titer
toalla *f* towel; —— **sanitaria** *or* **femenina** sanitary napkin
tobillo *m* ankle
tocar *vt* to touch
tocino *m* bacon
tocoferol *m* tocopherol
tofo *m* tophus
tolazamida *f* tolazamide
tolbutamida *f* tolbutamide
tolerancia *f* tolerance
tolerar *vt* to tolerate
tolueno *m* toluene
tomacorriente *m* electrical outlet
tomar *vt* (*una bebida*) to drink; (*medicamentos, etc.*) to take; **Tome una pastilla en la mañana y una en la tarde**..Take one pill in the morning and one in the evening; —— **aire** (*fam*) to breathe in; to catch one's breath; —— **el**

sol to get sun

tomografía f tomography; tomogram, (fam) CT scan; —— **axial computarizada** (TAC) computerized axial tomography (CAT); —— **computada** (TC) computed tomography (CT); —— **por emisión de positrones** (TEP) positron emission tomography (PET)

tomograma m tomogram

tónico -ca adj & m tonic

tono m tone; (sonido) tone, pitch; —— **muscular** muscle tone; **de** —— **alto** high-pitched; **de** —— **bajo** low-pitched

tonsilectomía f tonsillectomy

tonsilitis f tonsillitis

tópico -ca adj topical

torácico -ca adj thoracic

toracotomía f thoracotomy

tórax m thorax

torcedura f sprain

torcer vt, vr to sprain, twist, to get sprained o twisted; ¿**Cuándo se torció el cuello?**..When did you sprain your neck?

torcido -da adj crooked, twisted, bent

torniquete m tourniquet

torpe adj clumsy

torrente sanguíneo m bloodstream

torsión f torsion

tortícolis f torticollis

tortura f torture

torturar vt to torture

torunda f cotton ball, wad of gauze

torus m torus; —— **palatino** torus palatinus

torzón m (Mex, fam) abdominal cramp

tos f cough; —— **chifladora** (CA, fam), —— **de perro** (fam), —— **ferina**, or —— **perruna** (fam) whooping cough; —— **seca** dry cough; **jarabe** m **para la** —— cough syrup; **pastilla para la** —— cough drop

toser vi to cough; **Tosa fuerte**..Cough hard.

tosferina var of **tos ferina**

tostado -da adj (fam) tan

tostarse vr (fam) to tan, to get a suntan

total adj & m total

toxemia f toxemia

toxémico -ca adj toxemic

toxicidad f toxicity

tóxico -ca adj toxic

toxicología f toxicology

toxicólogo -ga mf toxicologist

toxicomanía f drug addiction

toxina f toxin

toxocariasis f toxocariasis

toxoide m toxoid; —— **diftérico** diphtheria toxoid; —— **tetánico** tetanus toxoid

toxoplasmosis f toxoplasmosis

trabajador -ra mf worker; —— **social** social worker

trabajar vi to work

trabajo m work, job

tracción f traction

tracoma m trachoma

tracto m tract; —— **digestivo** digestive tract; —— **respiratorio** respiratory tract; —— **urinario** urinary tract

traducir vt to translate

tragar vt, vi to swallow; —— **saliva** to swallow; **Debe chupar esta pastilla, no tragarla**..You should suck on this pill, not swallow it.

trancazo m (Mex, fam) dengue fever, dengue; flu

trance m trance

tranquilizante adj sedating, tranquilizing; m tranquilizer

tranquilizar vt to sedate, tranquilize; vr to calm down; **Ud. necesita tranquilizarse**.. You need to calm down.

tranquilo -la adj calm

transcurso m course

transexual adj & mf transsexual

transferencia f (psych) transference

transfusión f transfusion; **hacer una** —— to transfuse, to give a transfusion; **Tenemos que hacerle una transfusión de plaquetas**..We need to give you a transfusion of platelets.

transitorio -ria adj transient, temporary

translocación f translocation

transmisible adj communicable

transmisión f transmission

transmitir vt to transmit

transparente adj transparent

transpiración f perspiration

transpirar vi to perspire

transportar vt to transport

transporte m transport

transvestista mf transvestite

trapecio m (anat) trapezius

tráquea f trachea, windpipe (fam)

traqueítis f tracheitis

traqueobronquitis f tracheobronchitis

traqueostomía f tracheostomy

traqueotomía f tracheotomy

trasero m (fam) buttocks, bottom (fam)

trasladar vt (un paciente) to transfer, move

traspié m **dar un** —— to stumble, trip

trasplantar vt to transplant

trasplante m transplant

trastornado -da adj upset; crazy, mentally deranged

trastornar vt to upset; to drive (someone) crazy; vr to become upset; to go crazy

trastorno m disorder, disturbance; —— **bipolar** bipolar disorder; —— **de la personalidad** personality disorder; —— **del estrés postraumático** posttraumatic stress disorder; —— **del sueño** sleep disorder o disturbance

tratamiento m treatment

tratar vt (una enfermedad, un paciente) to treat

trauma m trauma

traumático -ca *adj* traumatic
traumatismo *m* trauma
traumatizar *vt* to traumatize
travieso -sa *adj* mischievous
trazadona *f* trazadone
trazas *fpl* trace(s)
trazo *m* (*de EKG, etc.*) tracing
trementina *f* turpentine
treonina *f* threonine
treponema *f* treponeme
tretinoína *f* tretinoin
triamcinolona *f* triamcinolone
triamtereno *m* triamterene
triazolam *m* triazolam
tríceps *m* (*pl* -ceps) triceps
tricocéfalo *m* whipworm
tricomoniasis *f* trichomoniasis
tricúspide *adj* tricuspid
Trichomonas Trichomonas
trifluoperacina *f* trifluoperazine
trigémino -na *adj* trigeminal
triglicérido *m* triglyceride
trigo *m* wheat; —— **integral** *or* **entero** whole wheat
trigueño -ña *adj* olive-skinned; *mf* olive-skinned person
trillizo -za *mf* triplet
trimestre *m* trimester
trimetoprim *m* trimethoprim
tripa *f* (*often pl*) gut, bowel, intestine
tripanosomiasis *f* trypanosomiasis
tripsina *f* trypsin
triptófano *m* tryptophan
triquinosis *f* trichinosis
trismo *m* trismus, lockjaw
trisomía *f* trisomy; —— **21** trisomy 21
triste *adj* sad
triturar *vt* (*form*) to crush, grind
trivalente *adj* trivalent
trocánter *m* trochanter
trocisco *m* lozenge, troche
trombectomía *f* thrombectomy
trombo *m* thrombus
trombocitopenia *f* thrombocytopenia

tromboembolia *f* thromboembolism
tromboflebitis *f* thrombophlebitis
trombosis *f* thrombosis
trompa *f* tube; —— **de Eustaquio** Eustachian tube; —— **de Falopio** fallopian tube
tronado -da *adj* (*Mex, vulg*) high (*on drugs*)
tronar *vt* (*la columna, los huesos*) to adjust, crack; **El quiropráctico me truena la columna**..The chiropractor adjusts my spine...¿**Es malo tronarse los dedos?**..Is it bad to crack your knuckles? *vi* (*las tripas*) to growl (*one's stomach*); *vr* (*una articulación*) to click, make a clicking sound; **Me truena el hombro cuando lo muevo**..My shoulder clicks when I move it; **tronárselas** (*esp. Mex, vulg*) to get high, to use drugs
tronco *m* (*anat*) trunk
tropezar *vi* to stumble, trip
tropical *adj* tropical
trotar *vi* to jog
trusa *f* (*Mex*) (men's) underpants
tuberculosis *f* tuberculosis
tubería *f* tubing
tubo *m* tube; —— **de drenaje** drainage tube; —— **de ensayo** test tube; —— **de ventilación** ventilation tube; —— **digestivo** digestive tract; —— **endotraqueal** endotracheal tube
tubular *adj* tubular
túbulo *m* tubule
tuerto -ta *adj* one-eyed
tularemia *f* tularemia
tullido -da *adj* disabled
tumor *m* tumor, lump, bump; —— **de Wilms** Wilms' tumor
tumorcito *m* small lump *o* bump
túnel *m* tunnel
tupido -da *adj* (*Carib, SA*) stuffed up, congested; **Tengo tupida la nariz**..My nose is stuffed up..I have a stuffy nose.
turbio -bia *adj* turbid, cloudy
tutor -ra *mf* (legal) guardian

U

úlcera *f* ulcer, sore; —— **de decúbito** decubitus ulcer, bedsore; —— **de estrés** stress ulcer; —— **duodenal** duodenal ulcer; —— **gástrica** gastric ulcer; —— **péptica** peptic ulcer; —— **por presión** pressure sore
ulna *f* ulna
ulnar *adj* ulnar
últimamente *adv* recently
último -ma *adj* last; **su última evacuación..** your last bowel movement
ultrasonido *m* ultrasound
ultrasonografía *f* ultrasonography
ultravioleta *adj* ultraviolet
umbral *m* threshold
uncinaria *f* hookworm
ungüento *m* ointment, salve
unidad *f* unit; —— **de cuidado coronario** coronary care unit; —— **de cuidados intensivos (UCI)** *or* **de terapia intensiva** intensive care unit (ICU); —— **internacional** international unit
uniforme *adj* uniform; *m* uniform
unirse *vr* to join
uña *f* nail; (*del dedo*) fingernail; (*del dedo del pie*) toenail; —— **enterrada** *or* **encarnada** ingrown nail
uñero *m* ingrown nail; (*fam*) hangnail
urbano -na *adj* urban
urea *f* urea
uremia *f* uremia
urémico -ca *adj* uremic
uréter *m* ureter
uretra *f* urethra
uretritis *f* urethritis; —— **no gonocócica** non-gonococcal urethritis
urgencia *f* emergency; **sala de urgencias** emergency room (ER)
urgente *adj* urgent
úrico -ca *adj* uric
urinálisis, urianálisis *f* urinalysis
urinario -ria *adj* urinary
urocultivo *m* urine culture
urodinámica *f* urodynamics
urogenital *adj* urogenital
urografía *f* urography; urogram; —— **excretoria** excretory urography; —— **retrógrada** retrograde urography
urograma *m* urogram, pyelogram
urokinasa *f* urokinase
urología *f* urology
urólogo -ga *mf* urologist
urosepsis *f* urosepsis
urticaria *f* urticaria; —— **marítima** swimmer's itch
uruguayo -ya *adj & mf* Uruguayan
usar *vt* to use
uso *m* use; **hacer** —— **de** (*Mex, fam*) to have intercourse with (*male as subject of sentence*); **la última vez que mi esposo usó de mí..**the last time my husband had intercourse with me; **para** —— **repetido** reusable
usual *adj* usual
usuario -ria *mf* user
útero *m* uterus
úvea *f* uvea
uveítis *f* uveitis
úvula *f* uvula

V

vaca f cow
vaciar vt to empty, to drain
vacío -a adj empty; m vacuum
vacuna f vaccine; —— BCG, DPT, Salk, etc. BCG vaccine, DPT vaccine, Salk vaccine, etc.; —— contra las paperas, —— contra la rabia, etc. mumps vaccine, rabies vaccine, etc.
vacunación f vaccination
vacunar vt to vaccinate
vagal adj vagal
vagina f vagina
vaginal adj vaginal
vaginitis f vaginitis
vago m vagus
vagotomía f vagotomy; —— selectiva selective vagotomy
vahído m dizzy spell, spell of lightheadedness
valgo -ga adj valgus
valgus adj valgus
valina f valine
valor m value
valoración f evaluation; —— Apgar Apgar score
valorar vt to evaluate
valproico -ca adj valproic
válvula f valve; —— aórtica aortic valve; —— mitral mitral valve; —— pilórica pyloric valve; —— pulmonar pulmonic valve; —— tricúspide tricuspid valve
valvuloplastia f valvuloplasty
vancomicina f vancomycin
vapor m vapor, steam, fumes; (cocido) al —— steamed
vaporizador m vaporizer; sprayer
variable adj & f variable
variación f variation
variante adj & f variant
variar vi to vary
várice f varix (en inglés se emplea casi siempre la forma plural: varices)
varicela f varicella (form), chickenpox (fam)
varón adj & m male; La señora Lugo tuvo un varón..Mrs. Lugo had a baby boy.
varo -ra adj varus
varus adj varus
vascular adj vascular
vasculitis f vasculitis; —— necrosante necrotizing vasculitis; —— por hipersensibilidad hypersensitivity vasculitis
vasectomía f vasectomy
vaselina f petroleum jelly
vasija f basin, bedpan

vaso m vessel; glass; un vaso con agua..a glass of water; —— sanguíneo blood vessel
vasoconstricción f vasoconstriction
vasoconstrictor m vasoconstrictor
vasodilatación f vasodilation
vasodilatador m vasodilator
vasopresina f vasopressin
vasospasmo, vasoespasmo m vasospasm
vasovagal adj vasovagal
VDRL m VDRL
vecindad f neighborhood
vecino -na mf neighbor
vector m vector
vegetación f vegetation; vegetaciones adenoides adenoids
vegetal m vegetable
vegetarianismo m vegetarianism
vegetariano -na adj & mf vegetarian
vegetativo -va adj vegetative
vehículo m vehicle
vejez f old age
vejiga f bladder; (fam) blister
vello m body hair
vena f vein; —— antecubital antecubital vein; —— femoral femoral vein; —— porta portal vein; —— safena saphenous vein; —— subclavia subclavian vein; —— varicosa varicose vein; —— yugular externa external jugular vein; —— yugular interna internal jugular vein
vena cava f vena cava; —— —— inferior inferior vena cava; —— —— superior superior vena cava
vencido -da adj (medicamento, etc.) outdated, out of date
venda f bandage; dressing material; —— elástica elastic bandage
vendaje m bandage
vendar vt to bandage, dress
veneno m poison, venom; —— para hormiga, —— para rata, etc. ant poison, rat poison, etc.
venéreo -a adj sexually transmitted, genital; enfermedad venérea sexually transmitted disease
venezolano -na adj & mf Venezuelan
venir vi —— de familia to run in one's family
venodisección f cutdown
venografía f venography; venogram
venograma m venogram
venoso -sa adj venous

ventaja f advantage
ventana de la nariz f nostril
ventilación f ventilation
ventilador m ventilator; (abanico) electric fan
ventral adj ventral
ventrículo m ventricle
vénula f venule
ver vt, vi (pp **visto**) to see
verano m summer
verapamil m verapamil
verde adj green
verdura f vegetable
vergüenza f shame, embarrassment; shyness; **Me da vergüenza**..It makes me feel embarrassed...**Tiene vergüenza**..He's shy.
vermicida m vermicide
vérnix caseosa f vernix caseosa
verruga f wart; —— **genital** genital wart; —— **plantar** plantar wart
vértebra f vertebra
vértigo m vertigo
vesícula f vesicle, blister; (fam) gallbladder; —— **biliar** gallbladder
vespertino -na adj (form) pertaining to evening, evening
vestido m dress
vestir vt to dress; vr to dress (oneself), get dressed
veterinario -ria adj veterinary; mf veterinarian
vez f (pl **veces**) time; **a veces** at times; **cada** —— each time, every time; **cuatro veces al día** four times a day; **de —— en cuando** from time to time; **la primera** —— the first time; **la próxima** —— the next time; **la última** —— the last time; **muchas veces** many times, often; **una** —— one time
vía f tract; **vías biliares** biliary tract; —— **corticoespinal** corticospinal tract; —— **espinotalámica** spinothalamic tract; —— **piramidal** pyramidal tract; —— **respiratoria** airway
viable adj viable
víbora f viper, (fam) poisonous snake
vibración f vibration
vicio m vice, bad habit
vicioso -sa mf addict
víctima f victim
vida f life; —— **media** half-life; —— **sexual** sex life; **con** —— alive
vidrio m glass; **un pedazo de vidrio**..a piece of glass
viejo -ja adj old; m old man, old person; f old woman
viento m wind; (flatulencia) gas; **tirar vientos** to pass gas
vientre m belly, abdomen; womb
vigilancia f monitoring, follow-up
vigor m stamina
vigoroso -sa adj vigorous, strong

VIH abbr **virus de inmunodeficiencia humana.** See **virus.**
vinagre m vinegar
vinblastina f vinblastine
vincristina f vincristine
vínculo m (psych, obst) bond
violación f rape
violar vt to rape
violencia f violence
violento -ta adj violent
violeta adj violet
viral adj viral
virgen adj & mf virgin
virginidad f virginity
vírico -ca adj viral
virilización f virilization
virología f virology
viruela f smallpox; **viruelas locas** (esp. Mex, CA) chickenpox
virulencia f virulence
virulento -ta adj virulent
virus m (pl **virus**) virus; —— **de Epstein-Barr** Epstein-Barr virus (EBV); —— **de inmunodeficiencia humana (VIH)** human immunodeficiency virus (HIV)
visceral adj visceral
vísceras fpl organ meats
viscosidad f viscosity
viscoso -sa adj viscous
visible adj visible
visión f vision, sight, eyesight; **visiones** (fam) hallucinations, the d.t.'s; —— **borrosa** blurred vision; —— **doble** double vision; —— **en túnel** tunnel vision; —— **nocturna** nocturnal o night vision; —— **periférica** peripheral vision; —— **profunda** depth perception
visita f visit; visitor; **visitas** (de los médicos) rounds; **pasar** —— to make rounds
visitante mf visitor
visitar vt, vi to visit
vista f vision, sight, eyesight; —— **cansada** or **fatigada** eyestrain; —— **doble** double vision; —— **empañada** blurred vision; —— **nocturna** nocturnal o night vision
visto pp of **ver**
visual adj visual
vital adj vital
vitamina f vitamin; —— **A, B₁₂, etc.** vitamin A, B₁₂, etc.; —— **hidrosoluble** water-soluble vitamin; —— **liposoluble** fat-soluble vitamin
vitamínico -ca adj pertaining to vitamins, vitamin
vitíligo m vitiligo
viudo -da adj widowed; m widower; f widow; **viuda negra** black widow
vivir vi to live
vivo -va adj alive, (virus, vacuna) live
vocal adj vocal
vocear vt to page (overhead)

voltearse *vr* to turn over, roll over; ¿Me **volteo?**..Should I turn over?
voltio *m* volt
volumen *m* volume
voluntad *f* will; **contra la** —— **de uno** against one's will; **fuerza de** —— will power; **por** —— **propia** of one's own free will
voluntario -ria *adj* voluntary; *mf* volunteer
volver *vi* (*pp* **vuelto**) —— **el estómago** (*esp. Mex, fam*) to vomit, throw up; **Volví el estómago**..I threw up; —— **en sí** to regain consciousness; *vr* **volverse loco** to go crazy, to lose one's mind
vólvulo *m* volvulus

vomitar *vt, vi* to vomit, throw up (*fam*); —— **en seco** to retch
vómito *m* vomit; **vómitos del embarazo** morning sickness; **vómitos en seco** dry heaves, retching
voyeurismo *m* voyeurism
voz *f* (*pl* **voces**) voice; **decir en** —— **baja** to whisper
vudú *m* voodoo
vuelta *f* turn; **darse** —— to turn; to turn over, roll over; to turn around; **darse media** —— to turn around
vuelto *pp of* **volver**
vulnerable *adj* vulnerable
vulva *f* vulva

warfarina *f* warfarin

xantoma *m* xanthoma

Y

yema *f* (*del dedo*) pad; (*de huevo*) yolk
yerba *var of* **hierba**
yerno *m* son-in-law
yeso *m* (*ortho*) cast, plaster (*for a cast*)
yeyunal *adj* jejunal
yeyuno *m* jejunum

yo *m* (*psych*) ego
yodo *m* iodine
yoga *f* yoga
yogurt, yogur *m* yogurt
yugular *adj* jugular

Z

zafada *f* (*fam*) dislocation
zafar *vt, vr* (*fam*) to dislocate, to become
   dislocated; **Me zafé el hombro..**I
   dislocated my shoulder.
zambo -ba *adj* bowlegged
zancudo *m* mosquito
zapato *m* shoe
zapeta *f* (*Mex*) diaper
zidovudina *f* zidovudine
zinc *var of* **cinc**

zona *f* zone; (*fam*) herpes zoster, shingles
zorrillo *m* skunk
zorro *m* fox
zumaque venenoso *m* poison oak
zumba *f* (*Es, Guat; fam*) binge
zumbar *vi* (*los oídos*) to ring, hum
zumbido *m* (*de oídos*) ringing, humming
zumo *m* juice
zurdo -da *adj* left-handed

APPENDIX

EJEMPLO DE HISTORIA CLÍNICA Y EXAMEN FÍSICO

SAMPLE HISTORY AND PHYSICAL

(Alternate terms and phrases appear in parentheses.)

HISTORIA CLÍNICA ACTUAL/PRESENT ILLNESS

Buenos días. Soy la Dra. Jones...Good morning. I'm Dr. Jones.
Buenas tardes. Soy el Dr. Smith...Good afternoon. I'm Dr. Smith.
Siéntese, señora...Have a seat, ma'am.
¿En qué puedo servirle?..How can I help you?
¿Porqué vino al hospital?..Why did you come to the hospital?
¿Dónde está el dolor exactamente?..Where is the pain exactly?
¿Puede enseñarme?..Can you show me?
¿El dolor se mueve a otros lados?..Does the pain move around?
¿El dolor se queda aquí?..The pain stays here?
¿Cómo es el dolor?..What is the pain like?
¿Agudo?..Sharp?
¿Sordo?..Dull?
¿Le arde?..Does it burn?
¿Cómo piquetes?..Like quick jabs?
¿Punzante?..Stabbing?
¿Cómo presión?..Like pressure?
¿Aplastante?..Crushing?
¿Es un dolor fuerte?..Is it a severe pain?
¿Moderado?..Moderate?

¿Suave?..Mild?

¿Cuándo le empezó el dolor?..When did the pain begin?

¿Cuándo fue la primera vez en su vida que tuvo este dolor?..When was the first time you ever had this pain?

¿Se quitó por un tiempo?..It went away for a while?

¿Solo? (¿Solito?)..By itself?

¿Cuándo le empezó de nuevo?..When did it begin again?

¿Le va y le viene el dolor?..Does the pain come and go?

¿Es un dolor constante?..Is it a constant pain?

¿Cuando le viene, cuánto tiempo le dura?..When it comes, how long does it last?

¿Qué tan frecuente le viene el dolor?..How often do you get the pain?

¿En la última semana, cuántas veces ha tenido el dolor?..In the last week, how many times have you had the pain?

¿Qué está haciendo cuando le viene el dolor?..What are you doing when the pain comes on?

¿A qué hora del día le viene el dolor?..What time of day does the pain come on?

¿Le viene más en la mañana?..Do you get it more often in the morning?

¿En la tarde?..In the afternoon?

¿La hora que sea?..Anytime?

¿Tiene relación al comer?..Does it have anything to do with eating?

¿Al hacer esfuerzos?..With exertion?

¿Hay algo que le agrava el dolor?..Is there anything which makes the pain worse?

¿Hay algo que le alivia el dolor?..Is there anything which makes the pain better?

¿Se alivia con el ejercicio?..Does it get better with exercise?

¿Se pone peor?..It gets worse?

¿Ha tomado medicamentos?..Have you tried medications?

¿Cuál medicamento?..Which medication?

¿Le ayudó un poco?..Did it help a little?

¿Hay familiares o amigos que tienen el mismo problema?..Are there relatives or friends who have the same problem?

¿Qué cree que le está causando el problema?..What do you think is causing the problem?

¿Ha visto a un médico por este problema antes?..Have you seen a

doctor before for this problem?

¿Qué le dijo que tenía?..What did he say you had?

¿Le hizo estudios?..Did he do any studies?

¿Le sacó sangre?..Did he draw blood?

¿Cuándo fue esto?..When was this?

¿Cómo se llama el médico?..What's the name of the doctor?

¿Sabe su número de teléfono?..Do you know his telephone number?

¿Porqué vino al hospital hoy en vez de algún otro día?..Why did you come to the hospital today instead of some other day?

¿Tiene otras molestias?..Do you have any other problems?

¿A propósito, cuántos años tiene Ud.?..By the way, how old are you?

¿Hace cuánto que está aquí en los Estados Unidos?..How long have you been in the United States?

¿Cuándo fue la última vez que salió del país?..When was the last time you left the country?

¿A dónde fue?..Where did you go?

ANTECEDENTES PERSONALES/PAST MEDICAL HISTORY

¿Tiene otros problemas médicos?..Do you have any other medical problems?

¿Desde cuándo tiene diabetes?..How long have you had diabetes?

¿Quién le atiende por su diabetes?..Who takes care of you for your diabetes?

¿Tiene un médico que visita regularmente?..Do you have a regular doctor?

¿Dónde está ubicado?..Where is he located?

¿Es un médico privado?..Is he a private doctor?

¿Cuándo fue la última vez que vio a un médico?..When was the last time you saw a doctor?

¿Ha estado hospitalizado alguna vez?..Have you ever been hospitalized?

¿Ha sido operado alguna vez?..Have you ever had surgery?

¿Ha tenido alguna enfermedad grave?..Have you ever had any serious illness?

¿Ha tenido alguna vez dificultades emocionales?..Have you ever had

emotional problems?

MEDICAMENTOS/MEDICATIONS

¿Está tomando medicamentos?..Are you taking any medications?
¿Ha tomado algún medicamento que se vende sin receta médica?..Have you taken any over-the-counter medications?
¿Está tomando píldoras anticonceptivas?..Are you taking birth control pills?
¿Trae sus medicamentos?..Do you have your medications with you?
¿De qué color son las pastillas?..What color are the pills?
¿Son tabletas o cápsulas?..Are they tablets or capsules?
¿Cuántas veces al día las toma?..How many times a day do you take them?
¿Quién le recetó las pastillas?..Who prescribed the pills for you?
¿Las toma todos los días o se le olvida de vez en cuando?..Do you take them every day or do you forget every now and then?
¿Por ejemplo, durante una semana cuántas veces se le olvida tomar las pastillas?..For example, in a week how many times do you forget to take the pills?
¿Cuándo fue la última vez que tomó esta pastilla?..When was the last time you took this pill?
¿Cuántas de estas tomó Ud. ayer?..How many of these did you take yesterday?
Enséñeme precisamente cuales pastillas tomó Ud. esta mañana..Show me exactly which pills you took this morning.
¿Cuándo se le acabaron las pastillas?..When did you run out of pills?

ALERGIAS/ALLERGIES

¿Es Ud. alérgico a la penicilina?..Are you allergic to penicillin?
¿Ha tomado penicilina alguna vez?..Have you ever taken penicillin?
¿Es Ud. alérgico a algún medicamento?..Are you allergic to any medication?
¿Ha tenido alguna vez una mala reacción después de tomar una medicina?..Have you ever had a bad reaction to a medicine?

¿Qué le pasó?..What happened?
¿Le cae mal la codeína?..Does codeine bother you?
¿Puede tolerar la aspirina?..Can you tolerate aspirin?

HISTORIA SOCIAL/SOCIAL HISTORY

¿Qué trabajo tiene Ud.?..What kind of work do you do?
¿Desde cuándo no trabaja?..How long have you been out of work?
¿Porqué no ha podido trabajar?..Why haven't you been able to work?
¿Qué trabajo tenía?..What kind of work did you use to do?
¿Había substancias químicas u otras cosas peligrosas donde trabajaba?..Were there chemicals or other hazards where you worked?
¿Qué hace Ud. durante el día?..What do you do during the day?
¿Come bien?..Do you eat well?
¿Duerme bien?..Do you sleep well?
¿Tiene donde vivir?..Do you have a place to live?
¿Con quién vive Ud.?..Who do you live with?
¿Fuma Ud.?..Do you smoke?
¿Fumaba?..Did you used to smoke?
¿Cuántas cajetillas fumaba al día?..How many packs a day did you use to smoke?
¿Cuándo dejó de fumar?..When did you quit smoking?
¿Acostumbra tomar bebidas alcohólicas?..Do you drink alcohol?
¿Vino?..Wine?
¿Cerveza?..Beer?
¿Tomaba?..Did you used to drink?
¿Hace cuánto que no toma?..How long has it been since you quit drinking?
¿Cuándo fue la última vez que tomó un trago?..When was the last time you had a drink?
¿Cuánto puede tomar cuando tiene ganas?..How much can you drink when you have a mind to?
¿Le tiemblan las manos a veces cuando deja de tomar?..Do your hands ever shake when you quit drinking?
¿Ha tenido alguna vez visiones al dejar de tomar?..Have you ever had the d.t.'s when you quit drinking?

*¿Ha tenido alguna vez convulsiones (ataques) al dejar de
tomar?*..Have you ever had seizures when you quit drinking?
¿Ha tratado de dejar de tomar?..Have you tried to quit drinking?
¿Qué pasó?..What happened?
¿Ha usado drogas alguna vez?..Have you ever used drugs?
¿Se ha inyectado drogas alguna vez?..Have you ever used I.V. drugs?
¿Cuál droga?..Which drug?
¿Tiene hábito o la usa de vez en cuando?..Do you have a habit or do
you use it occasionally?
¿Cada cuándo la usa?..How often do you use it?
¿Comparte agujas con otros?..Do you share needles?
¿Ha tenido relaciones con otros hombres?..Have you had relations
with other men?
¿Con prostitutas?..With prostitutes?
¿Usó condones?..Did you use condoms?
¿Ha recibido alguna vez una transfusión de sangre?..Have you ever
received a blood transfusion?
¿Le han hecho la prueba para el virus que causa el SIDA?..Have you
been tested for the AIDS virus?
¿Cuál fue el resultado?..What was the result?

HISTORIA FAMILIAR/FAMILY HISTORY

¿Hay familiares que tienen el mismo problema que tiene Ud.?..Are
there any family members who have the same problem you have?
¿Hay enfermedades que vienen de familia?..Are there any diseases
which run in the family?
¿Todavía viven sus padres?..Are your parents still living?
¿Tiene algún problema médico su mamá?..Does your mother have any
medical problems?
¿De qué murió su papá?..What did your father die of?
¿Qué edad tenía cuando murió?..How old was he when he died?

REVISIÓN DE APARATOS Y SISTEMAS/REVIEW OF SYSTEMS

General/General:

¿Ha cambiado de peso ultimamente?..Has your weight changed recently?
¿Cuántos kilos ha ganado?..How many kilos have you gained?
¿Cuántas libras ha perdido?..How many pounds have you lost?
¿En cuánto tiempo?..Over what period of time?
¿Tiene tanta energía como siempre?..Do you have as much energy as usual?
¿Desde cuándo se siente cansado?..How long have you felt tired?
¿Ha tenido fiebre?..Have you had fever?
¿Sudores durante la noche?..Night sweats?

Piel/Skin:

¿Tiene problemas con la piel?..Do you have problems with your skin?
¿Erupción?..Rash?
¿Picazón?..Itching?
¿Alguna bolita?..Any kind of lump?
¿Úlceras? (¿Llagas?)..Sores?
¿Cambios en el color de su piel en alguna parte?..Changes in the color of your skin anywhere?

Cabeza/Head:

¿Tiene dolores de cabeza?..Do you have headaches?
¿Se ha lastimado su cabeza ultimamente?..Have you hurt your head recently?

Ojos/Eyes:

¿Puede ver bien?..Can you see well?
¿Usa lentes?..Do you wear glasses?
¿Ve borroso a veces?..Does your vision get blurry at times?
¿Ve doble a veces?..Do you ever see double?
¿Se le ponen rojizos los ojos?..Do your eyes get red?
¿Tiene cataratas?..Do you have cataracts?
¿Glaucoma?..Glaucoma?

¿Ve Ud. halos (círculos) alrededor de las luces en la noche?..Do you see halos around lights at night?

¿Le han revisado la vista alguna vez?..Have you ever had your vision tested?

¿Cuándo fue la última vez que vio a un médico de los ojos?..When was the last time you saw an eye doctor?

Oídos/Ears:

¿Oye bien?..Do you hear well?

¿Oye igual en los dos oídos?..Do you hear equally well in both ears?

¿Oye menor con algún oído?..Do you hear less with one ear?

¿Se le ha empeorado la audición ultimamente?..Has your hearing gotten worse recently?

¿Tiene dolor de oído?..Do you have an earache?

¿Ha tenido infecciones del oído?..Have you had ear infections?

¿Le sale líquido del oído?..Is there liquid draining from your ear?

¿Siente como si el cuarto estuviera dando vueltas alrededor de Ud.?..Do you feel as though the room were spinning around you?

Nariz/Nose:

¿Le sale sangre de la nariz frecuentemente?..Do you get a lot of nosebleeds?

¿Es Ud. alérgico al polen?..Are you allergic to pollen?

¿Tiene sinusitis?..Do you have sinusitis?

¿Le dan resfriados muy seguido?..Do you get a lot of colds?

¿Puede distinguir bien los olores?..Can you smell all right?

Orofaringe/Oropharynx:

¿Le duele un diente?..Do any of your teeth hurt?

¿Tiene dientes postizos?..Do you have false teeth?

¿Qué tan frecuente se cepilla los dientes?..How often do you brush your teeth?

¿Le sangran facilmente las encías?..Do your gums bleed easily?

¿Cuándo fue la última vez que vio a un dentista?..When was the last time you saw a dentist?

¿Le duele la garganta?..Is your throat sore?

¿Le salen pequeñas úlceras en la boca frecuentemente?..Do you get canker sores frequently?

¿Le ha cambiado la voz ultimamente?..Has your voice changed recently?

*Cuello/*Neck:

¿Le duele el cuello?..Is your neck sore?

¿Tiene bolas (bolitas) en el cuello?..Do you have any lumps in your neck?

*Senos/*Breasts:

¿Tiene algunas bolas (bolitas) en los senos?..Do you have any lumps in your breast?

¿Le han hecho un mamograma alguna vez?..Have you ever had a mammogram?

¿Le sale leche de los pezones a veces?..Do your nipples ever give milk?

¿Algún líquido?..Any kind of liquid?

¿Sangre?..Blood?

*Pulmones/*Lungs:

¿Tiene dificultad para respirar?..Do you have trouble breathing?

¿Le falta aire?..Are you short of breath?

¿Puede subir escaleras?..Can you climb stairs?

¿Tiene que parar para agarrar aire?..Do you have to stop to catch your breath?

¿Cuántas cuadras puede caminar sin parar?..How may blocks can you walk without stopping?

¿Usa oxígeno en casa?..Do you use oxygen at home?

¿Tiene tos?..Do you have a cough?

¿Le sale flema?..Are you bringing up phlegm?

¿Cómo se ve?..What does it look like?

¿Es espesa?..Is it thick?

¿De qué color es?..What color is it?

¿Es como saliva?..Is it like saliva?

¿Le ha salido sangre cuando tose?..Have you coughed up blood?

¿Tiene chillidos en el pecho?..Do you have wheezing?
¿Tiene asma?..Do you have asthma?
¿Hay algo que le provoca ataques de asma?..Is there anything that brings on asthma attacks?
¿Tendrá relación con las estaciones del año?..Would it have anything to do with the time of year?
¿Tiene alergias?..Do you have allergies?
¿Hay mucho polvo en la casa?..Is there a lot of dust in your home?
¿Hay animales en la casa?..Are there animals in your home?
¿Ha tenido pulmonía alguna vez?..Have you ever had pneumonia?
¿Tuberculosis?..Tuberculosis?
¿Le han puesto alguna vez la prueba para la tuberculosis?..Have you ever had a TB test?
¿Cuál fue el resultado?..What was the result?
¿Le han tomado una radiografía del pecho alguna vez?..Have you ever had a chest x-ray?

Corazón/Heart:

¿Tiene problemas con el corazón?..Do you have heart problems?
¿Alta presión?..High blood pressure?
¿Cómo sabe que tiene alta presión?..How do you know you have high blood pressure?
¿Tiene dolor de pecho a veces?..Do you ever have chest pain?
¿Puede dormir plano en la cama sin dificultades?..Can you sleep flat in bed without problems?
¿Qué le pasa si duerme plano en la cama?..What happens when you sleep flat in bed?
¿Cuántas almohadas usa para dormir?..How many pillows do you use to sleep?
¿Ha despertado durante la noche alguna vez con una sensación de ahogo?..Have you ever woken up in the middle of the night with a smothering sensation?
¿Le han dicho alguna vez que tiene un soplo cardiaco?..Have you ever been told you had a heart murmur?
¿Cuando era niño, tuvo una enfermedad que se llama fiebre reumática?..When you were a child, did you have a disease called rheumatic fever?

¿Tuvo alguna vez una fiebre quizás con dolores de las articulaciones (las coyunturas, los huesos) o una erupción?..Were you ever sick with a fever and maybe joint pains or a rash?

Gastrointestinal/Gastrointestinal:

¿Tiene dificultades para tragar? (para pasar alimentos?)..Do you have trouble swallowing?

¿Se le atora la comida?..Does food stick in your throat?

¿Tiene dificultades para tragar (pasar) líquidos también?..Do you have trouble swallowing liquids too?

¿Tiene agruras?..Do you have heartburn?

¿Náusea?..Nausea?

¿Vómitos?..Vomiting?

¿Vomitaba de veras o solo tenía ganas?..Were you actually vomiting or did you just feel like it?

¿Vomitó sangre?..Did you vomit blood?

¿Tiene dolor de estómago?..Do you have a stomach ache?

¿Hay ciertas comidas que le provoca los dolores?..Are there certain foods that bring on the pain?

¿Tiene problemas para ir al baño?..Do you have trouble going to the bathroom?

¿Tiene estreñimiento?..Do you have constipation?

¿Diarrea?..Diarrhea?

¿Ha notado sangre en el excremento?..Have you noticed blood in your stool?

¿Ha tenido excremento negro como el asfalto de la calle?..Have you had stools that were black like asphalt?

¿Tiene hemorroides?..Do you have hemorrhoids?

¿Le han sacado la vesícula?..Have you had your gallbladder taken out?

¿Ha tenido hepatitis?..Have you had hepatitis?

¿Se le ha puesto amarilla la piel alguna vez?..Has your skin ever turned yellow?

¿Sus ojos?..Your eyes?

Genitourinario (general)/Genitourinary (general):

¿Tiene problemas para orinar?..Do you have problems urinating?

¿Orina más que de costumbre?..Are you urinating more often than usual?

¿Tiene que levantarse durante la noche para orinar?..Do you have to get up in the middle of the night to urinate?

¿Le arde al orinar?..Does it burn when you urinate?

¿Le arde por donde sale la orina o más a dentro?..Does it burn where the urine comes out or further inside?

¿Ha tenido alguna vez una infección de la orina?..Have you ever had a urinary tract infection?

¿Ha notado sangre en la orina alguna vez?..Have you ever noticed blood in your urine?

¿Ha eliminado una piedra en la orina alguna vez?..Have you ever passed a stone?

¿Ha tenido alguna vez una enfermedad venérea?..Have you ever had a sexually transmitted disease?

¿Es decir, una enfermedad que se transmite por tener relaciones sexuales?..That is, a disease you get from having sexual relations?

¿Lo trató un médico?..Were you treated by a doctor?

¿Tiene alguna dificultad sexual?..Do you have any sexual problems?

*Genitourinario (del hombre)/*Genitourinary (male):

¿Tiene que esforzarse para que salga la orina?..Do you have to strain to get your urine out?

¿Cómo es el chorro?..How is your stream?

¿Siguen saliendo gotas después de que haya terminado?..Do you have problems with dribbling?

¿Tiene úlceras (heridas) en el pene?..Do you have sores on your penis?

¿Le sale una secreción del pene?..Do you have a discharge from your penis?

*Genitourinario (de la mujer)/*Genitourinary (female):

¿Se le sale orina a veces sin querer?..Do you ever lose your urine accidentally?

¿Cuándo se rie o tose?..When you laugh or cough?

¿Todavía tiene su regla?..Do you still have periods?

¿Cuándo fue su última regla?..When was your last period?

¿Fue normal?..Was it normal?

¿Tiene dolores con la regla?..Do you have pain with your periods?

¿Sangra mucho durante la regla?..Do you bleed a lot during your periods?

¿Cuántas toallas usa?..How many sanitary napkins do you use?

¿Usa tampones?..Do you use tampons?

¿Vienen a tiempo sus reglas?..Are you periods regular?

¿Ha sangrado entre las reglas?..Have you had bleeding between periods?

¿A qué edad le vino la regla por primera vez?..How old were you when you had your first period?

¿Cuándo le vino la menopausia?..When did you go through menopause?

¿Ha sangrado desde entonces?..Have you had bleeding since then?

¿Le vienen calores? (bochornos? sensaciones repentinas de calor?)..Do you get hot flashes?

¿Cuántos niños ha tenido?..How many children have you had?

¿Tuvo problemas con alguno de los embarazos?..Did you have problems with any of your pregnancies?

¿Ha tenido abortos?..Have you had any abortions or miscarriages?

¿Con intención o natural?..An abortion or a miscarriage?

¿Cuándo fue la última vez que tuvo relaciones?..When was the last time you had sexual relations?

¿Usa algún método anticonceptivo?..Are you using any birth control?

¿La píldora?..The pill?

¿El diafragma?..The diaphragm?

¿Un dispositivo intrauterino? (aparato?)..An IUD?

¿Condones (¿Preservativos?)..Condoms?

¿Podría estar embarasada?..Could you be pregnant?

¿Tiene secreción (desecho, flujo) vaginal?..Do you have a vaginal discharge?

¿Cómo siempre o diferente?..As usual or different?

¿Cómo es?..What is it like?

¿Tiene úlceras (heridas) en sus partes?..Do you have sores on your private parts?

¿Tiene picazón?..Do you have itching?

¿Le duele cuando tiene relaciones?..Does it hurt when you have intercourse?

Musculoesquelético/Musculoskeletal:

¿Tiene dolores de las articulaciones? (las coyunturas? los huesos?)..Do you have joint pains?

¿Se le hinchan las articulaciones? (las coyunturas? los huesos?)..Do your joints swell up?

¿Se siente tieso en la mañana?..Do you feel stiff in the morning?

¿Le duele la espalda?..Does your back hurt?

¿Se siente débil?..Do you feel weak?

¿Le dificulta subir escaleras?..Do you have trouble climbing stairs?

¿Levantarse de una silla?..Getting up from a chair?

¿Peinarse?..Combing your hair?

Neurológico/Neurological:

¿Con cuál mano escribe Ud.?..Which hand do you write with?

¿Ha tenido un derrame cerebral? (una embolia?)..Have you had a stroke?

¿Se le ha puesto débil una sola parte del cuerpo alguna vez, como el brazo o la pierna?..Has a single part of your body ever turned weak, like your arm or your leg?

¿Se le ha puesto negra la vista en un solo ojo alguna vez?..Has your vision in one eye ever gone black?

¿Siente dormida alguna parte del cuerpo?..Does any part of your body feel numb?

¿Tiene hormigueo?..Do you have tingling?

¿Tiene temblores?..Do you have trembling?

¿Tiene dificultades para recordar cosas?..Do you have trouble remembering things?

¿Tiene mareos a veces?..Do you get dizzy at times?

¿Como si fuera a desmayarse?..As if you were going to faint?

¿Se ha desmayado?..Have you fainted?

¿Siente a veces como si el cuarto estuviera dando vueltas alrededor de Ud.?..Do you ever feel as though the room were spinning around you?

¿Ha tenido alguna vez una crisis convulsiva? (ataque?)..Have you ever had a seizure?

¿Cuando su cuerpo estaba moviendo sin querer?..When your body was moving involuntarily?

Estado mental/Mental status

Cómo se llama Ud.?..What's your name?
¿Sabe donde está?..Do you know where you are?
¿En qué tipo de edificio estamos?..What type of building are we in?
¿Cuál es la fecha?..What's the date?
¿Cuál año?..What year?
¿Sabe quien soy yo?..Do you know who I am?

Psiquiátrico/Psychiatric:

¿Está nervioso mucho? (¿Tiene nervios?)..Are you nervous a lot?
¿Hay algo que le molesta?..Is something bothering you?
¿Diría que padece a veces de depresión?..Would you say you suffer
    from depression at times?
¿Ha visto alguna vez a un psiquiatra?..Have you ever seen a
    psychiatrist?
¿Le ayudó?..Did it help?
¿Ha pensado alguna vez en suicidarse?..Have you ever thought of
    killing yourself?
¿Ha pensado en como lo haría?..Have you thought about how would
    you do it?
¿Ha pensado en hacerle daño a otra persona?..Have you thought of
    hurting someone else?
¿Puede valerse por sí mismo?..Do you think you can take care of
    yourself?
¿Podrá arreglárselas?..Are you going to be able to manage?

Endocrino/Endocrine:

¿Tiene problemas con la tiroides?..Do you have thyroid problems?
¿Se lo dijo un médico?..Did a doctor tell you?
¿Siente calor muy seguido?..Do you feel hot a lot?
¿Más que de costumbre?..More than usual?
¿Siente frío muchas veces cuando los demás no lo sienten?..Do you
    feel cold a lot when others don't?
¿Tiene mucha sed?..Are you thirsty a lot?
¿Tiene que levantarse durante la noche para orinar?..Do you have to

get up in the middle of the night to urinate?
¿Está comiendo mucho?..Are you eating a lot?

EXAMEN FÍSICO/PHYSICAL EXAMINATION

EXAMEN GENERAL/GENERAL EXAMINATION

Siéntese en la mesa de exploración (mesa de exámenes)..Have a seat on the exam table.
Quítese la chaqueta..Take off your jacket.
Necesito tomarle la presión..I need to take your blood pressure.
Enrolle su manga, por favor..Roll up your sleeve, please.
Deje caer el brazo, yo lo sostengo..Let your arm fall, I will hold it up.
Su presión es ciento treinta sobre setenta..Your blood pressure is one hundred thirty over seventy.
Desvístase, por favor, de la cintura hacia arriba..Take off your clothes from the waist up, please.
Quítese toda su ropa menos la ropa interior..Take off all your clothes except your underwear.
Quítese toda su ropa y póngase esta bata..Take off all your clothes and put on this gown.
Incluyendo su ropa interior..Including your underwear.
Puede usar la cortina..You can use the curtain.
Siéntese viendo esta pared, por favor..Sit facing this wall, please.
Siéntese con las piernas colgando..Sit with your legs dangling.
Déjeme ver su pulso..Let me see your pulse.
Siga mi dedo con sus ojos sin mover la cabeza..Follow my finger with your eyes without moving your head.
Mire mi nariz..Look at my nose.
Fije la vista en aquel punto en la pared..Stare at that point on the wall.

Siga mirando el punto en la pared..Keep staring at the point on the wall.

Trate de no mover los ojos..Try not to move your eyes.

Ahora mire la luz directamente..Now look directly at the light.

Levante las cejas..Raise your eyebrows.

Frunza el ceño..Frown.

Arrugue la nariz..Wrinkle your nose.

Sonría..Smile.

Enséñeme los dientes..Show me your teeth.

Apriete los dientes..Clench your teeth.

Empuje mi mano con su cara..Push against my hand with your face.

Levante sus hombros contra mis manos..Raise your shoulders against my hands.

Mire al techo..Look up at the ceiling.

Abra la boca..Open your mouth.

Levante la lengua..Lift your tongue up.

Saque la lengua..Stick your tongue out.

Muévala de lado a lado..Move it from side to side.

Diga "A"..Say "Ah".

Trague saliva (Pase saliva)..Swallow.

Le voy a examinar el corazón..I'm going to examine your heart.

No hable por un momento..Don't talk for a moment.

Inclínese hacia adelante..Lean forward.

Le voy a examinar los pulmones..I'm going to examine your lungs.

Cruce los brazos..Cross your arms.

Respire profundo con la boca abierta..Breathe deeply with your mouth open.

Afuera..Out.

Otra vez..Again.

Necesito examinarle los senos..I need to examine your breasts.

Quítese el brassiere (el sostén), por favor..Take off your brassiere, please.

Ponga las manos en la cadera y empuje hacia dentro..Place your hands on your hips and push inward.

Levante los brazos arriba de la cabeza así..Lift your arms above your head like this.

Ahora acuéstese..Now lie down.

Le voy a examinar el abdomen (la barriga, el estómago)..I'm going to examine your abdomen (belly, stomach).

Acomódese derecho en la mesa..Arrange yourself straight on the table.

Relaje los músculos..Relax your muscles.

No levante la cabeza..Don't lift your head.

Dígame si le duele..Tell me if it hurts.

Es necesario hacer un tacto rectal..I have to do a rectal examination.

¿Sabe que es un tacto rectal?..Do you know what a rectal exam is?

Necesito examinar su recto con mi dedo, usando guante..I need to examine your rectum with my finger, using a glove.

Voltéese a su lado izquierdo..Roll over onto your left side.

Doble sus rodillas hacia su pecho..Bend your knees toward your chest.

Puje como si estuviera defecando..Bear down as if you were having a bowel movement.

Apriete mi dedo..Squeeze my finger.

Necesito examinarle por una hernia..I need to examine you for a hernia.

Tosa, por favor..Cough, please.

EXAMEN GINECOLÓGICO/PELVIC EXAMINATION

Necesito hacerle un examen ginecológico..I need to do a pelvic examination.

Ponga los pies en los estribos..Put your feet in the stirrups.

Muévase hacia adelante..Move forward.

Hacia mí..Toward me.

Separe las piernas..Separate your legs.

Voy a introducir (meter) el espéculo..I'm going to insert the speculum.

Voy a hacer un examen de Papanicolaou (examen del cáncer)..I'm going to do a Pap test.

Falta poco para completar el examen..The exam is almost over.

Necesito examinarla con mis dedos, usando guante..I need to examine you with my fingers, using a glove.

Ahora le voy a examinar la vagina y el recto y el tejido entre ellos..Now I am going to examine your vagina and rectum and the tissue in between.

EXAMEN NEUROLÓGICO/NEUROLOGICAL EXAMINATION

Cierre los ojos..Close your eyes.

¿Siente un olor?..Do you smell anything?

¿A qué huele?..What does it smell like?

Voy a examinarle la visión periférica..I am going to examine your peripheral vision.

Tápese este ojo y con el otro mire mi ojo..Cover this eye and with your other eye look in my eye.

Ahora dígame "Sí" al momento que vea menear mi dedo..Now tell me "Yes" the moment you see my finger wiggling.

No mire mi dedo..Don't look at my finger.

Siga mirando mi ojo..Keep looking at my eye.

Cierre los ojos y no deje que se los abra..Close your eyes and don't let me open them.

¿Escucha el sonido de mis dedos frotando?..Can you hear the sound of my fingers rubbing?

Cierre los ojos y dígame al momento que escuche mis dedos frotando..Close your eyes and tell me the moment you hear my fingers rubbing.

¿En cuál lado suena más fuerte el diapasón?..On which side does the tuning fork sound louder?

¿O suena igual en los dos lados?..Or does it sound the same on both sides?

¿Cuál sonido le parece más fuerte, este?..Which sound seems louder, this?

¿O este?..Or this?

(Para preguntas adicionales sobre los nervios craneales, vea el EXAMEN GENERAL arriba. For additional questions concerning the cranial nerves see GENERAL EXAMINATION above.)

Póngase de pie, por favor..Stand, please.

Camine hacia la puerta..Walk toward the door.

Ahora camine para aca..Now walk to me.

Camine de puntillas..Walk on your toes.

Camine en sus talones..Walk on your heels.

Camine en una línea recta, poniendo un pie directamente enfrente del otro, así..Walk in a straight line, putting one foot directly in front of the other, like this.

Brinque en un pie..Hop on one foot.

Ahora en el otro..Now on the other one.

Póngase en cuclillas..Squat down.

Ahora levántese sin usar los brazos..Now get up without using your arms.

Párese con los pies juntos y los brazos extendidos enfrente, las palmas arriba, así..Stand with your feet together and your arms extended in front of you, palms up, like this.

Cierre los ojos..Close your eyes.

Mantenga los brazos extendidos..Keep your arms extended.

Voy a empujarlo un poco, para revisar su equilibrio..I'm going to push you lightly to test your sense of balance.

No le voy a dejar caer..I won't let you fall.

Siéntese aquí, por favor..Sit here, please.

Apriete mis dedos lo más fuerte que pueda..Squeeze my fingers as hard as you can.

Separe los dedos de la mano así y no deje que se los cierre..Separate your fingers like this and don't let me close them.

Haga un círculo así y no deje que se lo rompa..Make a circle like this and don't let me break it.

Jale contra mi mano..Pull against my hand.

Empuje contra mi mano..Push against my hand.

Más fuerte..Harder.

Haga un puño..Make a fist.

Doble la muñeca contra mi mano..Flex your wrist against my hand.

Levante los brazos contra mis manos..Raise your arms agains my hands.

Extiende la pierna contra mi mano..Extend your leg against my hand.

Jálela hacia atrás..Pull it back.

Empuje el pie contra mi mano..Push your foot against my hand.

Doble el tobillo hacia arriba..Bend your foot upward.

Levante su pierna contra mi mano..Raise your leg against my hand.

Toque su nariz con el dedo..Touch your nose with your finger.

Ahora toque mi dedo..Now touch my finger.

Siga tocando su nariz y mi dedo, uno y otro, rápido..Keep on touching your nose and my finger, back and forth, rapidly.

Toque la rodilla con el talón de la otra pierna..Touch your knee with the heel of your other leg.

Ahora con el talón recorra la espinilla hasta el pie..Now slide your
heel down your shin to your foot.

¿Siente vibrar el diapasón?..Can you feel the tuning fork vibrating?

Ahora no está vibrando..Now it isn't vibrating.

¿Siente la diferencia?..Can you tell the difference?

Cierre los ojos..Close your eyes.

¿Está vibrando o no?..Is it vibrating or not?

¿Ahora?..Now?

¿Puede sentir cuando le toco con este algodón?..Can you feel when
I touch you with this piece of cotton?

Cierre los ojos y dígame "Sí" cada vez que sienta el algodón..Close
your eyes and tell me "Yes" each time you feel the cotton.

Al momento que la sienta, me dice..The moment you feel it, tell me.

Voy a usar este alfiler para revisar sus sensaciones..I'm going to use
this pin to test your sensations.

Este es agudo..This is sharp.

Este es sordo (romo)..This is dull.

¿Siente la diferencia?..Can you feel the difference?

*Cierre los ojos y dígame "Agudo" o "Sordo" ("Romo") cada vez que
lo toco*..Close your eyes and tell me "Sharp" or "Dull" each time I
touch you.

¿Sintió algo?..Did you feel anything?

¿Siente este punto?..Do you feel this point?

¿Siente estos dos puntos separados?..Do you feel these two separate
points?

*Cierre los ojos y dígame "Uno" o "Dos" según cuantos puntos
sienta*..Close your eyes and tell me "One" or "Two" according to
how many points you feel.

Voy a revisar sus reflejos..I am going to check your reflexes.

Relájese..Relax.

Relaje la pierna..Relax your leg.